A Lamp for the
Dark World

A Lamp for the Dark World

Akbar, India's Greatest Mughal

Parvati Sharma

ROWMAN & LITTLEFIELD
Lanham • Boulder • New York • London

Published by Rowman & Littlefield
An imprint of The Rowman & Littlefield Publishing Group, Inc.
4501 Forbes Boulevard, Suite 200, Lanham, Maryland 20706
www.rowman.com

86-90 Paul Street, London EC2A 4NE

British Library Cataloguing in Publication Information Available

Library of Congress Control Number: 2023930529

ISBN 9781538177891 (cloth) | ISBN 9781538177907 (epub)

For Shahrukh
who is also quite great

Cast of Characters

Jalaluddin Muhammad Akbar: Third Mughal emperor. Ruled for just short of fifty years (1556–1605) and built the empire that bears his dynasty's name

FAMILY

Babur: Akbar's grandfather. Ruled in Fergana, Kabul and – very briefly – Agra, where he laid the foundations of his family's ambitions in Hindustan.

Maham Begum: Babur's wife, Humayun's mother (not to be confused with Maham Anaka, Akbar's nurse)

Khanzada: Babur's sister and trusted adviser to all four of his sons

Haider: Babur's cousin, Humayun's uncle. Commander and adviser in Humayun's court. Left to conquer Kashmir after Humayun's exile from Hindustan. Wrote a history of the Moghuls of Central Asia, the *Tarikh-i Rashidi*

Humayun: Babur's eldest son, Akbar's father. Lost Hindustan to Sher Shah Suri. Managed to reclaim his throne but died only months afterwards, leaving thirteen-year-old Akbar to inherit his conquest-in-progress

Hamida: Akbar's mother. Married Humayun, with reluctance, during his exile. Had Akbar when she was about sixteen and lived almost to the very end of his life and reign. Was deeply loved, respected and trusted by her son

Muazzam: Hamida's brother and Akbar's uncle. Eccentric, unreliable and increasingly violent, was eventually imprisoned by Akbar

Kamran: Akbar's uncle, Humayun's half-brother. Usually the villain in stories of Humayun's life

vii

Askari: Akbar's uncle, Humayun's half-brother, Kamran's full-brother – and his unimpressive second-in-command

Hindal: Akbar's uncle, Humayun's youngest half-brother. Brave, chivalrous and greatly mourned by his sister, Gulbadan

Yadgar Nasir: Humayun's cousin. Plotted against Humayun once too often, executed at Humayun's orders

Gulbadan: Akbar's aunt, Humayun's sister. Lived to old age in Akbar's empire. Made an adventurous journey to Mecca, and wrote an enjoyable account of Humayun's reign and exile, the *Humayun-nama*

Dildar: Hindal's mother. Persuaded a reluctant Hamida to marry Humayun, despite Hindal's objections to the match

Sultan Begum: Askari's wife and affectionate guardian to Akbar when he was held hostage by Askari

Mahchuchak: Humayun's youngest wife and mother of his second son, Hakim. Fiercely protective of Hakim's (and her own) right to rule Kabul

Hakim: Akbar's half-brother and embattled ruler of Kabul. Was proclaimed an alternative to Akbar more than once by disenchanted warlords in Hindustan

Faridun: Hakim's uncle. Blamed by Mughal historians for instigating Hakim's incursions into Hindustan

Khwaja Hasan Naqshbandi: A descendant of the Naqshbandi Sufis. Among Hakim's closest advisers. Married Hakim's sister

Abul Qasim: Kamran's son and Akbar's cousin. Kept imprisoned and possibly executed by Akbar's command

Sulaiman: Humayun's cousin, Akbar's uncle. Replaced Humayun as governor of Badakhshan, then became its ruler. Long hoped to rule Kabul, spent his last days as Akbar's refugee-guest in Lahore

Haram: Sulaiman's formidable wife, said to be the real ruler of Badakhshan

Shahrukh: Sulaiman's grandson, Akbar's nephew. Became a rival for Sulaiman's throne in his teens, later joined Akbar's court

Sharafuddin: A distant Timurid relative who came to offer his congratulations to young Akbar, remained to marry Akbar's sister, then rebelled against him

Mirza[1] Ibrahim Husain: Best known of 'The Mirzas' – a clan of Timurids who were frequently guilty of insubordination, and worse, to Humayun and Akbar. Ibrahim was married to Kamran's daughter, Gulrukh

Mirza Muhammad Husain: Mirza Ibrahim Husain's brother. Remembered for his shock when he heard that Akbar had chased after him from Fatehpur Sikri to Ahmedabad in nine days. Was defeated in the battle that followed

Bihari Mal: Embattled heir to the Kachhwaha throne. Became Akbar's first Rajput ally – and father-in-law – when he married his daughter, Harkha, to Akbar

Harkha Bai: Kachhwaha princess, Akbar's first Rajput wife and mother of his first son, Salim

Bhagwant Das: Harkha's brother and Akbar's brother-in-law. Attained high rank in Akbar's court; married his daughter to Akbar's firstborn son (also Bhagwant Das's nephew)

Man Singh: Harkha's nephew and brother-in-law to Akbar's firstborn son. One of Akbar's star generals and among the most powerful men in his court

Salim: Akbar's eldest son. Born of Harkha as the boon Akbar sought from God, Salim became the bane of Akbar's old age. Led the last prominent rebellion against Akbar and succeeded him as Jahangir

Man Bai: Salim's first wife, Bhagwant Das's daughter, and mother to Salim's first son, Khusro

Salima Sultan: Akbar's cousin, Bairam Khan's widow and thereafter Akbar's wife. A trusted adviser to the family, played a key role in negotiations between Akbar and Salim

Murad: Akbar's second son. A favourite of his Jesuit tutor Father Antonio Monserrate, unpopular with Akbar's nobility. Died while Akbar lived

Daniyal: Akbar's youngest son. Enjoyed hunting, horses and poetry. Died while Akbar lived, despite Akbar's desperate efforts to save him

Khusro: Salim's first son. A favourite of Akbar's and a contender for his throne

FOSTER FAMILY, FAMILY FRIENDS AND FRENEMIES

Maham Anaka[2]: Generally, and incorrectly, said to be Akbar's foster mother; more likely the superintendent of his nurses. Loving, protective and ambitious, she played a prominent role in the early years of Akbar's reign

Adham Khan: Maham Anaka's son. Memorably and brutally executed by Akbar for murdering Akbar's foster father

Shamsuddin Muhammad Ataka[3]: Akbar's foster father and his attendant from Akbar's infancy. Loyal and ambitious, rose to a high rank during Akbar's reign before being killed by Adham Khan. His family remained powerful and became known as the 'ataka khail' – clan of the ataka

Jiji Anaka: Wife of Shamsuddin and one of Akbar's most beloved foster mothers

Aziz Koka[4]: Son of Shamsuddin and Jiji. Akbar's milk brother, best friend and most outspoken critic

Zain Khan Koka: Another of Akbar's milk brothers. Best known for leading imperial troops against the Afghans of Swat and Bajaur and losing control of the campaign in which Birbar perished

Shihabuddin Ahmad Khan: Maham Anaka's friend, relative and second-in-command. Served in Akbar's court for decades after Maham Anaka's death

Abul Ma'ali: A great favourite of Humayun's; of handsome appearance and villainous nature. Plotted against Akbar and his family, briefly held the throne of Kabul

Bairam Khan: Became Akbar's regent when Humayun died. Without him, Akbar might not have had an empire in Hindustan. Generous, ambitious and sometimes vengeful, was ousted in a coup led – most likely – by Maham Anaka

Abdur Rahim: Bairam Khan's son. Orphaned at age four when Bairam Khan was murdered, brought up by Akbar in whose court he rose to Bairam Khan's rank of Khan-Khanan – khan of khans

Husain Quli Khan: Bairam Khan's nephew. Once disparaged by Akbar for not having fought so much as a chicken, his father was executed for supporting Bairam Khan's rebellion. Rose to high rank as governor of both Punjab and the east, yet never seems to have gained Akbar's affection, and was mistrusted by some of Akbar's Sunni warlords because he was Shia

Tardi Beg: A tight-fisted but ultimately loyal warlord who served Humayun and – very briefly – Akbar. Was executed at Bairam Khan's command

Munim Khan: Akbar's ataliq – guardian – when Akbar was a prince. Allied with Maham Anaka against Bairam Khan. Led Akbar's conquests into Bihar and Bengal, battling on Akbar's behalf into his eighties

Jouher 'Aftabchi': Humayun's ewer-bearer, served Akbar for decades and wrote an account of Humayun's reign, including his exile from and return to Hindustan, the *Tezkereh al Vakiat*

Ali Quli Shaibani: An Uzbek warlord who was loyal to Humayun and helped establish Akbar's rule in Hindustan. Led the Uzbek rebellion, the first serious insurrection against Akbar

Bahadur Khan: Ali Quli Shaibani's brother and co-captain of the Uzbek rebellion

Ibrahim Khan: Uncle to Ali Quli Shaibani, participated in the Uzbek rebellion

Sikander Khan: Uzbek fief-holder in Oudh. Participated in the Uzbek rebellion, pleaded his way back to Akbar's court

Shahim Beg: A soldier in Humayun's court, then Akbar's. The great and undeserving love of Ali Quli Shaibani's life

Abdullah Khan: One of the many Uzbek warriors who accompanied Humayun on his return to Hindustan. Governed Malwa briefly. Joined the Uzbek rebellion against Akbar

AIDES AND ADVISERS, COMMANDERS AND COURTIERS

Birbar (Mahesh Das): A minstrel who became one of Akbar's closest friends. Comrade-in-arms in Akbar's theological adventures. Died in a military mishap, leaving Akbar distraught. Lives on in popular lore as Birbal

Abul Fazl: Akbar's star historian, biographer and, eventually, friend. Paid with his life for Akbar's trust in him when he was assassinated by order of Prince Salim. Wrote the *Akbarnama* and the *Ain-i-Akbari*

Faizi: Akbar's poet laureate and close friend. Abul Fazl's elder brother

Shaikh Mubarak: Abul Fazl and Faizi's father. An outcast from the court ulema at the beginning of Akbar's reign, he rose to great power over time

Asad Beg: An old employee of Abul Fazl's, wrote an account of Abul Fazl's assassination. Led an embassy to Bijapur and introduced Akbar to the art of smoking tobacco

Abdul Qadir Badauni: Talented translator, enthusiastic warrior and bitter critic of Akbar's arrogance and heresies, of Akbar's favourites like Birbar and Abul Fazl, and of Akbar's self-important court clergy. Wrote a secret account of Akbar's reign, with all his complaints, as part of his *Muntakhab-ut-Tawarikh*

Nizamuddin Ahmad: Rose to the high post of bakshi in Akbar's army during the later years of the long Gujarat campaign. Wrote the most dispassionate contemporary account of the first forty-odd years of Akbar's reign, the *Tabakat-i Akbari*

Shaikh Abdun Nabi: Akbar's sadr, chief justice. A powerful scholar and jurist until he fell out of favour, was exiled and later imprisoned and murdered

Makhdum-ul-Mulk (Maulana Abdullah Ansari): A leader of the ulema in the Suri court, remained powerful in the first half of Akbar's reign. Was exiled along with Shaikh Abdun Nabi. Died of fright when arrested

Muhammad Yazd: A Shia scholar in Akbar's court. Initially favoured by Akbar, but later issued a fatwa encouraging rebellion against the emperor. Drowned in an 'accident' possibly engineered by Akbar

Pir Muhammad: Bairam Khan's arrogant and bloodthirsty deputy. Was exiled by Bairam Khan but returned as a commander to Akbar's court after the regent's downfall. Drowned in the Narmada when his horse was bit by a camel

Asaf Khan (Khwaja Abdul Majid): A clerk in Humayun's court. Became a military commander under Akbar. Led the conquest of Rani Durgavati's kingdom. Joined the Uzbek rebellion, but only briefly

Baba Khan Qaqshal: Leader of the Qaqshal clan of warlords who settled in eastern Hindustan and led the Bengal rebellion – the last serious attempt by Akbar's nobility to remove him from the throne

Shahbaz Khan: A hot-tempered Punjabi commander in Akbar's court; instrumental in subduing the Bengal rebellion

Todar Mal: Star financial adviser, reformer and general in Akbar's court. Led Akbar's armies (including against the Bengal rebels) as well as he led many of Akbar's administrative and revenue reforms

Muzaffar Khan: Another of Akbar's star financial advisers. Often fell out of favour because of his blunt manner. Redeemed himself with military success in the east. Executed by the Bengal rebels

Shah Mansur: One of Akbar's great accountants (and, like all his great accountants, greatly unpopular with Akbar's nobility). Was hanged at Akbar's command on false charges

Tansen: A singer of legendary talent, whom Akbar poached from Panna. Became one of the luminaries of Akbar's court

Hakim Abul Fath: A Sunni refugee from Shia Iran who became a great favourite of Akbar's. Was part of the disastrous military campaign in which Birbar died

Amir Fathullah Shirazi: A man of many talents, from astrology to mechanics. Was invited to Akbar's court and led some of his administrative reforms, though he did not encourage Akbar's theological adventurism

Bir Singh Bundela: Son of Raja Madhukar of Orchha. Allied with Prince Salim and assassinated Abul Fazl

MISSIONARIES

Father Rudolf Aquaviva: Leader of the first Jesuit mission to Akbar's court

Father Antonio Monserrate: One of the three priests who comprised the first Jesuit mission to Akbar's court (along with Father Rudolf Aquaviva and Father Francis Henriquez). Was appointed tutor to Murad and other children of the nobility. Wrote an account of his experiences, *The Commentary of Father Monserrate, S.J. on His Journey to the Court of Akbar*

Father Hierosme (Jerome) Xavier Navarrois: Leader of the third Jesuit mission to Akbar's court. Travelled with Akbar's camp to Kashmir and on his last campaign to Khandesh

CHIEFTAINS, KINGS AND QUEENS

Sher Shah Suri: Founder of the Suri dynasty. Evicted Humayun and his brothers from Hindustan

Salim (Islam) Shah Suri: Sher Shah Suri's son and successor. His death led to a succession battle that allowed Humayun to return to Hindustan

Muhammad Adil (Mubariz Khan): Claimed the Suri throne after Salim Shah Suri died, murdered Salim Shah's young son

Hemu (Raja Bikramjit): A grocer who rose to administrative and military command in the Suri court. Brilliant general and de facto regent to Muhammad Adil. Defeated Mughal forces in Delhi and titled himself Raja Bikramjit. Lost the second battle of Panipat a few weeks later and was executed

Shah Tahmasp: Ruler of Iran and unpredictable host to Humayun during Humayun's exile

Shah Abbas: Emerged as shah of Iran after a long and bloody succession battle following Shah Tahmasp's death. Had regular diplomatic relations with Akbar, whom he referred to as 'shah baba', or king father

Raja Maldeo: Ruler of Marwar. Refused Humayun shelter during his desperate journey through Rajasthan

Rana Prasad: Ruler of Umarkot. Offered shelter and an alliance to Humayun and Hamida during their exile. Akbar was born in his fort

Sultan Adam: Ruler of the Gakkhars. Refused an alliance with Kamran and handed him over to Humayun instead

Kamal Khan: Sultan Adam's nephew. Claimed the Gakkhar throne and took it from Sultan Adam with Akbar's support

Sultan Abdullah: Ruler of Turan, Akbar's neighbour to the north. Had regular and sometimes tense diplomatic relations with Akbar's Hindustan

Sultan Baz Bahadur: Ruler of Malwa, best known for his musical talent and love for Rupmati. Lost his kingdom to Mughal forces led by Adham Khan and eventually joined Akbar's court

Rani Durgavati: Ruler of Gondwana, greatly admired by Mughal historians. Lost her kingdom to Mughal forces led by Asaf Khan and took her own life

Rana Udai Singh: Ruler of Mewar when Akbar besieged Chittorgarh. Left the defence of Chittorgarh to Jaimal

Jaimal: Rajput commander, greatly admired by Mughal historians. Allied with Akbar's relative Sharafuddin in the conquest of Merta, then with Udai Singh in the defence of Chittorgarh. Shot by Akbar during the siege

Rana Pratap: Son and successor of Rana Udai Singh. Resisted the Mughal conquest of Mewar until the end of his life, most famously against Man Singh in the battle of Haldighati

Rai Surjan Hada: Ruler of Bundi, cousin of Udai Singh. Surrendered Ranthambore to Akbar and joined his court

Sultan Bahadur: Last prominent king of Gujarat's Muzaffarid dynasty

Muzaffar Shah (Nannu): Propped up as a scion of the Muzaffarid dynasty by the Gujarati nobility, considered a pretender by the Mughals. Led a long struggle against the Mughal conquest of Gujarat. Slit his own throat when caught

Chenghis Khan: Not to be confused with Akbar's famous ancestor and founder of the Mongol empire in the thirteenth century, this Chenghis Khan was one of several powerful chieftains who ruled various parts of Gujarat between the decline of its Muzaffarid dynasty and its conquest by Akbar

Sher Khan Fuladi: Among the Gujarati chiefs who resisted Akbar's incursions. Allied with Mirza Muhammad Husain against Akbar in the great battle for Ahmedabad in 1573

Itimad Khan 'Gujarati': Another powerful Gujarati chief, though more inclined to ally with Akbar than his peers. Sent Akbar an African elephant while Akbar was besieging Chittorgarh. Eventually joined Akbar's court

Sultan Sulaiman Karrani: Ruler of Bengal and able to keep Mughal ambitions in the east at bay until his death

Sultan Daud: Younger, and reputedly very handsome, son of Sultan Sulaiman Karrani. Far less successful than his father at maintaining either his throne or diplomatic peace with Akbar. Lost one battle after another, managed to sweet-talk a truce out of Munim Khan but was captured and beheaded – reluctantly – at Husain Quli Khan's orders

Yusuf Shah Chak: Ruler of Kashmir. Negotiated a truce with Bhagwant Das but to little avail. Was imprisoned by Akbar

Chand Bibi: Regent and de facto ruler of Ahmednagar, led the defence of the fort against the Mughals. Greatly admired by Abul Fazl – who negotiated with her at one point. Murdered by her own men

Sultan Raja Ali Khan: Ruler of Khandesh. Allied with the Mughals

Sultan Bahadur Shah: Son and successor of Sultan Raja Ali Khan. Broke Khandesh's alliance with the Mughals, was besieged in Asirgarh, eventually surrendered and was imprisoned

Contents

Acknowledgements

I can only hope that what I've written of Akbar's life is worthwhile, but that I've written it at all owes entirely to two people: Chiki Sarkar and Nandini Mehta.

I am deeply grateful to Chiki for convincing me to embark on a project I would have been far too shy to attempt on my own. And I cannot quite express how wonderful it has been to have had Nandini by my side these past years, with her perfect balance of enthusiasm and patience, encouraging me to write, allowing me to think – I could not have written this book without her. Many thanks also to the people who worked on Akbar with me. At Juggernaut Books: Parth Mehrotra, Arani Sinha, Devangana Ojha, Shreya Chakravertty, Shyama Warner and Gavin Morris. At Rowman & Littlefield: Ashley Dodge, Haley White, Laney Ackley, Alden Perkins and Kathi Ha, with Arun Rajakumar at Deanta.

Thank you to Priya Doraswamy, my agent.

I am grateful to BLink of *The Hindu Businessline* for the use of two passages that I first wrote for the newspaper; and to Juggernaut Books for the use of the map on page 303.

Thank you also to the French Institute in India and the Maison des Écrivains Étrangers et des Traducteurs in France for giving me two lovely months of leisure in Saint-Nazaire in which to finish the penultimate draft of this book.

Finally, and as always, I am hugely indebted to my family and my friends, some of whom have endured relentless conversation about Akbar these past years and all of whom have long endured me.

Prologue

Sometimes, in the dimly lit passages of time, there shines a light so bright it dazzles the ages. Such was the flare, at any rate, that burst across the Mongolian sky one dark night, blazing into Alanqoa's tent, her astonished mouth, and then her womb.

Who knows when Alanqoa lived? Over 2000 years before she saw the light of day, her luckless ancestor Qiyan had seen his entire tribe massacred. Only Qiyan, his cousin and their wives survived. The four found refuge in Arganaqun, an Edenic valley surrounded by high mountains, and here, upon a meadow lush with water and fruit, the tribe rebuilt itself. Eventually, when the valley would hold them no longer, the men and women travelled out, no longer fugitives but an unstoppable force. An iron mountain that blocked their way they melted with bellows. Two millennia after Qiyan's desperate escape, his descendants – the Qiyat – returned to rule Mongolia.

Alanqoa was a Qiyat, married to her cousin, the king – but when that light flew into her tent, the king was long dead and Alanqoa herself ruled the Mongols. Anticipating protests from literal-minded chieftains who might not understand how their widowed queen was suddenly with child, she commanded some trustworthy men to witness the miracle. They stood guard around her tent as the stars rose and the darkness grew, their silence interrupted by the unearthly sounds of night and the shuffling of feet. And then, as one, the men let out a cry. It was as Alanqoa had said! A magnificent light had made its unerring way across the sky and into the tent of their queen.

Nine months later, she delivered three boys: Baqun Qataqi, Bughutu Salji and Bodhonchar Qa'an. Few in the modern world will find their names familiar; yet few in the modern world will not have heard of their descendants. Chinghis Khan, Timur the Lame, Akbar the Great – men who would grab the world by the scruff of its neck and claim it as their own. And why should they not? They were, after all, the Niru'un. Born of Light.

Chapter 1

Exodus

'The first degree of dutiful obedience is not to scowl with knitted brows when trials befall, but regarding them as the bitter remedies of a physician, to accept them with a cheerful countenance.'

– Akbar, Happy Sayings, *Ain-i-Akbari*

Five thousand elephants draped in European velvet and Turkish brocade, hung with chains of gold and silver, lined the road to the newly built stone palaces of Fatehpur. Between every pair of these fluorescent beasts sat a cheetah upon a dais, dressed with equal excess in bejewelled golden collars and rich cloth. Arabian and Persian horses with saddles of gold were part of the spectacle, too; and, lest anyone find it wanting in glitter, oxen carts held up displays of gold embroidery.

The palaces were also decorated, the whole city was festive – as was only fitting. This was Akbar's city of victory. Only three years since its foundations were laid and, already, Akbar had marched west from Fatehpur and conquered Gujarat, sailed east from Fatehpur and conquered Bihar. Only two decades into his half-century-long reign, Akbar's Hindustan was becoming the pre-eminent power in the region, if not upon the globe: the rulers of Iran and Turan had sent envoys to their increasingly formidable neighbour; the Portuguese in Goa, Daman and Diu were 'submissive', and possibly of one mind with the Deccani chiefs 'greatly affected' by the sheer pace at which Akbar was expanding his realm.[1]

And yet, the elephants in all their finery, the cheetahs in their jewels and the tremendous quantities of gold gleaming in the late October sun were not in honour of yet another military triumph, nor meant to overawe yet another foreign ambassador. The reception had been arranged for a far more humble – you might even say pathetic – audience: the recently widowed, erstwhile

1

ruler of Badakhshan, who had spent the last two decades far less productively than Akbar, nursing a 'few paltry ambitions'[2] with little success, until he was evicted from the 'the stony land of his birth' by his own grandson.[3] This failed and hapless man had been accorded the greatest deference by Akbar's nobility all the way from the banks of the Indus to the imperial capital, where the glory of his reception so overwhelmed the poor man that, upon catching sight of Akbar, he leapt off his horse and ran towards the emperor, ready to fall at his feet.

Akbar, too, dismounted to greet his guest. The old man scurrying towards him, his Central Asian features lightly bearded and slightly flushed perhaps, was Akbar's uncle, Mirza[4] Sulaiman, the last of a generation of uncles who had conspired, it would seem, to give Akbar the worst possible start to his career – and the only one who remained, now, to witness his extraordinary rise. The glamour, the pageantry, was for his benefit, for what use is all the world's success if it cannot be flaunted to family?

Sulaiman was satisfyingly overawed, and Akbar was gracious in his majesty, speaking kindly to his aged relative, entertaining him at a banquet, and promising him troops to help him regain his lost kingdom. It was twenty years, at least, since uncle and nephew had met, and it isn't unlikely that the conversation turned to the past. Certainly, Sulaiman, as he marvelled at Akbar's court – the splendour of its gardens and buildings, the profusion of food and drink – must have marvelled, equally, at how things had changed since he last set foot in Hindustan.

That was almost exactly half a century ago. A younger, happier man, Sulaiman was part of the small army that battled Ibrahim Lodi on the plains of Panipat in 1526 and won his own uncle, Babur, a foothold in the north Indian plains. Sulaiman did not remain long in this newly conquered land, however; Babur sent his nephew to govern Badakhshan and died soon thereafter. As a result, Sulaiman did not witness his family's ignominious reverse migration across the blue waters of the Indus, when, barely fifteen years after that spectacular if all-too-fleeting victory at Panipat, Babur's sons abandoned their father's dreams of empire.

In the fifteen years that followed, however, Sulaiman had not only witnessed but even participated in the bloody and often melodramatic struggles for a kingdom in Kabul between his cousins – Humayun, Kamran, Askari and Hindal. Sometimes, Sulaiman had allied with Kamran, sometimes with Humayun; once, all five young men had formed an optimistic fellowship, planning to march on Samarqand. Sulaiman knew well, besides, how Akbar had spent his childhood hung in the competitive balance between his father and his uncles – how the boy was crowned king when his father died, how he was ruled by regents and challenged by warlords, how slim the chances were that he would survive. And now, having crossed the Indus a second time, no longer part of a conquering army but a lonely supplicant, Akbar's uncle would learn this, too: that all the operatic fury with which Sulaiman and his cousins had scrambled for a throne was only a pitiful game of musical chairs in the light of Akbar's achievement.

In July 1540, Mirza Haider, Babur's young cousin and uncle to his four sons – Humayun, Kamran, Askari and Hindal – arrived in Lahore and could hardly find a place to stay. The 'throng was so great', he wrote, 'that it was difficult to move about, and still more difficult to find a lodging'.[5] The crowds were not celebratory, however; no grand coronation was in the offing, no festival or pilgrimage in progress. Instead, a great darkness was descending upon the city. Its streets were panicked, its inns sold out and its gardens packed with tents; all for one reason: a kingdom was crumbling and Lahore was its last refuge.

A little over six weeks earlier, the armies of Humayun, the second Mughal 'padishah',[6] and Sher Shah, the ambitious Afghan general, had faced each other on the banks of the Ganga, in Kannauj. As the north Indian summer crept up on them, there was an occasional skirmish, and more than occasional desertion.[7] Haider, commanding a contingent of Humayun's troops, saw little more than reluctance animate his side. A 'heated feeling ran through the army', he would write later, caustically, 'and the cry was, "Let us go and rest in our own homes."' Thunderclouds gathered, 'with tumult, like rutting elephants',[8] showing more appetite for battle than the Mughal men. The rain was turning the ground to mush, making it impossible to camp and imperative, therefore, to battle. On 17 May 1540 – which was also Ashura, the tenth of Muharram, the day of Husain's martyrdom upon the bloody battlefield of Karbala – Humayun and his 40,000 men charged a 15,000-strong force led by Sher Shah at Kannauj. Perhaps 'charged' is not the right word. Haider remembers how there were twenty-seven Mughal contingents between him and the river, each marked by the fluttering banner of its commander. On the day of the battle, however, not one of these brave banners was to be seen, 'for the great nobles had hidden them in their apprehension'.

Defeated before the fighting began, the reluctant commanders packed off their untrained servants, *ghulams*, to the front. No sooner did these men see Sher Shah advance than they were possessed of an urge to get out of his way. The resulting chaos destroyed any semblance of discipline in the Mughal army – 'the whole array was broken', writes Haider – and before a gun could be fired or a commander wounded, it was each man for himself, commander and ghulam racing each other to the river in desperate flight.

Humayun's own fate was humiliating. His water carrier and future biographer, Jouher, recalls how 'an Afghan clothed in black' struck Humayun's horse with a spear.[9] Even with his horse injured and his army in a shambles

– Afghan soldiers were looting Humayun's artillery in front of his eyes – the emperor remained eager to fight, until a more sensible and anonymous hand grabbed the reins of his mount and led him to the river. Here, Humayun recognized an old elephant that had once belonged to his father, and climbed upon its back, only to realize that its driver was marching him towards the enemy. A eunuch he found hiding in the howdah whispered to Humayun to 'take off the fellow's head'.[10] Sensible advice, but Humayun knew nothing of driving an elephant; he would be stranded without a mahout. The eunuch assured the emperor that he knew a little about riding elephants and would take them to safety. Hacking at the treacherous driver with his sword, Humayun managed to push him to the ground, then, somehow, to cross the river – only to find the riverbank so steep he couldn't climb up it. Eventually, two camp men saw him and tied their turbans into a rope, by which the hapless emperor, soaked and dishevelled, clambered ashore.

Abul Fazl, Akbar's historian and greatest admirer, wrote the official and approved account of this debacle in his *Akbarnama*, ridding the story of its more farcical bits. In his telling, the emperor, 'mounted with firm foot on an elephant' – there is no mention of the eunuch who helped him ride it – made his way across the Ganga's swollen waters, and climbed ashore with manly dignity, aided by one Shamsuddin Muhammad of Ghazni, a soldier whose helping hand would gain him the highest rank in the years to come. For the moment, however, neither emperor nor soldier could hope for more than staying alive. That noon, writes Haider, Humayun had 17,000 men under his command; now, he rode alone upon a borrowed horse,[11] his head bare and his feet unshod.

It wasn't just his shoes Humayun had lost, but also his spirit. Riding ragged from Kannauj towards his capital, Agra, he began to speak of the women in his harem in doleful, ominous tones. Would it not be best to avert the dangers of defeat, the fate worse than death . . .? Humayun's youngest brother, Hindal, told the emperor to stop it. 'What it would be to your Majesty to kill a mother and a sister . . .!' cried the chivalrous prince. 'So long as there is life in me, I will fight in their service. I have hope in the most high God, that, poor fellow as I am, I may pour out my life's blood for my mother and my sisters.'[12]

The emperor was not wrong to worry, however. News of his defeat was travelling faster than he was: less than halfway to Agra, the retreating army was stopped in its tracks by 3000 villagers of Bhangaon, these 'peasants', writes Jouher, being 'in the habit of plundering a defeated army'. Humayun sent orders for his brothers Hindal and Askari, with their cousin Yadgar Nasir, to disperse the villagers, but the men began to squabble instead. Askari was fed up of fighting and 'delayed to proceed', at which Yadgar Nasir took out his horsewhip and began to ply it upon the recalcitrant prince, shouting that things would never have come to such a wretched pass if it weren't for Askari's 'discord'.[13]

His brothers, it is true, had not been pillars of support during Humayun's brief reign. Now, in almost as much danger of killing each other as of being waylaid by opportunist marauders – 'sedition raised its head on every side', writes Abul Fazl – the princes mustered the wits to drive back the men of Bhangaon, galloped to Agra, and from there, 'broken and dispirited',[14] fled north.

So it was that in July 1540, a decade after Babur died and left his progeny to grow his Hindustani kingdom – a brushstroke of land running south-east from Peshawar to Patna, with its capital in Agra, and precarious toeholds in Rajasthan and Malwa – his family huddled in Lahore, the only Hindustani city they had left, to see how, *if*, they might salvage their inheritance. Humayun, Askari and Hindal each arrived in Lahore separately and set up separate camps. The fourth brother, Kamran, was already in the city, having declined any part in the battle at Kannauj.[15] Besides the brothers, there was their cousin Yadgar Nasir, their uncle Mirza Haider, their various mothers, aunts, sisters and wives, and, of course, a great many chiefs of wavering allegiance.

For over two months, they held consultations, writes Abul Fazl, even managing to draft 'a deed of concord and unanimity', duly signed. Humayun delivered a rousing speech. 'With what difficulty had [Babur] . . . conquered Hindustan – so vast a country! If through your disunion it pass from our possession into the hands of nobodies what will the wise say of you? Now is the time to sink the head into the bosom of good counsel . . .'

It wasn't so much good counsel, however, as an outpouring of second thoughts that followed Humayun's oration. Why not move upon Sindh, proposed Hindal and Yadgar Nasir, and thence to Gujarat, and thus take on Sher Shah once again? Haider, having given Humayun a rather sharp lecture on his 'want of constancy and of purpose',[16] said let the princes and chiefs take over the hills while Haider went to Kashmir – he would send word when the valley was his, while Sher Shah would be unable to reach the Mughals in their heights. Even better, said Kamran, what if the padishah and princes marched into the hills or Kashmir as they liked, while Kamran took their women and families to Kabul? He would return to join them, of course – only later.[17]

The meeting broke up with nothing achieved. Meanwhile, every day brought news of Sher Shah's advance, and with it the realization that the princes might negotiate between themselves all they liked, but it was Sher Shah, the new star of Hindustan, who held their fate in his hands.

Kamran – always portrayed as the most self-serving of the four brothers – 'out of wickedness and blindness', writes Abul Fazl, sent a messenger to Sher Shah, offering himself as a kind of governor in Punjab. 'I will do a good job',[18] he promised eagerly. Sher Shah, 'a thousand times emboldened by the good news of disunion', accepted Kamran's petition and sent an envoy to Lahore. The faithless Kamran organized a party for this man – sworn enemy of his dynasty! – and even 'by entreaties induced' Humayun to come.

We are left to imagine that Humayun treated such pitiful scrambling for crumbs with the scorn it deserved, but here – as often, when it comes to the imperial family he chronicled and adored – Abul Fazl writes with an adorning pen. Gulbadan Begum, Babur's daughter and author of the *Humayunnama*, was in Lahore at this time, and she remembers it very differently. By Gulbadan's account, it was Humayun who wrote to Sher Shah, pleading for Lahore. After all, he wrote, 'I have left you the whole of Hindustan.'

The Afghan was unmoved. 'I have left you Kabul', was his frosty reply. 'You should go there.' Humayun's messenger, realizing that Sher Shah meant business, sent a runner to alert the emperor, who decamped immediately. 'It was like the Day of Resurrection', writes Gulbadan, a fearful scramble in which people left all they had except their money. Then, perhaps in hope of a sudden change of fortune, or perhaps unable to believe the end had come, Humayun pitched his tents across the Ravi river to the west of Lahore. Three days later, Sher Shah's envoy arrived – and Gulbadan writes that it was Humayun, not Kamran, who arranged a reception for him. Worse, he even composed a bit of verse for the victorious Afghan:

Although one's image be shown in the mirror,
It remains always apart from one's self.
It is wonderful to see one's self in another form:
This marvel will be the work of God.[19]

For all the sunny optimism of his couplets, Humayun could hardly have thought it 'wonderful' to have Sher Shah mirror his accession; and if, indeed, the padishah did bring himself to look at his reflection, he would have seen a failure that no amount of philosophizing would separate from his own self. It may be that Humayun went to sleep a defeated and lonely man that night, and in that sorrowful state, he had a dream. An old man came to him, dressed in green, and told him to cheer up.

'Do not grieve', said the vision, and gave Humayun the staff he held in his hand.

'Who are you?' asked Humayun.

'I am Ahmad of Jam', said the old man, 'and God shall give you a son of my blood. You will name him Jalaluddin Muhammad Akbar.'[20]

For some days, an unfamiliar optimism animated Humayun's camp. One of his wives, Bibi Gunwar, was in an advanced stage of pregnancy; would she have the promised boy? It was not to be; Bibi Gunwar had a girl.[21]

Humayun's dreams, like his reality, had disappointed him. What was the point, anyhow, of visions, no matter how propitious? Whether it was Kamran who schemed or Humayun who grovelled, there was little either man could do to stop Sher Shah – and when news arrived that the Afghan army had crossed the Beas river east of Lahore, the Mughals did the only thing they could. They ran away.[22]

In the way that it's usually told, as an interlude to better things, the story of Humayun is of a man undone by weakness, whimsy and sentimentality; a 'delicate king' (*padshahi latif*), as one of his own courtiers described him.[23] He was an emperor more interested in the movements of stars than in the affairs of men and far too indulgent of his brothers – Kamran foremost – who did all they could to undermine Humayun's authority and usurp his empire. It is possible, however, that Humayun was far less careless of his interests than he is reputed to have been. A soldier-historian called Nizamuddin Ahmad relates an odd bit of intrigue that casts a murky light on Humayun's seemingly effortless accession to his father's throne. The popular story is that Humayun fell ill and Babur offered God his own life in exchange for his son's. God accepted. Immediately, Humayun began to recover and Babur's health declined. With one last effort of will, the emperor pronounced his eldest son his heir, then took to his bed and died.

As Nizamuddin tells it, however, Babur's last days were spent against a backdrop of dizzy conspiracy. The story is this: a trusted, high-ranking chieftain in Babur's court, Mir Khalifa, conceived a mysterious antipathy towards the prince Humayun and proposed his own candidate for the throne: Mahdi Khwaja, a 'generous and liberal young man' who had the advantage of being married to Babur's beloved sister, Khanzada Begum. The idea gained traction, then quickly went to Mahdi Khwaja's head – so much so that he began plotting against his own advocate, Mir Khalifa, who promptly withdrew his support for the two-faced would-be heir, and had him arrested instead.[24]

Humayun, meanwhile, had long been aware of competing interests for Babur's throne, it seems. Sometime in the summer of 1529, eighteen-odd months before Babur died, Humayun left Badakhshan – his fief for almost a decade – and hurried down to his father's court in Agra. He went uninvited but, as he told his brother Kamran – surprised to see Humayun riding south through Kabul – 'he was always seeing [Babur] with his mind's eye, yet this was not equal to a personal interview'.[25]

Annette Beveridge, translator of both the *Humayun-nama* and Babur's memoirs, suggests that Babur wasn't flattered by such filial devotion. Badakhshan was not just a distant outpost of the newly formed empire; it was central to Babur's dreams for his dynasty. Though it appears historically inevitable, today, that the Mughals would rule Hindustan, Babur's great ambition had been to conquer the magnificent capital of his ancestor Timur – Samarqand; and even now, settled uncomfortably in the north Indian plains, Babur kept his two eldest sons north of the Indus – Humayun in Badakhshan, Kamran in Kabul – possibly to push conquests in that direction.

Humayun's unexpected arrival, however, was compounded by a stubborn refusal to leave. Soon after the prince appeared in Agra, there followed news that Badakhshan was besieged, but when Babur suggested that Humayun might like to go and defend his fief, the prince declared that having so long 'suffered' the lack of his father's presence, he had 'vowed . . . [to] never again . . . exile himself' from it. Thus it was that Babur's nephew, young Sulaiman, went to rescue Badakhshan – and went on to take it for his own – while Humayun settled in Sambhal, where he 'remained happily' for six months until he fell ill, thus setting the course for Babur's demise.[26]

Is it possible that if Humayun had followed his father's instructions, or Mahdi Khwaja had been less treacherous, the Mughal Empire would have grown towards Bukhara, not Bengal? 'There is mist over the scene', writes Beveridge, 'from which only the accomplished facts emerge'.[27] Humayun, that is, was neither too unworldly nor too abstracted to nurse ambition. He wanted Babur's throne in Hindustan and he got it.

And now, in 1540, he had lost it. All of it, even Badakhshan – now held by Sulaiman. At some point during those unhappy months in Lahore, discussing possibilities threadbare, Humayun had declared, rather disingenuously, that he would return to his old fief, a decade after abandoning it. The proposal never even reached Sulaiman. Kamran put his foot down at the very thought, declaring that Babur 'gave Kabul to my mother . . . It is not right [for you] to go to Kabul'.

This apparent non sequitur – Humayun had said nothing about Kabul, after all – was prompted by the fact that Kabul lay en route to Badakhshan, and Kamran may have suspected that, once in Kabul, Humayun wouldn't leave. Humayun's reply, in which he argued that Babur had intended his beloved Kabul to remain imperial land, unattached to any one son, only confirmed Kamran's suspicions. Thus, writes Gulbadan, let Humayun 'talk as he would, pacifying and conciliating . . . [Kamran] resisted more and more'. And why should he not? No matter Babur's sentimental attachment to Kabul, it was Kamran who had ruled that city before and after the late emperor's death. Why would he allow a potential rival into his realm? Babur might not have encouraged the idea himself; for all his talk about shared 'imperial' domains, he had also once quoted this bit of practical verse: 'Ten darvishes can sleep on one rug, but one climate cannot hold two kings.'[28]

Besides, numbers were on Kamran's side – he had a 'large following', says Gulbadan – and Humayun had to abandon the idea, though not, it seems, before making one last, indecorous attempt to race Kamran for it. Jouher describes how the two brothers met at an intersection near Kushab, some

250 kilometres west of Lahore. One road led north to Kabul, the other south to Multan. 'Unluckily', writes Jouher, 'the royal party and the followers of Kamran came to the pass at the same time'.

Humayun declared that he should get to go first, being the elder brother, but Kamran would not give way. After some wrangling and a stern lecture on propriety delivered by one of Humayun's chiefs, Kamran let Humayun and his men march ahead. But now, with Kamran watching hawk-eyed, and Humayun holding on to the vestiges of his dignity, the fallen emperor had little choice except to take the road south, away from the gardens of Kabul into the 'waterless wilderness'[29] of Sindh.

Humayun's long exile had begun.

It was fifteen years before Humayun returned to Hindustan; thirteen before he was able to establish unchallenged control over Kabul. He wandered, dishevelled and thirsting, through the deserts of Sindh and Rajasthan, treading diplomatic water in the realm of Iran, threatening retirement yet fighting battle after battle to remain a force in the world.

A full account of Humayun's adventures would arouse all the pity and terror of Greek tragedy and empty the ink from any storyteller's pen; it is a shame it isn't more often told. There is one occurrence from these times, however, that makes its way into every history of the early Mughals: it was now that Humayun met the girl of his dreams.

As the man in green had foretold, Hamida Banu was a descendant of Shaikh Ahmad of Jam, a renowned Persian saint of the twelfth century. She was also under fifteen years old and untouched by any desire to marry Humayun. For him, on the other hand, it was love at first sight.

They met in the camp of Humayun's youngest brother, Hindal, the gallant prince who had discouraged the despondent emperor from putting his harem to the sword after the rout in Kannauj. Ever since their escape from Lahore, the two brothers and their cousin Yadgar Nasir had been meandering through Sindh, neither in alliance nor at war – a 'blundering band',[30] as Haider puts it – scraping what living they could for their diminished armies. Humayun, for example, was camped by the Indus, trying to interest Mirza Shah Husain, the ruler of Sindh, in an attack on Gujarat, while also besieging one of his fortresses. As the siege dragged on and Shah Husain sent no clear reply, Humayun's soldiers were reduced to eating their own camels and horses.

It was at this point that Humayun decided to visit Hindal, who had camped a little downstream, in Patr (now Paat). Abul Fazl would like us to believe that Humayun had 'appointed' him there some months ago, but Gulbadan is more forthright. She says that Hindal had recently moved his camp across the river and the rumour was that he was planning to leave for Qandahar. That city, like Kabul, was ruled by Kamran, who also commanded the loyalty of his brother Askari. To have Hindal join that alliance would be another blow to Humayun's shattered fortune. He went hurrying to Patr, writes Gulbadan, to meet Hindal's mother, Dildar Begum, in the hope, presumably, that she would influence the prince in Humayun's favour.

When Humayun reached Hindal's camp, all the women of the harem came to greet him. Among them was Hamida. 'Who is this?'[31] asked Humayun, and was informed that she was the daughter of Mir Baba Dost, then employed as Hindal's teacher of religion. Hamida's young brother, Muazzam, was part of the gathering too; turning to him, Humayun remarked, 'This boy will be one of my kinsmen . . .' – and then, of Hamida, 'She, too, is related to me.'

Possibly, he meant they were all related through the venerable Shaikh Ahmad of Jam: Humayun's own mother, Maham Begum, was also a descendant of his. As a pickup line, the remark was more smug than charming and impressed neither Hamida nor Hindal. Some days later, when Humayun came to Dildar Begum and pressed the point more forcefully – 'Mir Baba Dost is related to us. It is fitting that you should give me his daughter in marriage' – Hindal exploded. According to Jouher, who was present at the spot, if not at the scene, 'Prince Hindal was very angry with his brother, and said, "I thought you came here to do me honour, not to look out for a young bride: if you commit this [ridiculous] action, I will leave you."'

Gulbadan, too, writes that Hindal kept 'making objections' to the match, arguing that he 'looked upon this girl as a sister and child of my own' and that Humayun couldn't afford to marry. Gulbadan adds that Hamida 'was often in [Hindal's] residence', thus allowing for the speculation that Hindal's interest in her was more romantic than protective. He was certainly closer to her in age: Hamida was fourteen, Hindal twenty-two, and Humayun a relatively ancient thirty-three.

Whatever the reason for his objections, Hindal was adamant and Humayun furious. He stormed out of Dildar's tent, and, according to Jouher, 'went on board a boat'. The frazzled begum took a stern line with both men. With Hindal, writes Jouher, she was 'very angry', telling him off for speaking rudely to his elder brother 'whom you ought to consider as the representative of your late father'. To Humayun, she wrote a calming but firm letter, comforting him with news that Hamida's own mother had shown interest in the match, but also expressing her own astonishment 'that you should go away in anger over a few words'.[32] The brothers duly chastened, Dildar went to Humayun, brought him off his boat and out of his sulk, and arranged a conciliatory party.

Dildar's greatest challenge was to come, however. She may have enforced a fragile peace between Hindal and Humayun, but how to persuade Hamida? A few days after Dildar's party, Humayun returned to his stepmother's tent and sent for his beloved. Hamida refused his invitation, point-blank. She had paid her respects when Humayun first arrived, 'Why should I come again?' Humayun persevered. He sent a messenger to Hindal, asking for help.

With grim satisfaction, perhaps, the prince told the messenger there was nothing he could do: 'Whatever I may say, she will not go. Go yourself and tell her.' The messenger arrived at Hamida's tent, but had no luck. 'To see kings once is lawful; a second time it is forbidden', she told him. 'I shall not come.'[33]

When has rejection diminished love's ardour? Hamida's stinging refusals did not discourage Humayun. Gulbadan writes that when his messenger returned, spurned and alone, all Humayun said was, 'If she is not a consort, we will make her a consort.'

Not only did Humayun press his suit with unflagging vigour, the courtship seems to have superseded all his other concerns – whether negotiations with Sindh or Hindal's possible defection. Hadn't the struggling emperor wanted Dildar to cement Hindal's loyalty towards himself? Instead, Humayun had roped her into his romantic schemes. For forty days, Dildar coaxed Hamida, who 'resisted and discussed and disagreed'. Eventually, Dildar produced the trump card often laid before reluctant brides. 'After all', she said, 'you will marry someone'. And who better to marry than a king? At this, Hamida made the reply for which she is famed: 'Oh yes, I shall marry someone; but he shall be a man whose collar my hand can touch, and not one whose skirt it does not reach.'[34]

This can be (and often is) interpreted to mean that Hamida felt Humayun was too exalted for her, that she was expressing a humble desire for a less august match (might she have meant Hindal?). On the other hand, given Humayun's circumstances at the time – he was living on a boat in the wilds of Sindh, eating horsemeat – it's possible, if less flattering, that Hamida was being sarcastic. If so, Dildar ignored her, and 'again', writes Gulbadan, 'gave her much advice'. Finally, Hamida relented. Humayun was thrilled. He did the astrological calculations himself, to find an auspicious date for the wedding. In September 1541, a year or so after losing his empire and fleeing Lahore, Humayun had won himself a bride.

Abul Fazl maintains a loyal, tight-lipped silence on all the drama that preceded the marriage; all he will say is that Humayun and Hamida's wedding was celebrated 'with lordly ceremonies and royal rites'. He does not say, either, that one member of the royal family found no joy in the occasion. Only Jouher writes of how Hindal marched off 'in an angry mood' towards Qandahar.[35]

Humayun may have triumphed in affairs of the heart, but in affairs of state he was more isolated than ever before. Indeed, in the first year of their marriage, the skirt Hamida could not reach would find itself straggling and torn upon barren ground; and the young bride would have more than one occasion to regret not having clung more firmly to her refusal.

By the spring of 1542, Humayun's Sindh 'campaign' was in a shambles. He had gained neither military victory nor strategic alliance, and his army – with neither food on their plates nor victory on the horizon – was haemorrhaging. Jouher recounts the pitiful tale of how Humayun had to stay up all night with two of his chiefs, Tardi Beg and Munim Khan, to 'prevent their going off '. In the morning, Humayun left the tent – presumably for his ablutions – but no sooner had he gone than the two men 'ran towards their horses'. Though Humayun's attendants called after them – stop! – they wouldn't listen until Humayun raced into view and 'with great difficulty prevailed on them to return'.

As summer stole upon them, Humayun and his few unhappy adherents took a decision born of desperation: they marched into the arid desert lands of Rajasthan, and the realm of Raja Maldeo of Marwar. The journey, writes Jouher, was 'horrid'; on one particular leg of it, they marched twenty-seven hours without finding water. Thirst is not a suffering that ennobles; it certainly did not bring out the best in Humayun. Soon after the enfeebled company found water, Humayun rode past a Mongol merchant lying on the road, too weak even to walk to the pond. As it happens, Humayun owed this merchant a great deal of money and saw a golden opportunity in his plight. He offered the Mongol as much water as he could drink in return for cancelling his debt. What could the merchant do but agree? 'A cup of water', he said, 'is . . . more valuable than the wealth of the whole world'. Even so, Humayun was canny enough to summon three men to witness the deal before giving the merchant his drink.

The Mongol lost but a small fortune; others in the camp were less lucky. 'Many of our people died', writes Jouher, 'and all suffered exceedingly'.

As the Mughals entered the land of Maldeo, it looked as if they might be coming into a bit of luck. Gulbadan says the raja sent them armour and money, and a generous message: 'You are welcome! I give you Bikaner.' Jouher writes that Raja Maldeo only sent them fruit, though even this, given the camp's wretched state, must have been welcome.

Hamida would have been pleased. In early July 1542, when Humayun entered the desert, Hamida was about six months pregnant. It is hard to imagine what her suffering must have been; endless marches under a blazing sky, the dust blowing in her eyes and her flask running dry. But clearly, the fifteen-year-old kept her spirit. 'In that waterless and grainless [desert] where it was difficult to find any trace of corn', writes Abul Fazl, Hamida declared she wanted a pomegranate. As she made this seemingly impossible demand, a man arrived with a sack of barley for sale. He opened the bag to show off his grain – and who would believe it! A 'large, juicy pomegranate' fell out.

Is this the miracle Abul Fazl declares it to be, or is he extrapolating matters from Maldeo's gift of fruit? At any rate, Hamida got her pomegranate, and Humayun looked like he might get a foot through the door of Hindustan. Soon, however, that hope was revealed to be no more than a desert mirage. Various sources credit the unmasking of Maldeo to various men.[36] The most apt of these stories is Gulbadan's. She recounts how her bibliophile brother's former librarian, one Mulla Surkh, found employment with Raja Maldeo after the 'downfall and desolation in Hind'. It was this librarian who sent urgent word of the raja's treachery. 'Beware, a thousand times beware of advancing', he wrote. 'March at once from wherever you are, for Maldeo intends to make you prisoner.' Sher Shah, it seems, had offered the raja Alwar and Nagor in exchange for Humayun in chains.[37]

As Humayun prepared to leave, two spies were caught and brought before him. It was in keeping with Humayun's luck that they managed to kill several men, women and horses[38] before being slain themselves, with the result that when the camp was ready to move Hamida had no horse to ride. Humayun, summoning what authority he could, asked Tardi Beg – whose desertion he had prevented mid-toilette – for his horse. It was one of Tardi Beg's horses that Humayun had ridden when he fled Kannauj, but now the chief had reached the shallow limits of his generosity. Unmoved by Hamida's swollen belly, Tardi Beg refused; Humayun had to give up his own mount and ride, for a while, on Jouher's camel.

Judger does not tell this story; his is worse. In his telling, an officer called Roshan Beg proved even more cold-hearted than Tardi – he took away the horse on which Hamida was already mounted, having lent her the animal previously and now lost his own. This story ends like the other: with Humayun, son of Babur, heir to the rich plains of Hindustan, the dynasties of Timur the Lame and Chinghis Khan, barely able to provide a horse for his pregnant wife, seeking shelter in the desert, lurching upon a camel.

And yet, he had reason to be grateful. There were many in the company, both men and women, who were on foot, and even the animals found it hard to carry on: the horses in particular 'kept sinking to the knees in the sand'.[39] Humayun appointed Tardi Beg and Munim Khan to hang back and guard the company's flank against any possible attack by Maldeo; himself, he rode ahead, with twenty-odd soldiers to protect the harem, the slaves and the court astrologer, Maulana Chand. 'On they went', this beleaguered party, 'thirsty and hungry', marching all night – the astrologer guiding them by the stars, perhaps – and at dawn they found a well. The horses, writes Gulbadan, had not had a drop to drink for three days.

The men and women, stiff-jointed, their feet blistered and throats dry, were only just moving towards the water when a moan spread through them, 'The Hindus are coming . . .'![40] Tardi Beg and Munim Khan, deputed to prevent exactly this attack, had 'lost their way and gone off in another direction'.[41] Humayun sent the few soldiers with him to fight – some had to borrow horses from the harem. The rest of the company turned from the water and resumed their long march again, 'slowly, slowly on',[42] too tired even to flee with speed.

Only Humayun, writes Gulbadan, 'was far ahead' – was he racing to save his own skin, or that of his wife and unborn child? At any rate, a galloping horse soon overtook him – did he wonder, perhaps, if this was the end? – but it was only a messenger from his men: somehow, the Mughal soldiers had fought off the attack. For now, they were safe; and there was even a bit of water nearby.

For the second time that day, Humayun got off his horse, and for the second time, there was the dust of horsemen on the horizon. Another cry: 'God forbid! Maldeo!'[43] But no, it was only Tardi Beg, Munim Khan and the others, catching up with the camp. Finally, the thirsty, dusty exiles were able to drink in peace. They would find no more water for the next three days. According to Jouher's account, this was not so much from a lack of wells, but because Maldeo had deputed his men to ride ahead of Humayun's party and fill the wells in their path with sand. The raja's intention, it seems, was to punish Humayun for allowing his men to capture and kill cows and buffaloes during their march. The raja sent two messengers to say so: having known that 'the killing of kine was forbidden in Hindu districts' and having 'nevertheless killed a number of these sacred animals', Humayun 'must take the consequences'.[44]

The consequences were dire. The exiles were specks in the endless sands of Jaisalmer; it was August and the sun rose ferociously high, day after day, in skies that held not a hint of rain. For three days they walked, sipping at their meagre reserves, and when, on the fourth, the company finally found some wells that held water, men and women threw themselves at the buckets that were hauled up, some with such force that they fell tumbling into the wells head first.

Nizamuddin the historian presents an even more pathetic picture. A bullock was used to draw out water, sunk so deep that you had to beat a drum when the buckets reached the rim, 'a call would not reach' the bullock driver. With water so close, this last, sluggish journey was too much for some to bear. As soon as the drumbeat sounded, they threw themselves at the well, thus breaking the rope and sending the longed-for bucket crashing into the dark, far below. Imagine the scene. 'Cries and lamentations' broke out, and some who could bear it no more 'cast themselves intentionally into the well'. So it was for many that their lives were quenched before their thirst, and few showed any pity for another's condition.

Certainly not Tardi Beg, that paragon of self-interest. This chieftain had commandeered a well for himself and was using it to pull out water for his own animals, denying access even to Humayun's horses and camels. Humayun's attendants came to complain, swearing that they would 'either have water or be killed'. Humayun had to intervene and more or less beg water from Tardi Beg, speaking to him in their native Turki: 'Be so good as to draw off your people for a short time . . .'[45] Tardi Beg complied and bloodshed was prevented, but still, whatever the curmudgeonly chief allowed the animals, it wasn't enough. Another march of a day and a night brought the company to a tank. Horses and camels, no longer dependent on the benevolence of their masters, saw the delicious wetness before them and waded in. Many drank so much that they died.

The pity of it was beyond description, and Jouher does not test his pen, writing only, and bluntly: 'the misery we suffered at this stage was intolerable'. It was also, however, near its end. On 22 August 1542, Humayun's company – only eight of whom still had horses left to ride[46] – reached the rounded turrets and thick walls of the fortress of Umarkot, and found shelter with its ruler, Rana Prasad.

Now that he had refuge, there were two matters that required Humayun's most urgent attention. One was clean clothes. Jouher offers the quite wonderful scene of his master lounging in his dressing gown, having sent his clothes – sweat-stiff and pungent, no doubt – to the wash. Second was money. Humayun didn't have any, neither to pay his men nor to offer the rana; and his chieftains, as Abul Fazl puts it, dismayed, 'grudged' him their wealth 'even when his Majesty asked for it!'

Once again, however, Humayun reveals himself to be a far more canny operator than his reputation suggests. He assembled all the chiefs in his tent, as if for a meeting, then sent some trusted men to ransack their baggage. This produced a small loot of money, jewels and clothes, of which Humayun ordered half to be returned. The remaining gems and coins he distributed among his 'servants and followers' – the clothes he kept for himself.[47] Thus, dressed in what finery he could muster and able to acknowledge Rana Prasad's hospitality with gifts of sword belts and armour, Humayun embarked on what he and his followers must have hoped would be a new and more fortunate chapter of his life. In this, they would be quite wrong; but that does not deprive Umarkot of significance in Mughal chronicles. It was here, after all, in Umarkot, where you could buy four goats for one rupee,[48] and mango trees perfumed the air, it was here, as the summer waned and the refugees began to recover their strength, that the very first words of another and more glorious life were written.

By Abul Fazl's account,[49] the seven weeks between 22 August and 15 October, the last two months of Hamida's pregnancy, were crowded with good omens. One day, for example, Hamida was riding in her litter through one of Umarkot's famous mango orchards, its trees as heavy with fruit as she was.

A sudden craving overtook her, and she sent her brother, Muazzam, to bring her an armful of mangoes. When the boy returned, he was half-blinded by the light reflecting off her brow, and asked, 'Have you put a mirror on your forehead?' Nothing of the sort, she replied, yet Muazzam could not look her full in the face, for all the 'glory of the divine light' that shone from it.

Light is the predominant theme of these omens. Jiji Anaka, future wet nurse to Hamida's child, told Abul Fazl of how a 'great light' settled on her bosom. 'I felt', she said, 'as if the world-warming Sun had fallen into my breast'. Humayun was not spared such visitation either. He was having a party in a room with a latticed window, the assembly was attempting to divine the date of the 'glorious birth', when '[s]uddenly rays of divine light shone from the lattices'.

The visions piled up, the day of the birth drew close, and yet, only three days before Hamida delivered her baby, Humayun left Umarkot. It's possible, of course, that Humayun didn't want to go. Why would he not want to welcome the new life that Hamida and he had managed, somehow, to preserve across the desert? But Humayun was a guest in Umarkot – more bluntly, a refugee – and guests cannot do as they please. Rana Prasad had helped Humayun because the rana wanted vengeance against Shah Husain of Sindh, whose territory Humayun had fled in such humiliating circumstances. Shah Husain had killed Rana Prasad's father, and the rana was willing to give Humayun troops, shelter and an alliance, if Humayun would help him obtain the shah's head.[50] Thus, on 11 October 1542, Humayun left Hamida and marched off with Rana Prasad towards Shah Husain's territory.

Humayun had to leave, but he left behind some instructions that reveal his keen interest in his prospective progeny. The emperor better known for his interest in astrology than in rule issued clear commands to Maulana Chand, his astrologer: be present at the birth and make precise note of the planets and stars that would reveal the newborn's fate.

Maulana Chand was nothing if not conscious of his responsibility, and zealous in discharging it. Not for him a merely clerical recording of the birth; he went above and beyond the call of duty and determined a wonderfully auspicious hour for it, too, 'such as does not happen once in a thousand years'. When Hamida went into labour some hours before this time, Maulana Chand was appalled. Not only was this not the best time to be born, it was, in fact, the worst. The astrologer hurried to the harem declaring, 'What an advantage if the birth could be delayed!'[51]

One can imagine how the women 'made light of' his idea, but little did they know. Fate had decided to favour the unborn child. A midwife arrived to deliver the baby; she was so utterly 'repulsive' that Hamida's contractions stopped in their tracks. Still, the astrologer's anxieties were not at an end. As night descended on Umarkot and the auspicious hour crept upon them, Hamida was fast asleep. Maulana Chand was 'disturbed', wishing perhaps to prod the girl awake. Again, her attendants were intractable. Hamida had fallen asleep 'after much suffering', they said, and they would certainly not wake her. 'Whatever Almighty God . . . has determined, must happen.'

God was of one mind with the maulana. Hamida's attendants were still arguing with the astrologer when she woke up in labour. Just a little past 1 a.m. that night, on Sunday, 15 October 1542, not a moment too soon nor a moment too late, Akbar – 'the greater' – was born.

Akbar was not Humayun's first son. Almost exactly fourteen years before, when Humayun was still discharging his duties in Badakhshan, he had a son whom he named Al-Aman. When news of this was brought to Babur in Agra, the emperor was displeased. Never particularly impressed with Humayun's literary instincts (he once wrote a letter to his son ticking him off for his convoluted style), Babur didn't like this newfangled name. It was unusual to prefix 'al' to a name, and even if Al-Aman meant 'peace' or 'security' in Arabic, in the family's native Turki it could easily be misheard as 'alaman', 'plunderer' or 'ilaman', 'I do not feel'.[52] It was hardly the kind of name a conqueror would want for his grandson, and, besides, it was entirely inappropriate for Humayun to name the boy without Babur's approval.

In a cold-hearted aside on the subject, Abul Fazl writes that displeasing one's father can bring about 'a hundred evils, external and internal'. Indeed, the infant died.

Once Humayun became emperor himself, his mother, Maham Begum, developed a burning desire for a grandson, such that, in Gulbadan's words, any 'good-looking and nice girl' she spotted was immediately recruited to the task. Among these was Maywa-jaan. Dutifully, Humayun married her. Three days later, Humayun's first wife, Bega Begum, arrived in Agra from Kabul – and was soon pregnant. Unhappy to lose her limelight, Maywa-jaan declared herself with child too, sending Maham Begum into ecstasy; she began collecting gifts while mouthing a refrain: 'Perhaps one of them will have a son.'

As it happens, Bega Begum had a daughter. Maham Begum focused all her attention on Maywa-jaan and the months passed by. Ten, then eleven. The young girl spoke cheerfully of an aunt who'd delivered in her twelfth month. 'But in the end', writes Gulbadan ruefully, 'everyone knew she was a fraud'.

It is easy, almost reflexive, to imagine Maham Begum flapping about in a womanly dither, to dismiss her ambitions as merely domestic. In fact, however, her impatience may have been for an heir, not a grandson – Humayun had just assumed his father's throne; one day, he would need a successor in turn.[53] Maham Begum died well before Humayun lost his inheritance; she was spared the humiliation of his collapse. Might she have endured it all for

the chance to exult in this longed-for moment; or would it have increased her
dismay, to have an heir born, finally, but with nothing to inherit?
Perhaps not. Kings, like artists, must live on hope. As Akbar was born,
in fact, Humayun had a vision of a magical new dawn. The padishah was
absorbed in meditation, sitting in a trance, when he called out, 'Praise be to
God . . . the lamp of our royal family has been relit.'
A chieftain who stood nearby – and later narrated the whole story to
Abul Fazl – asked what Humayun had seen. It was, said his emperor, as if a
bright star had risen over Umarkot, and 'as it ascended, its size and brilliance
increased, until its light had embraced the greater portion of the world'. What
could it be, this light? 'It was the light incarnate of my successor', came the
reply.

Regardless of visions and marvels, Akbar's very birth – that Hamida and her
unborn child had survived their trials under the desert sun – was something
of a miracle. His continued survival, moreover, was uncertain. Akbar was
born a refugee; his parents impoverished, beset by enemies on the one hand,
seeking kindness from strangers on the other. Given these circumstances, the
celebrations at Akbar's birth may not have been as extravagant as Abul Fazl
claims ('there is no need of explanation or description', he writes demurely,
after a page-full of 'Dark-haired maidens . . . Rose-cheeked damsels . . .
Red-garmented, sweetly-smiling nymphs . . . scattering saffron' as musicians
create 'enchanting ecstasy') – but they would have been heartfelt.
Jouher's account of Humayun's reaction to the news is more credible.
Humayun and his faithful water carrier were camped by a pond not far from
Umarkot when they saw a rider galloping towards them. By one account, this
was Tardi Beg, and Humayun showed his pleasure by forgiving the Chagatai[54] Scrooge his many sins.[55] Then he summoned Jouher to bring out what
little of the chieftains' confiscated wealth remained with him. The water carrier produced two hundred silver coins, a silver bracelet and a pod of musk.
The money and bracelet Humayun returned to their owners; the pod of musk
he broke upon a china plate. As the plate was passed around the tent, Humayun gave a short but moving speech, telling the gathered chiefs, 'This is all
the present I can afford to make you on the birth of my son.' Yet, he hoped,
his son's fame would one day fill the world 'as the perfume of the musk now
fills this apartment'.
Drums and trumpets completed the short ceremony. There wasn't time for
more; the camp had to resume its march.
All that Abul Fazl writes, meanwhile, of '[m]elodious musicians and
enchanting vocalists', harps, lutes, rebecs and tambourines filling the camp
air may be safely ignored, but the historian, giddy with joy, offers one little
anecdote that rings with truth. When Humayun saw his son's horoscope, the

new father locked himself in his 'private chamber' and here, alone and able to rejoice at ease, 'he fell a'dancing'.

Back in Umarkot, meanwhile, Akbar had had his first bath. Afterwards, wrapped in a soft blanket, he formed the first alliances of his long political career: the bond by milk with his wet nurses or foster mothers, his *anakas*. The first of ten to hold him was Jiji Anaka, wife of Shamsuddin of Ghazni who had rescued Humayun from the riverbank in Kannauj.[56] Akbar was smiling – another small miracle in an infant – causing hearts to 'rejoice' as the women fed him, then put him in a cradle of sandalwood and aloe, rocking him gently and singing him a lullaby made with the names of God.

Many of these women and their families would play critical roles in the life and reign of the baby they suckled now. For the moment, however, no one – not even Maulana Chand – could have predicted the course of their linked destinies. For the moment, the world turned very much as usual, as the newborn Niru'un took his first, small breaths of its air.

Chapter 2

Return

'Alas! that the Emperor Humayun died so early and that I had no opportunity of showing him faithful service!'

– Akbar, Happy Sayings, *Ain-i-Akbari*

A year had not passed when Akbar the refugee became also a hostage. For much of the first decade of his life, in fact, the prince was to be shunted between malevolent uncles and ministering aunts, in the wake of his father's fluctuating fortunes. For most of these years, any thought of resuscitating his rule in Hindustan must have retreated to the deepest recesses of Humayun's mind; his greatest challenge would no longer be Sher Shah, but Kamran, his greatest ambition no longer Delhi, but Kabul. To lower one's ambitions by such scale cannot be easy for anyone, let alone for a padishah, and it would be a while before Humayun was able to bring himself to do so. He would have to fall to the very pits of his fortune first, bereft of even a pebble to rule, bereft of even his son. And, as befits a life of such Grecian drama, the fall would be of Humayun's own making, the result of his own tragic flaw: self-indulgence.

Within days of Akbar's birth, Humayun had fought a quick battle and won a riverside town called Jun, then settled down in it for a prolonged rest. The expedition should have carried the momentum of its victory and marched on to attack Shah Husain in Thatta, his capital; and Gulbadan, for one, cannot understand why it didn't. 'It is a six days' journey from Jun to Tatta', she writes, but Humayun 'was as much as six months in Jun'.[1] Abul Fazl's description of Jun goes a long way to explain Humayun's decision. The town was beautiful, and beautifully located, built along the blue waters of the Indus, 'eminent . . . for its many gardens, streams, [and] pleasant fruits'[2]. Humayun had suffered a terrible two years; now, with his tents pitched in one of Jun's lovely gardens, surrounded by its orchards, soothed by the sounds of

21

the river nearby, the exiled emperor may have felt he deserved a little treat. Instead of ordering marches, then, he summoned his family.

On 9 December 1542, when Akbar was just under two months old, he met his father in a lovely little ceremony: Akbar's head was put to Humayun's feet, after which the father took the baby in his arms and kissed him.

Humayun's new-found domestic bliss was charming no doubt, but it was hardly calculated to overawe an enemy. Seeing Humayun so disinclined to march upon Thatta, Shah Husain brought his own army to the slack conqueror. Camped a few miles from Jun, the shah began to send skirmishing parties against Humayun's soldiers, and secret overtures to his commanders. Rana Prasad, meanwhile, had quarrelled with one of these Chagatai chiefs and was tiring of the endless wait. He left in a huff, exclaiming, as Jouher reports, that 'any attempt to assist the Moghuls was a loss of labour and time'.[3] With the rana went his men, at which the smaller chieftains of Sindh, who had allied with Rana Prasad and Humayun, abandoned the campaign, too, leaving Humayun 'alone, as before, with his own people'.[4] These people were not immune to temptation, as Humayun knew too well; one by one his commanders began to desert. Among them was that would-be turncoat Munim Khan – this time, Humayun was not alert enough to prevent his leaving.

Humayun's time in Jun was running out as fast as his men, but before it ended altogether, there was one man who joined him in his riverside garden; one man who was worth more than all the others put together in what he would do, not just for this emperor without a throne, but for his dynasty.

Abul Fazl gives Bairam Khan the hero's entrance he deserves. It was the spring of 1543, and Shah Husain's attacks were unceasing. There was one ongoing, in fact, as Bairam rode into view. Without pause, the soldier charged into the heart of the battle, as if from 'the secret army [of God]'. Humayun's men let out shouts of delight when they recognized him.

They would have met last at the rout in Kannauj. Bairam had joined Babur's service when he was sixteen,[5] and while he couldn't prevent Babur's heir's unseemly rout from Hindustan, the soldier had acquired a reputation for military prowess. So much so, in fact, that not one but two Hindustani rulers tried to poach him before he managed to rejoin Humayun's camp: Sher Shah the Afghan and Sultan Mahmud of Gujarat. Bairam refused Sher Shah's offer ('whoever keeps his loyalty, shall not stumble', he said with flair) and barely escaped the aggrieved shah's domain with his life.[6] When Bairam arrived in Gujarat, he had learnt not to offend kings; he did not refuse Sultan Mahmud's offer of employment, only asked if he might perform the pilgrimage to Mecca first. When the sultan allowed it, Bairam got on a boat and sailed to Sindh instead.

Such quick thinking gave Bairam Khan a reputation for military and political genius that has survived centuries, but even he couldn't rescue

Humayun's campaign against Shah Husain. Three months after Bairam arrived, in the summer of 1543, Humayun gathered his few remaining men and abandoned his ambitions in Sindh – and thereby any hope of a covert return to Hindustan via Sher Shah's western borders. Instead, he decided to venture into Kamran's realm. He would go to Qandahar.

As Humayun prepared to pick at the scabs of his fraternal feud, a new rivalry was developing in his harem. The idyll of that first nursing ceremony, Akbar suckling at the breasts of his many mamas – the affectionate term for mothers and mother figures in Turki – was too perfect to last. Now, Akbar was seven months old and his mamas were at daggers drawn. As Jiji Anaka fed the baby one evening, a woman called Maham Anaka, superintendent of Akbar's nurses, led a delegation of discontented foster mothers to Humayun, declaring, that Jiji was 'practising incantations so that . . . the prince . . . should not accept anyone's milk but her own'.

Humayun's response is unrecorded, nor is it the point of this story, told many years later by Jiji Anaka to Abul Fazl. The point is this: as Jiji sat disconsolate, the child in her arms began to speak. 'Be of good cheer', he said, 'for the celestial light of the *khilafat* shall abide in thy bosom and shall bestow on the night of thy sorrow the effulgence of joy. But see that thou reveal this our secret to no one, and that thou dost not proclaim untimely this mystery of God's power, for hidden designs and great previsions are infolded therein.' Jiji was surprised, naturally, by such portentous eloquence from the infant at her breast, but it had its effect: 'sorrow's knot was at once loosed from off my heart'. What was a little domestic friction, after all, in the face of divine revelation?

In obedience to the baby's command, and suspecting, wisely enough, that any mention of it would only attract unkind remarks about the 'weakness of [her] intellect' from unsympathetic rivals, Jiji told no one of the miracle. When, a few weeks later, the company set off for Qandahar, she alone knew that the youngest among them was also, perhaps, the most powerful.

Humayun never made it to Qandahar. He had been warned that his brother Askari, who held the city as Kamran's deputy, would not allow Humayun into it; that he would, in fact, attack and imprison his former king. Humayun responded with a reproving letter to his 'little-loving, disloyal brother' – but if he meant to induce any guilt in his kin, he failed. As Abul Fazl laments, 'where was there the reason-hearkening ear . . .?'

The very next day, a young Uzbek came galloping into the camp at full throttle, demanding to see Humayun. When a servant indicated where his master was resting and invited the Uzbek to get off his horse, the young man merely 'twisted the reins about his hand', rode behind the screen where

Humayun lay, and woke him up. 'Myrza Askery is coming to attack you', he said.[7]

Gulbadan writes that Humayun fled immediately and was 'two arrows' flight' gone before he sent for Hamida. Jouher and Abul Fazl both have the fallen emperor proposing battle, a brave idea vetoed by Bairam ('there are but few of us'[8]); but only Jouher tells of how, at this critical moment, Humayun was short, once again, of a horse for his wife. Once again, he asked that churl, Tardi Beg, to lend him one, and once again, Tardi Beg refused. This time, in fact, he refused any kind of service at all, having no more interest, evidently, in another bout of uncertain vagabonding in Humayun's company. With Tardi Beg so intractable and little time to lose, Humayun took Hamida upon his own horse and began to ride west, seeking no more kingdoms, but only refuge.

They left their son behind.

According to Gulbadan, this was because there was 'not a chink of time' in which to take him; according to Abul Fazl, it was because Humayun knew his son was protected by 'Divine love'. Neither explanation is very satisfactory. Jouher's unhappy scene, however, suggests a more credible cause for the abandonment: Hamida and Humayun, with one horse between them and no idea of their future, had every reason to think it more practical, even safer, to leave their son behind.

Back in the camp, Akbar would have food, at least, and warmth and loyal attendants. Jouher was among them, as were the two rival anakas, Maham and Jiji, and Jiji's husband, Shamsuddin Muhammad. Perhaps they huddled protectively around their charge – Akbar was barely one year old; perhaps they prepared to battle on his behalf. When Askari arrived, however, riding in with his troops only hours after Humayun's departure, he was less menacing than he was impudent.

Why had Humayun 'gone off by the desert'?[9] he asked Shamsuddin, claiming cheekily that he'd only come to pay his elder brother his respects. For Akbar, he sent some fruit, then settled down with a couple of clerks to take full account of whatever treasures Humayun had left behind. It was only the next day that Askari went to meet his nephew – imprisoning most of Humayun's chieftains on his way. (Among them Tardi Beg, who was forced to bail himself out with a small fortune, and thus, writes Abul Fazl with satisfaction, he 'got the retribution of his deeds'.)

Akbar was a cheerful child, generous with his smiles. Not so with his uncle. Though Askari came to him with 'a jubilant air', Akbar would not be moved to smile. And why should he? As Askari muttered sadly to himself, 'We can see whose this child is. Why should he be elated at seeing us?' Instead, he made a grab for the ring his uncle had strung around his neck. Eager for a little affection, Askari took it off and gave it to Akbar immediately, but received no reward.[10]

In mid-December 1543, Askari and his glum nephew arrived in Qandahar. Askari gave him a room near his own, at the very top of the fortress, and his own wife, Sultan Begum, for a mother.[11] It was here, in this eagle's nest, that Akbar began to walk.

He liked to tell the story himself. The wrench that took him from Humayun's camp to Askari's castle was the kind of memory that does not fade with time. 'I perfectly remember what happened when I was one year old, and especially the time when [my father] proceeded towards Iraq and I was brought to Qandahar.' Here, as Akbar took his first unsteady steps about his room, tumbling into his various mamas' laps, Maham reminded Askari of an avuncular duty. It was a custom that when a child started walking, his father, or grandfather – and failing either, now, his uncle – would roll his turban in the toddler's way, whose tripping and falling would divert the evil eye. '[I]mmediately', Akbar remembers, 'the Mirza . . . took off his turban and flung it at me, and I fell down.'[12]

Another ritual would follow soon. Akbar was ready for his first haircut; to bless the event, he was taken to the riverside shrine of Baba Wali, a popular Sufi saint of Qandahar. The details of the day, he would say later, 'are present before me as in a mirror'.[13]

While his son experienced such rites of passage, Humayun was acquiring indelible memories of his own. He had set off upon the second leg of his exile with barely forty men (and two women, including Hamida). Their first night was spent upon a snow-covered mountain, eating horsemeat boiled in a helmet. Humayun cooked his portion on one of the several campfires they had lit around them, though these were as useful as the burning stars against the bitter cold. 'My very head was frozen', Humayun would tell his sister, Gulbadan.

It would be almost a year and a half before Humayun returned to Qandahar, but most of this exile – unlike the last – was spent in far greater comfort than its first terrible night. The purported padishah of Hindustan was given sanctuary by the shah of Iran.

Shah Tahmasp, a man of grit and tremendous ego, had ascended to the Persian throne at the age of twelve and would rule for over fifty years. In terms of both career and character no two men could have been more unalike than Tahmasp and Humayun, and the months that Humayun spent in the shah's realm must have been among the most unnerving of his life. Not that Shah Tahmasp did not make his guest welcome, too much so, if anything. In one long letter of instruction to the governor of Herat, detailing reception and travel arrangements for his neighbouring monarch, the shah stipulates 100 horses with golden saddles, 400 suits of velvet and brocade, 500 dishes every day – bread kneaded with milk, marmalades of Mashhad apples and grapes, halwa, puddings, molasses, Chinese noodles scented with ambergris, all to be served on 'porcelain, gold, and silver' with sherbets 'cooled with snow and ice'. He orders bazaars in city gardens and entertainments on city streets ('the women will engage in pleasant sayings and doings with the comers and goers'), perfumed bathhouses, plush carpets, tents with brocade within and paisley without – and still the list is incomplete.[14]

Clearly, the shah's hospitality was designed to overawe as much as to please, and there was no end, besides, to the slights Humayun had to endure and the threats he had to evade. The shah insisted, for example, on referring to Humayun as his younger brother, although the exiled padishah was eight years his senior. Tahmasp also wanted Humayun to convert to Shiism. This was not, in itself, inimical to Humayun's religious sensibility, but it would have made him even less appealing to the chieftains of Kabul and Qandahar – all Sunni – than he was already. Several stories from this time reveal the nimble ducks and feints Humayun performed to keep his religion and his head. At their first meeting, for example, Shah Tahmasp offered his guest a *taj hyder*, a crown with veneration of the twelve Imams, integral to Shia Islam, built into its design. Humayun, most likely, was wearing a crown he'd 'invented' in Badakhshan – its distinguishing feature being the two '7s' in its design, 77 being the numerical equivalent of *izz*, that is, 'power'. Humayun had brought this *taj-i-izzat* as a gift for Babur when he came uninvited to Agra years ago, and it may have helped assuage Babur's displeasure at Humayun's dereliction of duty.[15]

Now, once again, Humayun was in the court of a great monarch, one he could neither charm nor afford to displease. Humayun took the taj hyder from Tahmasp and declared that since any taj – crown – was 'an emblem of greatness',[16] he would gladly wear it as such. The taj-i-izzat, Humayun's proud invention, was quietly set aside.[17]

The shah took sadistic pleasure, it seems, in reminding Humayun of how he had lost his throne, subjecting the exiled emperor to humiliations – fining Humayun's party for letting deer escape during a hunt – and hectoring lectures: 'It was a consequence of your foolish vanity, that you could not properly govern those *extensive* dominions; you were therefore driven away by the *villagers*. . . .'[18] At one point, the shah may even have thought of having his guest killed – it's unclear why – and both Jouher and Gulbadan agree that it was the shah's sister, Sultana, who saved Humayun's life 'when it was in the balance'.[19] All in all, with little to protect him from either the shah's relentless entertainment or his unpredictable moods, it is no wonder that Humayun called upon the faithful Jouher to *champoo* his head.[20]

But a head massage was only a palliative; what Humayun needed urgently was a way of keeping his dignity, of tempering the gratitude that kept him on such precarious terms with his host. The age-old manner of repaying hospitality is with gifts, of course, and luckily for Humayun he had managed to hold on to a great diamond and 250 Badakhshani rubies. Abul Fazl makes sure to write that these gems 'repaid more than four times over' all that the Persians spent on Humayun over the course of his exile. It is Gulbadan, however, who tells the wonderful story of how the gems were almost lost, and with them, perhaps, Humayun's chances of ever ruling his own kingdom again.

The story goes like this: Humayun kept his jewels in a small box that he would either wear around his neck or leave with Hamida. One day, when Humayun had left the case in her care, Hamida wrapped it in cloth, left it on their bed, and went to wash her hair. When she returned, the case was still there, but perceptibly lighter – someone had helped themselves to Humayun's rubies.

Distraught and ashamed, Hamida went to her brother, Muazzam, and asked for his help. Muazzam revealed himself a talented sleuth. 'One thing occurs to me!' he said. 'I, who am so closely connected with his Majesty, have not the means to buy even a poor pony' – and yet two men from the company, Raushan Koka and Khwaja Ghazi, had just bought themselves a fine pair of horses. Off Muazzam went to the horse trader and found that, yes, indeed, the two men had promised payment in rubies. Next, Muazzam had a casual chat with one of Khwaja Ghazi's attendants and discovered that the khwaja possessed no wallet nor chest, only a high cap, which he wore all day and clutched in his sleep all night.

The detective laid his trap. A boy known for eccentric behaviour, Muazzam began to play the fool around Khwaja Ghazi, teasing and making fun, until the older man learnt to deal with the annoyance by ignoring it. Thus, at an assembly, Muazzam was able to grab the hat from the khwaja's head. He found the rubies in it, of course, and laid them before Hamida and Humayun. So it was, writes Gulbadan, that Humayun was able to send an appropriate gift to Shah Tahmasp – the rubies were dazzling enough; the diamond may have been the Koh-i-noor – and 'the two sovereigns again became of one mind'.[21]

They held parties for each other, and the conversation was rather less tense than before: the shah was pleased with the Hindustani banquet Humayun arranged for him, a dish called *daal khuska* finding particular favour, and Humayun, no doubt, was pleased and relieved at the shah's gift of an army of 12,000 men.

The refugees might now try and win themselves a home.

Kamran wasn't happy to hear the news. It was his Kabul, after all, his home, that Humayun would come to claim. Worried, Kamran sent word to Askari in Qandahar: send Akbar to Kabul. To his credit, Askari was in two minds about giving Akbar over to Kamran's tender mercy; but Askari did little in his life to gain a reputation for courage, certainly not when it came to defying his older and greatly more forceful brother, Kamran. His timidity won over his concern and 'in the depth of winter', as the land was lashed with snow and icy rain, Akbar and his older sister, Bakshi Banu – two and three years old respectively – were taken out of the fort that had been their home the past year.[22] Babur's grandchildren were to enter their grandfather's beloved capital as hostages.

They were escorted by those three most intimate of Akbar's early guardians, Jiji Anaka, her husband Shamsuddin, and Maham Anaka, along with a small party of attendants, all under strict instructions to keep the children's identity secret. They were even given false names: Akbar was called 'Mirak', and Bakshi 'Bicha'.

This and other stories from Akbar's early childhood are told by Abul Fazl, who did a great deal of painstaking research, collecting testimonies, comparing interviews and slicing through the brambles of 'contradictions and imperfections'[23] that are the historian's lot, to produce one of the most masterful and comprehensive accounts of a man ever written by another: the *Akbarnama*. For all the achievement of his scholarship, however, Abul Fazl is rarely willing to see his subject as anything less than superhuman; a divine glow clings to his every description of Akbar, whose every word drips with a sacred nectar. It is a haze of adulation that makes it almost impossible to see Akbar as a real person, let alone a real child; but there are moments when even Abul Fazl's pen cannot quite hide an altogether human sight.

One such moment occurs here, on the cold and secret journey to Kabul. Every night, the travellers would stop at a friendly home, and, one night, the lamp in their room burnt out. Immediately, the child-prince burst into howls of protest. His 'nurses did their best [but] they could not . . . [soothe] him'; only the light of a fresh lamp stopped his tears. In Abul Fazl's telling, this is, of course, a sign of Akbar's supernatural origins; he was a Niru'un after all, descendant of Alanqoa and pure light – but it is easy enough to see him two years old, far from home, wide awake as the wind blows and grown-ups confer in low tones. It is easy enough to see a small child afraid of the dark.

If Askari had been a fond though unreliable uncle, Kamran was his sinister counterpart. Far from trying to make his little nephew smile, Kamran 'cringed' says Abul Fazl – when he met Akbar.[24] To make matters worse, Kamran had brought along a painted drum – not for Akbar, but for his own son, Ibrahim, who was a little older than his cousin. As soon as Akbar saw the drum, however, he wanted it. Kamran was not inclined to indulge his nephew, of course, but he thought he might get a little fun out of the situation. He made the drum a prize and told the boys to wrestle for it.

Akbar wasn't daunted by the idea of fighting the older, bigger Ibrahim; he was delighted. The podgy little toddler 'girt up his loins, and rolled up his sleeves . . . and stepped bravely forward'.[25] Soon, Ibrahim was flat on the ground, the spectators had erupted in cheers, and Kamran had stormed away. Later, his anger would give way to spite: Kamran ordered that Akbar be weaned; his fond mamas would no longer be allowed to suckle him.

If Kamran was cold and mean-spirited, however, there was another in Kabul whose love for Akbar overflowed. This was his great-aunt Khanzada Begum, Babur's older sister, trusted adviser to and intermediary between his squabbling sons. Khanzada was given charge of Akbar when he arrived in the city and was immediately besotted by her grand-nephew. As Gulbadan describes it, the elderly lady would kiss Akbar's hands and feet, exclaiming, 'They are the very hands and feet of my brother [Babur], and he is like him altogether.'

So, delighting in his drum and basking in the affection of his great-aunt, Akbar survived the winter darkness in Kabul; and, in the spring of 1545, news arrived that his father had besieged Qandahar.

The struggle for Qandahar was as much diplomatic as it was military. Urgent embassies travelled between Humayun at the gates of the fort, Askari within, and Kamran on edge in Kabul. Bairam Khan was among these confidential envoys and thus met young Akbar in a Kabul garden, neither of them knowing they would change the history of the world between them. When Bairam Khan arrived, Akbar was playing with Khanzada, who, too, was an ambassador between the warring brothers; it was, in fact, who went to Qandahar and negotiated the terms of Askari's eventual surrender so that, on 3 September 1545, six months after the siege began, Askari came out of the fort in all humility, his sword hung around his neck and Khanzada by his side, to be forgiven by his for-once victorious brother, Humayun.

Khanzada may have negotiated a relatively peaceful agreement between Askari and Humayun in Qandahar, but she'd had to leave Akbar behind to do so. Now, in Kabul, Kamran heard the news of Askari's defeat and took Akbar out of Khanzada's quarters and gave him to his own wife, Khanim Begum. Then, as if to make his mala fides crystal clear, he put Akbar's most loyal male guardian, Shamsuddin Muhammad, in prison. Clearly, Kamran was rattled, and with reason. He might have secured a valuable hostage, but news of Humayun's victory had loosened Kamran's grip on the men and women he had gathered around himself during Humayun's exile.

Among them was the youngest of the four brothers, Hindal. Having marched off in anger when Humayun married Hamida, Hindal had arrived in Qandahar, made some unsuccessful attempts to take it for himself, then become a virtual prisoner of Kamran's. Yadgar Nasir, their cousin, had remained in Sindh to try his luck; when he failed, he too had no refuge but Kabul and Kamran. Sulaiman, their cousin and ruler of Badakhshan, along with his wife Haram Begum and their son Ibrahim, was also among Kamran's unwilling guests – all of whom now took the opportunity to take their leave.

Not that Humayun was in any position to march upon Kabul. The victory at Qandahar was not really his own: four days after he entered the city,
Humayun handed it over to Muhammad Murad Mirza, the Persian shah's
infant son, who was in nominal command of the Persian army that had
helped Humayun defeat Askari. The Persian prince was too young to make
any claims or decisions himself, but his commanders – one Budagh Khan in
particular – were quite clear that the victory, and its spoils, belonged to their
shah. Much like Tahmasp's hospitality, his army, too, had strings attached,
and not half so finely wrought. Not only was Humayun unable to stop the
Persians looting the locals, he couldn't even persuade Budagh Khan to let
his harem stay in Qandahar while Humayun and his troops went on to Kabul.
Such was Humayun's ignominy that he was still camped outside the city
gates after having 'won' it, and was wondering if he should go to Badakhshan instead of Kabul and seek an alliance with Sulaiman, when, in a sudden
stroke of luck, the Persian shah's son died.

Humayun's chieftains wanted to chase the Persians away immediately.
Humayun, averse to any bloodshed that would 'look ill in the eyes of good
men'[26] – like Shah Tahmasp, presumably – proposed a less aggressive
approach. The chiefs prevailed: groups of them lay in ambush around the
several gates of the fort and stormed it at dawn with ruthless efficiency – one
gatekeeper who tried to resist had his hand cut off by a flashing sword. By
noon that day, Bairam Khan was governor of Qandahar, and Budagh Khan
had 'apologised for his offence' to Humayun, who reciprocated with a tactful letter for Tahmasp, assuring him that Qandahar's governor might have
changed from Budagh to Bairam, but the city remained the shah's.

Finally, Humayun set off for Kabul. He left Hamida behind but took
Askari (who had tried to run away and been found hiding under a blanket
in an Afghan's hut) and Khanzada Begum. Their venerable aunt was close
to seventy years old and had lived a life of unusual adventure. As a young
girl, she had been given as wife (and hostage) to Babur's great rival Shaibani
Khan, the Uzbek king of Samarqand; in middle age, she had been among
Babur's senior advisers, her husband Mahdi Khwaja had almost succeeded
him to the Hindustani throne; and now, in her old age, she had preserved what
little peace and goodwill she could between her brother's unhappy heirs. The
mission to Qandahar, however, was her last on the family's behalf; she died
on the way to Kabul.

More happily for Humayun – for whom the loss was not of an aunt alone,
but of a strategic ally – he was joined, en route, by his youngest brother,
Hindal. This was good news in itself, of course, but also because it signalled
a changing wind. As Abul Fazl puts it, Hindal's coming was a 'preface to
the advent of many others'. Such was the wave of allegiance that swept to
Humayun's side, in fact, that by the time the returning emperor's expanding

army came face to face with Kamran's, outside Kabul, that 'black-hearted . . . prince'[27] had decided to leave without a fight. As night fell, Kamran crept back into the fort, gathered his son Ibrahim and some of his women, and left.

Be jang girift mulk-i-Kabul az we was one chronogram for the date, 'without a battle he took the country of Kabul from him'.[28] On 17 November 1545, at an auspicious time two hours into the night, Humayun marched into the city in which he was born. After five long years of exile, he was finally home.

And he was hungry. It was the month of Ramzan and Humayun hadn't eaten all day, so he sent Jouher to one of the begums in the fort – a widow of Babur's – to ask if she would send him a little dinner from her kitchen. Of course she would: Jouher and a chamberlain were soon back with a broth and a meat-and-veg curry, both made of beef. The table was laid, Humayun was seated, his spoon held ready, when suddenly the emperor drew back his hand. Was it *beef* he was to eat? 'Oh, unfortunate Kamran!' he exclaimed. 'Was this the mode of your own existence? And did you feed the Asylum of Chastity [Babur's widow] on the flesh of cows? . . . What! Could you not afford to keep a few goats[29] for her subsistence? What! Could not we, his four sons, support . . . [her] as he did?' So dismayed was Humayun by this unfitting meal – beef was such poor fare to the Mughals, it seems – that he refused a single bite of it, only downing a glass of sherbet instead.[30]

Still, though dinner was a disaster, the emperor was able to satisfy a far deeper longing that night. Two years after he had left him behind, Humayun met his son. Humayun offered prayers of gratitude and alms in joy, but we must wait for Akbar's mother, Hamida, to arrive for a more touching scene of reunion. Hamida came to Kabul with the spring, riding up from Qandahar as 'violets raised their head from the stream's lip'.[31] When she reached, Humayun arranged a little game: he brought Akbar into the harem, carrying the three-year-old on his shoulders. When father and son were seated, side by side, the ladies streamed in and arranged themselves before the pair. Gulbadan would have been among them, and Akbar's many jealous mamas, and also, perhaps, Askari's wife, Sultan Begum, who had taken such loving care of the prince in Qandahar. Also among them was Hamida, deliberately unmarked in any way. Once the stage was set, Humayun told his son to find his mother – at which, the story goes, Akbar toddled straight into Hamida's lap. A painting of the scene shows a child with a determined chin falling into his mother's lap; what catches the eye, however, is the tenderness of the glance between Hamida and Humayun.[32] So much might have filled a look in that moment: the delight of parents in their progeny, the unspoken understanding of lovers in public, the quiet relief of an emperor and his queen with a city to rule, finally.

A 'shout arose', writes Abul Fazl, and its call for celebration can be heard across the centuries. As immediate cause, it was time for Akbar's circumcision; or, as Abul Fazl insists on putting it, 'for pruning the sapling of the divine garden'.[33] Circumcision was, and remains, a significant event in families across cultures and terrains, but circumcision alone cannot explain the sheer extravagance of the party. It went on for days – seventeen by one account – the decoration of the city's bazaars and gardens 'exceeds description'; the chieftains held wrestling competitions, received fiefs and titles and robes of honour, basking in 'the light of favour'.[34] There was feasting and giving of alms and granting of amnesty – to, among others, that fickle cousin Yadgar Nasir. 'Small and great', all were invited – 'high and low', all were favoured.[35] Such festivities were not to mark a milestone in Akbar's life alone, but also in his father's. After a three-year absence, Humayun wanted 'to restore his contacts with the nobility',[36] to let them know they had a new ruler to celebrate.

Many of them, while quaffing their drinks and cheering their prodigal padishah, may have wondered how long Humayun's new rule would last. There was, after all, the niggling fact that Kabul didn't really belong to him; it was Kamran's.

For the next seven years, these two older sons of Babur would be locked in seemingly endless and increasingly bloody tussles over the city in which their father was buried. The fault of this is often laid at Babur's feet; Abul Fazl suggests more than once that it was Babur who dinned an endless clemency for his brothers into Humayun's head, thus making it impossible for his eldest son to take definitive action against his insubordinate siblings. It is true that Babur once wrote to Humayun, 'Conduct yourself well with your younger brother [Kamran]. Elder brothers need to have restraint.' It is equally true, however, that in the lines immediately preceding this advice, Babur also wrote, 'You know that this rule has always been observed: six parts to you and five to Kamran. Always observe this rule and do not break it.'[37]

Now, when all that remained of Babur's bequest was Kamran's share, Kabul and Qandahar, and when it was Humayun, after all, who had lost the rest of it, was it not breaking Babur's rule to take Kamran's cities away from him? Certainly, Humayun knew that he did not possess the unquestioning approval of his kin, and he wasn't shy of suppressing their dissent. All through those seventeen days of celebration in Kabul, for example, Askari was kept in prison. Soon afterwards, their cousin Yadgar Nasir, recently returned to the fold, was found plotting rebellion again. Humayun had him killed. The impatient young man who had whipped Askari into action against plundering mobs was strangled with a bowstring. Then, Humayun went marching north to his old fief, Badakhshan, where Sulaiman was showing a Kamran-like disinclination to give up his land to his stateless cousin.

Humayun had a successful campaign in Badakhshan. Sulaiman fled the battlefield, and Humayun followed his success further north, so energetically that the northern kingdom of Turan was in 'dismay',[38] wondering if Babur's son would make a bid for its capital and the city of Babur's dreams: Samarqand.

As it happened, however, Humayun fell ill, and while he recovered soon enough, news of his ill health travelled as quickly to Kamran. The dispossessed younger brother had not been idle these past months: he had forged himself an alliance with Sindh by marrying the daughter of Shah Husain.[39] When he heard that Humayun wasn't well, he borrowed an army from his father-in-law and marched back home.

There was no one in Kabul to stop Kamran. Its governor, Muhammad Ali Taghayi, was recovering from a hangover in a hot bath, from which he was dragged out, naked, and killed. Others loyal to Humayun were as deftly murdered, blinded or imprisoned, and Kamran was swiftly repossessed of his old throne, surrounded by followers 'like flies at the stall of a sweetmeat-seller . . . falling upon one another'.

'How have I gone and how have I come back?' the prince asked one of them, and pat came the flattering reply, 'You went in the evening and you came in the morning.'[40]

Akbar became, once again, his uncle's hostage. He wasn't yet five years old, but it is a measure of how very soon a boy could be seen as eligible for a throne that two Persian soldiers, seeing Akbar in court, thought of staging an extempore coup in his favour, then and there. There is no record that Kamran thought of, or treated, his nephew as a threat just yet, but it was only a matter of time before he would.

Humayun abandoned his excursions into Turan (which was 'relieved') and returned to recover his kingdom and rescue his son.[41] Thus was laid the famous siege of Kabul, often recounted through a montage of Kamran's escalating cruelties. Gulbadan tells of how Kamran plundered Humayun's harem and locked the women in an improvised dungeon of 'bricks, plaster and dung-cakes'. A two-year-old girl among them would die before the siege was done. Next, Kamran began a grisly 'negotiation' with his besiegers, threatening Humayun's chiefs with the murder of their children and the rape of their wives unless they switched sides. One man's wife was 'suspended . . . by the breasts'. Another, Babus, had his three sons, all under seven, butchered and thrown off the fort walls, and his wife given over to 'the people of the bazaar'.[42]

The imprisoned begums sent word to Humayun to stop the siege. Humayun replied with reassuring messages and gifts: Gulbadan lists 'nine sheep, seven flasks of rose-water, one of lemonade', dresses and jackets, but no promises to reconcile with his brother. The begums were right, however: things were getting out of hand, and Kamran's worst was yet to come. As the siege continued despite his ferocious demoralizing tactics, as cannonballs and musket fire assailed the walls of Kabul, Kamran had Akbar exposed upon the battlements – a child turned into a shield.

'What . . . demon has such principles?' cries Abul Fazl. It is not the anguished historian but Gulbadan – sister to both Kamran and Humayun – who offers the most measured account of this ignoble act. On the one hand, she suggests that Humayun was well aware of the need to calibrate his assault on Kamran to keep Akbar safe; that he even wrote, 'if we had used force against the citadel, Mirza Muhammad Akbar would have disappeared'. His garrison, on the other hand, was losing patience – and no wonder, given the brutalities Kamran was inflicting on them. One day, one of the besiegers fired his gun at Kamran directly, at which the rattled prince decided to use his nephew as a deterrent. Meanwhile, she adds, Humayun's men put Askari – Kamran's blood brother – in the line of fire 'and made fun of him'.

The historian Nizamuddin's version is more dramatic. Not only did Kamran's 'dastardly feeling' make him expose Akbar, but he did so at exactly the spot where 'balls and shot . . . fell thickest'. Seeing this, Maham Anaka, the mama who had once complained about Jiji Anaka monopolizing Akbar's attentions, grabbed the child 'in her bosom' and held him safe from the fusillade.

Whatever the truth of Kamran's offence (Jouher, for example, doesn't mention it at all), and whatever the extent of Maham Anaka's devotion (if the harem was locked away, how did she escape to the turrets?), the siege went in Humayun's favour. In April 1547, a year or so after those glorious springtime celebrations to proclaim his rule, Humayun marched into Kabul a second time, was reunited with Akbar a second time, and mounted the throne[43] a second time.

The sense of déjà vu would continue: another year didn't pass before Humayun was besieging his brother again. Kamran had fled Kabul and gone northwards, hoping to form an alliance with Sulaiman of Badakhshan, whom Humayun had defeated in battle but reinstated when he came rushing back to Kabul. Kamran's attempted alliance was unsuccessful.

Gulbadan tells a wonderful story that may be from this time and explains Kamran's failure. Sulaiman was married to a woman called Haram Begum, and it was well known that if Sulaiman was the chief of Badakhshan, Haram was its ruler. Thus, when Kamran wished for an alliance with Badakhshan – and its army – he did not approach Sulaiman but sent, instead, a proposal of marriage to his wife. As Kamran's messenger woman 'wept, and moaned, and coaxed', pressing his suit upon the queen, Haram sent for her husband and son, thundered at them for being cowards and wondered what a man like

Kamran should deserve, 'who fears neither me nor my son'. As for Kamran's proposal – she had his messenger torn from limb to limb.

Thus rebuffed, Kamran began to attack Badakhshan instead of allying with it; and Humayun, still in Kabul, began to make plans to march north in his pursuit – plans interrupted by the sudden defection of several of his chiefs. Among them, inexplicably, was Babus, the man whose sons had been flung at him from Kabul's walls, and whose wife had been thrown to Kabul's bazaar. Does Babus's defection say a great deal for Kamran's charisma, or very little for Humayun's leadership? It's hard to say – and Humayun couldn't do much about it. According to Jouher, he thought of sending Akbar as mediator to the chiefs, 'to make friends of them', but gave up the idea when he was told it might backfire should the chiefs make a hostage of the young ambassador. All Humayun could do in the end was give the defectors rude nicknames: Babus Daiyus (cuckold) being a particularly unkind example.[44]

By the summer of 1548, however, Humayun had rallied enough support to besiege Kamran in the fortress of Taligan, near Badakhshan. The siege lasted a month, during the course of which Sulaiman and his son came to Humayun's aid with their army. According to Gulbadan, the formidable Haram Begum had ridden with her troops some distance before sending them to battle – and win – against her cheeky suitor.

Humayun, on the other hand, was keen to make peace, asking Kamran – 'O evil brother and beloved war-seeker' – to stop and spare a thought for all the unnecessary blood being spilt in their quarrel. Kamran replied valiantly of kingship belonging to he who kisses 'the gleaming . . . lip' of the sword, but when the reinforcements he was expecting didn't arrive, he changed his tune. '[N]ow I repent of the past', wrote Kamran in a letter that he shot into Humayun's camp on the edge of an arrow. He asked for an envoy to whom he might surrender. When the envoy arrived, Kamran was the very picture of submission. 'I've sinned, I've sinned', he said, head bowed. 'I'll do whatever you order.'

The stage was set for a grand reconciliation. The defecting chieftains appeared before Humayun, one by one, swords hanging from their necks. 'What ailed *you*, and what made *you* go away?' asked Humayun of one of whom he'd expected better. But the question was rhetorical. Humayun knew what had happened: ''Tis the fortune of war, such accidents as this must happen.' A few days later came Kamran's turn. The rebel prince humbled himself before his brother, making all the requisite salutes and prostrations. Then, Humayun pulled him into a hug: 'Now come and let us embrace like brothers.' With Kamran firmly in his grip, Humayun burst into tears.[45] Such tendency to weep has given Humayun his reputation for sentimentality, though it might be that he wept as much to wash away his own sins as those of his brother.

Both had a chance to redeem themselves now. Not just Humayun and
Kamran, but all Babur's sons – and their cousin Sulaiman – were together,
seated on the same carpet, eating off the same cloth. They were even to wash
their hands in the same basin. The protocol of age decreed that Humayun
went first, followed by Kamran, then Sulaiman, Askari and Hindal. Sulaiman
of Badakhshan, unused perhaps to the courtly ways of Kabul and Agra, took
to the hand-washing with more aplomb than decorum, possibly he blew his
nose. At this, the younger brothers exploded in protest against such 'nose-
wagging performances', crying, 'What rusticity is this?'[46]

Poor, abashed Sulaiman may have cheered up as the celebration progressed:
the bright, vibrating sounds of harp, rebec and qopuz filled the air, men sang
and ate and talked until the sun set. So convivial was the atmosphere that,
the next day, the Timurid men even plotted a joint campaign against Balkh.

The what-ifs of history are tempting detours. What if, now, the brothers
had attacked Balkh?[47] On the borders of Turan and only 500-odd kilometres
south of Samarqand, Balkh would have been a launching pad into Timur's
great capital; its conquest might have shaped a wholly different destiny for
his descendants. When they parted, at Taligan, the brothers and Sulaiman
sealed their fellowship by drinking from the same cup; together, they would
revive the name of the Timurids in their ancestral land. Only months later,
however, when Humayun set off for Balkh, Kamran reneged on his promise.
And such was Kamran's reputation that when he didn't show up, Humayun's
soldiers assumed he'd gone to Kabul instead and began to desert. Or, as
Gulbadan puts it, 'the royal army ran away'. Humayun was forced to abandon
his campaign ('after a thousand struggles with his spirit'),[48] bitterly disappointed, and return to Kabul, where rumours of Kamran's renewed rebellion
were proven false.

But what if Kamran had not played spoilsport – would the Mughals
have had an Indian empire at all? Abul Fazl isn't sure, thanking God for
the rumours and defections, if not for which 'the work of the helpless ones
of India would have been hindered by the undertaking of the conquest of
Transoxiana'.

Indeed, Humayun did not abandon Balkh easily. He tried to enlist Kamran's support once again, and once again Kamran replied obligingly and
did nothing. Eventually, Humayun realized that he would have to battle his
brother before he could battle Balkh – to stop him 'wandering about the
country with bad intentions', as Jouher puts it – but he did not realize that
the loyalty of his chiefs had sprung leaks again. They fed him incorrect intelligence, enabling Kamran to launch a surprise attack in which Humayun's
soldiers were butchered, and Humayun injured. As he was led away from the
carnage by a few faithful men, Humayun lost his *jubba* – a quilted, protective
jacket that would propel a twist in the act to come.

The jubba was brought to Kamran's camp and taken to imply Humayun's death. Kamran, so delighted that he 'could not contain himself', marched to Kabul, where he used the jacket to convince its governor that Humayun was no longer alive to assert any claim on the city.[49]

Humayun's son, on the other hand, was a different matter. Akbar wasn't a child any longer, to be allowed to play in court. He was eight years old, Humayun's sole heir, and potential anchor of any rebellion by Humayun's loyalists. Kamran put him in prison. How the news of his father's demise and his own imprisonment affected the boy isn't recorded. If he was grief-stricken and afraid, he may also have derived some comfort from knowing that his family's fortunes tended to see-saw with manic speed. True enough, it was only three months before Kamran was marching at a very living Humayun once again. This time, he took Akbar with him.

Perhaps it was knowing this – and fearing how his son might be treated, now that he was no longer protected by infancy – that Humayun tried to prevent a battle.[50] He sent Kamran an envoy proposing peace and tempting him with a joint conquest of Hindustan. Kamran's reply was that they must sort out their Afghan holdings first. Let Humayun keep Qandahar and return Kabul to Kamran, only then would he join the march to Hindustan. Humayun suggested a tweak to the arrangement: how would Kamran like to marry his daughter to Akbar, and let the boy have Kabul while the brothers marched south? 'Both Kabul and Hindustan would then . . . belong to the two of [us]', the emperor concluded with disingenuous satisfaction.

Not surprisingly, negotiations broke down; battle was joined and swiftly lost by Kamran, who fled the scene. He left Akbar behind, as also two camels carrying Humayun's books – lost in the battle of the missing jubba. Both reunions gave the emperor great joy; his brother's prospects were dimming, meanwhile.

The defeat didn't break Kamran's spirit, but it did reduce his circumstances. His brother Askari, who had drifted back to Kamran's side, was caught by Humayun and promptly exiled.[51] In fact, very little of Kamran's army seems to have survived the battle un-killed, uncaptured or undeterred: he had no more than eight men with him when he fled. A year or so later, he had only managed to gather enough warriors for night raids, not wars. Even so, it was a raid that would hurt Humayun – and Kamran, too; the whole family, in fact – more than any previous battle between the brothers.

'The night was dark', writes Abul Fazl. News of a raid had reached Humayun's camp earlier that evening; the men were on guard, Humayun and Akbar had ridden up a hill, from where they kept watch. It was November, and cold. Hindal, the youngest, was wearing a greatcoat on top of his armour and a black fur hat.

Kamran and his men stormed the camp, and Hindal rode out to the trenches. He heard a voice calling for help – it was Hindal's *tabaqchi*, his master of plate (or loosely, his waiter). Ever gallant, Hindal got off his horse. In the darkness and confusion, no one followed him; and two of Kamran's men ambushed the prince. The first Hindal managed to wrestle aside, but the second cut him dead with a spear and stole his bag of thumb rings as a prize. It was a while before anyone realized the prince was dead.

Kamran's raid was repelled, and he retreated with his men, taking stock of their plunder. The soldier who brought him the thumb rings was an Afghan mercenary, not a Chagatai who might have known the prince, and might even have spared him. Kamran, however, recognized the little bag of rings immediately. He took off his turban and threw it to the ground in grief, crying 'Hindal had been martyred'.[52]

Humayun, meanwhile, was calling out for Hindal in the dark, over the sound of his men celebrating victory. He got no reply; it would be a while before he understood why.

The prince who had once vowed to protect his mothers and sisters with his last breath did, in fact, die with chivalry, defending someone in danger – not a woman from his harem but a servant from his household. He was buried at his father Babur's feet in a Kabul garden, but the anguish of his passing lived on. Decades later, his sister Gulbadan was still struck with grief when she wrote the lines that tell of his demise: 'Would that merciless sword had touched my heart and eyes . . .!'

And what, meanwhile, of Akbar? Only a few days previously, the nine-year-old prince had forgotten his turban when riding out to greet his father. Seeing his nephew in breach of protocol, Hindal had taken his own turban off and put it on Akbar's head.[53] Did they share the kind of affectionate, joking relationship that often exists between young uncles and their nephews and nieces? Perhaps. Does Akbar's bare-headed appearance reveal a loose, careless swagger, even an impatience with conventions? It's not unlikely.

Akbar had grown, and his personality was showing. Six-odd months after he was dangled over the battlements of Kabul, when he was exactly four years, four months and four days old – the auspicious age for beginning a child's education – he was given his first tutor: Mullazada Mulla Isamuddin Ibrahim. Much ceremony was attached to the event; Humayun had divined the perfect hour in which to begin Akbar's lessons – but, like many children on their first day of school wish they could, Akbar 'disappeared' when the appointed moment arrived; 'no trace of him could be found'.[54]

If Mulla Isamuddin hoped that Akbar would grow fonder of his company over time, he was wrong. In fact, the teacher was soon dismissed. According to Abul Fazl, Isamuddin's fault was his all-absorbing devotion to pigeons. Perhaps the tutor was an avid pigeon flyer; it was a popular sport. Babur's father died, famously, falling from his dovecote. The historical evidence, however, suggests that the poor mullah was only trying to keep pace with his young student. As shy as Akbar was of study, so he was besotted by animals. Abul Fazl puts it in most lofty terms. If the prince was fascinated by the camel's 'strange make and ways', delighted in leading one about by the reins, or feeding brambles to another, laughing with joy and alarm, perhaps, when the large animal plucked its food from his small hand, this was a form of serious reflection 'under the guise of amusement'. Similarly with Akbar's 'thoughts to the delight in an Arab horse', and the spread of 'the wings of his genius' through pigeon-flying – for all that Abul Fazl will try to mould his subject into the shape of a little philosopher, Akbar's mind in 'the guise of sport perform[ing] the work of adoration' even when he was playing with his dogs ('inwardly it was quickening the senses') you cannot but imagine a boy tearing through the grounds of Kabul fort, delighting in the flap of pigeons, the panting of hounds and the thunder of horses.

Isamuddin could not lure Akbar to the classroom, nor could his successor, Maulana Bayazid. Eventually, Humayun had to draw lots to find a tutor for his son; the job fell to Mulla Abdul Qadir, who found no more success in his thankless job than had his predecessors.

Akbar's attendants, less inclined to regard their charge with the worshipful gaze of his future historian, complained to Humayun about the boy. Akbar was about nine years old at this time and had just returned to Kabul after Kamran's raid and Hindal's death. Humayun was still away on Kamran's trail. When complaints about Akbar reached him, Humayun sent his son a letter. Abul Fazl finds the idea preposterous. 'For what need has he who has been taught at the Divine school – of human instructions?'[55] As if to make up for Humayun's faux pas, Abul Fazl cites another miracle. A man sent to look for Akbar when he was skipping school yet again found the prince sleeping with a 'lustrous countenance', talking with 'the holy ones of heaven's court', his hands moving as if in a contemplative trance, and speaking: 'God willing, I'll bring the cream of earth's surface under my sway and fulfil the desires of the sorrowful of the seven climes.' Evidently, Akbar's visionary pronouncements had grown no less flamboyant since he assured Jiji Anaka of his divine favour.

Still, for all the hyperbole and devotion of Abul Fazl's defence, he wasn't entirely off the mark. Akbar may not have spent much time at his books, but he was acquiring responsibility and ambition both. When he was six years old, just before Humayun besieged Kamran in Taligan, Akbar had been put in charge of Kabul, howsoever nominally, with his mother and a *darogha*, an officer, to guide and serve him. Two years later, Kamran's eight-year-old nephew was old enough, and a threat enough, to be imprisoned and taken into battle. When Humayun won, Akbar received his reward, like the other men on the battlefield: a village called Charkh to hold in fief. A year later, Akbar received his second fiefdom, inheriting all of Hindal's territories in Ghazni, as also Hindal's men.

The fiefs and men would mean nothing, of course, if Akbar treated them with the disdain he showed his studies. There is a wonderful story that reveals how Humayun, while keeping one eye on Akbar's education, had another firmly focused on his son's future relationships with the men who would be his to command one day. Among them was Munim Khan, whom Humayun had made Akbar's *ataliq*, or guardian. It was a position of great trust and intimacy, so Munim had clearly redeemed himself for his inconstancy during Humayun's exile.

Clearly also, Munim was an indulgent ataliq. Once, for instance, he gave Akbar the day off when the prince wanted, as ever, to give school a miss. Humayun heard about it, was upset and scolded Akbar. However, he didn't tell the boy that it was his ataliq who had ratted him out but put the blame on one Haji Muhammad instead. Later, Humayun would explain to Munim that he didn't want Akbar, future padishah, to be prejudiced against him. Haji Muhammad, on the other hand, 'was an impertinent person and deserved any harm that may come to him'.[56]

Given Humayun's evident concern for his son's well-being, present and future, it is easy to imagine how 'his heart was greatly delighted',[57] and relieved, when, sometime after that complaint about Akbar's indiscipline, Humayun received another, altogether different kind of report about his son. Akbar had gone to hunt at the foot of a range of snow-capped mountains outside Kabul. His idea was to have his dogs catch deer, to which effect he commanded one group of men to chase deer down the mountain slopes, and another to release the dogs at their approach. The latter lot of men grew peckish as they waited; when the deer came hurtling down, they were eating. The dogs were not released.

The men, writes Abul Fazl, had misunderstood the prince's 'tender years and boyish appearance'. His wrath they would appreciate all too clearly. The men were put in collars and chains, like the dogs they had failed to let loose, and 'led round the camp'. When Humayun heard the news, he understood his son was learning – if not his alphabet, then how to rule.

The lessons were not all easy. An ability to command would attract followers, naturally; and it was equally, perhaps instinctively, clear to Akbar, who had grown up in plain sight of the fleeting loyalties of his father's and uncle's chiefs, that he must be wary of their flattery. Perhaps instinctive suspicion falls to the lot of those born to rule. There is even a theory that both Akbar's name and birth date were changed during the festival of his circumcision, 'to protect him against the perils of malignant sorcery'.[58] Thus, anticipating betrayal since infancy, Akbar would get angry if a courtier spoke too eagerly of the glorious future that awaited the prince when he became king.

What kind of well-wisher encouraged a prince to covet his father's realm? 'They [were] imagining evil for me in thinking of the decease of His Majesty [Humayun]', Akbar would say of the wagging of their tongues; they were 'gathering my temporal good from my spiritual ill'.[59] At nine, Akbar wasn't just learning how to master animals and men, he was also acquiring a bleaker talent: to appraise the people around him and gauge their ambitions, to measure the worth of his own life in their eyes. At ten, he would learn the most chilling lesson of his young life.

For a year and more, Kamran had sought shelter and allies among the Afghan tribes of his erstwhile kingdom, while Humayun's troops drew ever closer on his trail. After one particularly narrow escape, Kamran decided to try his luck in Hindustan, offering himself in alliance to Salim Shah, son of the Sher Shah who had chased Kamran's family out of Bengal, then Agra and Lahore. The son was no more favourable to the Timurids than his father; according to Abul Fazl, he treated Kamran worse than he would 'enemies or street-dogs', and it soon became clear that all the territory Kamran could reasonably expect from the Afghan king was a dungeon cell. He managed to escape, with some help from two rajas of Punjab and a disguise of women's clothes, and returned across the Indus to the court of Adam, sultan of the Gakkhar tribe.[60] Deep in the winter of 1552, a messenger from Sultan Adam arrived in Humayun's court. He carried a letter, in which the sultan professed concern for Kamran's 'vagabond' state and a desire to 'do homage' to Humayun. The messenger's oral report was less circumspect: he told Humayun the whole sorry tale, including the fact that Kamran was trying to get Sultan Adam to join his rebellion. It is some indication of Kamran's burning ambition that even now, reeling from defeat after defeat, abandoned by mercenaries and disdained by kings, he remained intent on his throne. And not even now, when Kamran was no more than the unwelcome guest of a distant tribe, could Humayun afford to think of his brother as a spent force. He hurried west, taking Akbar with him. They made it just in time. According to Abul Fazl, Sultan Adam had developed 'misplaced apprehensions' when Humayun arrived, and it took some 'cajolery and stratagem' to remind him of his lately professed loyalty.[61] Kamran was taken prisoner, but now it was Humayun who seemed to be suffering a change of heart. His urgent journey west may have suggested that Kamran would meet the fate of Yadgar Nasir, or Askari. No bowstring, however, was coiled around Kamran's neck that night, no men dispatched him to Mecca in chains. Instead, Humayun invited him to a feast. Much as he had done after the siege of Taligan, Humayun called Kamran to sit by his side. There were no brothers to join them this time: it was Akbar, now ten, who sat on Humayun's other side. Jouher tells of how Humayun called for a watermelon and cut it in three parts, one each he gave to Akbar and Adam, and one he shared with Kamran – as he had once shared a washbasin and a goblet with his brother. Two nights were spent thus, 'in jollity and carousing'[62] – it was Ramzan, besides, and a time for feasting at night – but eventually the gathered chieftains staged an intervention. What was Humayun playing at? The padishah – if, indeed, he wished to be padishah – must end his troubles with Kamran the only way they could be ended: once and for all, with the sword.

According to Jouher, Humayun delayed the matter by throwing yet another party, this one to honour Sultan Adam. According to Abul Fazl, he dragged his feet until the chieftains drew up a writ, duly witnessed by jurists and clergymen, listing Kamran's misdeeds and arguing for appropriate punishment. Humayun sent the writ to Kamran, who replied: '[T]hose who today had put their seals for his death, were the men who had brought him to this pass.'

Kamran's bitterness was justified. The chieftains, cutting and running from side to side during the long fraternal strife, had hardly covered themselves in glory. Not only this, they had bullied an oath out of Humayun, making him swear compliance to their will in exchange for their loyalty. And now their will was crystal clear: 'If you wish to act as a brother, abandon the throne.'[63] What kind of dynasty would the Mughals have been if their kings abandoned thrones? Early next morning, Humayun rode away from the camp, leaving orders that his brother be blinded in his wake.

The faithful Jouher had spent the previous night with Kamran, giving the melancholy prince a champoo. 'Do you think they will kill me?' Kamran asked him, and would Jouher keep the remaining fasts of Ramzan on Kamran's behalf? Jouher tried to give comforting answers, but there was little he could say to lift the prince's mood.

In the morning, two men, Ali Dost and Ghulam Ali, joined Jouher in Kamran's tent and began squabbling over who should put out his eyes. An absurd horror followed, as the men passed the buck to each other as if it were a ticking bomb, each arguing with bureaucratic obduracy that while they both had instructions to blind the prince, neither had been clearly designated the blinder.[64]

Eventually, Jouher said he would ride after Humayun and ask him; Ali Dost followed closely behind. Humayun wasn't happy to see them, nor to hear from Ali Dost that 'No one will perform the business'. Humayun swore at him and snapped, 'Why don't you do it yourself?'

Ali Dost returned to Kamran with his orders; Kamran declared he would rather be killed. It isn't hard to understand why: what would it be for a man of his ambition and energy to live the life of an enfeebled prisoner, groping in the dark? A fate far worse than death.

'We dare not exceed our orders', said Ghulam Ali, with bleak, pedantic finality. Then, as if in a sudden hurry to get the unpleasant task over and done with, Ghulam Ali and Ali Dost stuffed a handkerchief into Kamran's mouth, dragged him out of his tent, laid him down and pierced his eyes with a small, sharp knife. 'This they repeated at least fifty times', writes Jouher, but Kamran made not the slightest moan – until, in the end, they squeezed lemon juice into his ravaged eyes and he cried out, 'O Lord, O Lord, my God . . .'

Some days later, Kamran appeared before Humayun, to seek his permission to go on the pilgrimage to Mecca, a common form of exile or retirement. Humayun agreed and asked if any of the prince's retainers would accompany him. 'No one came forward', writes Abul Fazl. Humayun had to send his own table attendant with his brother.

Thus, alone and unmourned, Kamran left his home, his kingdom and his family behind, sailing down the Indus to Sindh and then to Mecca where, five years later, he died.

In history, too, Kamran has been a lonely, unmourned figure, the faithless brother and evil prince. There are only the rarest glimpses of the younger brother's tragedy and the older brother's guilt. Jouher's 'very melancholy mood' after the blinding, for example, suggests that Kamran was not the unpopular villain he's made out to be[65] – 'more sinned against than sinning', as a modern historian puts it.[66] A year later, in the winter of 1553, when Humayun returned to Kabul, he didn't want to celebrate the end of his long feud, let alone talk about it. When the women of the harem came to greet him, he told them not to congratulate him on Kamran's defeat, for 'it was as if he had struck at his own eyes'.[67] In fact, by this time, all three of Humayun's brothers, not just Kamran, were either dead or exiled, if not by Humayun's doing, then in the service of his ambition. Far from sharing an empire with them, as their father might have hoped, he had lost his inheritance and snatched what remained for himself. If guilt spoiled some of the pleasure of being the unchallenged master of Kabul, it would be unsurprising.

There is no record of what Akbar felt about his father's triumph in the war between brothers that began before Akbar was born, no record of what he felt about his uncle's friendless end, and certainly no record of Akbar's feelings when, in Kabul that spring, Humayun's youngest wife gave birth to Humayun's second son. If Akbar looked upon his newborn half-brother and saw, already, a sword and shield in his little fists, that would be unsurprising – but Akbar kept any such thoughts to himself.

Perhaps he had no time for such forebodings. By the following year, in the winter of 1554, Kabul was abuzz with news from Hindustan. Salim Shah Suri[68] was dead. Salim's father, Sher Shah, had died almost a decade earlier, having achieved a lifetime's worth in his five brief years of rule – from occupying Ranthambore and Chittorgarh without battle to introducing a standardized 'rupee'. When Sher Shah choked to death in the smoke of explosives during a siege, he was succeeded by his son, who kept the Suri empire stable and, more recently, quashed Kamran's hopes for an alliance. Salim's own son, however, was a child when the shah died, and was murdered almost immediately by his uncle. A fractious battle for succession had begun, the Suri dynasty might well be in collapse, and it was the perfect time for rival claimants to swoop down upon Hindustan. In short, would Humayun march east and win his throne back?

He would; he did.

In mid-November 1554,[69] Humayun left Kabul with an army of 3000 men. Among them were some old familiars: Tardi Beg, no doubt hoping to recover what treasure he'd lost during Humayun's decline; Muazzam, Hamida's younger brother and one-time sleuth; Shamsuddin Ataka, Akbar's faithful foster father; even Babus, that most tragic of turncoats; and, of course, Bairam Khan, who had kept guard over Qandahar these past years. There were some newcomers, too, whom Humayun had recruited during his long exile: Bairam Khan's brother-in-law Wali Beg and his two sons Husain Quli and Ismail Quli; some Uzbek warriors, including Abdullah Khan and a swashbuckling homosexual called Ali Quli Shaibani; and Shah Abul Ma'ali, a man of gorgeous looks and treacherous sensibility, whom Humayun had recently adopted as a favourite. Finally, there was Akbar, who, for all his precocious experience of betrayal, cannot have suspected how much trouble many of these men would soon give him – nor how many of them he would have killed.

If Akbar was innocent of his future, Humayun may have guessed at it. At one point during the journey, Humayun called for his son. Jouher was sent to bathe and dress the prince, and bring him along. Akbar was twelve years old and he bristled, as any twelve-year-old would, at the idea of being bathed by the retainer. 'I cannot bathe, nor appear naked before you', he declared. The prince got ready – 'in private' – and went to meet his father.

Humayun was sitting under a clear sky, facing the moon as it sank into the dark horizon. When Akbar arrived, Humayun asked him to sit before him. The boy would have eclipsed the moon. The emperor began to read from the Quran, and at the end of each verse he looked at his son and '*breathed*' upon him, each time 'so delighted and happy, it might be said that he had then acquired all the good fortune of this world, and the blessings of the next'.[70]

There are several fleeting moments in the chronicles that reveal the love between father and son. Humayun's giddy dance when he saw Akbar's horoscope. The little game he arranged to reunite Akbar with his mother, Hamida. A passing observation in Jouher's memoirs, of Humayun kissing Akbar's forehead and eyebrows when they met after yet another Kamran-induced separation. Humayun's worry for his son's education and his relief at the prince's growing ability to command. And, finally, this mystical and lovely ceremony: an almost ethereal moment of quiet, a father's prayers on his breath, blessing his child.

There was little quiet ahead of them. Between February 1555, when Humayun's army entered Lahore, and July of that year, when Humayun was enthroned in Delhi, the Mughal army fought four battles of varying intensity in Punjab, against Afghan armies trying to keep them out. The last of these, at Sirhind, dragged on for almost forty days, with Humayun, Bairam and Abul Ma'ali leading battalions against Sikandar Suri – most daunting of the several Suris now fighting over Hindustan – and his army of 80,000 horsemen. 'The rush of arrows and the clash of swords / Tore the marrow of elephants and the gallbladders of tigers' – and there were some who lost heart at the very sight. Hamida's own brother Muazzam, for example, was so sure of defeat that he wrote to Sikandar Suri pledging his support to the Afghan.[71]

Muazzam did not realize that the luck of the Mughals had changed. Humayun won all his battles in Punjab, including Sirhind. He 'undid' the debacles that had propelled his clan from Hindustan, writes a modern historian, and 'sealed the fate of the Afghan empire of Sher Shah'.[72]

And yet, it seems, his victories brought little cheer to the reinstated padishah.

Half a year after Sirhind, Humayun, seemingly well settled in Delhi, had begun to nurse morbid thoughts. If Abul Fazl is to be believed, it was difficult to get him to stop talking about his imminent demise; indeed, he 'took pleasure in speaking on the subject'. At one point, Humayun told Akbar and his courtiers of his 'inevitable doom' and consoled them. He liked to tell the story of a man who was inspired to die by the cemetery of Ghazni, declaring he felt the same upon seeing Delhi's shrines. Another time, a voice spoke to him after his dawn prayers, reciting a quatrain that began, 'O God, make me wholly Thine.' Tears flowed from Humayun's eyes as he recited the poem. Later, he would inscribe another bit of melancholy verse upon an arch in his Delhi fort: 'I've heard that on this gilded dome [the sky] 'tis writ / The end of all things is praiseworthy.'[73]

Finally, to hammer home the point, Humayun put seven days' supply of opium on a piece of paper and announced: 'This is all the opium we shall eat.'

On the seventh day, a Friday in late January 1556, Humayun called for rose water and swallowed the last of his opium – there were four pellets remaining – and had an unexceptional day. In the late afternoon, he received visitors: a group of men returning from the Haj pilgrimage, another from Gujarat, a third with letters from Munim Khan, Akbar's easy-going ataliq, who had been left in charge of Kabul and the imperial harem.

It may have been one of those clear, sunny days that grace Delhi in winter because Humayun chose to meet his visitors on the roof of the Sher Mandal, a squat little tower of red sandstone that the emperor used as a library. Meeting on the roof had another advantage: people gathered in the neighbouring mosque for Friday prayers would be able to catch a glimpse of their ruler. Meetings concluded, Humayun summoned his mathematicians, wanting them to confirm his calculations that Venus would rise that night. If it did, he wanted to use the auspicious hour to hand out promotions.

Humayun was in this cheerful, generous mood as evening began to fall. Thoughts of death, it would seem, had left his mind. 'But now', writes Nizamuddin, 'a most extraordinary event occurred . . .'

The sudden chill of winter evenings may have pierced the air and the emperor's coat. Humayun rose and began to climb down the Sher Mandal. He had a staff to help him negotiate the steep and slippery staircase. Just then, the muezzin of that nearby mosque called out the azaan.

'Allah . . . u Akbar!'

Humayun was a pious man. Nizamuddin writes that the padishah would not take God's name until he had performed his *wazu*, ablutions – so much so that he once referred to a man called Abdul Hai as merely 'Abdul' because 'Hai was a name of the Almighty' and Humayun hadn't yet washed.

So, now, as the melodious call for prayer reached him, Humayun bent to kneel in respect. His foot caught in the hem of his coat; his staff slipped. Down fell the emperor, headlong on hard stone, rolling to the end of the stairs. His attendants rushed to their king, his form spreadeagled – or contorted, it might have been – on the ground. A small, ominous trickle of blood began to flow from his right ear.

Humayun means 'the fortunate' – and for all that historians have written wryly of the man who 'tumbled through life, and . . . tumbled out of it',[74] there is no doubt that it was he, of Babur's four sons, who found his fortune. When Humayun held court on his library's sunny roof, two of his brothers were exiled and one was dead. All had risen against him, whether periodically or persistently; all had failed. The exile, meanwhile, the refugee, had clawed his way back to the thrones of Kabul and Delhi. But now, even Humayun's abundant fortune had run out. Seventeen days after his fall, the emperor died.

Chapter 3

The Veil

'It was the effect of the grace of God that I found no capable minister, otherwise people would have considered my measures had been devised by him.'

– Akbar, Happy Sayings, *Ain-i-Akbari*

Akbar was not in Delhi when his father died. He was with Bairam Khan, chasing Sikandar Suri, who had retreated to the great fortress of Mankot, far west of Sirhind, near the Chenab. He had been in battle camps for over a year, but it is unlikely that he was fatigued, or craving a return to the relative comforts of Kabul or – God forbid! – the classroom. Until his father died, in fact, Akbar's Hindustani adventure had been going rather well. It wasn't all battles and marches, first of all. A painting from this time shows Akbar on a horse, stirrups adjusted for his height, wearing yellow pyjamas and a red shirt, a jaunty feather in his turban, out for a day's hawking in Punjab with Bairam Khan.[1] One can imagine the thrills of discovering new animals, new vistas, new hunts, for a boy of his temperament. It was here, in Punjab, that Akbar discovered the two animals he most adored through his life. Bairam's brother-in-law, Wali Beg, gave the prince his first cheetah, along with its keeper, Dundu. Dundu would become a royal huntsman under Akbar, and the sight of trained cheetahs, streaks of lightning striking prey, would never cease to delight his master. But even cheetahs might be forgotten in the face of elephants.

Elephants! Abul Fazl tells us their names: the one Akbar first rode – Dal-singar; the one Akbar first rode without a keeper – Faujbidar; the one Akbar first rode while it was *musth* – Damudar; the one Akbar first rode while it was musth *into* a fight with another – Jhalpa. All in a matter of two years, between the ages of twelve and fourteen, and each one, it is clear, etched in Akbar's

Figure 3.1   Young Akbar hunting with falcons. Dressed in jaunty yellow pyjamas, Akbar is possibly accompanied by his future regent Bairam Khan. A scene from before Humayun's death and the end of Akbar's (relatively) carefree youth. Attributed to Abd al-Samad, c. 1558–60. *Source*: The Cleveland Museum of Art, Public domain.

memory; who else, after all, would have recited the names of these long-ago beasts when Abul Fazl began to write his history?[2]

Elephants were the joy of Akbar's life – he collected them like stamps, he mastered them like rhyme, and he coveted them like gold. By contrast, his father, having spent years in Hindustan, had never learnt – as was clear in Kannauj – to drive these animals. Akbar was riding musth elephants in two years: astride their necks, adrenalin aflow as the animals bellowed, making them fight.

The boy wasn't just acquiring new pets in Hindustan, but also new prey. On the very day that Humayun entered Delhi, news arrived that Akbar had killed a nilgai with the strength of his own sword. Impressed, Humayun ordered some of its flesh preserved – he had sworn off meat for Ramzan, a vow to aid his conquest of Hindustan, but would keep this for when his fast was over.[3] It was also in Punjab, around the time of that nilgai's demise, that Akbar began to learn how to shoot; he would acquire an almost legendary skill with the musket.

None of this was either surprising or unusual; a prince must know how to kill.[4] Akbar's role in Humayun's return to Hindustan wasn't only to see the sights and acquire a menagerie, he was expected to participate in its conquest. Thus, for that great forty-day battle for Sirhind, the prince was given command of a battalion. Historians are coy about what the boy did, exactly, with his troops. Even Abul Fazl only describes Akbar standing on a rooftop, watching the vast spread of a 'hostile army' in the distance, and uttering one of his prophecies: 'that in a short time "our" men would disperse it'.

It is not surprising or shameful that Akbar wasn't on the front lines at Sirhind. Hunting animals is not the same as killing men, and it would be a while before Akbar was able to bring himself to shed human blood. He was only thirteen years old, after all.

And now, with a sudden thunder of galloping hooves at his camp, and urgent confabulations in Bairam's tent, Akbar was also king.[5]

He was crowned upon a throne of brick in Kalanaur, today a small tahsil in Punjab, just this side of India's border with Pakistan. Decades later, the most acerbic historian of Akbar's reign, Abdul Qadir Badauni, would write of how, 'to this day, they have not yet finished laying out' the gardens around the throne.[6] If those gardens were ever laid, they have long disappeared. The 'throne' – a bare seat of plastered brick on a discoloured platform – stands as unadorned as it must have been when Akbar sat upon it.[7]

Akbar was unadorned, too, save a black crown and a golden robe. In paintings of the time, he has a slight frame, and a round face; at thirteen, the vestiges of childhood clung to him still. The paintings do not show that he was distraught.

For Abul Fazl, Humayun couldn't die soon enough. Finally, after so many reams spent setting the scene, the historian could get to the good bits, 'as the moment of time arrived which the heavens had been expecting for so many cycles'. Not so for Akbar. When news of his father's death arrived, he cried, and no one could console him, though many tried.[8] Akbar's mother, Hamida, was far away in Kabul – still unaware that she was widowed – but he had another mama by his side, Maham Anaka. He had a father figure, too, in Shamsuddin Ataka – husband of Maham's rival Jiji Anaka, the man who had helped Humayun escape the rout in Kannauj and watched over Akbar through the many years he spent hostage to his uncles. And there was, of course, Bairam Khan, Akbar's 'Khan Baba' and now his regent, taking pride of place by Akbar's side, and so too in the history of his young, heartbroken king's rise.

Besides these three, the most intimate of Akbar's early counsellors and guides, there were many other men, and a few women, who would play crucial roles in the early years of Akbar's reign. His coronation, for example, might have been a much more fraught affair if it hadn't been for the tight-fisted Tardi Beg, who took charge of Delhi when Humayun broke his crown. Over the next few days, Tardi Beg took several critical decisions: he appointed a lookalike to appear in public as Humayun so the city wouldn't panic and rival claimants wouldn't storm its gates, and he sent Akbar the insignia of rule, with declarations of his loyalty – and Mirza Abul Qasim.

This young prince is a shadowy character in the history of this time, and for good reason. Abul Qasim was Kamran's son, elder brother to the Ibrahim whom Akbar had once wrestled for a drum. He was also a Timurid, Akbar's cousin, older than him by several years, and a perfectly likely rival for his throne – if not from ambition of his own, then as a rallying point for ambitious chieftains.

Akbar's world did not lack for ambitious chieftains. Tardi Beg himself, for example, might have crowned Abul Qasim king and declared himself his regent, leaving Akbar and Bairam stranded in Punjab. There is something touchingly generous, in fact, about the irascible Beg's loyalty to Humayun's son, given how much cause he had to be suspicious – not of Akbar, but of Bairam. The two senior commanders had been at loggerheads for a while. Only a few months earlier, Tardi Beg and Bairam Khan had disagreed on whether or not to pursue some enemy troops; the fight escalated until Humayun had to call a peace meeting to sort things out.

Tardi Beg was not the only thorn in Bairam Khan's side. There was also the good-looking Shah Abul Ma'ali. The two men hated each other. Bairam Khan was descended from a high-ranking nobleman; his family had been marrying Timurids for five generations; his father had joined Babur's forces before Babur held Kabul, let alone Agra, and Bairam had stuck by Humayun's side through some of the emperor's worst times. Abul Ma'ali, claiming sayyid descent,[9] had arrived on the scene only recently and, for no clear reason except that he was exceedingly handsome and flaunted both courage and impudence, he had gained Humayun's favour.[10]

Besides, Bairam Khan was Shia, and Abul Ma'ali was not. A year or so earlier, Humayun had gone to visit Bairam Khan in Qandahar. Abul Ma'ali, who was part of the emperor's entourage, had taken particular dislike to a Shia he found in Bairam's service – a defector from Iran who had gained the khan's protection and wanted to join Humayun's court. Abul Ma'ali would often declare, in public, that he would 'kill this heretical fellow'.[11]

Such threats were evidently not uncommon, because Humayun took it 'as a pleasantry', until Abul Ma'ali did, in fact, murder the poor Shia.[12] When summoned by Humayun, Abul Ma'ali 'swaggered drunken into the royal assembly',[13] wearing the dead man's clothes and the sword he'd used to kill him. His gall inspired Bairam Khan to recite an impromptu, enraged bit of verse, 'His dishevelled locks of hair / Lo! a blazing proof is there . . .'[14]

Humayun applauded the rhyme but let the criminal go free. If he hoped the two men's differences would dissolve in the camaraderie of the Hindustan campaign, he was wrong. Bairam Khan and Abul Ma'ali both led troops in the battle of Sirhind, and afterwards they both stood bristling before Humayun, demanding sole credit for the victory. Once again, Humayun took the path of least resistance and declared the victory Akbar's. But now, Humayun was gone, and with him any hope of even such unsatisfying compromise.

For the moment, however, they held their peace, Tardi Beg and Abul Ma'ali, not to mention all the other equally authoritative, egoistic warlords who had marched across the Indus with Humayun. Akbar was able to claim his makeshift throne unopposed, uncontested – though not even the bricks he sat on were his. Akbar had inherited no kingdom – 'less than a petty district',[15] in fact. The Mughals had hardly been back in Hindustan a year, and barely held two cities, Lahore and Delhi. What Akbar had inherited was a conquest in progress, its future as uncertain as the course of a dream, and while his Khan Baba and Shamsuddin Ataka and Maham Anaka might console their charge for the death of his father, all of them must also have been fighting fears about the turns his fortune, and their own, could take.

The first of many such swerves in Akbar's destiny occurred within days.

'This man was a dullard', writes Badauni of Abul Ma'ali; he was 'drunk on old wine and read last year's calendar',[16] says Abul Fazl. Of all the late padishah's courtiers, Abul Ma'ali had most reason to long for the past. Humayun had favoured him, but Akbar was guided by his bitter rival, Bairam Khan. Understandably wary, Abul Ma'ali did not attend Akbar's coronation. A message arrived afterwards, demanding his presence at a celebration some days later, but the 'self-conceited fool' replied he was still mourning Humayun's death.[17] No doubt he was. The last time he met Akbar, Abul Ma'ali had boasted of his place in Humayun's affections, of how they had drunk from the same cup, and complained that Akbar wasn't even inviting him to share his cushion. This time, would he be allowed to sit at all? Abul Ma'ali sent back word: 'how would His Majesty . . . behave to him, and where would he sit in the assembly . . .?' He would only come if he were seated on Akbar's right.[18]

It was agreed. Abul Ma'ali arrived and sat in pride of place; the banquet was laid out and the courtier held out his hands to wash. Immediately, one

Tulak Khan Qauchin 'appeared on the scene like a spider's web',[19] grabbed Abul Ma'ali from behind, and put him in chains.

Bairam Khan was itching to execute him, but Akbar wouldn't agree. He didn't want to spill blood – least of all sayyid blood – so close to his coronation. (Sayyids claim descent from the Prophet Muhammad; Akbar's own Muslim antecedents numbered only about ten generations – it was in the thirteenth century that Timur's great-grandfather embraced Islam.) Abul Ma'ali was bundled off to prison, unharmed, but it must have been clear to the gathered chieftains and to all those who heard of this inglorious affair that a new rule had begun and that it was not Akbar's alone but Bairam Khan's – and that Bairam Khan would have his revenge.

It might seem as if in all this celebration of Akbar's accession and plotting against Abul Ma'ali the young emperor had ample time to settle into his new role, and his regent to settle old scores. They did not.

On 14 February 1556, when Akbar put on his black crown, he was one of half a dozen claimants to the throne of Hindustan. Its last competent ruler had been Sher Shah Suri's son, Salim; the dynasty had fractured after his death. Now, four Suri rivals of varying talent were in competition. Only two of them are of immediate interest. One was Sikandar Suri, whom the Mughals had defeated at Sirhind. The other was Muhammad Adil,[20] a man as vicious as he was cowardly. He'd murdered his own nephew, a child, for the throne; once, he'd hidden in the women's quarters to escape a brawl in his court. The only good history has to say of him is that he had an ear for music – he is said to have tutored the legendary Tansen, no less[21] – and an eye for talent. Adil appointed a supremely gifted general to lead his army, a general who won him twenty-two straight victories and emerged as the last and most surprising of Hindustan's potential emperors.

Hemu of Rewari began life as a grocer. His was not a large business; in fact, Abul Fazl describes him as one of 'the petty hucksters' in his town, hawking saltpetre in the back lanes of Rewari. Nevertheless, Hemu was enterprising enough to attract the attention of Salim Shah, Sher Shah Suri's son and successor, who gave Hemu a commission to the Suri court. The grocer rose rapidly, until he was handling administrative and financial affairs as the king's trusted aide. When Salim Shah died and the Suri rivals revealed themselves like so many daggers drawn, Hemu was allied – whether by chance or design – with Muhammad Adil. Soon, Hemu discovered that this was not so much an alliance as an opportunity; his position was very similar to Bairam Khan's, in fact, for his king was 'careless of worldly affairs'.[22] Unlike Bairam Khan's young protégé, moreover, Adil was unlikely to develop an ability to rule, while Hemu's talents were only just beginning to flower.

Even Abul Fazl, whose resentment of Hemu's challenge to Akbar knows few bounds, admits that he 'waged great wars . . . [with] valour and daring' and 'performed great deeds'. Badauni, too, has a bias against Hemu, though his grudge is more personal: Badauni's father's library was destroyed during one of Hemu's campaigns. It is Badauni, moreover, who provides a glimpse of Hemu's ruthless pursuit of victory.

As various would-be monarchs marched across the north Indian plains, the people of Hindustan faced a far more pressing concern – they were battling a famine. The hunger was particularly severe around Delhi and Agra. People ate whatever they could find: thorns, herbs, animal hide – even each other. Some 'would join together and carry off a solitary man and make him their food', writes Abul Fazl; Badauni swears he saw it with his own eyes. It was under such grim conditions that Hemu launched a three-month siege of Bayana, south of Agra, and throughout, writes Badauni, while 'the people died with the word "bread" upon their lips', Hemu fed his elephants rice, sugar and butter and would host a grand public meal every day himself, encouraging his Afghan soldiers to eat in 'large handfuls . . . "How can you with such a slender appetite expect to fight with any rascally Mughal"'!

It is possible that Badauni is exaggerating or ill-informed; he would have been a boy at the time and an unlikely witness to the scene. On the other hand, a show of plenty was commonly used as psy-ops during a siege[23] – it would be testament to Hemu's strategic mind, not a condemnation of his cold heart.

Whatever the case may be, Hemu won the siege of Bayana, as he won every battle he fought on Adil's behalf, while Adil appeared nowhere on the scene. It was only a matter of time, then, before the general's eye turned to the crown, and thus, to Delhi.

On 6 October 1556, eight months after Akbar's enthronement in Kalanaur, Hemu led 50,000 men and 1000 elephants, equipped with 500 mortar guns and fifty-one cannons, to the outskirts of Delhi. Akbar was still in Punjab, with Bairam Khan; they had resumed their pursuit of Sikandar Suri. It was Tardi Beg who remained in charge of Delhi, though several Mughal chiefs joined him in the city's defence. Among them were Bairam Khan's deputy, Pir Muhammad, and one of Humayun's Uzbek recruits, Abdullah. The battle began rather well. The Mughal vanguard – including Abdullah the Uzbek – led a terrific charge that scattered Hemu's forward battalions, killed 3000 of his men, and captured 400 elephants. The vanguard galloped away in pursuit of the enemy – and plunder – but when they came back a little later, expecting the remaining army to have secured a victory, they found a scene of abject defeat instead.

What happened between the vanguard's triumphant chase and bemused return isn't clear. Hemu, it seems, took command of some 300 elephants and a battalion of soldiers and entered the fray. Meanwhile, the Mughal chieftains who remained with Tardi Beg were far less inclined to fight than those who had galloped away. Some, writes Abul Fazl, 'did not behave with courage', while Pir Muhammad simply turned tail and 'chose flight'. He did so, Abul Fazl continues, in order to 'ruin the Commander-in-chief-ship of Tardi Beg Khan' – and why he might have wanted such a thing will be clear soon enough. For the moment, however, Tardi Beg seemed willing to give up of his own accord; he, too, left the battlefield, and with victory in their grasp, 'there came [instead] a catastrophe'.

News of the rout reached Akbar on 13 October 1556, two days before his fourteenth birthday. The padishah was in Jalandhar, but quickly handed the campaign against Sikandar Suri to his aunt Gulbadan's husband, Khizr-Khwaja Khan, and marched south. It was in Sirhind, site of the great victory that had only just won them a stake in Hindustan, that Akbar's 'scattered Amirs came to salute him'.[24]

They brought with them an equally scattered resolve. According to Ferishta, a seventeenth-century historian, a 'majority of the officers' wanted to go home.[25] Hemu's army had too many men, too many elephants, and far too great a chance of defeating the Mughals. It was almost two years since Humayun had left Kabul; now, if only his son agreed, the soldiers and warlords who came with him might all return to their fiefs and families, enriched with plunder and possessed of their lives. Perhaps they were even a little nostalgic for the familiar, familial squabbling over Kabul. Delhi could wait.

Bairam Khan disagreed. Not only should Akbar stay, he must march upon Delhi at once; they might still surprise Hemu with speed if not overwhelm him with numbers. The choice was clear: did Akbar wish to be emperor of Hindustan, or would he retreat to the comforts of Kabul and remain a provincial padishah?

It's equally possible that there was no such choice at all – that Bairam Khan was more interested in asserting his own authority than in building Akbar's future. It could be, as Abul Fazl suggests, that Bairam Khan's deputy, Pir Muhammad, ran away from Delhi to demoralize Tardi Beg's troops and put him in exactly this embarrassed situation: a veteran commander having to explain himself to a fourteen-year-old.

Tardi Beg had not challenged the ambitious regent so far, and Bairam Khan deferred to the older soldier, calling him *toqan*, 'elder brother'[26] – but there was little family feeling between the two. Bairam was a Persianized Turk, his clan historically associated with the descendants of Timur. Tardi Beg was a Chagatai, proud of his Mongol lineage, and imagining himself, as Ferishta once wrote of Chagatai chiefs generally, 'at least equal to [the legendary Persian kings] Keikobad and Keikaoos'. One was a talented general, relatively young, a tactician and diplomat who had stuck by the Mughals since he was sixteen; the other a grizzled nobleman with a keen interest in the health of his treasury, who would well remember how Humayun once ran after him, begging for his loyalty. Finally, Bairam was Shia and Tardi Beg was Sunni. Little wonder, then, if both were looking for ways 'to ruin one another'.[27]

Tardi Beg's retreat from Delhi gave Bairam a perfect opportunity to strike. He did not waste it.

Akbar was out hunting. The boy had prevented Abul Ma'ali's execution and Bairam was not inclined to take such a chance again. Quickly, as Akbar rode through Sirhind with his sparrowhawks, his regent sent a friendly message to Tardi 'toqan', inviting him to his tent. No one knows what they talked about. Perhaps Bairam let the commander reinvigorate himself with old war tales. Perhaps he let him imagine that Bairam sought his advice; that he, too, was anxious to return to his fort in Qandahar. They might even have had an avuncular chat about Akbar and the boy's uncertain destiny. Whatever it is, Tardi Beg seems to have been at ease, suspecting nothing, when Bairam got up to wash before the evening prayer. This was a signal to his men, who fell as one on Tardi Beg and killed him.

When Akbar returned that evening, Pir Muhammad brought him the news. Bairam had sent an equivocal apology with his deputy: 'He hoped that [Akbar] would approve of him with the glance of pardon so that other evildoers might take warning.'[28]

If Akbar was unhappy or upset by the sudden execution of a familiar face, he said nothing. Besides, Bairam was busy planning a strike on Hemu; Tardi Beg was already old news. Any talk of him would be a distraction from the business at hand – getting Akbar an empire.

Nor was Hemu resting on his laurels. Having heard that the Mughals were planning to retaliate, he sent his artillery ahead to Panipat, and prepared to follow. Bairam, too, had dispatched an army of 10,000 men under Ali Quli Shaibani, an outstanding Uzbek warrior who would soon display his flair for battle. The Mughals weren't far from Panipat when Hemu's guns and cannons arrived. Immediately – with the reflexive speed that would become a hallmark of Akbar's own military strategy – Ali Quli Shaibani raced ahead with a small detachment of men, surprised the commanders guarding the artillery, and took it from them.

Hemu wasn't dismayed by the setback; instead, he left Delhi 'with consummate pride and great celerity'.[29] The distance from Delhi to Panipat is under 100 kilometres. Famine still held sway over the region, so there would have been little sign of life along the way, the fields untended or even unsowed as Hemu and the 'black mass of his army'[30] marched by. His cavalry alone comprised 30,000 'practiced horsemen',[31] Rajput and Afghan, and there were anywhere between 500 (Abul Fazl) and 1500 (Badauni) elephants, wearing bright armour, spears and daggers tied to their trunks, carrying musketeers and archers on their backs.

Never before had many of the Mughals seen these 'mountain-like and dragon-mouthed' creatures in such grand array. Abul Fazl's description catches something of the open-mouthed gasps of awe that may have filled the air as the two armies came face to face on 5 November 1556 upon the battle-weary plains of Panipat. How could a description of these 'rushing mountains be strung on the slender thread of words'? An elephant could outstrip the fastest Persian horse – indeed, it could lift both horse and rider in its trunk and '[fling] them into the air'.

The Mughal horses, as new to Hindustan as their masters, 'had never seen such terrific forms', and would run amok at their approach. No wonder that 'perturbation found its way into the hearts' of the Mughal men.[32] Still, Abdul-lah the Uzbek was among them, as also Ali Quli Shaibani, and several others who rallied the troops. On the other side, Hemu, bare-headed, shouting war cries, 'went forth with scowling brow'[33] on his elephant, Hawai – airborne. His attack was swift and strong, and threw both left and right wings of the Mughal army 'into great confusion'.[34] Central Asian horsemanship was not to be taken lightly, however. Instead of charging at the elephants, head first, they rode into Hemu's ranks diagonally, slashing with their swords, aiming to unseat enemy soldiers and trample them under 'the dagger-hooves of swift, fiery horses'.[35]

'Like thunder in April and lions in the thicket', writes Abul Fazl, the two armies 'roared and charged each other'.[36] A painting of the scene shows a man who has lost his helmet, trying to keep his long, loose hair out of his eyes with one hand and control his horse with the other; his shield flies behind him like an umbrella in a storm. Another man is caught and twisted out of shape in an elephant's trunk. A white horse's neck is splattered with blood. 'You'd say the air was all crimsoned daggers / Their steel had all become solid rubies.'[37]

Ali Quli Shaibani, in command of the centre, was holding strong, thanks to a large ditch between his men and Hemu's elephants. His archers fired volley after volley of arrows at the enemy, but nothing, it seems, would make the battle turn their way.

Some 15 kilometres away, Bairam Khan was preparing the reserves, riding through the ranks and delivering 'promises of favour and anger'.[38] It was do or die; there would be no second chances.

Did Akbar know, did he realize that Panipat was his family's second chance?[39] He wasn't a diligent student, and there is nothing to suggest that he had, as yet, acquired any interest in history, or even his own ancestry. On the other hand, it's hardly possible that Babur's great victory of 1526 on this very battlefield wasn't a familiar story to his grandson. He must have known how Babur had routed Ibrahim Lodi's army of 100,000 men – even more than Hemu's – with only 10,000 of his own. But then, Akbar would also have known that Babur had a secret weapon. Gunpowder.[40] Thrown into utter confusion by unexpected explosions, Lodi's army had been routed by noon. Thirty years later, Akbar had no secret weapon. Gunpowder was so commonplace now that Akbar had ordered his chief of artillery to stuff an effigy of Hemu with it and have it blown up, as a way of cheering his troops and, as likely, himself. All he could do, as he put on his armour and rode those last dusty kilometres towards Panipat, was hope for a miracle.

A miracle is what he got.

Hemu had broken two wings of the Mughal army. Now, he watched as Ali Quli Shaibani's centre unleashed its barrage of arrows across the ditch, and Hemu's embattled elephants retreated just enough to allow the Mughals to charge. Unfazed, Hemu launched a counter-attack with a platoon of musth elephants that roared and 'dislodged many . . . soldiers of the sublime army'.[41] The Mughal position wasn't getting any better. Ploughed through by demented elephants, Ali Quli's cavalry fired desperate arrows into the air.

One of them found its mark.

Hemu the grocer had never learnt to ride a horse. This explains, partly, why he was riding an elephant; though an elephant was also a way for a commander to remain visible, at a height, to his troops. That may be why Hemu wasn't wearing a helmet – so that his men might recognize him easily, and gain heart from his bare courage. It was a brave but reckless decision. The air was thick with arrows and one struck Hemu in the eye, piercing his skull so that, in Badauni's graphic description, 'his brain passed clean out from the cup of his head'.

Ferishta writes that Hemu did not give up despite the mortal blow; that he 'drew the arrow and with it the eye out of the socket, which he wrapt in his handkerchief . . . [and] continued to fight with unabated courage'. Perhaps that is true; Hemu's ambition for power was no less than Akbar's would become. He had even vowed, some say, to convert to Islam if he defeated the Mughals.[42] But willpower alone cannot staunch the effects of an arrow through the eye.

Hemu slumped upon his howdah, unconscious.

It is a telling indictment of warfare in general that if the leader of a battle was killed, his army lost all interest in the fight. Thus, when Akbar and Bairam reached Panipat, they did not find a battle to join, but a victory to celebrate. Hemu's army had disintegrated like chalk to dust; his elephant Hawai, meandering off the battlefield, had been captured, and Hemu was in chains.[43]

The grocer who became a general, the shopkeeper who dreamt of empire, the champion of over twenty battles who now lay bleeding and breathing his last, was brought before Akbar, a boy who still needed his stirrups shortened to ride a horse. Bairam Khan did not – or could not – see the asymmetry. He, too, had lost his father young and joined Babur's army when he was sixteen, only two years older than Akbar was now. He told the newly crowned padishah to execute his foe: it would be an act of 'holy combat', a blow for empire and for Islam.[44]

Looking at the man before him, with his horrible wound and his rasping breath, Akbar hesitated. He made excuses.

'I have already torn him to pieces', he said. 'One day in Kabul I was practicing drawing . . . I drew a picture of a person with disjointed limbs.' When someone asked him what he was trying to draw, he said, 'It's a picture of Hemu.'[45]

It is impossible that Akbar had heard of Hemu until a few months before the man himself was brought before him. For Abul Fazl, this is, of course, the miracle of the drawing. There are other ways to look at it, too. A child drawing cartoonish scenes of graphic violence, as another might play with dolls by tearing their limbs apart. A boy inspired by stories of his father's enemies in a faraway land, mangling one of them on paper: I'll beat him, I'll kill him. A man, a little embarrassed by his adolescent inhibitions over spilling human blood, camouflaging the fact in stories.

A cacophony of voices rose to support Bairam's suggestion. Akbar must kill the enemy! Abul Fazl writes that the more they 'pressed him' to do it, the more Akbar resisted. Ferishta says that the boy compromised by touching Hemu with his sword. Some later historians, from Vincent A. Smith to Harbans Mukhia, believe that Akbar did, in fact, use his sword more forcefully. Whether this is true, that Akbar took his first human life in Panipat, or whether, as is more generally believed, it was Bairam who finally swung his own sword in an impatient arc and cut off Hemu's head, the fact is that Akbar's official history overflows with regret for Hemu's death. 'Would that [the emperor] had come out of his veil', writes Abul Fazl; would that Akbar had forbidden Hemu's execution and inducted him into his own service instead. A man of such 'lofty spirit' under Akbar's patronage, 'what works might he not have performed?'

Thus, at any rate, the Second Battle of Panipat was won, but Hemu was hardly the only challenge that Akbar and Bairam faced during these first months of what was, in effect, their joint reign. Back in Badakhshan, Sulaiman – seniormost in the family after his cousin Humayun's death – had taken over neighbouring fiefs while their holders were in Hindustan,[46] and besieged Kabul, where he was held at bay by Munim Khan for several months until Sulaiman retreated in September 1556, only weeks before Tardi Beg lost Delhi. The intrepid Ali Quli Shaibani's brother, Bahadur Khan, had made a move on Qandahar, forcing its Mughal governor to seek Persian help. As is only too likely to happen when flies invite spiders home, Qandahar surrendered, some months later, not to Bahadur but to the mighty Shah Tahmasp, chafing, no doubt, ever since Humayun swiped the city from under his nose.

Closer home, a former governor of Sher Shah Suri's, Hajji Khan, had commandeered Narnaul, south-west of Delhi, and marched upon Alwar.

It was in pursuit of Hajji Khan that Pir Muhammad, Bairam's deputy, now set off. En route, he found Hemu's wife, fleeing with 'elephants laden with gold'.[47] The widow who might have been queen managed to escape, but her elephants and riches fell to the Mughals, the neighbouring villagers, and the ground – there was so much gold that they were picking it up by the shield-full, writes Badauni; years later, lucky travellers might still find 'gold coins and ingots' along the way.

Understandably, the loot delayed Pir Muhammad, and Hajji Khan had long escaped when the Mughal army reached Alwar. Pir Muhammad had, in any case, found himself a more tempting and remunerative target: he rode on to Deoti, where the rest of Hemu's baggage train was camped. More bounty fell to the Mughals, and also, more tragically, Hemu's eighty-year-old father. Pir Muhammad offered him his life in return for converting to Islam, but after eight decades of having 'worshipped my God according to [my own] religion' the old man was not inclined to change. 'Why should I change it at this time', he said, 'and . . . merely from fear of my life, and without understanding it come into your way of worship?'[48]

Pir Muhammad was not a man to be diverted by theological debate. Hemu's father was killed.

Hajji Khan, meanwhile, arrived in Ajmer, and took it.

The story of Hajji Khan is one of hundreds of digressions that flow like rivulets from the long-flowing river that is Akbar's life. Not every stream is worth paddling into, and Hajji Khan, though evidently an able commander, might have been safely ignored if his story did not introduce a far more significant character into Akbar's world.

In 1547, a decade earlier, the raja of the Kachhwaha Rajputs had died, leaving behind two embattled sons, Bihari Mal – or Bharmal – and Askaran. It was Hajji Khan, governor of the region, who negotiated a compromise and divided the land between them. The fall of the Suris and Humayun's return brought about a predictable slide in Hajji Khan's fortunes; he lost his territories. When Humayun died, the khan lost no time in winning back his land. Thus it was that Hajji Khan besieged a Mughal commander called Majnun Khan Qaqshal in Narnaul, with Bihari Mal by his side.

It was a tricky situation for the Rajput king, having to choose between a once-powerful Afghan governor and a rising Mughal star, but he managed to keep his bridges intact long enough to pick the right side.[49] Bihari Mal negotiated Majnun Khan Qaqshal's surrender, sending him back to court safe and sound, and, when Hajji Khan fled to Ajmer, his Rajput ally returned Narnaul to the Mughals, too.

Thus, Bihari Mal gained the Mughals' gratitude without arousing Hajji Khan's enmity, and when Akbar arrived in Delhi from Panipat, the Kachh-waha chief was among the elite invited to meet and congratulate him. Some days later, having established diplomatic relations with the young padishah, the raja and his kin came to take their leave. Akbar was riding a musth elephant, 'rushing in every direction',[50] and causing havoc, presumably, while Bairam tried to hold court on his behalf. As the chaos increased and people fled, the elephant turned upon the Rajputs – who, unlike the rest of the court, remained in place. Akbar was impressed – the first of many times that he would be impressed by Rajput courage – impressed enough, in fact, to ask to know more about the raja. He did not know that he was enquiring after his future father-in-law, nor how their lives would intertwine until their very blood was one.

Five years would pass, however, before the two met again; five years in which Akbar would leave his childhood behind.

Akbar's inattention in court on the day the Rajputs were leaving – his active disruption of it, in fact – was clearly not uncommon. Abul Fazl expends a great deal of his ink, at this point, on expanding metaphors of the veil – here equivalent to the proverbial bushel under which Akbar was hiding his light. It was the veil, therefore, that stopped Akbar from halting Hemu's execution. At other times, he was living 'within the veil of indifference', 'clad . . . in a garb of estrangement', or 'pretended not to notice' – all this apparent distraction a guise to 'test the powerful . . . under the veil of inattention'.

As always with Abul Fazl, there is a great deal of myth-making in the metaphor. The veil carried many political connotations. For one, as Azfar Moin writes, 'The veiling of the face . . . was a mark of the awaited savior who had yet to manifest his true nature.'[51] It might also hint at a person, particularly a ruler, being a representative of God – conceived as pure light in Islamic theology. Thus, Harbans Mukhia tells of how the thirteenth-century Sultan Balban, having declared himself God's shadow, appeared in court with his face literally veiled, 'lest even the shadow of the powerful light blind an onlooker'.

On the other hand, Abul Fazl's enthusiasm for myth-making is matched by an equally fierce commitment to creating an accurate historical record. He wasn't making it up: Akbar was distracted, but that doesn't mean that Akbar wasn't paying attention.

Glimpses of his childhood in Kabul – the complaints to Humayun, the rapid turnover of tutors, the obsession with animals – suggest a kind of wilful energy, a mind too busy with its own delights to have time for duty. It was this very Akbar, however, who would grow into a man of remarkable intelligence, with a fine memory, endless curiosity and love of detail. These qualities must have existed in him, if in germinating form, when he was a boy, and it is entirely possible that Akbar was watching and learning, observing and absorbing far more than he let on.

What would such a boy do when a sudden load of responsibility fell upon him, when it was in his name that battles were fought and men were killed? In the second year of his reign, Akbar did what unhappy children often dream of doing: he ran away from home.

The signs of stress had been showing. The only real order Akbar gave in his first year as padishah was to call for the harem. It was an 'imperial command driven by great yearning', writes Abul Fazl.[52] Bereaved, enthroned and overwhelmed, it is little wonder if Akbar was missing his mother. But the women were delayed; first, by Sulaiman's siege of Kabul, ably defused by Munim Khan; then by Hemu's challenge. It was only in the spring of 1557, a year after Akbar had called for them, that the harem arrived in Hindustan.

Akbar was camped outside Mankot, a little north of Multan, on the borders of Hindustan. Bairam Khan had resumed the campaign against Sikandar Suri, who was waging an increasingly hopeless resistance from within the Mankot fort, a grand and solid affair built on four hills by Salim Suri with the express purpose of repelling attacks from across the Indus. After the horrors of Panipat, the Mughals seemed to be taking the siege as an opportunity for showmanship. On the very first day, Maham Anaka's son, Adham Khan, had made a solo charge at a troop of soldiers from the fort – racing at them, sword in hand, slashing several to the ground 'in dust and blood' before making an about-turn and returning to 'shouts of Bravo!' Every day, writes Abul Fazl, 'war-loving . . . men' followed Adham Khan's example and made such brash attacks.

It may have been Akbar who told Abul Fazl of these exploits; perhaps he watched them with a mixture of admiration and envy, dying to make heroic dashes himself. No matter how intently he watched the siege, however, he kept one eye on the road to Lahore. Maham Anaka had gone to escort Hamida and the ladies to Mankot from that city. When he heard they were nearby, Akbar left the siege and went to meet them, to 'mutual rejoicings'.[53]

The harem brought good luck with them. In summer that year, Sikandar Suri gave up the fight and offered to surrender. Shamsuddin of Ghazni, Akbar's *ataka*, went into the fort to negotiate terms: all Sikandar wanted was to retire somewhere in the east. He sent 'money and goods' to bolster his case, though not to Akbar, nor even to Bairam, but to Pir Muhammad – some indication, perhaps, of Bairam's deputy's rising influence.[54] Then, on 24 July 1557, he gave up the keys to the fort and went away to Bihar. The east, Bihar and Bengal, would be the heart of vigorous Afghan resistance to Akbar's rule for years to come, but it would not feature Sikandar. He died in two years' time.

The Mughal camp should have been full of joy and bonhomie, the men reunited with their wives, their last real Suri challenger defeated. Instead, bad feeling filled the air.

Much of it was concentrated in Bairam Khan's tent, where Akbar's regent was laid up with a painful case of boils. Akbar doesn't seem to have been very concerned; he was busy fighting his elephants. One day, a particularly lively bout careened its way towards Bairam's tent – trumpeting animals, cheering spectators, exactly the kind of commotion designed to send an ill man into a rage.

What crime had he committed, Bairam railed to Maham Anaka, that Akbar had let 'furious elephants . . . loose against my tent?'[55]

Why would Bairam imagine that Akbar set the fight by his tent on purpose? Both Abul Fazl and the historian Nizamuddin say that gossips and troublemakers put the idea in the regent's head. Maham tried to 'quiet his disturbed mind', says Abul Fazl; Nizamuddin adds that Bairam was not to be soothed. In fact, he insisted that Maham convey his displeasure to Akbar.

Is it possible that Bairam was beginning to tire of the padishah's veil? Did he feel that Akbar was spending too much time fighting elephants and too little strategizing with Bairam? One day, some years later, Akbar would remind Bairam of how he'd often 'said . . . that it was time we dealt with affairs of state'.[56] Was Bairam's impatience exacerbated by paranoia, the fears of a Shia Turcoman who had imprisoned a Sunni rival, Abul Ma'ali, and executed a Chagatai nobleman, Tardi Beg? Bairam had every reason to believe that the Chagatai nobility mistrusted him. Munim Khan, Akbar's ataliq not long ago, was escorting the harem to Hindustan when he heard what Bairam had done to Tardi Beg. Promptly, the cautious khan turned back around. Was Bairam really contemplating a further purge of Akbar's court? If so, he must have known that his plan would require the young padishah's deference and that deference was not Akbar's strong suit.

And what of Akbar? How would he have felt being told off by his regent for a bit of hijinks with elephants?

'At this time a strange thing happened', writes Abul Fazl. Akbar, who had once put men in dog leashes for their slackness, 'began to chafe' until his indignation 'broke out into anger'. Shouting let no one dare follow him, not even his 'grooms and such like persons', he got on his best horse, Hayran, unequalled for speed, and galloped away.

After a while, Akbar got off, but Hayran, wild and 'fiery' like his rider, continued to run, until he was out of sight. Akbar was entirely alone, not even the impatient whinnying of a horse to distract him. Maybe this is what he wanted. A moment away from the unending drumroll of events that had filled his life since Humayun died, a moment away from Bairam's nagging annoyance and Maham's solicitous advice. Abul Fazl says that Akbar prayed, 'communing with his God'.

Time passed. Having left the camp of annoying adults in a rage, Akbar may have begun to wish he hadn't. Especially now that he had no horse to return upon, Hayran having disappeared across the horizon. He was wondering what to do, beginning to worry, maybe, in his helpless, unaccustomed solitude. Just then, Hayran returned, galloping to Akbar from wherever it is he'd gone to douse his own fury, and coming to a tame halt by his young rider's side. Akbar 'mounted the noble animal', astonished – an astonishment that he must have communicated to his historian, years later, for Abul Fazl's description of the scene is rather more overwrought ('to noble discourse of this kind there is no limit!') than the reunion warrants.

Still, you cannot discount Akbar's joy at Hayran's return. Akbar loved animals, and animals can love back in a way that no human can; the wildness of the horse and the fury of the boy may have been like balm to one another. Akbar got back in his saddle and returned to camp, his temper restored. His relationship with Bairam, however, had only suffered the first of many bumps in a long and rocky decline.

Five days after Sikandar Suri surrendered, the victorious Mughal army packed up and went to Lahore. Akbar raced ahead, hunting all the way. Bairam brooded. In Lahore, says Nizamuddin, the regent 'still harped upon' the elephant fight – but his suspicions had shifted from Akbar to his ataka, Shamsuddin Muhammad Khan.

Like Bairam, Shamsuddin began his career as a soldier. Unlike Bairam, he had no claim to any kind of name. Bairam descended from a well-known clan of Baharlu Turks; his father was governor of Ghazni under Babur, the very province in which Shamsuddin's father was a farmer. The class difference is clear in the fact that Abul Fazl doesn't include Shamsuddin in his list of commanders who came to Hindustan with Humayun; Shamsuddin was part of the retinue, yes, but he came as an attendant, not a warrior.[57] The two men did have one thing in common, however: they were both hugely ambitious.

Back on his farm in Ghazni, a twenty-two-year-old Shamsuddin had dreamt of holding the moon in his arms. Following the lucky accident by which he rescued Humayun in Kannauj, the young soldier had gained a place of intimate trust in Humayun's life. His wife, Jiji, was one of Akbar's many affectionate anakas – in fact, she had been the first foster mama to hold the newborn. Their son, Aziz, was Akbar's *koka*, milk brother, and would remain his friend until the end of Akbar's life. The padishah was the moon of Shamsuddin's dreams – and a man who had held Akbar in his arms from infancy would have a far greater hold on his love, and trust, than Bairam could hope for. Might the ataka, then, usurp the regent's role?

Bairam turned on him. Akbar's seeming 'disfavour' Bairam could only blame on Shamsuddin's 'calumnies'. Why, asked Bairam, was Shamsuddin 'thirsting for my blood', and turning Akbar against him such that the young emperor would 'even go so far as to [make an] attempt [on] my life?'

Bairam was a powerful man, and Shamsuddin did not take his melodramatic allegations lightly. He went to Bairam with all his sons and relatives and swore 'solemn oaths' of allegiance – he had never spoken ill of the regent, he never would. Finally, Bairam Khan 'came to his senses'.[58]

The saga was not yet ended, however. Having complained to Maham and terrified Shamsuddin, Bairam decided to punish Akbar. He confiscated the boy's beloved elephants, distributing the imperial herd among his own men. Akbar said nothing, and Abul Fazl can't believe it. 'Good God! What width of capacity! And what gentleness!' Not only did the padishah not protest his deprivation, he even rewarded his regent a few months later, marrying him to his cousin, Salima.

Poor Akbar. Was it the loss of his elephants that hurt more, or the realization that in Bairam Khan, now his brother-in-law, he was stuck with a tutor he could neither evade nor dismiss?

And poor Abul Fazl, too, anguished on his emperor's behalf. Few biographers, even fewer biographers of pre-modern monarchs, can have written at such length, in such detail and with such feeling for their subjects as Abul Fazl of Akbar. And yet, though the *Akbarnama* and the *Ain-i-Akbari* deliver, between them, such plentiful detail about Akbar's life and reign, from the founding myth of Alanqoa to what he fed his best elephants (rice cooked with chillies and cloves was part of the menu), it is maddeningly difficult to get an unhindered view of Akbar himself, wrapped as he is in the blinding embrace of Abul Fazl's adoration.

Only occasionally can you see him in flesh and blood: a child afraid of the dark, a boy missing his mother, an adolescent in a rage. Now, in the third year of his reign, another glimpse of his character emerges: he was deeply uncomfortable with homosexual love.

Specifically, of the love that Ali Quli Shaibani, the brilliant Uzbek warrior who stole Hemu's artillery and held his place against Hemu's elephants, espoused for a beautiful flirt of a man called Shahim Beg.

Ali Quli was one of the great warlords of his age.[59] His role in Panipat was second only to that of the anonymous arrow that blinded Hemu (and the arrow was probably shot by one of his troops); thereafter, he played a considerable role in clearing Afghan resistance from Sambhal and Lucknow. It wasn't just courage Ali Quli possessed, but also considerable flair. In Lucknow, being told mid-meal that 20,000 Afghans were marching at him, Ali Quli finished eating and began a game of chess before he rose to slay the enemy.

Badauni, who relates this anecdote with much admiration, describes Ali Quli's campaigns as 'a bright page in the annals of the time'. A later historian, Heinrich Blochmann, goes so far as to say that, after Bairam Khan, it is Ali Quli who deserves credit for 'the restoration of the Mughal Dynasty'.[60] And yet, soon after his impressive victory in Lucknow, the talk at Akbar's court turned from Ali Quli Shaibani's sangfroid to his fevered passion for Shahim Beg.

Shahim Beg was a *quorchi* – part of an elite class of soldiers at the Persian court, where his father held charge of the shah's camels, for which reason Abul Fazl refers to Shahim, sneeringly, as 'a camel driver's son'. Badauni tells the story with more sympathy. Shahim Beg, who had joined Humayun's court and remained in Akbar's, was a man of 'good looks, good disposition, and approved manners'; indeed, he embodied 'the beau ideal of the age', and Ali Quli had been smitten by him ever since Humayun's campaign for Hindustan began.

For a while, Ali Quli contented himself, in the manner of lovers, by writing moony poetry. 'Who else, as I for love of thee, lives such a weary life?'[61] But poetry, no matter how lovelorn, cannot take the beloved's place, and Ali Quli Shaibani was an intrepid man, after all. He sent a secret delegation to Delhi, where Shahim Beg was in attendance on Akbar, and smuggled his knight away.

Stories of Ali Quli's 'wonderful affection' began to spread: he would call Shahim 'my king', and wait on him 'like an ordinary servant', remain standing in his lover's presence. More: Shahim was a pious man, it seems, and to please him, Ali Quli 'became adorned with scrupulous regard for the Law' – presumably the sharia – even sending out officers to 'abolish all wanton and forbidden practices' in his camp.[62]

It may seem almost numbingly ironic to modern readers that a man embraced religious law in adoration of his gay lover, but there was clearly no insurmountable contradiction between homosexuality and Islamic piety – not for Shahim Beg and Ali Quli, nor for Badauni, bitter critic though he was of Akbar's later heresies. Ali Quli was 'following the manners of Transoxiana', writes Badauni, as an aside more than a reproach. Love between men wasn't reprehensible in Central Asia. Babur's first love was a young man called Baburi, of whom he wrote, 'I was so bashful that I could not look him in the face.'[63] Bairam Khan, too, did not disapprove of Ali Quli's affections; in fact, he 'took the part of 'Ali Quli Khan and . . . regarded his lawless acts as unacted'.[64]

It is Abul Fazl, the progressive to Badauni's conservative, who bristles at 'the wicked spirits of Transoxiana', and at Ali Quli's temerity in giving 'this outburst of . . . bestial desire the name of Love'. It is Abul Fazl, too, who records that Akbar sent Ali Quli a letter, inviting him to 'repent of your deeds and amend your evil-doings', reinforcing his reproof via 'a number of brave men' sent to appropriate fiefs in Ali Quli's vicinity, and thus keep an eye on him. As it happens, Ali Quli had already assigned one of these fiefs to one of his own men, who did not surrender his claim without a fight.

With battles breaking out in his backyard, and the wild throbbing of his heart shaking the scaffolding of Akbar's nascent kingdom, Ali Quli sent an emissary to Delhi. This man, one Burj Ali, did not plead his case before Bairam or Akbar. Like Sikandar Suri in Mankot, he approached Pir Muhammad. Bairam Khan's deputy's career was careening upwards: he was 'all powerful', writes Abul Fazl, and cruel, as Burj Ali would discover.

Pir Muhammad had Ali Quli's emissary beaten and thrown off a tower. Not content with killing the man, Pir Muhammad made a callous little pun on his name, too; 'Burj' means 'tower'.

A battle and an execution already in its wake, Ali Quli's love affair was about to enter its final, tragic, act.

Though Abul Fazl insists that 'the wicked ways of Transoxiana' are bereft of all worthy emotion, 'neither consuming nor melting, neither love nor friendship', few readers will deny that Ali Quli's love for Shahim possessed such noble qualities, sometimes in too great a measure. At some point, his previously pious knight shifted his affections from God to a dancing girl called Aram Jaan. Aram Jaan was not only 'very fascinating, and graceful in her movements', as Badauni puts it, she was also Ali Quli's wife. But what could the besotted commander do? 'No one can force the affections of the heart', writes Badauni, wisely. Ali Quli surrendered his wife to his lover.

Meanwhile, Akbar had decided to drown Ali Quli's passion in work – an order arrived for the warlord to leave Lucknow and go conquer Jaunpur. Ali Quli obeyed; when he went to Jaunpur, he even sent Shahim Beg away, though not without another poem – 'The [cold] wind of absence knows no bounds.' Shahim Beg was to leave, Aram Jaan in tow, and lie low a while in Sarharpur, a fiefdom not too far from Jaunpur. Ali Quli hoped they would be reunited once the 'wrath of the Emperor . . . abated'.[65]

Ali Quli might have thought he had it all figured out, but he hadn't taken his lover's fickle heart into account. Shahim Beg did go to Sarharpur, but once there he appears to have surrendered both his affection and Aram Jaan to its fief-holder, Abdur Rahman – then demanded her back. When Abdur Rahman refused, Shahim Beg tied him up and ran off with Aram Jaan. They were dallying in amorous if strategically unwise solitude when they were interrupted by Abdur Rahman's brother, who arrived with a posse of armed men, one of whom killed the faithless knight.

Abdur Rahman hurried to Akbar's court, hoping to present the whole affair as 'good service'[66] – his own bright idea, that is, to rid the world of Shahim Beg's intoxicating influence. Ali Quli's love, meanwhile, had wilted not a jot from Shahim's faithless behaviour. He was in mourning, and galloping on Abdur Rahman's heels, having hot words, at the very least, to exchange with the man who murdered his philandering lover. But when it became clear that Abdur Rahman would reach Akbar before Ali Quli caught him, the heartbroken warrior reined in his horse and returned to Jaunpur. Here, he buried the undeserving Shahim Beg by the side of a lake and built a grand tomb for the man who stole his heart. 'Night put on mourning black, and Morn / Raised a cold sigh, and rent its dress', writes Badauni. Abul Fazl wastes no time on condoling verses; for him, this was only another example of how resistance to Akbar invited a bad end.

Thus, the 'insane affair'[67] was ended, though neither man tells us what happened to Aram Jaan – that 'street-walker', Abul Fazl hisses, 'that wanton [woman]'. In what may be a painting of the brawl that claimed Shahim Beg's life, we may imagine her not overly perturbed by the commotion of armed men around her, nor by the spreadeagled form of her lover with an arrow through his chest.[68] Perhaps she was glad to have survived the dangerous infatuations of susceptible men and hoped to spend the rest of her life in peaceful obscurity.

And what, meanwhile, of Akbar's disapproval? Badauni records that the padishah's 'wrath knew no bounds'. When love between men was so common that even Badauni's orthodoxy didn't blink at it, why should Akbar find it so disturbing? Was it the impropriety of luring away one of his quorchis that galled the padishah? The theory might be credible, if it weren't for the fact that, soon after the Ali Quli affair began, Akbar had another of his courtiers separated from the young male dancer he had taken as companion. This courtier, Shahquli Khan, was so dismayed at his love being locked away that he 'set fire to his name . . . put on the dress of [a] yogi'[69] and retired from the world. A great deal of coaxing was required to bring him back – Bairam Khan even wrote him a ghazal – but the beloved dancer was never returned to him.

It may be pointless to speculate about Akbar's anachronistic homophobia. Still, there is something intriguing about it, particularly in a man whose male friendships would acquire legendary status – the Akbar and Birbal stories of popular culture, for example. Soon after the unhappy end of Ali Quli's tale, in the fourth year of Akbar's reign when he was seventeen, we hear of Akbar holding 'a wine party' for the first time.[70] Such assemblies would be commonplace in the years to come: Akbar's would be a garrulous court, and Akbar himself its beating heart. At the moment, however, Akbar was a beardless adolescent surrounded by Central Asian chiefs, each with more experience and clout than the other. Is it beyond belief that Akbar wanted to discourage potential romantic overtures?

An intriguing essay by Ali Anooshahr bolsters the idea. Revisiting the story of Babur and his beloved Baburi, Anooshahr notes that Babur was not indiscriminately in favour of sexual relations between men. He writes with strong disapproval, for example, about an uncle of his called Mahmud Mirza who, spying any 'comely, beardless youth in his realm' would do all he could to 'turn him into a catamite'. The point to note is that this uncle was also eyeing the kingdom of Fergana, which a pre-pubescent Babur had inherited from his father. 'Now', writes Anooshahr, 'coupled with this threat of political subjugation by his uncle was the possibility of a sexual dominance as well. For Babur clearly states that Mahmud Mirza's love for beardless youths was not checked by any social taboos and even extended to his own family.'[71]

For Akbar, too, homosexuality among the men in his court, particularly the more powerful men in his court, may not have breached religious or social prohibitions as much as it posed a political threat. Such a man might well nurse the idea of taking Akbar into his bed as a way of taking over Akbar's throne – on which, some might say, Bairam Khan was already keeping a chaste but too possessive eye.

The fourth year of Akbar's reign – March 1559 to March 1560 – may have broken Ali Quli's heart, but it brought him some poetic justice, too. Pir Muhammad, the man who killed Hemu's aged father and Ali Quli's envoy, was exiled.

Bairam's deputy had been outgrowing his boots for a while. He had joined Bairam's retinue as an impoverished mullah, and risen rapidly so that he held the reins of all 'political and financial affairs' by this time.[72] It was to him, writes Nizamuddin, that 'the nobles and officers had to make their applications', and it's clear these applications enriched the mullah's treasury as much as they inflated his ego. Once, for example, when offering Bairam Khan an impromptu snack during a hunt – 'whatever may be at hand', he said, coyly – Pir Muhammad produced '3000 drinking cups and 700 porcelain dishes'.[73]

Pir Muhammad was not only corrupt, he was bloodthirsty, too, and frighteningly flippant about taking human life. Once, to decide whether Bairam Khan should or shouldn't kill yet another of his enemies in court, the mullah proposed a gruesome little game. Pir Muhammad took two pieces of paper, one inscribed 'Release', the other 'Death'. The chits were drawn up and thrown in the air; Death landed face up. The courtier lost his life.

Thus, the mullah's wealth and power grew unchecked. '[O]f the many, high and low, who attended at his door', Nizamuddin continues, 'he admitted hardly anyone'. One day, however, he went too far. Pir Muhammad was too unwell – or, according to Nizamuddin, too arrogant – to leave his tent. Bairam Khan went to visit him and was stopped by a Turkish slave at the door. 'Let me tell him you're here', said the slave, sending the regent into a rage. Pir Muhammad came rushing out with profuse apologies, to little effect. The slave had not recognized the regent, he explained; Bairam was unconvinced. How would Pir Muhammad know 'what the slave thought'?[74]

Bairam went away, frowning and plotting revenge.[75] Pir Muhammad received his marching orders a few days later: it would be better, wrote Bairam, if the mullah took a break from his exalted duties and '[sat] down in a corner' to work on 'amending of your disposition'.[76] After a brief spell in jail, Pir Muhammad was sent away on a pilgrimage to Mecca – the euphemism for exile.

It may have seemed to Bairam that in getting rid of his uppity deputy he was merely continuing a purge that had begun with Shah Abul Ma'ali, the handsome villain; that he was ridding Akbar's court of overly ambitious, overbearing men, threats to Bairam's influence and hurdles to conquest. He could not have known that the apparently seamless expulsion of Pir Muhammad was also the beginning of his own banishment.

Pir Muhammad was travelling through Gujarat, to the ports where pilgrims set sail for the Middle East, when he received a letter telling him to stop 'and await events'.[77] The message was from two men: Mirza Sharafuddin Husain, a Timurid from Kashgar who came to console young Akbar on Humayun's demise, and remained in his realm; and Adham Khan, the daredevil who led a solo charge to inaugurate the siege of Mankot, and who was, more importantly, Maham Anaka's son.

And who was Maham Anaka? For a woman who plays such a remarkable role in history, there is remarkably little known about her, and not all that is known is true. To begin with, she is usually said to be one of Akbar's foster mothers, one of the women who suckled him when he was born and thus bound the prince to her with ties of milk. The fact that she is called 'anaka', foster mother, seems to confirm that impression. However, Abul Fazl does not name Maham in his list of women who fed the newborn Akbar. Henry Beveridge, in his translation of the *Akbarnama*, suggests that she was not a wet nurse at all, but rather the 'Head or Superintendent of the nurses'.[78]

It furthers this theory that Adham Khan was older than Akbar – a dashing soldier at Mankot when Akbar was fourteen. Maham could not have nursed Akbar unless she had an infant of her own to nurse, too; this child, if male, would be Akbar's koka – his milk brother. Aziz, son of Jiji Anaka, is often referred to as Aziz Koka, for example; not so Adham Khan.

Adham is only known, in fact, as his mother's son; his father's name is missing from the record, an exceptional omission that suggests to the translator and historian Heinrich Blochmann that Adham was a 'royal bastard'[79] – an epithet that would soon be proven at least figuratively accurate. No husband of Maham's is ever mentioned. Indeed, the only man, besides Akbar and her son, to play any significant role in her life is one Shihabuddin Ahmad Khan, her 'relation and friend'.[80] Their names are joined in the chronicles: it is likely that Shihabuddin helped to build Maham's mosque, the beautifully spartan Khair'ul Manazil that stands across Delhi's Old Fort;

and he was certainly Maham's ally in her better-known historical legacy: the plot against Bairam.

Was it Maham who told her son to send that letter to Pir Muhammad? Possibly. Adham Khan's own life doesn't reveal a man capable of subtle conspiracies, and halting Pir Muhammad's exile was nothing if not a long game. The message began the plot against Bairam as the tuning of instruments begins a concert. For months afterwards, everyone went about their business as usual. Two attempts at expansion – Ranthambore and Malwa – didn't quite take off; Akbar took his hunting cheetahs to Gwalior; and Bairam acquired a new right-hand man, as influential as his predecessor – a Shia cleric called Shaikh Gada'i, given to holding 'singing parties'[81] at which Bairam and Akbar were regular guests.

Then, at the very beginning of Akbar's fifth regnal year, in March 1560, the orchestra struck its first, ominous chord.

It was the trumpet, once again, of elephants.

One of Akbar's elephants went wild and gored one of Bairam's. The regent, in a fury fit to match the elephant's, had its mahout – who was Akbar's own personal elephant-keeper – executed.

Another time, one of Akbar's elephants 'rushed into the Jamna'.[82] And who but Bairam should happen to be cruising on the river, just then! Unerring as fate, the elephant made for the regent's boat – only this time, thank God, its mahout managed to control the animal before it could do any harm. Akbar sent the keeper, in chains, to Bairam: a generous gesture that should have inspired an equally magnanimous forgiveness. Instead, the regent had this mahout killed, too.

As he had done after the first debacle with his elephants in Mankot, Akbar said nothing. Instead, he went 'travelling and hunting', writes Abul Fazl, or 'worshipped the incomparable Deity'. This time, however, Akbar was four years older.

How much a person changes from fourteen to eighteen. Akbar's voice would have broken. He would have experienced that sudden spurt that stretches a boy like bamboo in rain. He would be stronger, more skilled with sword and musket; the boy who put grown men in leashes at nine would be even more adept at exercising authority. Meanwhile, it is an unfortunate truth that the allure of power begets impatience; princes are not known to await their turn at the throne with equanimity. How much more frustrating it must have been, then, to occupy the throne but 'not [have] absolute power in his own kingdom'?[83]

It was Bairam who exercised authority on Akbar's behalf, Bairam who controlled the treasury, and Bairam, most crucially, who promoted his own favourites and persecuted his own enemies. Back in Kabul, a decade ago, ambitious chiefs had gathered around Akbar because the child was heir to

Humayun. How long would it be before men and women in Delhi, whose ambitions were being thwarted by Bairam, made their own claims on Akbar, now that he was king?

'[E]nvious, malignant men' came to him, whispering complaints, writes Nizamuddin. To ask whether it was Akbar's own annoyance or the influence of Bairam's enemies that finally tipped the scales against the regent is like asking about the chicken and the egg. Whatever the whispers in his ear, Akbar had grievances of his own to match them. Bairam was not the kindly sort of guardian Munim had been, allowing Akbar to skip school and fly pigeons. Instead, Bairam had confiscated Akbar's elephants, killed Akbar's mahouts and didn't even allow the padishah a privy purse.[84] So, writes Abul Fazl, it was Akbar who revealed Bairam's 'evil intentions' against him to Maham Anaka, Adham Khan and Mirza Sharafuddin. Later, a council was held, and Maham's friend Shihabuddin Ahmad Khan was inducted into the circle of conspirators. On 18 March 1560, Akbar left Delhi, 'determined to do the deed'.[85]

From Abul Fazl's telling of the following days, however, it is hard to tell if what happened next was meticulously planned or entirely ad hoc; whether Akbar was directing the play, or merely guessing at its plot.

'Ostensibly', when Akbar left Delhi, it was to hunt. He didn't go very far, only across the Yamuna river. Then, as if by chance – '[as] he had no residence' there – he spent the night at the house of one Hakim Zambil.[86] So far so good, but Abul Fazl follows this straightforward narrative with a maddeningly suggestive non sequitur about Kamran's long-forgotten son:

> Since Bayram Khan had shown his affection and inner preference for Mirza Kamran's son Mirza Abu'l Qasim, and since the malevolents of Bairam's coterie kept him under a constant watch, the prince had been summoned to come via the river and participate in the hunt lest he . . . assist in any way those path beaters in the desert of sedition and corruption. In truth it was a good plan, and it happened exactly as it had been suggested to the emperor.[87]

One can only admire the sheer audacity of reintroducing Abul Qasim into the narrative five years after Akbar's cousin arrived in Kalanaur, never to be heard of again. There had been no evidence, all these years, to suggest that Bairam ever thought of replacing Akbar with his cousin; the regent may have curtailed Akbar's authority, but he had no plan to remove Akbar from his throne. Abul Fazl himself doesn't repeat the allegation, almost as if embarrassed by it.[88] The plan of summoning Abul Qasim 'had been suggested to the emperor', he writes, without saying by whom. Could it have been Maham?

Akbar's anaka came with Akbar on this hunting trip, and, according to Nizamuddin, she 'seized every opportunity of saying something to set the mind of the Emperor against Bairam Khan'. Was Abul Qasim brought sailing down the dark waters of the Yamuna to further Maham's case against Bairam: a hapless captive presented to Akbar as proof of conspiracy against him? Is it possible, too, that Akbar didn't buy it? He had real resentments against his regent and would soon be sending angry messages to Bairam detailing them, but he never, not once, accuses him of contemplating treason.

Whatever happened that night, the hunting party did not return to Delhi the next day; instead, it went further south towards Agra, where Bairam was camped. It might be the case that Akbar wanted to confront his Khan Baba face to face and demand answers to Maham Mama's allegations. And it is certainly the case that Maham made every effort to prevent such a meeting.

'The mystery of the world is like the course of the ass', writes Badauni, quoting an Arab proverb, 'when it goes forward it does go forward, when it goes back it does go back'. Bairam's fortune, too, had changed its direction. Thus, when Akbar and his entourage reached Agra's outskirts, Maham tried to enlist another relative into her plot. He refused and sent word to Bairam instead, telling him what was going on. The regent wouldn't believe it.

How often, in the months to come, he must have kicked himself for ignoring so clear a warning. But the ass had begun its backward course. Not only was Bairam blind to signs of danger, he did not hurry to meet Akbar either – expecting, it seems, the padishah to come to him. Maham, meanwhile, convinced Akbar to leave without meeting his proud regent.

According to Abul Fazl, Akbar used a clever 'motive' for returning to Delhi – that his mother, Hamida, was unwell in that city. It's a revealing story: that Akbar should need excuses to leave without paying court to his own regent. Badauni tells a messier tale. According to him, it was Maham who told Akbar that Hamida was ill and insisted he return to Delhi. Did Maham feel that if Akbar met Bairam, the regent would convince him of his loyalty, leaving Maham and her associates exposed to the regent's revenge? She knew full well how Bairam treated his enemies.

It had been nine days since Akbar had left on his purported 'hunt'. For nine days, Maham had argued against his regent, perhaps even painting frightening pictures of Bairam's plot to overthrow him. Now, she played her trump card.

Maham Anaka came to Akbar overwrought. When Bairam found out that Akbar had left for Delhi at Maham's say-so, he would 'avenge himself ' on her, she cried. Maham, poor woman, had 'no power to resist' the regent; all she could hope for was Akbar's permission to leave for Mecca.[89] She would anticipate her own punishment and banish herself. In faraway Mecca – according to Nizamuddin, who tells a similar story – Maham might pray for Akbar, even if she could not see him or serve him in any other way.

Akbar's love for his mother and mother figures is one of his defining traits. He was closer to Hamida and his anakas, Jiji and Maham especially, than to any other woman in his life, reliant upon them for both affection and advice. The thought of Bairam attacking Maham, of forcing her to leave, was unbearable.

'The Emperor', writes Badauni, 'could not make up his mind to part with [Maham Anaka]'. They sailed back to Delhi; Shihabuddin came out and had 'the bliss' of escorting them to the city.[90]

Instead of a frank conversation with his protégé, therefore, Bairam received an arch message from him: 'Since without your leave and approval I have journeyed thus far, all my attendants are in the uttermost terror . . .' It would be well if Bairam showed himself 'amicably inclined' towards them.[91] Soon enough, Bairam would get even more puzzling news: Akbar had issued an edict declaring that Bairam was 'banished from our sight'.[92]

The regent had been sacked.

Too late, Bairam felt the reins slipping from his hands. He sent urgent messages to Delhi protesting his good faith, but Shihabuddin had already fortified the city and, with Maham, was sending news of Bairam's fall far and wide. The plot, as one historian puts it memorably, 'was carried out at the point of the tongue'.[93] Talk of such reversals travels fast: 'One by one, and two by two', writes Abul Fazl, the chiefs abandoned the regent and converged upon Delhi, to be greeted by Shihabuddin and Maham, who had taken over Bairam's office together and were promising lavish rewards to all comers.[94] Too late, Bairam held a council. Some among his remaining loyalists – these included Shaikh Gada'i of the singing parties and Wali Beg, the man who gave Akbar his first cheetah, both Shias – suggested war. Too late, Bairam decided to go and speak to Akbar instead.

Having spent such energy in keeping them apart, Maham would hardly allow a meeting now, with victory in her grasp. If Bairam came to Delhi, said Akbar's advisers, the court should 'go to Lahore before he arrived'. If Bairam followed, Akbar 'should go to Kabul'.[95] The very thought of Bairam coming for a chat was so daunting, it seems, that it would send Akbar's court scurrying back to Kabul as even the threat of Hemu's fearsome elephants had not.

Akbar put his foot down. He would not leave. But – and with, perhaps, the fear of Maham's exile in mind – he would not meet his ex-regent either. He sent men to block Bairam's way and tell him to stay away: 'for [the emperor] would not see him'.

Bairam did not insist. Instead, he declared he would go to Mecca. Clearly, however, he was seething. He released two political prisoners, including the very first of Akbar's disaffected nobles, Shah Abul Ma'ali. It was a bit like leaving the gas to leak in a house as you leave it. Did Bairam hope Akbar would panic at the thought of 'experienced troublers'[96] on the loose, and call his Khan Baba to set things right?

Akbar did, in fact, send Bairam two messages, but neither revealed any change of heart. The first was a letter[97] in which Akbar offered Bairam cold encouragement for his journey to Mecca and a fief to sustain him. It may be as a result that Bairam began to march northwards, heading to Punjab, it seems, rather than the ports of Gujarat. Akbar rode out of Delhi with an army to block Bairam's way, sending a messenger ahead. This second message was oral, to be conveyed by Mir Abdul Latif, recently appointed Akbar's tutor.

Abdul Latif was a congenial man. Abul Fazl and Badauni, for example, who could hardly agree on what day of the week it was, both write of him with admiration.[98] If Akbar – or his advisers – intended to soothe Bairam's ruffled feathers, Abdul Latif was the man for the job.

While Akbar was young, said the amiable tutor, he had left governance to Bairam, but now that he had turned his attention to 'affairs of government', it would be best if Bairam went on the Haj. He had often longed to do so, after all, 'in public and in private', and Akbar would be more than happy to give him 'whatever place and whatever extent of land' in Hindustan to support his journey.[99]

Bairam Khan hesitated. Instead of marching to Lahore, he remained in Mewat, somewhere between Alwar and Delhi. Akbar, too, returned to Delhi, and with the imperial troops so close by, a fresh wave of desertions hit Bairam. In May 1560, as summer set in, the ex-regent gave up. He sent a letter 'full of supplication and . . . excuses'[100] – along with his elephants, his standard, his banner and drums and symbols of command – and asked for permission to leave for the Middle East.

This time, Bairam did head west, into the sunset. Akbar's court heaved a sigh of relief. Then, writes Abul Fazl, 'a report suddenly sprung up' that Bairam had turned towards Punjab – again! – and was in open rebellion. Abul Fazl's explanation for this change of course is that Bairam realized, belatedly, that he had been undone by rivals in court, '[e]specially Maham [Anaka], who . . . was making it her business to ruin him', and decided to avenge himself. Other historians tell a different tale.

Many of Bairam's foes had thronged to Akbar's court after the regent's fall. Munim Khan, for example, having stayed away all these years after hearing of Tardi Beg's execution, was on his way from Kabul. Pir Muhammad, having cooled his heels in Gujarat, had already galloped back east. Akbar was pleased to see him and gave him a title, Nasir-ul-Mulk, 'friend of the realm'. His first task in this capacity was to ride after Bairam, his former master, the very man who had raised him to his former glories, and, in Badauni's words, 'pack him off as quickly as possible'.

Bairam Khan, the man who held on to a grudge over an elephant fight all the way from Mankot to Lahore, was furious at this final indignity. He abandoned any idea of leaving quietly and made a vengeful about-turn. War was imminent.

Once again, Akbar sent him a message, which Abul Fazl quotes in full. This third and last of Akbar's missives to his Khan Baba is the most revealing of all – both agitated and cold, a seventeen-year-old trying to articulate his sorrow and resentment at outgrowing his mentor, his pain at having to accept the inevitability of his own adulthood, his discomfort with taking difficult decisions smothered in anger at long-ago injustices, silently endured.

'[W]e have . . . not quarrelled with you on any matter', said Akbar, '. . . we have not gone against your advice in anything'. And yet, did Bairam remember how his servants committed 'murder, theft, highway robbery' and got away with it, while Akbar's men – he may have meant those wretched mahouts – were punished for the 'slightest infraction'? Bairam's men were titled 'sultan and khan', but others who had served the family since Humayun's reign had only 'scraps of bread'. Forget the men, Akbar himself had suffered such indignities! One of Bairam's men had refused Akbar's orders, another 'replied so rudely to us that he should have had his tongue cut out', a third 'said such an impolite thing' he should have lost his life.

Some of these grudges sprang from court animosities as much as from Akbar's bitter memories. Akbar's letter begins, for example, with a complaint against Shaikh Gada'i, at whose parties Akbar was a regular, presumably happy guest. Now, however, he complained that the shaikh was so favoured by Bairam that he would not even bow to Akbar but come to him on horseback and shake his hand – and, moreover, 'was set above all the sayyids of true lineage'. Resentment against the Shia shaikh in a largely Sunni court was strong. Badauni writes of how other, less-favoured clerics went 'mourning from house to house' at Gada'i's elevation, while 'the princes and nobles of the kingdom . . . flew into a rage at [his] advancement', composing disgruntled verse to vent their feelings, as for example: 'Mention not Gada-i's name, eat not his bread.'

Bread, metaphorically speaking, was as much a cause for contention between these factions as faith – Gada'i was appointed *sadr*, chief justice, and had immense power to give out grants of land. So, of course, had Bairam, and again it may have been the mutterings of unhappy chiefs that made Akbar write about the regent favouring his nephew, Husain Quli, with rich fiefs, though Husain Quli had never so much as 'fought . . . a chicken', while 'great khans [had] to make do with ravaged lands'.

Still, Akbar might have disregarded it all – 'you were dear to us', he said, 'we . . . relied absolutely on your word and deed' – until he heard that Bairam was planning to take away his closest companions. Was this a reference to Maham? Had she said to him, Bairam will banish me across the ocean, and then, one by one, drive away all those you love? Bairam 'intended to deprive

us of the few people who accompany us and leave us alone and unattended',
said Akbar – and there is a terrible frailty in the words. What is a king without
supporters, a boy without his mothers?

But Akbar was not alone; he would not be threatened, nor told what to do.
'[W]e have sought to please you over the last five years and not quarrelled
with you', he said, but now, 'you will hear and obey this command of ours'.
If not, there was no doubt: 'we will crush you'.[101]

Thus the letter ended, and battle began.

In August 1560, five months after Akbar left on his fateful 'hunting' expedition, two small armies met across a rice field in Gunachaur, north-east of
Ludhiana. The imperial side was led by Shamsuddin of Ghazni, Akbar's
ataka, whom Bairam had so terrified some years ago. It is worth noting
that Shamsuddin's army did not include Adham Khan, whom his mother,
Maham, had kept away from 'maternal solicitude'.[102] For all that the ataka
and anaka may have shared views on Bairam, they were not fighting on the
same side. Bairam, meanwhile, had few men, but loyal – Abul Fazl admits
that 'they were of good quality'. In fact, loyalty to Bairam seems to have
spilled over to the imperial side: Shamsuddin 'was not certain of his men',
writes Abul Fazl, many of whom were sending messages of support to their
old commander. When the battle began, therefore, Bairam's troops charged
with much 'valour' while many imperial soldiers fled. It was only because
Bairam's elephants got stuck in the muddy rice fields that Shamsuddin managed to fight back and defeat him.

Bairam Khan fled into the Siwalik hills.[103] Two months later, in October,
the month in which Akbar would turn eighteen, the padishah and his troops
followed Bairam. A contingent went up into the hills, there were 'great
onsets on both sides',[104] but it was Bairam who surrendered. However, just
as he doesn't tell the story of Pir Muhammad sent to chivvy the regent,
Akbar's historian leaves out a critical detail in his telling of Bairam's final
defeat.

Bairam Khan may not have allowed Akbar a privy purse – perhaps he
thought the padishah would spend it all on elephants – but he was a generous
man. Badauni, always approving of generosity in noblemen – all potential
patrons – describes how Bairam gave 100,000 coins to his favourite musician,
Ram Das of Lucknow.[105] Another time, he bestowed a similar bounty upon a
poet. In the post-battle loot upon the fields of Gunachaur, Shamsuddin found
a richly decorated *alam*, a holy standard 'worked with pearls and gems',[106]
intended for a Shia shrine. 'The sum of the whole matter', writes Badauni, 'is
that 100,000 were to the liberal mind of the Khan as one'. Besides a liberal
mind, Bairam possessed a noble disposition, too, as evidenced by the loyalty
of his former soldiers, sending him messages of support across enemy lines.

There is certainly something both generous and noble about Bairam's surrender as Badauni describes it.

A young soldier 'of great beauty . . . and bravery' died during the battle in the Siwaliks. He was fighting on Akbar's side, and Bairam's men brought him the soldier's head, thinking their commander would be pleased. Instead, Bairam Khan covered his face and wept. The young man had once been in Bairam's service. 'A hundred reproaches on this life of mine!' he exclaimed, that so many like this man had died because of him. But now, no more. Bairam sent a messenger to Akbar, declaring surrender.

Sometime in the autumn of 1560, in the month of Muharram, when Bairam Khan, like Shias across the world, would have been mourning the martyrdom of Imam Husain, the ex-regent prostrated himself before the youthful padishah whom he had guided so well and for so long. By all accounts, the meeting was emotional, perhaps even healing. Bairam fell to the ground, weeping; Akbar raised him up and hugged him, wiped the tears from his cheeks and seated him where the regent always sat in court, to Akbar's right. They spoke, Akbar talking with 'kindness and favour'[107] to put Bairam at ease. When they rose, Akbar took off his own robe and gave it to his Khan Baba. Thus, the two men parted. They would never meet again – though only a year later, Akbar would find himself looking after Bairam's fatherless son, as Bairam had once looked after him.

Bairam left Akbar's court, but he may have carried the hope of another change in his fortune. On his way, he had 'reproached' one of his old friends, grumbling to him, 'you forgot all your old obligations'.[108] The man who had kept the Mughal padishah on the Hindustani throne these past five years still had his grudges, his ambitions and his access to power. He was married to Akbar's cousin, Salima Begum, a Timurid. In their caravan of travellers to Mecca, he met a Kashmiri widow of Salim Shah Suri's, with a young daughter. Bairam promptly arranged the marriage of this little Suri princess with his own son. If, in a year or two, Bairam Khan had returned to claim justice, allied to the houses of Timur and Sur – with Central Asians and Afghans – would the history of Hindustan itself have taken a new course?

Bairam's story never charted such tempting terrain; it reached an abrupt end instead. He stopped for a few days in Patan, then the capital of Gujarat. He went boating with his family; when they came ashore, a crowd of men were waiting for them, as if to pay their respects. Suspecting nothing, Bairam signalled for them to approach. It was a large group and Bairam was soon surrounded. Still, he suspected nothing. As Bairam talked and listened, one of the men standing behind him took out a dagger and stabbed him in the back, 'with such force that the point came out at his breast'.[109]

The assassin was an Afghan seeking vengeance for his father, killed in one of those early battles in Punjab that cleared Humayun's way to Delhi.

Whether he wanted to or not, Khan Baba died in service of Babur's dynasty, his own future trickling to the dust like the blood from his chest.

Back in Akbar's court, the wheels of government continued to turn. Munim Khan had made his way to Hindustan from Kabul, and been given Bairam Khan's position and title – that is, he was made Akbar's deputy, or *vakil*, and titled Khan-Khanan, the khan of khans. He was not, however, the former regent's sole replacement. Indeed, it speaks for the extent of Bairam's influence that his powers spilt across two, if not three, factions. On par with Munim Khan, if not a bit above him, was Maham Anaka, who 'took charge of affairs',[110] assisted by Shihabuddin, the friend whom Abul Fazl describes as one of Maham's 'tools'.

In clear opposition to this group was Akbar's ataka, Shamsuddin. It was Shamsuddin who had defeated Bairam on the rice fields of Punjab, and been rewarded with Bairam's standard, banner and drum, his fur robe and the 'choicest parts of the Punjab',[111] and titled Azam Khan – the greatest khan. This was not nearly enough for the ataka, however. Abul Fazl records – without comment – a letter that Shamsuddin wrote to Akbar soon after his victory over Bairam. Though couched in deference – 'prayers and expressions of devotion' – Shamsuddin's message was aggressive and clear. The recent battle had not been against Bairam alone, but also against the meddling of veteran commanders and the sniping of others to 'the Mother', that is, Maham Anaka. It was Maham, wrote Shamsuddin, who represented his cautious march through muddy fields as cowardice. 'God deliver us!' – if Shamsuddin had lost the battle, anyone can imagine how vicious the whispers in court would have been. Even the victory's aftermath was perverse: people who took no part in the battle received rewards 'tenfold', but no one bothered to ask about those who did the actual fighting – among them, Shamsuddin reminded Akbar, the ataka's own twelve-year-old son.

'Protector of the world', Shamsuddin continued, like Mark Antony to the Roman mob, 'this well-wisher regards [Maham] as a mother, and says no evil of her' – but he did wish to point out that none of the nobility had left their fiefs to help Akbar's 'old servant' as he battled in the mud and managed, somehow, to win. Now, he had only one small request. Akbar had already given him Bairam's insignia, from his banner to his robe, would he not give him Bairam's rank too?

For all Shamsuddin's self-deprecation, his power – and that of his family – was only increasing. Indeed, Shamsuddin's brothers and sons – not one of whom was among Humayun's commanders six years ago – would soon have enough influence to merit their own collective noun: they would be called the *ataka khail*, the clan of the ataka.

As Maham's coterie and the ataka khail tested their new authority, a third power centre began to emerge. Mirza Sharafuddin – the Timurid relative from Kashgar who had sent that conspiratorial letter to Pir Muhammad – now married Akbar's sister, Bakshi Banu, and became, therefore, the padishah's brother-in-law, his dignity 'enormously exalted',[112] and his story about to unravel.

As for the padishah himself – for all the drama of the last few months, all the declarations of taking on the mantle of his own rule – he had retreated, once again, behind his veil. When Bairam left for Mecca, Akbar returned to Agra, and put on his old 'disguise of inattention'.[113]

The fall of Bairam had not, after all, signalled the rise of Akbar; indeed, you could even argue that Akbar only played a supporting role in a coup against his regent, engineered by his nurse. But now, at the end of this turbulent fifth year of his reign, a chain of events was set in motion, a chain in which Akbar's veil would find itself entangled and finally ripped off.

Chapter 4

The Fist

'On the completion of my twentieth year, I experienced an internal
bitterness . . . my soul was seized with exceeding sorrow.'

— Akbar, Happy Sayings, *Ain-i-Akbari*

Some eight months after Bairam's murder, his son, Abdur Rahim, was
returned to court, and Akbar adopted him. It was September 1561; Abdur
Rahim was just short of five years old, and Akbar of nineteen. In a painting
of the scene, Abdur Rahim is being taught how to bow to the padishah, who
reaches out to him, one hand resting on the boy's back, the other taking one
of his little hands into his own.[1] Given the aesthetic conventions of medieval
and pre-modern art, Abdur Rahim has a rather adult face; you might even say
that it is Akbar who looks the younger of the two.

The emperor would be fully grown by now, though he was never very tall;
even Abul Fazl admits Akbar was 'of middle height'.[2] But he was strong; it was
only months earlier that he had killed a lioness single-handed, and months later
that he would knock a man to the ground with a single blow. Even so, though
later visitors would describe Akbar as broad-shouldered and 'exceedingly
well-built',[3] for the moment he appears rather slight, his frame not quite full,
and hints of boyishness in his small, round face, with its wisp of a moustache.

There is nothing childlike about his expression, however; instead, an age-
less tenderness fills his eyes. He knew what it was to lose a father, and now,
in fact, a father figure, too. In the fifteen-odd months after Bairam Khan's
death, Akbar would lose a great deal more, besides: friends and faith in his
administrators, his shyness of shedding human blood, and, worst of all, the
privilege to shrug off the burdens of rule.

It began with the blood-soaked conquest of Malwa.

Malwa, which corresponds roughly to western Madhya Pradesh today, was then ruled by Baz Bahadur, who enjoys a historical reputation on two counts – his talent for composing Hindi songs[4] and his love for Rupmati, 'renowned throughout the world for her beauty and charm',[5] for whom, in fact, he sang his compositions. As far as the history of Akbar is concerned, however, Baz Bahadur's pre-eminent contribution was to give the padishah or his historians – the logic of his imperial design. Thus, writes Abul Fazl, the ruler of Malwa was 'immersed in bestial pleasures'. Or, as Nizamuddin puts it, 'Baz Bahadur had given himself up to sensuality, and cared nothing for the country'. To take that country from him, therefore, was only Akbar's duty; indeed, the emperor's 'justice' (Abul Fazl), the very 'honour of the imperial throne' (Nizamuddin) demanded conquest so that the dissolute sultan's wretched subjects might find 'peace and security'.[6]

Until now, Akbar's chieftains had fought to preserve their presence in Hindustan, battling to stay in place, more or less. Thus, Mirza Sharafuddin – now Akbar's brother-in-law – was off seizing forts in Rajasthan, while the lovelorn Ali Quli Shaibani was in Jaunpur battling Afghans with his usual flair. This was a tried-and-tested method of maintaining the momentum of a conquest while also maintaining the conquerors. The nascent Mughal 'empire' had no steady flow of revenue, but it did have warlords, none of whom were in the business for their health. Babur's solution to the problem was to assign territory to his commanders, 'often . . . resistant cities' from which they were to 'extract . . . their expenses for maintaining their soldiers, households and pleasures',[7] and send the rest back to the ostensibly 'imperial' treasury.

The conquest of Malwa, in the way that it is officially described, reversed this logic, in that its beneficiary was no longer the conqueror but the conquered – as, much like US marines transporting American democracy to the world, Akbar's troops now embraced the responsibility of foisting his justice upon the many kingdoms of Hindustan they would engulf.

They could not have had a more ironic start.

Adham Khan, Maham's son, was in command of the troops, with Pir Muhammad, Bairam Khan's arrogant deputy, by his side. The Mughal and Malwa armies met outside the town of Sarangpur. Every day, they skirmished without clear result, and every day, the Mughal troops sent scouting parties to spy on the enemy and block their access to grain. One day, these scouts were late returning and, losing their way in the dark, they rode right into the Malwa camp. A fast, furious and very unexpected battle later, Baz Bahadur was routed and fled.

His exit inaugurated no sudden shower of peace and prosperity, however, but a debauchery of gore. Badauni, who was present at the scene, describes how Adham Khan and Pir Muhammad had 'troop after troop' of the defeated brought before them and executed, so that 'blood flowed river upon river'. Pir Muhammad, true to form, kept up a flow of jesting commentary: '[W]hat a plague of a strong neck this victim has, and what a power of blood has poured from it!' It was, writes Badauni, as if human heads were so many 'radishes, and cucumbers, and leeks'. Disgusted and horrified by such 'terror, like that of Judgement day', Badauni pleaded, through a friend, for it to stop, but Pir Muhammad was unmoved – he'd taken such an abundance of prisoners overnight, where was he to put them except in their graves?[8]

In the palace of Sarangpur, meanwhile, another kind of slaughter was under way. Baz Bahadur had left instructions that, should he be defeated, his women and dancing girls were to be killed.[9] Thus, writes Abul Fazl, many of these 'fairy-framed' women were put to the sword; Rupmati, too, had been wounded when the imperial troops came galloping in.

They were led by Adham Khan, keen to lay his hands on Baz Bahadur's treasures, of which his beloved Rupmati was, of course, the pearl. When the poet-sultan's muse heard that Adham Khan had arrived, she did not wait, but 'bravely quaffed [a] cup of deadly poison' and left this world – thus taking 'her honour', notes Abul Fazl approvingly, 'to the . . . chambers of annihilation'.

Rupmati may have escaped his unwanted attentions, but still a great bounty flowed into Adham Khan's arms. Not only women whose 'heart-ravishing charms were sung of in the streets' but also all manner of 'rare and exquisite articles . . . and buried treasures'.[10] Of this rich loot, Adham Khan sent only some elephants to Akbar.

Did Adham Khan assume that Akbar – younger than Adham and nursed all these years by Adham's mother – lacked Adham's worldly appreciation of gold and women, and cared only to play with elephants? Or, less patronizingly, was Adham only abiding by the conventions of conquest and income that Akbar's father and grandfather lived by? Adham had taken Malwa so he was entitled to its riches.

Back in Agra, Akbar was beginning to realize the great disadvantage of this franchise model of empire-building: his commanders might be expanding his frontiers, but his treasury was empty. Bayazid, an old soldier of Humayun's, tells the famous story of Akbar's treasurer unable to find seventeen rupees for the padishah.[11] Maham, who eventually gave Akbar the money from her own purse, is sometimes accused of running a corrupt government that led to this pitiful state of affairs. It's also said that Munim Khan, who couldn't force Akbar to school, was far too placatory of the Mughal commanders – some of whom, including Ali Quli Shaibani, were none too happy with Bairam's abrupt removal – and allowed a 'slackening' in their remittances.[12] In fact, at about the same time as Adham's victory in Malwa, Ali Quli had won a great battle, too, but not a copper coin of his loot – or even an elephant – had reached Akbar's court.

The padishah had had enough. With the same burst of temper that sent him galloping on his fiery Hayran, years ago, Akbar went racing from Agra to Sarangpur.

He left in relative secret, 'without informing the great officers and Eyes of the State'. Munim Khan knew, writes Abul Fazl, but he says nothing about Maham Anaka.

If Akbar didn't tell her, believing that she might make excuses for her son, Maham found out. She sent 'swift couriers' to warn Adham, but Akbar was far swifter. He made it from Agra to Sarangpur, over 500-odd kilometres of 'ascents and descents', in just over two weeks.[13]

This wasn't the last time that Akbar's sheer speed befuddled his foe. On 13 May 1561, Adham Khan was riding out of Sarangpur, in all tranquillity.[14] As he rode on, however, Adham noticed the soldiers ahead of him behaving oddly. Peering into the distance, he saw them getting off their horses and throwing themselves to the ground. 'Good God', wondered Adham Khan, 'to whom are they paying such reverence?'[15] Spurring his horse forward, he was amazed to find Akbar the cause of his army's mid-march prostrations. Adham Khan got off his horse and kissed Akbar's saddle in deference. Akbar, too, dismounted, as a way of reassuring Maham's son. The two men rode back to Sarangpur in apparent amity.

The good feeling didn't last. Back in the palace, Adham made a belated presentation of 'things rare and beautiful', but to little effect. Whether because Adham's offerings were still too miserly or because they only confirmed the extent to which Adham had defrauded the treasury, Akbar's 'soul . . . did not open out towards him'.[16]

Indeed, no matter what Adham Khan did to win him over, it 'was not approved of '. When Adham brought out a change of clothes for his guest to wear after the 'dusty ride', Akbar refused. Adham panicked, stumbling 'in the net of agitation', asking others to plead his case until, finally, the padishah 'took compassion on his misery' and relented.[17]

That night, Akbar slept on Adham's roof – a wonderful image, the eighteen-year-old 'stretched out'[18] under the sky on a summer night. Adham didn't sleep a wink. According to Abul Fazl, he lurked about in the hope that Akbar – having travelled without his women – would be tempted to sneak into Adham's harem for the night; such gross violation of protocol would allow Adham to attack the padishah. It isn't clear why Adham might have wanted to kill Akbar, unless he was foolish or enraged enough to imagine that his mother would put him on the Mughal throne in Akbar's place. The idea seems preposterous, but only Akbar could have proposed it to his historian, so perhaps the padishah did feel threatened that night, having ridden with a small guard into hostile terrain. Perhaps that is precisely why he slept on an open roof, avoiding the potential trap of a closed room. It is far from Abul Fazl, of course, to admit any such fear in his hero. Akbar had travelled a long way. 'The last thing on his mind was Adham Khan's gloomy harem', sniffs the historian.[19] The padishah slept.

The next day, Akbar's own harem arrived, led all the way by Maham Anaka – a woman whose physical strength clearly matched her talent for intrigue. She left later than Akbar yet reached only a day after he did. Maham wasted no time in mending the growing rift between Akbar and Adham, arranging a 'great entertainment' and taking her recalcitrant son in hand, so that Adham finally presented all the tribute he should have before – all the treasure, all the musicians, all the women.[20]

Well . . . not all the women. On 17 May, four days after he had arrived, Akbar left Sarangpur. As was customary, Adham Khan escorted the padishah part of the way, and on the night of their first halt, he had some 'evil thoughts'. Having plotted with some of his mother's servants – Maham ruled the imperial harem – Adham managed to filch two 'special beauties' from it.[21] Akbar discovered the loss and had the women found and returned. He wasn't allowed to investigate their disappearance, however. A 'severed head makes no sound', as Abul Fazl writes: Maham Anaka had them both killed before they could be questioned.

Akbar didn't ask her what happened. Perhaps he didn't want to know; he was still behind that veil of his, he 'had not yet revealed himself'.[22] Instead, he continued his journey back home. On the way, he fought and killed a lioness – less daunting a creature, it appears, than Akbar's formidable nurse.

The sixth year of Akbar's reign abounds with examples of his growing, sometimes reckless courage. Five years ago, it was a nilgai Akbar had killed on the side of the road; now, a lioness with five cubs stood in his way. Akbar approached her on foot and killed her with one blow. It was in this year, too, that Abul Fazl reveals another of Akbar's dangerous pleasures: he liked venturing into public, incognito. One night, in Agra, he was wandering through a great crowd, gathered for an *urs*, a Sufi celebration, when he was recognized. Who knows what might have happened next if Akbar hadn't thought on his feet. He squinted and contorted his features, edging his way, thus disguised, from the crowd back to the fort.

It wasn't, however, that Akbar was shy of appearing in public as himself. Once, famously, he rode an enraged elephant through Agra, chasing its rival across a pontoon bridge – built on boats that sank in and out of the water under the weight of the 'two mountain forms', while Akbar's retainers threw themselves into the river, swimming alongside their apparently deranged padishah.

Among those watching in panic was Akbar's ataka, Shamsuddin. In another reckless act that year, Akbar had decided to accept his foster father's petition

Chapter 4

for a promotion, called him to Agra and made him vakil, or deputy, stripping the title from Munim Khan, and also, more importantly, from Maham Anaka, 'who regarded herself as the [vakil]'.[23] Six months had passed since the whole Adham Khan affair, but some suspicion of him and his mother may have lodged itself in Akbar's head. Maham was 'displeased at this', writes Abul Fazl – Munim Khan was still Khan-Khanan, at least; what was Maham supposed to do with herself and her abundant intelligence? Akbar didn't care. Having put Shamsuddin Ataka in the crosshairs of Maham's resentment, Akbar also recalled Adham Khan from Malwa, thus bringing all the major players in the factions of his ataka and anaka dangerously close to one another.

At this precise moment, however, the greatest threat to his empire's stability was Akbar himself, creating a royal commotion on his musth elephant – his bare feet gripping its harness, a metal goad at its head, while crowds gathered, mouths agape. Shamsuddin took off his turban in agitation, pleading for the padishah to get off. Akbar was disgusted. 'If you don't stop', he yelled, 'I'll at

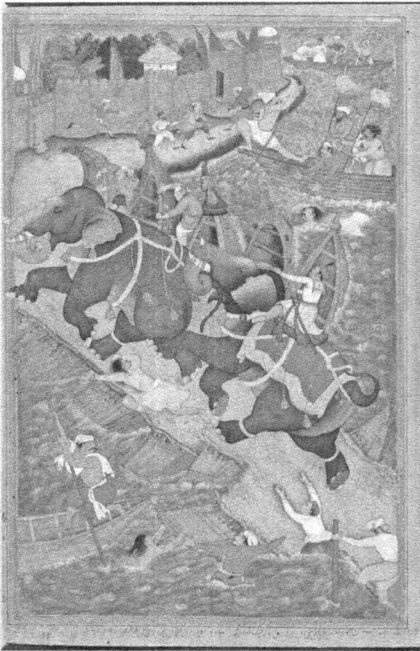

Figures 4.1 and 4.2 Akbar rides the musth elephant Hawai across a pontoon bridge in Agra while his horrified subjects wonder if their padishah has lost his mind. Riding musth elephants was one of Akbar's passions and became one of his defining traits. He said he did it to gauge God's will. Attributed to Basawan and Chatr, c. 1590–95. *Source*: Victoria and Albert Museum, Public domain, via Wikimedia Commons.

once throw myself down from the elephant.'[24] A painting of the scene shows Shamsuddin standing with hands raised in helpless prayer, as the boats keeping the bridge afloat slide this way and that under the pounding of elephant feet.[25]

Michael H. Fisher defines 'musth' rather wittily as 'seasonally aggressive behavior associated with testosterone surges in the elephant (and perhaps in the rider as well)'. The nineteen-year-old emperor may have needed release for his stores of energy. And he would not be the first human being to become addicted to danger. Years later, however, Akbar would explain what it was that made him ride musth elephants, the more bloodthirsty the better – elephants that had killed their mahouts and trampled bystanders, elephants that no one dared approach – in very different terms. Akbar did it, he said, because he wanted to know if he had 'taken a step . . . displeasing to God'.

Could he have meant that he was no longer interested in the advice of his retainers, nurses and foster fathers, no matter how loving or loyal? He wanted his opinions from God, and if God did not approve of Akbar's actions, well then, 'may that elephant finish us'.[26]

He 'sought for truth', writes Abul Fazl, '. . . and consorted with every sort of wearers of patched garments such as *jogis, sanyasis* and *qalandars*, and other solitary sitters in the dust'. One day, riding out of Agra on a hunt, Akbar came across some 'Indian minstrels . . . singing enchanting ditties about the glories' of their *pir*, the Sufi saint Khwaja Moinuddin Chishti. Enthralled, Akbar declared he would visit the saint's tomb in Ajmer. The trip was completely unplanned and even advised against – presumably since many Rajput kingdoms were at war, as much with each other as with the Mughals. But Akbar 'did not give heed',[27] and who knows, perhaps it was God who nudged him to go, for it was on this trip that Akbar not only formed one of the most fruitful spiritual associations of his life but also agreed to a marriage that would transform the very face of his dynasty.

It was en route to Ajmer that Akbar met Raja Bihari Mal Kachhwaha again. Five years had passed since the Rajput's brave showing at Akbar's court, and the raja's fortunes had declined in the interim. For all that Bihari Mal may have impressed Akbar, it was a rival of his called Suja who had managed an alliance with Akbar's brother-in-law, Sharafuddin, who governed this area as independently as Adham had hoped to rule Malwa. Suja, therefore, occupied the Kachhwaha throne, while Bihari Mal 'had taken refuge in the folds of the hills',[28] forced to pay Suja tribute and let him keep his son hostage. At the moment, therefore, the raja's situation 'was by no means enviable', as a modern historian writes, 'but it improved rather unexpectedly . . .'[29]

Seeing that Akbar was travelling through his land, and remembering, perhaps, the padishah's friendliness from some years ago, Raja Bihari Mal sent him a message, asking for an audience.

Akbar agreed. Not only that. A few days later, when Akbar and the Rajput king met near Bihari Mal's capital, Amber,[30] Akbar also agreed to give him back his hostage and his throne and to marry his daughter.

It doesn't seem to have taken much for the raja to bring Akbar to his side. Abul Fazl implies that the padishah made up his mind when he saw how people fled at his advance through Rajasthan. 'We have no other intention than to do good to all mankind', he had said in dismay. 'What can be the reason of the flight of those people?' Clearly, he continued, they were reacting to the 'oppression they have undergone'. Sharafuddin liked to extract obedience through fear; this was not Akbar's way.

Sometime between his gallop to Malwa and this meeting in Amber, Akbar had also ridden a short distance east, towards Ali Quli Shaibani in Jaunpur and all his unsettled dues. Ali Quli, cleverer than Adham, had hurried to meet Akbar on his way and handed over a substantial bounty. Ajmer was Akbar's third excursion into a commander's 'fief' in nine months; and it's possible that the restoration of Bihari Mal and the marriage to his daughter was another sharp signal to his scattered warlords: not only the riches of his realm but also the decisions about its rule were Akbar's and Akbar's alone.

The chroniclers do not underscore the fact of Akbar's marriage with drumrolls. Abul Fazl, Badauni and Nizamuddin merely describe a ruler adding another 'honourable lady'[31] to his harem. Perhaps the fact of a Rajput bride entering the Mughal dynasty is remarkable only in retrospect. Akbar himself wasn't overly self-conscious about it. The match settled, he rode off to Ajmer and visited the shrine he had set out to see. On his return, he stopped for a day in Sambhar, where Raja Bihari Mal arranged a wedding in a 'most admirable manner';[32] then, making sure that Sharafuddin kept Akbar's promises to the Rajput king, the padishah returned to Agra, galloping some 300 kilometres in less than three days.

In a fascinating essay on the evolution of Rajput loyalties to the Mughal state, Norman P. Ziegler notes that a critical marker of a Rajput's identity was his '*saga*': 'those to whom he gave his daughters and/or from whom he received wives in marriage'. As was the case across the world until very recently, a marriage was not just (or even) an agreement between two people, but an alliance between families and clans – even nations. Thus, writes Ziegler, the 'term in Marwari (western Rajasthani) for both betrothal and alliance is *sagai*, a derivative of *saga*'.

Ziegler goes on to note the Rajput custom of '*sala katari*' by which a Rajput would expect gifts of land from his sister's husband. This tradition applied across religions. Ziegler offers an example from the fifteenth century, in which two scions of Jodhpur acquired land by marrying their sister to the Muslim ruler of Nagaur.[33]

Whether it was framed in terms of 'sala katari' or not, Akbar's marriage to a Kachhwaha princess did ensure that it was her father, Bihari Mal, who retained his land, and not his rival, Suja, who had formed a less rewarding alliance with Sharafuddin.

And what, meanwhile, of Bihari Mal's daughter, with whom Akbar returned to Agra in February 1562? Often misidentified as Jodha Bai when her name was Harkha, the princess is also frequently miscast as the great love of Akbar's life. It is likely that Harkha and her husband had much to talk about; they were both intelligent, ambitious people. Indeed, Harkha doesn't exist only as Akbar's bride in history; she is known for her formidable trading business, too. It is also likely that she was a great influence on Akbar – along with the several other Rajput princesses the padishah would marry; that she swayed his thoughts on religion, policy and even diet (Badauni complains that Akbar's Rajput wives made him give up onion and garlic). And, of course, Harkha gave Akbar his first son and eventual heir.

But the chronicles say nothing about love.

It is not necessary, of course, for an emperor to love a wife, but there is something stark about the utter lack of documented romance in Akbar's life, especially given the amorous tendency in his dynasty. It wasn't just Humayun who fell madly in love with Hamida, but Babur with Baburi, Jahangir with Nurjahan, Shahjahan with Mumtaz and even the allegedly ascetic Aurangzeb with a dancing girl called Hira Bai, for whom the strict believer was willing to down a goblet of wine. All that the records contain of Akbar's feelings for his wives is a lament by the emperor himself. 'Had I been wise earlier', he once said, 'I would have taken no woman from my own kingdom into my seraglio, for my subjects are to me in the place of children.'[34]

There is a deep sadness in the sentiment, whether he intended it or not; the same sadness that fills his eyes in that painting with the fatherless Abdur Rahim. The young man whose passions overflowed upon the backs of testosterone-fuelled elephants, the nineteen-year-old who jousted with God, could he not – would he not – allow himself to dally awhile in a lover's arms?

There is no account, then, of Akbar's feelings for the 'gentle daughter'[35] of Amber, nor vice versa, but his intense, rewarding and often tempestuous relationships with her less-than-gentle kin spill over the pages. Best known of these new allies are the princess's brother Bhagwant Das and his son Man Singh, both of whom accompanied Harkha to Agra. Within months, Bhagwant Das was riding into battle by Akbar's side. Man Singh, eleven years old at the time, was given a different kind of command and put in charge of little Abdur Rahim. Such was the bond, it seems, that developed between Man Singh and the boy – both grew up to become Akbar's trusted conquerors-in-arms – that Abdur Rahim's children would call Man Singh 'Dadaji', grandfather.[36]

Akbar had not just brought home the mother of his eventual heir, he had also planted the seeds of profound transformation in the very nature of his court.

Even if the facts are linked by chronology alone, it is interesting to note that soon after Akbar married his Rajput bride, Abul Fazl has him giving audience to a brahmin petitioner. Hapa was his name, and he had come to complain about a group of eight villages called Athkanya, not far from Agra. The name 'eight maidens' suggests otherwise, but these villages contained a wicked lot, it seems, known for their 'insolence, robbery, manslaughter . . . and turbulence'.[37] They had killed Hapa's son and stolen all he owned. Akbar promised him justice.

It was delivered a day or two later, in the village of Paronkh. Some 400 men from the eight villages gathered here to resist Akbar's punitive force, which numbered about 200 soldiers and an equal number of elephants. As the smoke of battle filled the air, a disheartening sight filtered through it – far from storming the gates of Paronkh, many of Akbar's men were sheltering under trees and looking for other 'safe corner[s]' in which to hide. It was clear to him, as it must become clear to all people of ambition one day: if he wanted something done, he must do it himself.

Without wasting time reproving his reluctant soldiers, Akbar drove his elephant, Dalsingar,[38] into the narrow village lanes. All was confusion, 'a rain of sticks and stones and arrows'. Akbar thought he recognized one of his men by his yellow vest, wrestling on a roof, and charged towards him. Dalsingar's foot caught in a pit of grain; behind them, another elephant running at full speed wasn't expecting Dalsingar's sudden stop. It was an elephant pile-up! Somehow, Akbar manoeuvred Dalsingar out of the pit. Most of the rebel villagers had retreated into a fortified compound; Akbar drove Dalsingar towards it, with Raja Bhagwant Das riding by his side.[39]

One of the enemies appeared before them, slashing at Dalsingar with his sword. It struck a heavy iron ring of a kind put around elephants' tusks 'for strength and for show' – metal on metal threw sparks in the air. Startled and angry, Dalsingar trampled the man – just as a boy of fifteen fell from the roof onto Dalsingar's back. Akbar's men would have killed him, but Akbar wouldn't allow it.

Instead, speed on! They reached the compound – a contingent of soldiers had surrounded it as the villagers fired volley after desperate volley upon them. Seven arrows struck Akbar's shield, five pierced through. 'Who are you', cried one of Akbar's soldiers, impressed with his courage, 'that I may praise you to His Majesty?'

Akbar lifted his visor in reply.

He drove Dalsingar at the compound wall and others joined him. The wall fell, the villagers retreated. Now, they were all trapped in a house. Akbar ordered a hole made in its roof, and fire thrown in. Night fell as flames con-sumed the rebels. There is no record of how long Akbar watched them burn; whether he basked in the glow of victory or retreated as the scent of burning flesh filled the air.

Paronkh was no Panipat, no defining battle for the books, but it was the first that Akbar led, and he won. Similarly, appointing Shamsuddin Ataka his vakil may not have been the most important administrative decision that Akbar ever took, but it was a decision he took alone – and he stuck by it. In the second month of his seventh year on the throne, Akbar's veil had become decidedly worn and translucent with age.

Still, it hadn't slipped away.

A little after Paronkh, Shah Tahmasp of Persia finally sent condolences for Humayun's passing. The embassy, led by the shah's cousin,[40] may have signalled an emerging respect for Akbar in the region. After seven years on the throne, he was more than a flash in the pan; though in a painting of the scene, he hasn't quite outgrown his boyhood. Slim, beardless, his moustache an adolescent wisp, Akbar looks almost as young as the pageboys standing behind him. At least, in the painting, the emperor is enthroned and attended upon with some formality;[41] Abul Fazl describes the event with all the requi-site pomp: great gifts from each side to the other, the ambassador reading out the shah's letter after 'kissing the carpet'. In fact, as an eyewitness describes it, the bemused ambassador may have had some trouble identifying his host.

Cries of 'Badshah Salamat' filled the air, writes Rafi al-din Ibrahim Shi-razi, a Persian immigrant at the scene, but it was impossible to tell who they were hailing. 'I looked to my left and right but did not find anyone having the appearance of a king. As I turned around, I saw standing there a young man of about twenty years.' The young man had rested one hand on a friend's shoulder and tilted his head upon that hand – a casual, almost slack pose that communicated itself to his audience. 'I could guess he was the king', writes the immigrant, appalled. 'But the men continued to stand around rubbing shoulders with each other. No one observed the etiquette of showing respect to the king.'

Scandalized, Rafi asked bystanders what was going on, and was told that Akbar was 'an exceedingly informal person'. How was it possible, in his unceremonious presence, to 'observe etiquette'?[42]

In keeping with such informality about official business, on 16 May 1562, Akbar skipped 'court day . . . in the royal hall'. The padishah felt no need to attend. This is how it had been with Bairam, too. The regent would hold a couple of meetings every week, with all the chiefs, and fill Akbar in after-wards. Now, it was Shamsuddin, his vakil; Munim Khan, his Khan-Khanan; and Shihabuddin, Maham Anaka's representative, who sat with other, lesser lords, 'transacting public business', while Akbar remained upstairs.[43] It was a summer day and the padishah was fast asleep in the cool chambers of the harem. Afterwards, if an evening breeze stirred, he might have planned to fly a kite – as Rafi had once seen him do, running about the palace roof in a *lungi*, his head uncovered.[44]

He woke at a sudden clamour. What was going on? Akbar wrapped on his lungi,[45] walked out and leaned over the parapet to look into the courtyard below. There was Rafiq, an old retainer. What was going on?

Abul Fazl has Rafiq spell out an impressively coherent narrative of the chaos engulfing the palace. More likely, the old man could only point at the corpse in the courtyard and call out the urgent facts: Adham has killed your ataka!

This is what had happened: only moments ago, Adham Khan swaggered into the council meeting with his men. The lords of the council rose to greet him; even Shamsuddin, who had no love lost for Maham's son, 'rose half-up'. Adham strode up to Shamsuddin, hand on his dagger, and snapped at his crew, 'Why do you stand still?'[46]

One of the men stabbed Shamsuddin in the chest. Shocked yet still alive, Akbar's ataka staggered out of the door into the courtyard. Another of Adham's men slashed at him with his sword. Twice.

Shamsuddin of Ghazni, who dreamt of the moon in his arms, the farmer's son who became imperial vakil in Hindustan, fell to the ground, butchered in the palace of the foster child he had served and protected from the day that Akbar was born.

Akbar couldn't believe it; 'he asked again'.[47] Rafiq pointed at the dead man.

And Adham Khan? He had rushed upstairs, 'sword in hand'.[48] Even now, he was standing at the door to the harem, locked just in time by its guard, demanding to be let in. In a blaze of fury, Akbar went to Adham, though not through the door at which Adham stood. He took another way, not even bothering to pick up his sword – a servant gave him the weapon as he walked past.

'Spoiled child', he cried, from behind Adham, 'why did you kill our ataka?' This is the translation that William M. Thackston, most recent translator of the *Akbarnama*, offers, but it is hardly satisfactory. Other translators have alternatives. '*Bacha-i-laada*' is what Akbar said; he might have meant 'son of a fool' (Beveridge) or, perhaps, 'son of a bitch' (Blochmann). Only Bayazid Biyat, the old soldier, has Akbar swearing in properly and unambiguously filthy terms at the man who had just killed his foster father. '*Kandu!*' – or *gandu* – he screamed. 'Assfucker! Why did you kill my ataka?'[49]

Adham Khan rushed to Akbar and grabbed his hands. What did he mean to do, to say? Did he want to explain? Akbar let his own sword fall, wrenched his hands free and reached for Adham's blade, just as Adham, too, grabbed at it. Would he really have stabbed his padishah?

We will never know. As Adham took up his sword, Akbar let go of the weapon. He did not need sharp edges and polished steel. He had his fury. He made a fist.

The punch that landed on Adham Khan's face was so hard, so swift, it knocked him to the ground, unconscious.

Five years earlier, when Bairam Khan invited his young lord to execute his first enemy, the fourteen-year-old had refused. Bairam had had to pick up a sword and cut off Hemu's head himself.

But how long can a king baulk at vengeance and hope to retain his throne? At nineteen, having slammed Adham unconscious with his fist, Akbar did not think of trials and prisons, he did not think of Maham; he did not let calm reason come between him and his pitiless justice.

Akbar had Adham thrown head first over the balcony on which they stood. The balcony wasn't all that high; Adham didn't quite die. Akbar had him dragged back up the stairs, by the hair. In the time that Adham's injured body returned – screaming, moaning, weeping, or all three – Akbar's adrenaline would have begun to subside; he would have had time for second thoughts. But no: an emperor cannot betray his own decisions.

Akbar had Adham turned upside down and flung down again. This time, Adham's neck broke; his head must have been twisted at an unnatural angle, with the soft jelly of his brain spilling out.

Looking down at Adham's broken body, his own pulse racing, what did Akbar think? It was the first execution he'd ever ordered; it remains a milestone in the chronicles of his rule, proclaiming the dawn of his authority, as naked and compelling as his fist. Did he marvel a little at what he had done, what he was capable of? Or did the pounding fury in his head overpower all thought?[50]

'Mama, we have killed Adham.'[51]

Maham Anaka was ill and resting when Akbar went to tell her what had happened. Bayazid writes that he told her point-blank, but Abul Fazl presents a scene of greater ambiguity, as if Akbar did not have the heart to put the brutal fact of her son's execution in so many words: 'Adham killed our Ataga, we have inflicted retaliation upon him.'

'You did well', Maham replied.

She didn't believe Akbar had killed her son. It was another visitor who told her. Pale but composed, Maham went to Akbar and asked if she might see Adham one last time. Already, his mangled body had been inspected on behalf of the ataka khail, Shamsuddin's brothers and sons threatening civil war unless they were avenged. Akbar made sure they were satisfied, but he wouldn't let Maham near the body.

Figure 4.3   The execution of Adham Khan, son of Akbar's beloved Maham Anaka. Adham spearheaded the murder of Akbar's equally beloved foster father Shamsuddin (lying in a pool of blood at bottom left). Akbar's fury in the aftermath is often portrayed as the beginning of the end of his innocence of political affairs. Attributed to Miskin and Sankar, c. 1590–95. *Source*: Victoria and Albert Museum, Public domain, via Wikimedia Commons.

Perhaps he was trying to protect her – just as she had, perhaps, protected him on the ramparts of Kabul, or against the machinations of Bairam Khan. He could hardly protect her from her own grief. Forty days later, she died.

When he heard that Maham was gone, writes Abul Fazl, Akbar cried.

Chapter 5

Mutiny

'In a storehouse, mice and sparrows and other animals have a common interest but from ill-nature each thinks the place his own.'

– Akbar, Happy Sayings, *Ain-i-Akbari*

'this is one country – Mine.'

– Irwin Allan Sealy, *Zelaldinus: A Masque*

That one punch to Adham Khan's face ripped the veil off Akbar's. It wasn't just his bloody execution. Adham cost Akbar two of his most trusted and beloved advisers, his foster father and foster mother, both of whom he lost within weeks of each other. The third, his old ataliq Munim Khan, had proved himself either complicit in Adham's plot or incapable of preventing it. For the first time in his life, Akbar had no choice except to direct his own fortunes – and those of his realm.

What was this realm, though, and how much was it really his? Kabul, the family seat, was still caught in the family squabble – this time, between Humayun's youngest wife, Mahchuchak Begum, mother and regent of Akbar's half-brother Muhammad Hakim, and Akbar's uncle Sulaiman, now the seniormost Timurid in the region and, spurred by his command-ing wife, Haram Begum, keen to expand the scope of his authority. Punjab was enfeoffed to the ataka khail, a clan now led by the fallen Shamsuddin's brother, Mir Muhammad Khan, and including, also, Akbar's closest friend in the years to come, Shamsuddin's son, Aziz. Akbar himself was enthroned in Agra, in an unimpressive palace of brick in which Shamsuddin was murdered.

To his west, his brother-in-law Sharafuddin was making his own alliances with the desert lords of Rajasthan, one of which Akbar effectively subverted when he married Bihari Mal's daughter. To his east, the valiant Ali Quli Shaibani held Jaunpur but had made little headway into neighbouring Bihar, held by Afghan chiefs hoping to revive the fortunes they had enjoyed under the Suri dynasty. The southern fief of Malwa had lost both its original conquerors – Adham Khan to Akbar's vengeance; Pir Muhammad to the high waters of the Narmada, as he tried to cross the grand old river on a horse. (Thus, writes Badauni, recalling the commander's pitiless executions, 'he went by water to fire. And so the sighs of the orphans, and weak, and captives were his ruin.'[1]) Baz Bahadur had reclaimed his kingdom when it was thus unhelmed, but he was soon ousted by another of Akbar's great commanders, Abdullah Khan the Uzbek, who had led the briefly victorious Mughal vanguard against Hemu during Tardi Beg's ultimately shambolic defence of Delhi. And farthest of all, some 700 kilometres south of Agra and over double that distance from Kabul, pushing into unknown land in search of fortune, there was a man called Asaf Khan, about to take on the formidably rich and famously beautiful queen of Gondwana, Rani Durgavati.

Was it an empire, however, that Asaf Khan sought to expand? And if so, whose? In the few months of Humayun's second innings in Hindustan, the padishah had had a republican dream. '[R]epeatedly', according to Abul Fazl, Humayun had declared that he would 'make several seats of government' across the region 'for the regulation' of Hindustan. Thus, 'Delhi, Agra, Jaunpur, Mandu, Lahore, Qanauj' would all be 'under the charge of a prudent, farseeing, subject-cherishing, and just officer', capable of handling his territory independently, so much so that Humayun imagined he would need no more than a modest cavalry of 12,000 for his own imperial needs.[2] Indeed, Humayun had put his plan into practice: Nizamuddin writes that the chiefs who accompanied Humayun on his return to Hindustan 'were most liberally rewarded, and each one was made the ruler of a province'. Humayun had had long years, after all, to think of how internal dissension – not least by his own brothers – had weakened his hold over the Hindustan he had inherited from Babur and tried to expand under his own banner. Perhaps he hoped that a more decentralized rule would also be more stable, or longer lasting.

Such proto-federalism was, in any case, the logic of the 'conquest state': to allow the most powerful military commanders to extract their own 'salaries' from assigned territories, and to pay others from the 'treasuries of defeated enemies'.[3] This was why Adham Khan, Ali Quli and Sharafuddin were in the process of carving out virtually independent fiefdoms when Akbar interrupted them, causing understandable distress and resentment.[4]

It was not as if Akbar had any undisputed right to their loyalty, let alone any inalienable right to rule over them.

Leaving aside, for a moment, Abul Fazl's epic tale of the Niru'un, there is a broad historical consensus that Babur and his progeny were uniquely placed to rule because of the two currents of blue blood that ran in their veins – Babur was descended from two world-conquering kings, the Mongol Chinghis Khan and the Turk Timur. Thus, Stephen Dale writes of how the 'Mughal rulers' . . . genealogies were the envy of their contemporaries' in Turkey and Iran.[5] Such may well have been (or become) the case in neighbouring empires, but on the ground in the Central Asian lands from where the Mughals came – and in the minds of the warlords who came with them – things were more muddled.

Take, for example, Babur's descent from Chinghis Khan, which he claimed from his mother's side, which was Chagatai – descended from (and named after) Chinghis Khan's second son. Chinghis Khan had four sons, however, among whom he parcelled out his empire. The eldest, Juchi, ruled over land inhabited by Uzbeks – some of whom, like Babur's great enemy Shaibani Khan (as also Ali Quli Shaibani), claimed descent from Juchi himself. Besides, it is not as if Juchi or Chagatai, or Chinghis Khan himself, for that matter, was the last word in Mongol nobility. Central Asia also had a population of confusingly named Moghuls, descendants of the very first Mongol, Moghul Khan – ancestor not only of Chinghis Khan but of Alanqoa, too. These 'pure' Mongols considered themselves far superior to both the Chagatai, whom they called 'half-breeds' and the Timurids, whom they used to regard as 'nökör', their servants. Thus, as Ali Anooshahr argues, 'Babur's supposedly impeccable lineage, which modern scholars assume gave him legitimacy, in fact counted for little among Moghul aristocrats.'[6]

Not that the Chagatai and Timurids took this lying down. Anooshahr notes how the Chagatai called the Mongols 'bandits', and Abul Fazl clearly speaks for the Timurids when he describes the early Mongols with some disdain, as living 'far from civilisation', eating 'the produce of hunting and fishing' and wearing 'the skins and fur of . . . animals'.[7]

If Humayun's story shows him unable to control his chiefs, it is not because he was weak, but because they were strong; even Babur, much more authoritative and charismatic than his son, had to deal with noblemen who gave themselves all kinds of airs. This was partly because, as Iqtidar Alam Khan explains, the traditions laid down by Chinghis Khan, the *yasa-i-Chengezi*, did not allow for 'absolutism': 'In the empire founded by Ghengiz Khan the principle in force was that "the empire belonged not to the ruler, but to the ruling family".'[8] Thus, any of the many Chagatais among Babur's commanders had equal rights to Babur's rule.

With that rapid, furious march to Adham's court in Sarangpur – even more than with the furious fist to Adham's face – Akbar had indicated that his ideas of rulership did not match his predecessors'. In the years to come, Akbar would march out with his army many times, to the deserts of Rajasthan and the seas of Gujarat, eastwards down the Ganga and southwards to the Deccan, up into the high valley of Kashmir and even back to Kabul – but his march would be most rapid and most furious not when he was embarking on a conquest of foreign land, but when he was out to subdue yet another obdurate chieftain unwilling to allow that Akbar was anything more than a lucky first among equals.

To the last man, they would realize they were wrong.

The first of them, after Adham, was Sharafuddin, last seen menacing Raja Bihari Mal, and previously conspiring with Adham Khan to prevent Pir Muhammad's exile. Now, both Adham and Pir Muhammad were dead, and Raja Bihari Mal was Akbar's father-in-law, all of which may have raised apprehensions in Sharafuddin's mind. Still, it isn't as if Akbar planned a purge after Adham's execution. Men who were far more closely and publicly allied with Adham Khan were spared. Munim Khan, for example, bore great suspicion of colluding with Adham in the murder of Shamsuddin – who was, after all, Munim Khan's rival for the post of vakil. So convinced, in fact, was Munim of receiving his share of blame and punishment for Akbar's ataka's death that he fled the court, and was well on his way to Kabul when he was caught. Back in Agra, however, Akbar wasn't inclined to linger on the past; he made no investigations into Munim's conduct, and he did not even keep him under probationary scrutiny. Instead, he received his Khan-Khanan 'with boundless favours'[9] and gave him a promotion, allowing him Shamsuddin's office of vakil.

Sharafuddin, too, was left undisturbed in Rajasthan. A few months after the Adham affair, he came to Agra with his father, one Khwaja Mu'in from Khurasan, who had come to visit his son in Hindustan. Both 'father and son', writes Abul Fazl, 'were encompassed with favours'. Then, for no clearly stated reason, Sharafuddin ran away. Akbar heard the news of his sudden and suspicious departure with 'complete surprise and amazement'; Abul Fazl writes that Akbar often spoke of how his kin's 'narrow capacity could not stand' his patronage.

He went westwards, beaten out of Rajasthan by Husain Quli Khan, Bairam's nephew, the young man whom Akbar had once disparaged for not having fought so much as a chicken. Sharafuddin may have hoped to find refuge in the independent kingdom of Gujarat, which would shelter many rebel chiefs in the years to come. On his way, as luck would have it, Sharafuddin met the very first disgruntled nobleman of Akbar's reign, Shah Abul Ma'ali, favourite of Humayun. Released by Bairam Khan during the upheavals that unseated the regent, Abul Ma'ali was imprisoned by Akbar once again and exiled to Mecca to mend his ways. When Sharafuddin met him, the handsome sayyid had just returned to Hindustan, his malevolence intact.

Sharafuddin and Abul Ma'ali concocted a plan. Abul Ma'ali would lead a contingent of men against Husain Quli Khan in Rajasthan, then proceed to Kabul, from where he would extract Akbar's half-brother, the young Mirza Muhammad Hakim, and bundle him across the Indus – the first of many times that Hakim would be dreamt of as an alternative to his intransigent older brother. Sharafuddin's contribution to the effort, rather more vaguely described, would be to 'do all he could to promote a rebellion'.[10]

Abul Ma'ali's offensive against Husain Quli and others loyal to Akbar was an utter failure, and it wasn't long before the 'wicked . . . one'[11] was winding his way through byways and hidden tracks to Kabul, no longer in search of a new king but rather of refuge. Before his temporary disappearance from the tale, however, Abul Ma'ali took one last shot – literally – at destroying the young padishah under whose rule the proud sayyid's flourishing career was so abruptly forestalled.

He hired an assassin.

In the winter of 1563, Akbar was hunting in Mathura when he heard that Abul Ma'ali was back from Mecca. Akbar sent a few commanders after the sayyid and rode to Delhi himself. Abul Fazl suggests that Akbar's idea was to probe the 'condition of the people without . . . intermediary' – to investigate, perhaps, how far discontent had spread through the ranks of his nobility. Badauni agrees, writing that Akbar set off for Delhi 'immediately' upon hearing of Abul Ma'ali's onslaughts, 'with the intention of quelling the disturbance'.

It is the same Badauni, however, who proposes a sudden twist in Akbar's intentions; for now, he writes, the padishah decided to get himself some Delhi brides. Perhaps he meant to gain, thereby, the loyalty of Delhi's nobility, but the plan backfired: 'a great terror fell upon the city'. It is easy enough to understand why: Akbar's first Delhi bride was 'wonderfully beautiful', but also, already, another man's wife. Once the padishah desired her, however, her husband was bound to relinquish his claims. The 'virtuous lady entered the Imperial Harem' and her husband left to nurse his wounds in the Deccan.

According to Abul Fazl, Akbar arrived in Delhi on 10 January 1564, and if Badauni's story is more than backdoor gossip, then Akbar's courtship must have been as swift and certain as his future military campaigns. Only two days after his arrival, Akbar had already claimed his bride and was now seeing the sights. He had visited the dargah of Nizamuddin and was on his way back, riding past the Khair'ul Manazil madrasa built by Maham Anaka, when an arrow struck him.

According to Badauni and Nizamuddin, the arrow only grazed Akbar's shoulder, but Abul Fazl insists it struck deep, piercing the padishah's flesh 'about the length of a span'. Ten days later, it was still difficult for Akbar to ride, so that he returned to Agra in a '*sukasan*', a litter or, more poetically, a 'boat of dry land'.[12] At any rate, the man who shot him was quickly caught. Qutlug Fulad, the 'presumptuous iron-hearted one',[13] had been standing by the madrasa. According to Ferishta, he was pretending to shoot birds, when suddenly he lowered the angle of his aim and sprung his arrow at Akbar instead. Badauni says the sniper may have been delivering a message from Delhi's discontented nobility, for Akbar now gave up any thoughts of further nuptials in the city. Abul Fazl, however, declares without doubt that Qutlug Fulad, a former slave of Sharafuddin's, had been delegated to Abul Ma'ali, who, in turn, dispatched him on this murderous mission. History might have been less divided on the matter if Akbar had permitted an investigation, but he didn't. Instead, he ordered the assassin 'quickly torn to pieces lest a group of the imperial family be accused in the affair'.[14]

It was only some eighteen months since Akbar had suffered betrayal from those he considered his own. This year, he didn't want to know.

The number of Akbar's detractors would grow until the very end of his life, but so too would his realm. Sharafuddin's desertion, for example, only served to increase Akbar's territory: the troops he sent after his insurgent brother-in-law not only retained the fortress of Merta, which Sharafuddin had conquered some years previously, but also took the fort of Jodhpur nearby. This may have been particularly pleasing news to Akbar's ears – Jodhpur was then ruled by Chandrasen, son of the Raja Maldeo who had caused Humayun and Hamida such distress during their desperate exile in the desert.

The fury of the ataka khail at Shamsuddin's murder, too, Akbar was able to channel in a more productive, though unscrupulous, direction. He sent them off to depose Sultan Adam of the Gakkhars, the man who had imprisoned the vagabond Kamran and handed him over to Humayun. A young Akbar had travelled to Gakkhar territory with his father, shared a watermelon of amity with Humayun, Kamran and, indeed, Sultan Adam. He must have known, or realized by now, that if Kamran had remained free to launch his untiring assaults on Kabul, Humayun could not have ventured a return to Hindustan. The family owed a debt to the Gakkhar sultan.

And yet, Akbar betrayed the man. As it happens, Sultan Adam's estranged nephew, Kamal Khan, was a favourite of Akbar's. Shortly before Sharafuddin's rebellion, Kamal Khan claimed the Gakkhar throne, and Akbar declared that Sultan Adam must share his kingdom with his nephew. In his telling of the tale, Abul Fazl makes only the most oblique reference to the obligation Akbar owed the sultan, dismissing his long-ago 'small service' as hardly worth talking about. The sultan would not have forgotten, however, and besides, he was the ruler of an independent realm, why should he listen to Akbar's orders? Sultan Adam refused to give half his land to his nephew. At this, Akbar sent the ataka khail to march against him with Kamal Khan, and they won.

Kamal Khan kept his uncle in jail 'to the end of his days'[15] and became sole ruler of the Gakkhars. And Akbar? He may not have shown the most laudable ethics in his conduct vis-à-vis Sultan Adam, but he had not only managed to keep the ataka khail away from court – and retaliatory bloodshed[16] – but also reversed the flow of obligation between the Gakkhars and his family. As long as he lived, Kamal Khan would not waver in his loyalty to the man who made him king.

Far, far south of Kamal Khan's newly acquired kingdom, meanwhile, a Tajik clerk was plotting to depose a Chandel queen.

Khwaja Abdul Majid had been a clerk in Humayun's employ and continued as an adviser to Akbar, who titled him Asaf Khan, after the wise vizier who served King Solomon. It wasn't for his counsel, however, but for his military skill that Asaf Khan would be remembered. In the early years of Akbar's reign, the scribe rose '*az qalm-b-ilm*', from the pen to the military standard,[17] and Akbar's eighth year as padishah began, in fact, with welcome news of Asaf Khan's victory over Raja Ram Chand of Panna.

Only a little while earlier, the raja had allowed an envoy of Akbar's to take away a most valued musician called Tansen, of whom Akbar had heard great things. Abul Fazl writes of how the raja considered the envoy's arrival 'an honour', but it is more likely that Ram Chand resented the loss of Tansen's legendary talent – not to mention all the 'elephants of fame and valuable jewels' he sent as tribute besides. He had a chance to express his unhappiness soon enough. An Afghan called Ghazi Khan[18] raised his banners against Akbar, and the raja gave him alliance and refuge.

Asaf Khan, who held a fief in central India, sniffed an opportunity in the raja's insubordination. He sent Ram Chand a message, telling him to surrender Ghazi Khan and proclaim his allegiance to the Mughal throne. When the raja refused, Asaf Khan attacked – Ghazi Khan was killed, and Ram Chand surrendered his fragile independence along with '[i]mmense spoil'.[19]

It may have been hope of a similarly rich haul that turned Asaf Khan's gaze southwards a year later to the rich and forested realm of Rani Durgavati. The rani, whom all contemporary historians describe as most beautiful – 'a lady of great loveliness and grace', writes Badauni – was also the most powerful ruler in Garha-Katanga, a region of 'populous cities and towns' measuring 150 by 80 *kos* (or about 675 by 360 kilometres), south of Panna and north of the Deccan, inhabited mostly by Gonds.[20] Of the people Abul Fazl is less admiring than of their country; he says 'the people of India despise them'. The historian feels no need to investigate this contempt; indeed, he seems to share it, dismissing the 'low-caste tribe' as preoccupied with carnal concerns, 'eating and drinking and venery'.

No such scorn, however, attaches to their queen. Daughter of a raja in Bundelkhand, Durgavati had been married to the king of Garha, Raja Dalpat, who was socially her inferior but financially better off. As happens even to kings, Durgavati's father had fallen 'on hard times'.[21] Little is known of Raja Dalpat, except that he lived long enough to produce an heir, then died. Their son Bir Sah being only five years old, the rani took charge of the realm, and managed it exceptionally well.

Garha-Katanga was divided into several small kingdoms, writes Abul Fazl, but such was the rani's 'courage, counsel and munificence' that she brought 'the whole of that country under her sway'. Of its 70,000 villages, one-third were hers, and the rest 'were subordinate . . . their headmen . . . under her control'. Her courage and skill, Abul Fazl continues, was paramount; her intelligence enabled her to do 'great things'; she could shoot arrows or bullets with equal ease; and she had a passion – in common with Akbar – for hunting. So much so, says Abul Fazl, that should a lion be sighted anywhere in her terrain, she would not drink water until she'd shot it down.

And, of course, as her father had intended, she was rich. It was the rani's 'abundant . . . treasure', writes Abul Fazl, getting to the rub, that inspired Asaf Khan's 'desire of lordship' over her land. The eager commander began with 'coquetry and toying, and put out his hand to touch the . . . mole of the beauty' of Gondwana – Abul Fazl's fondness for metaphor makes it difficult to tell if Asaf Khan actually flirted with the idea of marrying his fortune rather than conquering it[22] – but then, in 1564, Akbar made the decision for him: he sent word for Asaf Khan to march upon the queen.

Rani Durgavati's reputation for valour rests on the war that followed. In brief, the story is that the rani, mounted on her best elephant, a 'lofty and swift' animal called Sarman, fought bravely until, on the cusp of defeat, her neck bleeding from an arrow wound, the queen of the Gonds drew out her own dagger and took her own life.[23]

A more elaborate account reveals that Rani Durgavati was let down by her own side as much as she was defeated by Asaf Khan's. It was the rani, first of all, who gave her 5000-odd troops the appetite for a fight, declaring they might leave if they liked but she would not, for how long was she to hide 'among trees'? She would 'fall or she would conquer'. Then, putting 'armour on her breast and a helmet on her head', she led her men – including her now-adult son Bir Sah – at the far larger Mughal army (10,000 cavalry alone) and made a successful onslaught. Three hundred of Asaf Khan's men were killed, writes Abul Fazl; the 'Rani was victorious'.

That evening, however, the queen's luck turned. She held a council and proposed a surprise attack that very night, to deny Asaf Khan any opportunity to fortify his position. 'No one agreed', writes Abul Fazl. She proposed the idea again, this time to a smaller council of her most loyal men. They, too, let the moment pass.

The next morning, Asaf Khan was, indeed, better positioned. Still, the rani's men fought their best. It was a bloody, exhausting struggle; for three watches of the day, the battle raged, men falling one upon the other. At one point, writes a contemporary historian called Shaikh Illahdad, soldiers on both sides threw away their 'guns and arrows . . . seized each other's collars, and fought hand to hand'.[24] Bir Sah, the young king in whose stead his mother had ruled these past sixteen years, broke through enemy ranks thrice until he was wounded. The rani ordered her son taken away.

She had let maternal instinct get the better of martial reasoning. It may have been the rani who led the men upon her elephant, but when Bir Sah left, most of her army followed him.

Left with barely 300 men, Rani Durgavati 'continued to wage hot war' until she was struck by two arrows, one in the temple, the other in the neck. She fainted.

When the queen came to, her elephant was being driven to safety by a loyal chieftain called Adhar – the last man Rani Durgavati would ever lay eyes on, and the last of many who let her down. She asked him to kill her but Adhar refused. Furious at his 'soft heart', writes Abul Fazl, the rani drew out her dagger and committed her final act of courage upon herself, on her own.

A thousand elephants and 'much other booty' fell to Asaf Khan,[25] but this was nothing to the treasure that was to come. Bir Sah had fled to the fort of Chauragarh, long a base for Gond rulers and repository for their treasure. Two months later, Asaf Khan's troops arrived at his gates, the young king was killed, and the Mughal soldiers found themselves arms-deep in riches worthy of legend, including 100 literal pots of gold.[26] Four days into their delighted exploration of the fort, the conquerors made a more grisly discovery. Opening yet another door, they found a room full of charred bodies.

Like Baz Bahadur in Malwa, Bir Sah rode out to his final battle leaving two men behind – Bhoj Kayath and Mian Bhikari Rumi – with orders to organize a *jauhar* of the women in the fort should he lose the fight. They lit a fire – Bhoj beheading, besides, any woman who protested her fate – and, in Abul Fazl's words, 'that harvest of roses [was] . . . reduced to ashes'.

Two buds survived the carnage. One was an unnamed princess, the other was Rani Durgavati's sister, Kamlavati. Both were hiding behind a piece of wood so large that it saved rather than burnt them. The two royal women were sent to Akbar's court, along with a measly tribute of 200 elephants – and not a single jewel.

Much like Adham, Asaf Khan did not seem to think that the fruits of his labour belonged to the throne. This time, however, Akbar paid no mind. Commanders coy about parting with their spoils were less of an emergency, after all, than warlords in full-fledged rebellion.

Abul Fazl doesn't record the date, but Rani Durgavati is generally believed to have killed herself on 24 June 1564. Akbar may not have heard of her defeat – and certainly not of the plunder at Chauragarh, which took place a full two months later – when, on 1 July 1564, for the second time in three years, he left Agra and began to ride south towards Malwa.

Word had reached his court that Abdullah Khan the Uzbek, who had replaced Adham Khan and Pir Muhammad in Malwa, was showing worrying signs of independence. No details are given, but Akbar thought the matter serious enough to warrant personal investigation. Still, this was not the secret and lightning dash he had once made with a handful of men to reach Adham Khan. It was, instead, a well-attended, leisurely journey, in which the hunting of wild elephants occupied the padishah as much as the chastisement of restive chiefs.

'A separate volume would be required', Abul Fazl once wrote, 'to describe [the elephant's] . . . [wondrous] deeds' – and it is something of a marvel that Akbar didn't commission him to write one, so evident is the padishah's boundless love for the animal. Pure joy animates the few days of Akbar's journey spent in elephant-rich forests near Narwar, in which the 'closeness of the trees and the thickness of the branches' would barely allow the 'north or east winds to penetrate'. One day, Akbar and his men caught as many as seventy elephants. The padishah was delighted, but the hunt had gone on so long it was too late to return for the night. Instead, his carpenters built a cosy little camp in the forest: a wooden platform spread with 'scarlet cloth'. On it slept Akbar, encircled by his companions, including his best friend and milk brother Aziz, Shamsuddin Ataka's son.[27]

The next morning, while he waited for a troop of tame elephants to arrive from his main camp – they were needed to escort their wild, captured fellows from the forest – Akbar treated himself to another kind of entertainment. Seated with his friends on his wooden perch, Akbar called for Darbar Khan, his *dastango*, to come and tell him stories. So, to the sound of magic tales in the dense forest, with thoughts of his wonderful new menagerie in mind, the elephant-catching, rebel-subduing, kingdom-usurping padishah took a short pause in the endless adventure of his own life.

The interlude could not last forever. The camp marched on. The monsoon had broken; there was lightning and flooding, and a 'vicious mud' that forced the imperial stallions 'to swim like hippopotami' through it. It was a slow, inching progress, and somewhere along the way, Akbar lost patience. There are endless accounts of Akbar doing this in the annals – if there is one thing he couldn't bear, it seems, it was a sedate pace. Leaving the main camp by some meadows where his animals feasted on 'fresh and moist grass', Akbar galloped ahead. He had reached Dhar, barely 40 kilometres from Mandu where Abdullah governed, when he heard that the Uzbek chief had not greeted news of Akbar's arrival with any great joy; in fact, he had fled the city at night.

Over the next few rain-drenched days and nights, Akbar's men would chase Abdullah Khan westwards until the Uzbek abandoned his possessions and most of his family, escaping to Gujarat with his young son. Akbar rode against Abdullah himself, against the advice of one of his chiefs, Khaksar Sultan, who suggested, unwisely, that Akbar hang back a little from the front lines. Akbar was incensed, so much so that the terrified Khaksar Sultan leapt off his horse and ran for his life, ducking and feinting his way between a maze of horses' legs. Not to be outdone, Akbar got off his horse too, chased the chieftain down and hit him with his sword – a double-edged '*khanda*' blade, long used in Indian warfare, that did not, fortunately, kill the wretched man. Others, too, tried to stop him as the arrows flew thick and fast, one right past Akbar's head. Munim Khan suggested 'in a despairing voice' that they wait for reinforcements; another courtier even grabbed Akbar's reins. The padishah paid no attention to either.

He knew what he was doing. Just as a general's fall could destroy his army's morale, so the sight of a king riding into battle could trounce his enemy. So it was now – Abdullah Khan and his men, though they numbered over 1000, fled before 300 under Akbar's command. On 10 August 1564, Akbar marched in triumph into the citadel of Mandu.

Two months later, he was back in Agra, having ridden much of the way on musth elephants, including one particularly bad-tempered beast called Khandi Rai. If Akbar was seeking God's opinion on his handling of the Abdullah affair, God must have approved, because Akbar survived his ride on the mad animal, driving the sharp point of one goad into his head, and striking him with another. In the long term, God was right: Akbar's march against Abdullah was to the padishah's advantage. In the immediate future, however, it would provoke the most dangerous insurrection of Akbar's short reign: the rebellion of the Uzbeks, led by none other than Ali Quli Shaibani, lord of Jaunpur, scourge of the Afghans, and heartbroken lover of Shahim Beg, the camel driver's son.

But first, another interlude. In the half-year or so before Akbar left Agra for Jaunpur, he had twin sons, Hasan and Husain, born to a nameless mother. '[M]eadows of roses of joy blossomed',[28] wrote Abul Fazl, but their petals soon withered and their scent turned sour. The boys died a month after they were born.

Akbar grieved, but he recovered soon enough. The twins were born in October 1564, the month of Akbar's twenty-second birthday. He was a young man just hitting his stride; the death of infants was not unusual – Akbar's own elder brother, the unfortunate Al-Aman, had died similarly, and a man who could tame mad elephants could surely produce more sons. Why waste time in mourning? Akbar decreed a pleasure dome. Barely 5 kilometres from Agra was a village called Kakrali, a 'land of flowers' with the perfect climate for hunting and other pleasures.[29] Let a city of ease be founded here – Akbar named it Nagarchain and ordered architects to build him pavilions and gardens. His nobility hastened to follow suit, and soon the refashioned village was filled with courtiers and their amusements, Akbar at their centre, immersed 'sometimes in chougan-playing, sometimes in racing Arabian dogs, and sometimes in flying birds of various kinds'.[30]

Along the eastern borders of Akbar's kingdom, meanwhile, Ali Quli Shaibani was contemplating a more dangerous game. About the time that Abdullah the Uzbek began showing signs of his disaffection, Ali Quli was more productively occupied, fighting off ambitious Afghans in and around his fiefdom. The fief was Jaunpur – Ali Quli had conquered it, now he ruled it, though in the teeth of the resistance of its former Afghan lords, now settled farther east in Bihar and Bengal. Foremost among these were Fath and Hasan Khan, brothers who ruled the sprawling, well-equipped fort of Rohtas, and Sulaiman Karrani, the sultan of Bengal. Rohtas and Bengal both offered wary lip service to Akbar's throne, just as Akbar's representative, Ali Quli, offered them a watchful peace – it was a fragile, three-cornered balance, in which no party ruled out exploratory forays into others' territories.

Now, Fath and Hasan Khan had attacked some of Ali Quli's holdings and even found a surviving Suri prince to proclaim king. Ali Quli and his men defeated the Afghans and returned to Jaunpur, triumphant yet increasingly mistrusted, it seems, by the padishah. Only months after Ali Quli's victory, Akbar sent an envoy east, one Qilich Khan, who was to bypass Jaunpur's commander and negotiate directly with Fath Khan of Rohtas – the very man Ali Quli had just defeated.[31]

Not long after, another envoy left Akbar's court, heading east to yet another Uzbek's fief. This envoy was to meet Sikander Khan Uzbek, a fief-holder in Oudh, and encourage him to present himself in court, rumours of his 'brainless head . . . affected by seditiousness'[32] having preceded him there. Sikander made every show of respecting Akbar's messenger except actually obeying his instructions. Instead of going to Agra, he hurried to meet a neighbouring chieftain, an older Uzbek called Ibrahim Khan – who also happened to be Ali Quli's uncle – and both of them decamped to Ali Quli in Jaunpur. The padishah's messenger they put in chains.

The Uzbek rebellion had begun, and it would take no half measures. The whole soaring saga of it could fill a book of its own, and yet, such is the force of Akbar's historiography that even the names of the men who formed the first major resistance to his rule are largely forgotten.

At the time, however, Ali Quli and his brother Bahadur, their uncle Ibrahim and Sikander Khan Uzbek of Oudh were the most urgent talk of the court.

The Uzbeks had cause to be upset with the padishah. Leaving aside the competing genealogies of Uzbek versus Chagatai, Timurid, or Moghul, these particular Uzbeks in Hindustan had every reason to believe that they had done more than enough to deserve pride of place in Akbar's court and realm. These men had been steadfast in their loyalty to Humayun through his battles with Kamran.[33] A modern historian tells of how, after a long march, Humayun once lay down with his head in Ali Quli's brother Bahadur's lap as Bahadur sang him to sleep.[34] When they crossed the Indus with Humayun, the Uzbeks were highly ranked and prized, and their contribution to the conquest of Hindustan and the expansion of the realm fully justified their favoured position.

On the other hand, the Uzbeks were warlords, powerful and proud. Ali Quli and his brother Bahadur, for example, were very unhappy with Bairam's overthrow and furious with how his supporters were treated. One of these was Wali Beg, Bairam's brother-in-law, and procurer of Akbar's first cheetah. Wali Beg was killed during the coup against Bairam, and his head sent to the eastern provinces. When the butchered head of his friend arrived in Bahadur's fief, he was so incensed, he cut off the messenger's head.

Clearly, the Uzbek brothers were not to be messed with; following her coup against Bairam, the powerful Maham Anaka was concerned enough about their displeasure to offer Ali Quli the rank of vakil.[35] Over the next few years, the Uzbeks' power would only increase. Just before the rebellion, as Afzal Husain explains it, Uzbeks held two large chunks of the empire, Malwa and the east, and were beginning to develop ties with neighbouring kings, in Gujarat, Rohtas, Bihar and Bengal.

Akbar, meanwhile, was increasingly disinclined to treat these warlords with either Maham's kid gloves or Bairam's friendship – let alone Humayun's trust. Already, long ago, he had meddled in Ali Quli's love life, and things were only getting worse: now, he was demanding account of their revenue and their administration – chasing Abdullah Khan Uzbek out of Malwa and going over Ali Quli Shaibani's head in dealing with Rohtas.

Thus, the two sides arrived at a point of no return. Just as the Uzbeks were settling down to become the kind of virtually independent rulers that Humayun had imagined managing his realm, Akbar was making it ever more clear that Hindustan would have one lord, and one lord alone: the padishah himself.[36]

It was a fundamental misunderstanding of roles that could only be resolved by war.

Akbar set himself to work 'from early morning till the end of day' on preparing an army, which included selecting the 2000 elephants, no less, that
would march with him.[37] Never yet, in his decade's worth of reign, had Akbar
led such a large force; nor, indeed, faced one. Even Hemu had only 1500
elephants, at most, in Panipat, but Akbar was taking no chances against the
very men who fought that battle for him. Could it be that the Uzbeks who had
marched into Hindustan with Humayun would snatch the realm from his son,
turn him into just another fief-holder among raucous, rival commanders, just
another zamindar in a land full of petty kings?

No, Akbar was taking no chances. On 24 May 1565, Akbar rode out of
Agra, having given yet another, more secret, order. Mirza Abul Qasim,
Akbar's cousin and Kamran's son, had lived in shadow his whole life and in
the dungeons of Gwalior these past years. He was to be killed.

It is popularly held that the shedding of family blood among Babur's
descendants began with Shahjahan – Akbar's grandson – who had all his
male relatives killed when he took the throne. To find Akbar killing his
cousin, too, comes as a bit of a shock; even more since it follows Humayun's tearfully held resolve to spare this very Abul Qasim's father, the far
more threatening Kamran, again and again.[38] Akbar himself was not keen to
publicize his decision – it is not recorded by any contemporary chronicler;
not Abul Fazl, not even Badauni, who rarely misses a chance to condemn his
king. Many later historians, however, agree that Akbar's departure from Agra
was also the time of his cousin's demise – there was the risk, no matter how
remote, that Abul Qasim would become the Uzbeks' figurehead, giving their
revolt its cause.[39]

Thus unencumbered by his inconvenient cousin, Akbar set off. The burning
north Indian summer had begun, so the army marched at night – one can only
imagine the scene, the dark silhouettes of 2000 elephants, troops upon troops
of cavalry, the endless thud of feet and hooves, the drumbeats to guide the
way, the burning torches held up in pitch darkness. When they reached the
Ganga, Akbar was gripped by a familiar impatience. It would take ten days
for the whole army to cross the river, but Sikander Khan Uzbek was close
by, it was said, in Lucknow, seemingly unperturbed by the imperial advance.
Akbar took a few men and 'at midnight went off on horseback'.[40] Sikander
fled at news of his furious approach.

Satisfied, Akbar waited in Lucknow for his army to catch up, then marched
on to Jaunpur. Here, Asaf Khan re-enters the story. It was a splashy entrance.

Newly enriched with Gond wealth, little of which had made it to Akbar's
treasury, Asaf Khan brought tributes for the padishah, along with 5000 cavalry freshly bought with the gold of Chauragarh. The padishah was pleased;
some days later, in mid-July 1565, he sent Asaf Khan and his prime troops in

pursuit of the Uzbeks. But only two months afterwards, in September, Asaf Khan abandoned his mission and took flight himself, and in the late spring of 1566, he joined Ali Quli's rebellion.

Asaf Khan's desertion did not share the communal logic of the Uzbek uprising – he was Tajik, not Uzbek – but it does illustrate something of the layers of suspicion, resentment and ambition that animated the feuds between Akbar's nobility at this time and reveal how fear – of an increasingly powerful padishah and the decreasing autonomy of his chiefs in their fiefs – might tip a man out of the fold.

At the heart of it, of course, is that Asaf Khan had gained a vast booty and sent nothing of it to court, hoping to protect himself by bribing the palace accountants. These men began to mutter about his 'former unwillingness to hand over the spoils' and suggest that even now he had retained more than he had revealed.[41] It may also be the case, as both Nizamuddin and Badauni suggest, that it was Akbar's new vizier, a stickler called Muzaffar Khan, who threatened to charge Asaf Khan with financial fraud, at which the covetous commander, his heart full of 'suspicion and anxiety',[42] ran away.

Muzaffar Khan was one of Bairam Khan's men, parsimonious and outspoken, but talented enough to have attracted Akbar's attention and favour. He worked with another of Akbar's new recruits, Todar Mal – both men charged with supervising the chieftains' revenue and ensuring that an adequate share of it came to the imperial treasury. This did not endear the two men to the chiefs; the indignant fief-holders couldn't decide which one of them they hated more. Badauni quotes 'a certain wit' who put the dilemma in verse: 'A dog of a Raja is better than Muzaffar Khan / Although a dog is a hundred times better than a Raja.'[43]

Munim Khan, Akbar's old ataliq and current Khan-Khanan, had more reason than most to despise Muzaffar Khan – an accountant who had once served Munim's own household. Now, Akbar had made Muzaffar Khan his vizier, thus turning Munim's subordinate into his superior.[44]

Just as Asaf Khan disliked Muzaffar Khan's interference in his finances, so Munim Khan resented Muzaffar Khan's promotion in court – but this mutual animosity did not make Asaf and Munim allies, as it might have. Quite the opposite, in fact: Asaf Khan was actually being propped up against Munim by a non-Chagatai faction in Akbar's court. The grand parade of 5000 soldiers that Asaf Khan arranged was designed to impress Akbar and gain Asaf Khan command of the expedition against the Uzbeks, thus sidelining Munim, his ageing Chagatai chief.

The whole messy melting pot of rivalries came to a boil when Asaf Khan ran away. As Akbar railed against the 'Tajik dwarf', Munim Khan burst into tears, protesting that Asaf Khan's defection was not his fault: it was Khwaja Jahan – another one of Akbar's new recruits – who backed Asaf

Khan as commander, and Khwaja Jahan who had been so terribly insulting of Munim's lineage, declaring that 'even a single hair of Asaf Khan is better than the entire Chagatai clan'.[45]

While Akbar consoled his weeping Khan-Khanan, Ali Quli Shaibani and his brother Bahadur were more productively engaged. They had crossed the Ganga into Bihar and forged an alliance with Bengal's Afghan sultan, Sulaiman Karrani. Together, the sultan and the Uzbeks were besieging Rohtas when Akbar sent his envoy Qilich Khan to the fort, once again, to ensure its allegiance. With so many covetous glances turned in its direction, Rohtas decided to play its own game. Its lord, Fath Khan, let out that he was now Akbar's ally, at which Sulaiman Karrani – fearing a battle with the vast Mughal army – lost his nerve and abandoned his siege. Immediately, Fath Khan – 'who was nothing if not two-faced', grumbles Abul Fazl – stocked the fort with supplies and reneged on his promises of fealty to Akbar.

The Uzbeks, meanwhile, split forces. Bahadur and Sikander were to 'ravage and plunder' in Bihar,[46] possibly to keep the pressure on while Ali Quli launched the first in a series of negotiations with Akbar. He did so via his old friend Munim Khan.[47]

Between these two men, comrades-in-arms from Humayun's time, 'there was an old and warm friendship', writes Nizamuddin, and after several months of talks the two of them did manage to hammer out a truce. Its details were fixed mid-river. Ali Quli and Munim Khan met on the Ganga, at Buxar. Behind each of them, the riverbanks were teeming with soldiers, prepared to attack at a moment's notice.[48] Ali Quli clambered into Munim's boat, they embraced, tears were shed and promises made – and over two days of banquets and negotiations, it was decided that both sides would suspend hostilities and that Ali Quli would send his mother and his uncle, Ibrahim, to Akbar's court, as sureties for Ali Quli's submission.

Again, Akbar agreed, stipulating only that Ali Quli stay on his side of the river as long as Akbar remained in the east.

Only 100-odd kilometres away, in Sarwar, Ali Quli's brother Bahadur's rebellion was proceeding in a very different way. While Munim could build peace on the scaffolding of his old friendship with Ali Quli, the commander pursuing Bahadur, Mir Muizzulmulk, had no such affection for Ali Quli's brother. Muizzulmulk refused all attempts to negotiate, declaring that the Uzbeks' crimes could only be washed away 'by the bloody deluge of the shining sword'.[49] He was greatly encouraged, it seems, by Todar Mal – the 'oil of naphtha' on Muizzulmulk's ire.[50]

As it happens, however, the commander's anger exceeded his ability: Bahadur won the battle between them and followed his victory with a daring raid on Jaunpur – 'throwing up a noose, [he] climbed into the fortress'[51] – to rescue his and Ali Quli's mother, so recently made guarantee of her sons' good behaviour. Not to be outdone, Ali Quli broke the pact that required him to stay on his side of the Ganga while Akbar toured the east.

Akbar was enraged. He even threatened to move his capital from Agra to Jaunpur until the Uzbeks came to heel. At this, Ali Quli sent renewed pleas for peace – and his newly rescued mother, back again – to Munim, and, once again, the Uzbek's friends in Akbar's court persuaded the padishah to give him another chance.[52]

Akbar returned to Agra, and Ali Quli to his rebellion. The Uzbek may have made a show of repentance to get Akbar to leave, but he had no intention of letting the boy win. He was damned, in fact, if a so-called padishah with only a battle against villagers in Paronkh to his name would tell him, grizzled hero of Panipat, what to do.

Many agreed with him. Abdullah the Uzbek, whom Akbar had chased out of Malwa, returned from Gujarat and joined Ali Quli. Asaf Khan, too, having hidden 'like a wild beast . . . in the forests'[53] for a while, decided to take his chance with the Uzbeks – as did a new posse of insurgents, known to history as the Mirzas: Timurid princes chafing at Akbar's increasing authority. Ali Quli's Jaunpur, as a modern historian puts it, 'was fast becoming a rendez-vous of disgruntled elements'.[54]

Unfortunately for him, Ali Quli had remarkable spirit for insurrection but little talent for binding men to his cause.

At their very first meeting, Asaf Khan was put off by the Uzbeks' arrogance and 'did not like their company'. His dismay only increased, presumably, when he saw Ali Quli 'cast eyes . . . on his property'. Asaf Khan plotted an escape, losing a finger and the tip of his nose in the process, and returned, sheepishly, to Akbar's fold. As for the Mirzas, their alliance with the Uzbeks was equally short-lived, 'for every one in his folly wanted to rule',[55] a desire that does not make for lasting unions. The Mirzas, like Asaf Khan, soon left. This didn't worry Ali Quli overly; in fact, it seems to have spurred him and his kin to set their sights on a far more ambitious coalition. Not for them Asaf Khan's Gond gold, nor the Mirzas' proud disaffection. The question was no longer of fighting Akbar's authority, but of denouncing it entirely. Akbar was not, after all, the only one of Humayun's descendants with a claim to Humayun's throne.

The ghostly Abul Qasim, Akbar's cousin, might be no more, but what about Humayun's other son, Akbar's half-brother, tucked away in Kabul?

In March 1567, almost exactly a year after he left Jaunpur, Akbar held a most magnificent – and outrageous – hunt on the outskirts of Lahore.

The hunt was of the '*qamargah*' style, in which beaters encircled a large area of forest land and closed in, thus increasing the density of animal life within their circumference. In this case, several thousand soldiers had been enlisted to enclose an area of over 20 square kilometres – 'from near the mountains on the one side, and from the river [Jhelum] on the other'. For a month, these men, 'both high and low', had moved forward, step by coordinated step, pressing animals into grounds as 'capacious [as the] hearts of princes'.[56] When the qamargah was ready, Akbar rode in with only one man by his side, Aziz, Shamsuddin Ataka's son and Akbar's favourite milk brother. The two friends hunted their fill for five days, Akbar aiming 'the arrow, the sword, the lance and the musket', swinging lassos to catch 'lightning-footed deer'.[57] The rest of the nobility was camped on the qamargah's borders, watching to see that no animal escaped in the day, keeping guard with flaming torches at night.

When Akbar was satisfied, the nobility had their turn, and so down the ranks to the foot soldiers until every man had taken what life he was entitled to, and all turned their backs on the blood-soaked plain. It was an extravagance of gore, the sheer spectacle of which suggests that Akbar had not come all the way from Agra to Punjab for a hunt.

He had come to frighten his little brother.

Mirza Muhammad Hakim, over a decade Akbar's junior, was an infant when Humayun left Kabul to recover his home in Hindustan – and never returned. He was brought up, therefore, by his mother, Mahchuchak ('Moonflower') Begum, whose dramatic and tragic struggle to ensure her son a throne deserves to be better known.

Humayun had left Kabul in Munim Khan's charge, and, as long as Bairam Khan held sway over Akbar's throne, the Chagatai nobleman remained where he was. During Bairam's ouster, however, when Akbar summoned his old ataliq across the Indus, Munim left Kabul in charge of his son, Ghazi Khan. Ghazi Khan was not a popular administrator; or, perhaps, Mahchuchak had had enough of being supervised by her stepson's aides. One day, he returned from touring some melon fields outside Kabul only to find the city gates locked against him – giving Abul Fazl the chance to quote an apt proverb: 'Eat the melons, what business have you with their beds?'

Sheepishly Ghazi Khan rode off to Hindustan, and Mahchuchak 'undertook the affairs of Kabul'.[58]

The dowager queen had three advisers, including Munim's brother and nephew, all of whom were killed in a churn of bloody intrigue. (Munim's nephew, for example, was invited to a drinking party, decapitated when drunk, and his body 'flung down from the citadel'.)[59] Her fourth adviser she may have married; he was allowed to live, at any rate, while he served as her son Hakim's vakil.[60]

It was in Hakim's name, and for his sake, that Mahchuchak did what she did. Merely being born in Kabul did not make it his; the city was as much in contention now as it had been when Humayun and Kamran fought over it.

Within moments of Humayun's death, it would seem, Sulaiman of Badakh-shan had marched upon the city, and though he was eventually dispatched by Munim, surely his wife Haram Begum's ambitions would send him marching this way again.

Across the Indus, meanwhile, Akbar's power was only increasing. Soon after executing Adham Khan, Akbar ordered Munim to recover Kabul and take charge of Hakim as his ataliq – guardian, tutor and mentor rolled into one. The news did not gladden Mahchuchak's heart: she had driven out Munim's son and presided over the brutal murders of his brother and nephew. She could hardly expect a warm reunion with her son's new adviser. Instead, therefore, she rode to war.

Munim Khan was defeated, comprehensively. Not only did he lose the battle, he lost many of his men to Mahchuchak's side, and most of his pos-sessions – 3 million in cash according to a member of his retinue. It was only because the winning army was so busy with its loot, in fact, that Munim didn't lose his liberty, too, and escaped with his life.

Thus, tail between his legs, Munim Khan returned to Akbar's court, and Mahchuchak rode in triumph to Kabul. Unfortunately, this moment of great victory was also the beginning of her fall.

It came in the treacherously handsome form of Humayun's favourite sayyid, Shah Abul Ma'ali, last seen making a discreet exit from Hindustan after hiring a sniper to shoot Akbar down.

It was around the time of Mahchuchak's victory that Sharafuddin and Abul Ma'ali had joined forces against Akbar – even pre-empting the Uzbeks' idea of putting Hakim on the throne. They had failed; Sharafuddin disappeared, for the moment, from the story, and Abul Ma'ali arrived at Kabul's gates.

He sent Mahchuchak a poem.

'We are not come to this door, for the sake of pomp and grandeur / We are come here as a refuge from the evil of circumstances.'

Mahchuchak was not shy of butchering her rivals nor afraid of riding into enemy troops, but she was susceptible, it seems, to self-pitying verse. 'Show kindness and alight, for the house is thy house', she replied.[61]

Perhaps, having shut her gates in Akbar's face, and knowing that Sulaiman of Badakhshan and his wife Haram Begum still looked upon her realm as their prey, Mahchuchak felt the need for an ally. Not only did she invite Abul Ma'ali into her citadel, she married him to her daughter. But Mahchuchak had misjudged her new son-in-law. Kindness was not his strong suit, and her house would soon be his, alone.

Abul Ma'ali was 'obviously vile',[62] writes Abul Fazl – and no one can accuse the historian, here, of exaggeration. What followed was horrific.

Hakim was eight years old at this time but, as Babur's grandson, he commanded a certain customary allegiance from the people of Kabul, and was an
asset, therefore, to anyone who sought to rule the city. His mother was not.
The scene is gruesome. Abul Ma'ali stormed into Mahchuchak's house,
with two other men. There was a group of women, one of whom looked a
bit like the queen; they killed her first and realized their error later. The three
men resumed their search for the begum, striding through the house, weapons
drawn. She had locked herself in a room; they broke down the door – you
can imagine the sound of their hammering and the screams of the women
behind them. There is no account of whether Mahchuchak cowered when
they barged in or put up a fight. Perhaps the begum had time to let fly a round
of curses on their heads. But then, they stabbed her.

Leaving Mahchuchak's butchered body behind, the three men went to look
for the children and plucked Hakim from among them. The eight-year-old
orphan went straight from the nursery to the throne.

Abul Ma'ali would not enjoy his ill-gotten gains for long. The child-
king's supporters had him write to his uncle, Sulaiman of Badakhshan, and,
'accompanied by Haram',[63] no doubt with some glee, he rode to the rescue.
Abul Ma'ali was defeated in the battle that followed, caught and hanged – on
the day of Eid after Ramzan. (A painting shows him strung up in a public
square – there is even a blackbuck among the watching crowd, looking on
approvingly.)

Hakim may have taken solace in the swift justice that swallowed his mother's murderer, but his troubles were far from over.[64] Sulaiman and Haram,
having been invited into Kabul, were not inclined to leave. They married
Hakim to one of their daughters and redistributed most of Kabul's provinces
to Badakhshani chiefs, creating such resentment among the Kabulis that, in
the winter of 1564 – only months after Sulaiman and Haram had 'liberated'
the city (and months before the Uzbek rebellion broke) – several Kabuli chiefs
smuggled Hakim across the Indus and sent word to his half-brother for help.

Akbar was building Nagarchain, his city of ease, practising his polo and
racing his dogs. As he listened to the news of the goings-on in Kabul and
heard his young brother's appeal, did Akbar reflect that, but for a series of
fortunate events – that he wasn't a few years younger when his father died,
that he had Bairam and Maham by his side – he, too, might have suffered as
his brother was suffering? Did he marvel at how the canvas of his own life
was expanding by the day, across the rivers and plains of Hindustan, while
the family he left behind was still squabbling over Kabul? Did he feel a pang
of guilt – or even sorrow – at the brutal murder of his father's youngest wife?

There is no record of Akbar's feelings, but he did send help. That legion
of great commanders in Punjab, the ataka khail, was told to escort Hakim to
Kabul and take it back from the Badakhshanis. One of the clan, Qutubuddin

Khan, 'distinguished for his ability and trustworthiness', was also appointed Hakim's tutor, an older, wiser head to guide the boy.[65]

Only half of Akbar's plan worked. Kabul fell to his men in an hour as Sulaiman and Haram '[d]isheartened . . . decided upon flight'; Hakim regained his home. He was less lucky with his new tutor. It turned out that Qutubuddin Khan was more interested in visiting his homeland, Ghazni, 'where he had been born and brought up', than in nurturing the prince. Having left to satisfy his homesickness as well as he could – meeting 'all his clan, and . . . all his friends . . . laying the foundations of stations, gardens and buildings' – Qutubuddin Khan swapped his tutor's duties with Mir Muhammad Khan.[66]

Mir Muhammad, who had led the Mughal forces to Kabul, was Shamsuddin Ataka's elder brother, and it might have been that he gave Hakim the affection, protection and loyalty his brother had lavished on Akbar. But what have might-have-beens to do with history? Mir Muhammad was loyal to the family, but he was also known for his 'impetuosity and roughness' – one night, incensed, he stormed out of Kabul, leaving the child-king in his realm and to his fate.[67]

According to Abul Fazl, this was because Hakim lacked 'inborn goodness . . . sound reason, and . . . honest and loyal servants'. He might also have added, the young ruler of Kabul was barely ten years old – and a great temptation to ambitious and unscrupulous men. One of these had appeared on the scene – Khwaja Hasan Naqshbandi – and contrived, somehow, to have Hakim marry him to his sister, the very same princess who was lately widowed (and thankfully rid) of Abul Ma'ali. It was the fact that the marriage was arranged without his counsel and consent that sent Mir Muhammad into a rage, and back to Punjab.

Two years later, in 1566, Akbar was back from his bout against the Uzbeks and recuperating in Nagarchain once again – this time experimenting with firelit balls that allowed for games of night polo[68] – when fresh news of his brother's unhappy adventures arrived. Sulaiman and Haram had made another – their fourth! – bid on Kabul; Hakim had fled across the Indus and needed Akbar's help again.[69]

Akbar had already dispatched a man called Faridun – a courtier and also Hakim's uncle – to advise his brother and keep him safe from malevolent influence. Now, he sent a messenger – the aptly titled Khushkhabar Khan, lord of good tidings – with money, a robe of honour, a horse from Akbar's own stables, all for Hakim, along with instructions for the ataka khail to set out for Kabul a second time.

The two men arrived within a few days of each other, and while Khushkhabar Khan brought no disgrace to his name, Uncle Faridun revealed himself 'a regular leprous spot'.[70] Having been entrusted with keeping 'seditious men' from 'speaking to the [prince]', Faridun went and proposed a brash sedition of his own. Let Hakim take Lahore! There was nothing to it, 'it would be easy'.[71] The thirteen-year-old – the same age as Akbar when Bairam crowned him in Kalanaur – and accustomed all his short life to accepting the instruction and aid of aggressive adults, agreed.

It was a pathetically weak-kneed siege. Hakim camped in a garden outside Lahore; Akbar heard the news, the 'flames of [his] wrath . . . burst forth' and he marched out of Agra. He had only reached Delhi when Hakim ran away terrified by 'the reverberation' of Akbar's approach.[72] Akbar continued his march anyway, and so we reach the scene of his vast and bloody qamargah hunt.[73]

The sheer scale of it – 15,000 animals, according to Badauni, were trapped in the qamargah circle – suggests that it was a means to shock and awe in the absence of a war. Even so, the enormous hunt did not sap all of Akbar's adrenalin and anger, still burning in his brother's wake. He returned to Lahore at a full gallop, insisting on swimming his horse to the city across the Ravi river. The accompanying nobility plunged in behind him, dutifully, and two of them drowned, including the messenger Khushkhabar Khan – perhaps unpopular despite his name, for his sudden death elicited a cruel rhyme that begins 'Khushkhabar Khan is bad news . . .'.[74]

There is a telling parallel to this anecdote from Humayun's life. During one of his eternal pursuits of Kamran, Humayun rode across a stream on horseback. As Abul Fazl tells it, not one of his chiefs followed; instead, they meandered away, 'seeking a safe passage'.[75] Humayun was upset; he told them all a peevish tale of how a Persian shah's followers had thrown themselves off a cliff to catch his falling handkerchief. His chiefs, no doubt, pretended to listen.

How things had changed. The Ravi, writes Abul Fazl, 'flows with ocean-like majesty', yet the force of Akbar's authority was stronger still. Unfortunately for Ali Quli and the Uzbeks, they could not see, or would not accept, the changing protocols of court – just as they were ignorant of, or unwilling to accept, news of Hakim's humiliating retreat. Thus it was that now, as Akbar secured his borders in the north, word arrived from the east: the unrelenting Uzbek warlords had proclaimed the boy in Kabul their king.

The Uzbek saga was drawing to its end. What kind of truce would hold good any more, now that they had proposed an alternative head for the crown of Hindustan?

On 23 March 1567, only days after Akbar heard of their proclamation, he left Lahore for his final campaign against the mutinous Uzbek siblings, Ali Quli and Bahadur. As it happens, two of his elephants died on the way, both on the same day. Unperturbed, the padishah saw in this an omen for the end of the 'two unlucky brothers' of Jaunpur.[76]

He was not, it seems, inclined to flatter them with any show of anxious hurry in their pursuit. He 'indulged in hunting' all the way back from Lahore, writes Abul Fazl; halfway to Agra, he even stopped to witness a pilgrimage in Kurukshetra. A great crowd of pilgrims and ascetics had gathered around the town's lake – the pilgrims in prayer, the ascetics receiving alms, 'gold and silver, and jewels and stuffs'.[77] Suddenly, the cheerful bustle turned aggressive. Two groups of ascetics that had converged on Kurukshetra, the Kaurs and the Puris, were arguing over turf. The Puris had long been positioned along the banks of the lake, within easy and profitable reach of alms-givers emerging from a cleansing dip in its holy waters. The Kaurs wanted to take their place.

The two sects decided to settle the matter with their fists. Akbar did not object to such violent resolution to the dispute; perhaps he even saw an omen in it. He, too, was going to battle a rival for land. As the ascetics began to bombard each other with rocks and arrows, the padishah pitched in to even their chances, lending some of his own men to the Puris, who were outnumbered by the Kaurs. The Puris won the day, and Akbar, having 'delighted [in the] sport' with all the gusto of an ancient Roman at the Colosseum, resumed his journey.[78]

At this leisurely pace, it was the first week of May before Akbar finally gathered his men and his elephants, and set out from Agra. As on his previous expedition to Jaunpur, summer had set in; the sun so hot, writes Badauni, 'that the marrow of creatures melted in their bones'.

A month later, marching in the relative cool of night, the Mughal army reached Rae Bareli, and news arrived that Ali Quli and Bahadur were heading to Gwalior. Catching scent of his prey, Akbar was no longer languid but tense for the chase. Despite objections from his courtiers,[79] on the evening of 7 June 1567, Akbar galloped away from his own camp.

With the reckless bravado of his dash across the Ravi, Akbar took a risky shortcut through a forest in which several of his already small troop of soldiers got lost. Near Manikpur, where they needed to cross the Ganga, Akbar would not wait to build a bridge but drove his elephant into the river, swollen with the rains that had just begun. Abul Fazl reports that only eleven commanders came with him – among them Aziz, his milk brother, and Darbar Khan, the dastango – and Nizamuddin records that over 1000 foot soldiers swam alongside. Thus, the air resounding with the splashing of his men and the 'raging and roaring' of his elephants – Balsundar, Khudabaksh, Tufan Masti – Akbar forded the river and camped for the night.[80]

As he would do again and again throughout his life, Akbar had taken his foe by surprise. Ali Quli and Bahadur were less than 10 kilometres away, but utterly ignorant of the padishah's presence. They were having a wild night of it, in fact, with dancers to entertain them and plenty to drink.

'O all ye doomed ones . . . !'[81]

A voice in the dark called out to the brothers. Akbar was nearby, the voice went on, but the brothers paid no heed. That informer, as Abul Fazl tells it, belonged to an 'ignorant loyalist' of Akbar's, hoping to prevent a confrontation between the Uzbek brothers and the padishah's relatively smaller force. Perhaps it was one of Munim Khan's men, commissioned by Munim[82] to make one last effort to help his obstinate Uzbek friend.

Whoever he was, he failed. Ali Quli was not the kind of man to retreat from a battle. Besides, a man who could finish a game of chess while battle raged was not to be put off his drink by disembodied voices. The revelry continued, for tomorrow is always another day, even if, in this case, it was to be the last day of Ali Quli's life.

On 9 June 1567, Akbar climbed upon Balsundar and, with Aziz sharing his howdah, marched upon the Uzbeks.

Ali Quli was sleeping off the night's carousal when Akbar's army arrived. Unruffled, the Uzbek got on his horse and rode into Akbar's vanguard. It was not a propitious start: in the chaos of the fight, Ali Quli's turban fell off. 'At the sight', writes Badauni, Ali Quli's brother, Bahadur – the man who had scaled the walls of Jaunpur to rescue their mother – made a furious charge at Akbar's archers. He was going strong until his horse was wounded and, rearing up in pain,[83] threw Bahadur to the ground.

Meanwhile, in another part of the battlefield, two of Akbar's elephants were settling a personal score – one of the hazards, it seems, of taking musth elephants into war. Chitranand charged at Gaj Bhaunr. The latter's mahout was a man of quick wit, however; he drove Gaj Bhaunr into enemy ranks, where his getaway would be of greater service to Akbar's army. Thus it was that Chitranand, racing behind, came face to face with an Uzbek elephant called Avidya. Impatient, perhaps, with the stranger coming between him and his feud with Gaj Bhaunr, Chitranand attacked Avidya with a 'mountain-breaking blow' – and felled him to the ground.[84]

With one of their best elephants down for the count and Chitranand charging madly after Gaj Bhaunr through their ranks, with Ali Quli turban-less and Bahadur out of sight, the rebel army began to lose steam.

In the chaos of the losing battle, amid the screams of wounded animals and the scramble of retreating feet, Ali Quli – like Bahadur – was thrown off his horse. As he looked around, in hope of another mount or a helping hand, one of Akbar's elephants approached. This one was called Nainsukh and he was missing a tusk; lost in another war perhaps.

Ali Quli, with not even a turban on his head, was less easily identified. The Uzbek called out to Nainsukh's mahout, 'I am a great leader, take me alive . . . '[85]

Bahadur, meanwhile, had already been captured by Akbar's men, and stood, head bowed, before the padishah. Once, long ago, Akbar's father had laid his head upon the warlord's lap, as Bahadur sang him to sleep. Akbar may have known the story. If not, it was below Bahadur's pride to remind him of it. He would say nothing, indeed, neither in anger nor apology; only, at the end of many questions, 'God is to be praised, whatever happens.'[86]

Abul Fazl says that Akbar did not want to kill him; Badauni adds that Bahadur asked for water, and Akbar gave him his own canteen. Akbar's commanders, on the other hand, wanted blood, and Akbar acquiesced. Two men stepped forward and cut off Bahadur's head.

But what of his brother?

One of the Uzbek's men, now in chains, spoke up. He had seen Ali Quli being killed by a one-tusked elephant. Nainsukh was promptly identified, as was his mahout Somnath, now brought out to tell his story.

'I am a great leader, take me alive to the king and you will get a great reward', Ali Quli had yelled.[87]

Whether it was because he did not recognize Ali Quli, or because Somnath's blood was in as much of a boil from battle as that of the elephants he drove, the mahout paid no heed. He drove Nainsukh forward, step by heavy step. The elephant knew what to do. He crushed Ali Quli 'with its trunk and feet', writes Badauni, '. . . and made his body like a bag full of chess-pieces'. Akbar wanted proof; he wanted Ali Quli's head. A gold coin, he declared, for anyone who brought him the trophy – and a rupee, to boot, for every Hindustani head besides. 'The crowd ran off' on their grim treasure hunt,[88] and one by one the heads began to roll in, each to be inspected for signs of Ali Quli's features.

It wasn't only soldiers who went head-collecting, but all the many types of people who marched with an army: accountants, cooks, painters. It was a clerk who found Ali Quli's broken body. He was sauntering back to claim his gold when he came across a slave. Perhaps they knew each other; perhaps the clerk was unwise enough to boast of his find. At any rate, the slave quickly divested the clerk of his prize and brought it to Akbar, claiming to have found the head under a tree.

But now, another problem arose. A man crushed by an elephant does not retain his looks. Yes, this head seemed to match Ali Quli's, but how to be sure? Badauni writes that a former eunuch of Ali Quli's stepped forward, describing how his late master's habit of chewing *paan*, betel leaves, had blackened the teeth on his right side. Thus, the mutilated head passed from hand to hand, its jaws examined by appraising eyes. It was Ali Quli's vakil, a minor raja, according to Badauni, who took the head in his hands and identified it with cries of 'Alas! Alas!'

Alas, indeed, for the Uzbek of melting heart and strong arm; the warlord who would wait upon a lover as his slave, but would defer to no man as his emperor; alas for Ali Quli, as he faded from the pages of history, his bid for power as ill-fated as his pursuit of love.

Chapter 6

Bloodthirsty Sword

'With the help of our bloodthirsty sword we have erased the signs of infidelity from their minds and have destroyed temples in those places and also all over Hindustan.'

– *Fathnama* proclaiming Akbar's victory over Chittorgarh

'The words of kings resemble pearls. They are not fit pendants to every ear.'

– Akbar, Happy Sayings, *Ain-i-Akbari*

The village near which the Uzbek siblings and their revolt died was renamed Fatehpur, city of victory. It is one of the pitfalls of writing history that facts – and certainly names – seldom arrange themselves for narrative convenience. There are at least three 'Muzaffars', for example, crowding the annals of Akbar's reign. There are also, it turns out, two 'Fatehpurs'. This one, a village near Allahabad that never attained the glory of the city of stone that Akbar would build near Agra, might not have been worth the confusion of mentioning at all, if the grandness of its title, thrust upon an obscure hamlet, did not suggest how important this win was for Akbar, how close Ali Quli came to plunging Akbar's realm into chaos.

Far from the Uzbeks' eastern stronghold, on the gossiping streets of Agra, writes Badauni, 'news-mongers, and especially drug and opium takers, used every day . . . to spread gloomy reports'.[1] Nizamuddin the historian was in the city at the time, an eyewitness to how 'designing men spread disastrous news'.[2] Such rumours were dangerous; they could topple thrones. Nizamuddin decided to float his own counter-story on the streets. 'Let us say', he told a friend, 'that news has come that they are bringing in the heads of [Ali Quli] and Bahadur Khan'.

Abul Fazl tells a similar tale, featuring Munim Khan, left behind as governor of Agra, and Abul Fazl's father, the scholar and theologian Shaikh Mubarak. Munim, too, was troubled by 'empty-brained and talkative' rumour-mongers, and came to Shaikh Mubarak 'for moral support'. The shaikh offered to undertake a Sufi meditation that evening and had a comforting vision; the very same, in fact, as Nizamuddin's strategic rumour.[3]

Between them, Nizamuddin and Munim won the information war, and, lucky for them, the prophesied heads did roll soon enough. Still, that Agra was gripped with such anxiety while it waited doesn't indicate widespread confidence in the stability of Akbar's rule. As one modern historian puts it, north India had grown accustomed, over centuries, to the 'ephemeral nature' of dynasties; the land was littered with 'pretenders', all with some connection, however tenuous, with dynasties that had once reigned, all of them convinced that 'the Mughal . . . [was] only a temporary occupant of the supreme seat of power, to be replaced, as fortune might direct, possibly by one of themselves, possibly by a new invader'.[4]

Besides local opposition to Mughal rule, there was, of course, the competition that the Mughals brought along with them. The Uzbeks might have been subdued, but Akbar's Timurid relatives, the troublesome Mirzas, were only waiting in the wings to take their place; as, after them, Akbar's nobility in Bengal would rise against him. Indeed, in the half-century that Akbar ruled, it was the rare year – the rare month – that did not include some discontent brewing, if not always bursting, in some part of his realm. Akbar, meanwhile, never slackened in weeding out opposition to his rule. Not for him the careful calibration of power that had characterized the political understanding of Humayun and Babur, for whom their chiefs were more allies than subordinates. Abul Fazl may write of Akbar offering his own water to Bahadur and not wanting the Uzbek killed, but there was absolutely no show of pity in how Akbar treated Bahadur's supporters. Many of these men were old companions of Humayun's and may have remembered how Humayun understood and forgave wavering allegiance. ''Tis the fortune of war', he had said once, 'such accidents . . . must happen'.

But this was the world of Akbar, and such accidents were terminal. Akbar held court in Jaunpur, meting out his punishment. The rebels were trampled by musth elephants – 'What bloodshed took place!'[5] was a chronogram for the date. One of them, Mirak Mashhadi, suffered nerve-racking torture. For five days, one after the other, he was brought before the padishah in chains, and set upon by an elephant – without orders to kill. The elephant only 'caught him in his trunk and squeezed him . . . and flung him from one side to the other', the petrified man expecting his death at any moment, yet released every day after the elephant had its play.[6]

Eventually, Mirak's sayyid ancestry saved him; he was pardoned – though his disappearance from the records indicates a subdued, even smothered, future career.

On the other hand, when the Mirzas began to try their luck on the heels of the Uzbeks' defeat ('the army was not yet rested from its labours'),[7] Akbar ignored them. It would be 'contrary to the canons of reason', writes Abul Fazl, for Akbar to deal personally with such men. It may be that Akbar realized he couldn't spend all his time racing about his realm, swatting at insurgent warlords. He needed, also, to strengthen his own position. The Hindustan he ruled had not grown an inch in the three years since the Uzbek troubles began:[8] scattered holdings in Rajasthan, some cities in Malwa, the eastern provinces he had just wrested back from the Uzbeks, and Agra, Delhi and Lahore. Akbar still needed to build the empire he would one day rule, and he needed, also, more land, more revenue, for the armies that would help him build it and the officers who would help him run it.

In short, he needed conquest.

It began with a joke. Or that, at any rate, is how Abul Fazl tells it. Akbar returned from Jaunpur to Agra and set off, almost immediately, on a hunt to Bari, a favourite hunting ground for cheetah and deer nearby.[9] Afterwards, Akbar continued to march, now heading east to Dholpur, then south to Gwalior. No one was sure where the padishah was going; certainly not Sakat Singh, a Rajput prince from the kingdom of Mewar who was travelling with him.

One day, it seems, Akbar remarked to Sakat Singh that while so many chiefs of Hindustan had acknowledged Akbar's suzerainty, the Rajput's father, the rana of Mewar, was yet to do so. The padishah 'proposed to march against him and punish him' and asked 'what service [Sakat Singh] would render in this case'. It was not the most amusing of pleasantries, but it stuck in Sakat Singh's mind. Some days later, the Rajput prince ran away. 'He did not know that it was all a joke', says Abul Fazl. Why would Akbar, after all, 'proceed against such landholders'?

'Landholder', 'landlord' – zamindar – is what the Mughal administration called the kings of Rajasthan, among whom the ranas of Mewar had long held semi-mythical status. Like Akbar and the Niru'un descendants of Alanqoa, many Rajput dynasties claimed descent from light – the greatest light of all, in fact, that of the sun. The colonial administrator, adventurer and aficionado of Rajput lore, Colonel James Tod uses this fact, among others, to trace a Central Asian lineage for the Rajputs, even proposing an etymological link between 'Sakadwipa', 'Scythia' and 'Chagatai'. The Rajput could hardly be more different, Tod continues, from 'the meek Hindu . . . worshippers of kine'. It is 'his horse, his sword, and the sun' the Rajput worships, 'and attends more to the martial song of the bard than to the litany of the Brahman'.[10] Tod has been described as 'notoriously a partisan of the Rajput princes',[11] an accusation that would, one day, be hurled at Akbar, too. Whether or not they shared Central Asian ancestry, the Mughal warlords and the Rajputs did share a 'warrior ethos'.[12] Thus, Bihari Mal's poise in the face of Akbar's excited elephant had impressed the boy at first sight. Many years into his reign, Akbar would talk of how he had grown his hair 'from sympathy with the natives of India'[13] and also, perhaps, in imitation of their martial ways.

Among these Rajput warriors, the ranas of Mewar claimed first place, and Chittorgarh was their pre-eminent bastion. This magnificent fortress, towering over the surrounding plains, had not always belonged to Mewar – it was conquered[14] in the eighth century by a Mewar king of legendary fame, Bappa Rawal. In 1303, some half a millennium after Bappa's rule – and his retirement, some say, to Khorasan[15] – Chittorgarh fell out of its rana's hands, to Alauddin Khilji. Two centuries later, the fort fell again, this time to the sultan of Gujarat – but also, in a sense, to dissensions within the Mewar dynasty.

Rana Bikramjit, who held Mewar's throne before and after the sultan of Gujarat's brief occupation, was not a popular king, being 'insolent, passionate, and vindictive, and utterly regardless of that respect which his proud nobles rigidly exacted'.[16] So detested was he – and so bereft of the qualities of his father, Rana Sanga – that his chiefs conspired to kill him, and engaged an illegitimate scion of the dynasty, one Rana Banbir Singh, to assassinate the king.

Having done the deed, Rana Banbir entered the nursery where Rana Sanga's infant son, Udai, had just fallen asleep after his meal of rice and milk. Banbir meant to kill the child and thus rid himself of any future contender for the crown of Mewar. It was the quick thinking of his nurse that saved the boy – she put her own son in Udai's bed, and gave the prince to the cook, who smuggled him away.

And yet, writes Tod, excitable chronicler of the desert kings, the nurse's terrible sacrifice was in vain. Indeed, when Banbir stormed into the nursery with his dagger, 'well had it been for Mewar had the poniard fulfilled its intention, and had the annals never recorded the name of Udai Singh in the catalogue of her princes'.

Tod's scathing indictment of the man under whose rule Chittorgarh would fall for the fourth and final time may sound hyperbolic, but the fact remains: Udai Singh fled his fort even before Akbar arrived.

On 23 October 1567, days after his twenty-fifth birthday, when Akbar pitched his tents below Chittorgarh, it seemed as if the fortress, too, had upped and left. A great rain was falling, hurled about from side to side by a 'storm of wind' as lightning flashed across the sky.[17] Of the fortress, hidden by clouds, there was no sign.

On a clear day, Chittorgarh would have been hard to miss. The hill on which it rises is the only elevation on a flat landscape. At its base, the hill's perimeter measures 5 or 6 kos, or about 20 kilometres, and the fort itself is among the largest in India, spread across 700 acres. 'Travellers do not speak of any fortress like this in the whole habitable world', wrote one Mughal historian.[18] Its immense height and thick stone walls made it almost impossible to breach, whether by cannon or rock-hurling catapults. There was water and ammunition aplenty within; Rana Udai Singh had left his army with 'provisions . . . for several years' – and destroyed the countryside so there was 'not even . . . grass in the fields' let alone grain for the Mughal army to eat.[19]

The rana had also left his stronghold in capable hands. Jaimal, the rana's commander in Chittor, passes the ultimate test of ability and worth – the admiration of his foes. Badauni calls him 'brave and chivalrous'; another Mughal historian describes him as 'infidel yet valiant'.[20] In fact, Jaimal was not always an enemy of the Mughals. When, long ago, Sharafuddin (Akbar's brother-in-law gone rogue) had embarked on his conquests in Rajasthan, he had defeated the ruler of Merta with the help of Rajputs who 'had an old quarrel with the garrison' of the fort.[21] One of these was Jaimal, who was given command of Merta after its fall. When Sharafuddin rebelled, however, Jaimal's own loyalty to Akbar became suspect. Unsure of his future in the Mughal court, the Rajput came to Mewar.[22]

Thus, now, Jaimal commanded the defence of Chittorgarh, but other contingents, from other lands, had come to Mewar's aid, too – Rathaurs led by Sahib Khan; Chauhans under Isar Das; a contingent of expert marksmen led by a musketeer called Ismail; and, finally, Chittorgarh's civilian population (people's houses rose 'several storeys over each other'[23]), tens of thousands of residents who would fight for their fort. When these defenders saw Akbar's army, so far below, men of flesh and blood peering up at rock and stone, they jeered.

Undaunted, Akbar mounted his siege, as slowly, as methodically as one of his beloved cheetahs stalking its prey. It took a full month to position his commanders and their soldiers around the base of the hill. Some of these chiefs would take it upon themselves to charge at the fort in flights of valour – much like Adham Khan had once charged at Mankot – but Akbar discouraged such showboating. It was as useless, in any case, as throwing pebbles at the sky. No matter if the Mughals fired their muskets with flair – they would hit only the air, and find themselves, or their horses, shot and killed.

To make any kind of dent in the fort's defences, Akbar needed to get much closer to it. He issued two orders. Five thousand men, 'carpenters, stone-masons, smiths, and sappers',[24] were to work night and day building a *sabat* – a 'sinuous' tunnel with roofs of hide and 'broad, mud wall[s] . . . that balls could not penetrate'[25] – through which the Mughal army might approach the fort in relative safety. Meanwhile, another group of men were to dig their way in secret to the fort walls, pack them with gunpowder and blow them apart.

The second mission was a disaster. The tunnellers did reach the walls, yes, and found not one but two adjacent spots to pack with gunpowder – 120 and 80 *maunds* of it, respectively. On 17 December, having lit two fuses for the two 'mines', Akbar's troops waited impatiently to charge their way in. The fire reached the ammunition, there was a great explosion. A whole tower with gunpowder beneath it 'was sprung into the air', and with it the soldiers fighting from its heights.[26] As the tower and its men came crashing to the ground, the Mughals charged. Chittor was breached, they were in!

But no.

Only one of the two stacks of gunpowder had caught fire; the second had a slower fuse. It caught just as the Mughal troops reached the broken tower.

If heavy rocks were propelled several kilometres by this second explosion, then what of men? Soldiers, Mughal and Rajput, 'flew about like moths in that flood of fire';[27] their burnt remains littered the surroundings. Others were crushed where they stood, by falling stone. A whole platoon of forty men, crouching in a crevice, ready to pounce, was buried alive in flying debris.

'A cry of horror', writes Badauni, 'arose from the people of Islam and from the infidels'. Another historian describes how the air was full of 'dust and smoke', how the army could only stare in shock as 'stones, corpses, and limbs fell from the air'. It was a scene of hellish despair.[28] Between 200 and 500 of Akbar's men died; the rest were 'sore distressed, and ready to succumb'.[29] Pouring salt on the Mughals' gaping wounds, the Rajputs, having escaped with fewer casualties, 'made fun of the accident'[30] from upon their bastions.

Chittor stood as solid, as unshaken, as ever.

So did Akbar. Neither his own army's wretched fear nor his enemy's piling of insult on injury would distract him. 'Patience and planning were necessary', writes Abul Fazl, and Akbar had plenty of both. Inch by inch, his sabat drew closer to his prey.

Akbar's sabat was a truly Herculean undertaking: wide enough to allow ten horsemen to march through it abreast, tall enough for a man to ride through on an elephant, holding up a spear. The tunnel was also, of course, a highly visible target. And the closer it got the more vulnerable it became. Building the sabat was lethal work, in fact, and Akbar paid for it accordingly: 'silver and gold were reckoned at the rate of earth', writes Abul Fazl; or, he might have added, of life. Between 100 and 200 men would die every day, building the tunnel, and even in death they would serve Akbar's single-minded vision of conquest, their bodies stuffed into the walls of their sabat, like bricks.

Whatever the cost, Akbar had decided that a sabat was 'the best mode of capturing a fortress'. Two commanders, Todar Mal and Qasim Khan, were deputed to supervise its construction, and Akbar himself inspected its progress regularly: 'frequently' he rode through its macabre walls, climbed upon its roof and fired at the fort's defenders.[31] It was Akbar and his musket on his sabat that managed to kill Chittor's star shooter, Ismail, leader of the fort's artillery corps and a menace to the Mughal troops.[32] And finally, one night, it was Akbar and his musket on his sabat that won Chittor.

It was the last week of February, four months after Akbar arrived at Chittorgarh in a storm. Its defenders and the Mughal troops remained equally well matched, equally unrelenting. The night before, every single Mughal contingent surrounding the fort had charged upon it simultaneously. The fighting had raged all night and day, and now on the second night of continuous battle, the sabat had snaked its way close enough to the fort for Akbar's soldiers to breach one of its walls.

Akbar was perched on top of his tunnel, musket in hand, watching the stone from the broken wall fall.

Jaimal's soldiers gathered at the site of the damage, fending off Mughal attacks and filling the breach with 'muslin, cotton, wood and oil',[33] intending to erect a wall of fire to replace the stone. A man wearing a breastplate called '*hazaar-mikhi*', spiked with 1000 nails and reserved for chiefs,[34] strode among the Rajputs. Every so often, fire or fusillade would light up the bastion.[35]

At each burst of light, Akbar aimed his musket. 'A mortar brazen-bodied, dragon-faced',[36] a poet would write of it. Its weight would have been familiar in Akbar's hand; it was his favourite gun[37] and he had named it Sangram. War.

Sangram, writes one admiring historian, was 'deadly as the darts of fate', and Akbar's aim was true. He fired, then turned to the two men by his side, Shajaat Khan and Bhagwant Das (brother of Akbar's wife, Harkha Bai). He had felt the 'pleasure and lightness of hand' that he often experienced when he knew his shot had struck home. He knew that 'he had hit the man'.[38]

A little later, the men guarding the breach disappeared. They had left kindling in the gaps unlit; instead, the Mughals noticed small fires coming alight deep within the fort. It was Bhagwant Das who told them what the flames signified. Jauhar. The Rajputs were burning their wives and mothers and daughters alive and preparing for their very last fight.

The man with the spiked breastplate, his form lit by gunfire, shot down by Sangram, was none other than Jaimal, commander-in-chief of Chittorgarh. When Jaimal fell, the fortress fell with him. Some 8000 Rajputs – Sisodiyas,

Rathaurs, Chauhans – lit funeral pyres, burned 300 women and prepared themselves to die.

'At the white dawn', the Mughal army poured into the fort – along with many war elephants, whose feats, often enough, get more space than those of soldiers in Akbar's chronicles.[39] One Jangiya, for example, had his trunk cut off by a Rajput's blade, which 'makes life difficult', as Abul Fazl admits. Still, Jangiya killed another fifteen men, on top of the thirty he had already slain, before he died. Another, Madhukar, seems to have killed the Chauhan chief, Isar Das, as he grabbed the animal by a tusk and stabbed him with his dagger.

Akbar rode 'an elephant, majestic as heaven', through the bloodied streets of Chittor, watching its final battle.[40] 'In every street and lane and bazar', one historian writes, 'there was desperate fighting'.[41] By the end of the day, all the Rajput soldiers had fallen to Mughal shafts, blades and spears, or taken their own lives, preferring death to disgrace.

Among the scenes that Akbar would recall, years later, was that of an anonymous Mughal soldier refusing his friend's help in hand-to-hand combat with a Rajput, declaring that it was against 'the rules of chivalry and courage' to offer such aid. Later, the padishah looked for the 'brave . . . man', but he was nowhere to be found – perhaps he was an apparition, Abul Fazl muses, come 'to help' the emperor.

How he was meant to help is not clear, for Akbar did not follow his example of chivalry in his victory. In fact, he ordered a massacre.

One of the many legends of Mewar that James Tod tells with gusto is that of the Goddess of Chittorgarh. The Goddess, he writes, had long stipulated the blood of kings in exchange for her presence in the fort. Thus, twelve kings gave their lives against Alauddin Khilji, and Chittorgarh eventually returned to Mewar. This time, however, 'no regal victim appeared to appease the Cybele of Chitor, and . . . retain its "*kunguras*" [battlements] as her coronet. She fell!' – Chittorgarh, that is – and 'the charm was broken'.

Udai Singh was far away and Jaimal was dead. Chittor's 8000 soldiers had perished to a man and the Goddess had withdrawn her blessing. But still, Chittorgarh held one last group of defenders, who were now completely unprotected.

Some 40,000 civilians had 'shown great zeal' in fighting for the fortress. In the long and gory hours after Chittor fell, three-fourths of them were killed – 30,000 in all – until there was 'no house or lane, or passage where there were not heaps of dead'. Only one Mughal soldier of note lost his life.[42]

In the extensive, sometimes exhausting, annals of Akbar's conquests, the bloodiness – and bloody-mindedness – of Chittorgarh is exceptional. Why would Akbar, whose policies in Rajasthan would be defined by co-option, not decimation, order such a massacre? Iqtidar Alam Khan traces the origins of the padishah's sudden vindictiveness to the recently concluded Uzbek revolt and the changing demographic of Akbar's nobility.

'It is interesting', he writes, 'that soon after the suppression of the Uzbek rebellion Akbar's attitude towards the Rajputs changed radically'.[43] He had beaten down the Uzbeks without mercy, but the Mirzas had sprung to action immediately after. Both groups had Central Asian roots, and Central Asian noblemen still comprised a large proportion of Akbar's court. Akbar, meanwhile, had begun to induct a new and diverse nobility into his service. These 'upstarts',[44] whom Munim and Ali Quli might have grumbled about to each other, included not just non-Chagatais and non-Timurids, but also non–Central Asians, non-Persians and non-Muslims. As Iqtidar Alam Khan demonstrates, two important new groups of people began to populate Akbar's court from about 1560 onwards (the year, perhaps coincidentally, of Bairam's fall). The first were 'Indian Muslims', including 'Shaikhzadas', descendants of earlier Muslim immigrants to Hindustan, or of converts.[45] The second, of course, were Rajputs.

In 1564, a year after he married Harkha Bai and some three years before the siege of Chittorgarh, Akbar had abolished the *jizya*. Translated rather inscrutably as 'poll tax', the jizya becomes more controversial, indeed incendiary, the further it recedes into the past. Simply put, it was a tax collected by Muslim rulers from their non-Muslim subjects that has been variously understood and interpreted – from wilful humiliation of non-believers, on the one hand, to a more dispassionate method by which non-Muslim subjects would have to pay the equivalent of zakat, the annual charity that is part of the Islamic faith.

Banning the jizya would have pleased Akbar's new Rajput commanders, and that is quite likely why he did it. Now, it seems, Akbar was making 'efforts at placating orthodox Muslim sentiments'.[46] Thus, Iqtidar Alam Khan continues, the padishah 'adopted a vigorous policy to reduce [Rajputs] into submission by force' – such as the gratuitous bloodshed at Chittorgarh. As if to prove Khan's point, Akbar issued an aggressive *fathnama*, a proclamation of victory, afterwards, 'full of intolerant professions and sentiments', declaring the 'fall of Chittor . . . as the victory of Islam over infidels'.[47]

Abul Fazl, writing many long years after the fall of the fortress, when any such policy of performative aggression against Rajput – or non-Muslim – subjects had fallen by the wayside, does not breathe a word of this fathnama. Instead, he removes the sting of sectarian slaughter from the tale by turning Chittorgarh's civilian population into a battle force. Thus, Akbar's historian writes of how, when Alauddin Khilji took the fort, he had left its inhabitants unharmed, but only because they had 'not engaged in fighting'. This time, the citizens had fought Akbar; their subsequent 'excuses . . . were of no avail', so they were killed.

The butchery went on from dawn to noon. Only Chittor's musketeers escaped it: pretending to be Mughal soldiers, tying up their families and chivvying them along like prisoners of war, they slipped out in plain sight of the Mughal army, as audaciously as they had shot at them these past four months. Akbar, meanwhile, did not linger to savour his victory. Only three days later, disappointed, perhaps, at having been cheated of his revenge on the marksmen who had plagued him, Akbar left Chittorgarh and set off on his first-ever pilgrimage of thanks to the dargah of Moinuddin Chishti in Ajmer.[48]

He went on foot. It was a vow he had made, in the hope of divine blessing for his campaign, but walking was also one of Akbar's many passions. Some years before, after a hunt in Mathura, he declared he would walk back to Agra. His unhappy courtiers had little choice except to stumble along behind their king as he strode the full 60 kilometres back home. None but three men, according to Abul Fazl, 'were able to keep pace with him'. Now, on 28 February 1568, as Akbar set off 'stage by stage over the burning desert-sands' his hapless nobility and harem were constrained, once again, to 'do as he did'. Chittorgarh to Ajmer was no 60-kilometre stroll, however. At some point, his walking companions seem to have gathered their flagging energies to sabotage their padishah's plan. One-third of the way through their journey, in Mandal, an envoy of Akbar's who had gone ahead to apprise the Chishtis of his arrival, returned with some ascetics from the dargah. Shaikh Moinuddin himself had come to them in a dream, said the fakirs, urging them to dissuade Akbar from coming, for 'If he knew the amount of his own spirituality he would not bestow a glance on me . . .'

Immediately, Akbar decided to ride the rest of the way. Not even Chishti saints from heaven could dissuade the padishah once he'd made up his mind, but it might yet be possible for earthly mortals to manipulate his will – whether by threatening rebellion or, more simply, flattery.

From Abul Fazl and Badauni onwards, Akbar's biographers have tended to be of two broad types: those who write with breathless awe and those who write with scorn. These reactions are not always triggered by the same causes – if Abul Fazl finds in Akbar a perfection of human attributes, a colonial historian called G. B. Malleson admires the unifying imperative that guided Akbar's policies. If Badauni railed against Akbar's religious experiments, Vincent A. Smith is provoked by his appetite for conquest.[49]

It is true that Akbar brought the same obsession to expanding his realm as he did to any of his passions, whether elephants or theology. So unflagging was his energy for conquest, in fact, that in the later years of his rule it wasn't uncommon for his generals to try and slip out of yet another campaign, or meekly petition their padishah to abandon the idea of yet another march far away from home. Akbar, himself, wasn't shy about his hunger for territory. 'A monarch should be ever intent on conquest', he would say, 'otherwise his neighbours rise in arms against him'[50] – passing lightly over the fact that the aggressive neighbour was often him.

Thus, the year after the collapse of Chittorgarh, Akbar marched on Ranthambore, held by Rai Surjan Hada, king of Bundi, and cousin of the recently defeated Rana Udai Singh of Mewar. Twice already, in the fourth year of his reign and then in the thirteenth, Akbar's troops had made failed attempts at this hilltop fort. This time, in February 1569, Akbar pitched his own tent at its feet.

It was said of Ranthambore, built upon a craggy mountaintop, protected by surrounding hills, that 'all other forts are naked, while this is mail-clad'. Let alone conquerors, even 'the bird of thought' hesitated to soar upon it.[51] Akbar had it writhing in his talons in six weeks.

His siege lasted through the month of Ramzan; his bombardments escalating until, on the day before the festival of Eid-al-Fitr, Akbar issued an ultimatum. Rai Surjan Hada could either submit on Eid or fall with his fortress. Much to the dismay of Rajput bards like Nainsi[52] – who writes that Akbar commissioned a statue of the rai shaped like a dog – Rai Surjan sent his sons to Akbar's camp and followed a few days later himself to give up the gold and silver keys of Ranthambore.

It was not unknown, and certainly no unmitigated disgrace, for a Rajput to leave his fort and live to fight another day. As Cynthia Talbot writes, there was even a term for it: 'going through the door of dharma' – leaving by a side-gate, that is. Besides, alternative versions of the surrender, as told in the *Surjancharita*, for example, restore much of the rai's dignity. In this narrative poem, Rai Surjan is shown fighting single-handed against a near-divine Akbar who has conquered every other inch of the world. And even so, the story goes, Ranthambore only falls through diplomatic manoeuvring; it does not surrender to force.[53]

James Tod, Rajput-manqué, tells a similar tale. According to him, Kunwar Man Singh, Harkha Bai's nineteen-year-old nephew, went to Ranthambore to negotiate with Rai Surjan. The two Rajput royals sat and conversed, while Man Singh's mace-bearer stood behind him, quiet and unnoticed. As the negotiations dragged on, Rai Surjan's uncle's eyes drifted to Man Singh's attendant.

The uncle sprang up – this was no mace-bearer, it was Akbar! The elder Rajput took the mace from the young king's hands and offered him a cushion. Unfazed, Akbar sat down and said, 'Well, Rao Soorjun, what is to be done?'[54]

Rai Surjan was king of Bundi and pledged allegiance, like many kings of Rajasthan, to the rana of Mewar, in this case his cousin, in whose name, in fact, Surjan held Ranthambore. Akbar's proposal was that Rai Surjan transfer his allegiance from Mewar to the Mughal; in return, he would be made an honoured commander in Akbar's court, with fifty-two districts to rule as he would and the liberty to name his terms.

The idea would not have sounded foreign to Rajput ears. It was an established tradition of Rajput lords to have dependent clients called 'chakars'. The term, writes Norman Ziegler, 'carries the general meaning of servant, but in Marwari usage, designates a "military retainer", one who held rights over villages on the condition of provision of arms to a superior, or who was included as a member of his patron's personal household'.[55] These were essentially the terms, if on a grander scale, that Rai Surjan was being asked to consider.

Eventually, the rai agreed, though with conditions. The first of these, writes Tod, was that no bridal procession would ever leave Bundi for Akbar's harem. The authenticity of this treaty is disputed, but if, indeed, the king of Bundi insisted on a frosty barrier between his political alliance and the implied honour of his blood, Akbar seems to have shrugged it off. Alauddin Khilji, the thirteenth-century emperor with whom Abul Fazl often compares Akbar's achievements, had taken a whole year to break Ranthambore 'with great difficulty';[56] Akbar had done it in just over a month. In the spring of 1569, Akbar rode into the grand fortress and raised his banners from its bastions.

Cries of 'Allah-u-Akbar' echoed across the hilltops, writes Abul Fazl, and they carried their message far across the desert land. First Chittorgarh, now Ranthambore had fallen. The great Rajput clans crumbled in their wake, one by one. Five hundred kilometres east of Ranthambore, Raja Ram Chand of Panna had only to hear of Surjan's surrender to send Akbar the keys of his own fort, the mighty Kalinjar. The last man who tried to breach Kalinjar's thick walls had perished in the attempt – Sher Shah Suri was shot through with shrapnel and suffocated from his own mine, trying to blast his way in. Akbar didn't so much as step in its direction.

Kalinjar's keys arrived in August 1569; by the winter of the next year, Akbar had also received princesses from Bikaner and Jaisalmer, as well as homage from Marwar. Chandrasen, whose father, Maldeo, had once hunted Humayun across a burning desert, had submitted to Humayun's son.[57]

To gain the fealty, one after the other, of these Rajput chiefs was Akbar's first truly great achievement. Without it – without the men who now filled his court and expanded his armies – Akbar's empire might never have stretched as far nor settled as deep as it did. It wasn't just the military might they gave him, nor the political legitimacy. Rajasthan was also economically vital to the health of any Hindustani empire, allowing, as it did, trade between the bustling ports of Gujarat and the north Indian plains.[58]

Abul Fazl makes a none-too-subtle allusion to this at the very beginning of the *Akbarnama*, when expanding on one of the several horoscopes made for the padishah. Not Maulana Chand's jottings, which made Humayun dance in private, but a horoscope cast by a Persian scholar called Amir Fathullah Shirazi, three decades into Akbar's reign. Naturally, then, Amir Fathullah's predictions carry more than a hint of hindsight, as, for example, in his calculations that show how Humayun will 'depart to the eternal city' when his son reaches 'the years of discretion'. It is Fathullah's horoscope, too, that has Akbar marrying women from 'the ruling families of India'.[59]

That is to say: whether any holders of 'orthodox Muslim sentiments' liked it or not, Akbar was joined to the Rajputs by the stars. And now, by blood: in the very month that Kalinjar's keys arrived in his court, Akbar also received the joyful news of the birth of his first son, born to his first Rajput queen – the prince he named Salim.

Chapter 7
Legend

"'Tis not the chain of insanity on the neck of the afflicted Majnun
Love hath laid a loving hand on his neck.'
 — A verse by Akbar, quoted in the *Akbarnama*

Akbar was a few weeks short of twenty-seven years old when Salim was born, in August 1569. A little late in the day, perhaps, for an emperor of fourteen years' standing to produce his first child and heir.

There had been children born or conceived over the years. Hasan and Husain who died in infancy five years previously, and others too, perhaps. Abul Fazl mentions 'various stories'[1] circulating in the city, and a later visitor to Akbar's court, the Jesuit Father Monserrate, relates one of them. Just before Akbar left on his first campaign against Ali Quli, in 1565, the padishah had given orders for the old, brick-built citadel in Agra to be torn down – it had 'become ruinous', writes Nizamuddin[2] – and replaced by a grand monument of red stone. Its walls, 2.5 metres thick, were to rise 50 sheer metres into the air, towering, as they do even today, over visitors squinting up at their heights from the streets below. As this grand fortress was being built – it took eight years, at least, to complete – a rumour spread that it was 'overrun with ghosts, which rushed to and fro' destroying the emperor's belongings, terrifying his harem, and murdering his newborn children.[3]

It wasn't enough anymore for God to offer his opinions on Akbar's policies via the emperor's elephant rides; now, Akbar needed His active aid. A child is the only thing, according to Abul Fazl, that Akbar ever prayed for,[4] and he did it in his usual comprehensive style, rallying 'dervishes, ascetics and theologians' to his cause, as if rousing soldiers to battle. Finally, and famously, one of them succeeded in his plea – Shaikh Salim of the same Chishti order as Ajmer's Moinuddin. As the Rajput kingdoms had fallen, so

135

now sons were born 'one after another': Salim in 1569, Murad the year after, and Daniyal in 1572.

In gratitude, as it is often said, Akbar ordered his best-known architectural project: a whole new city in the small village outside Agra where Shaikh Salim lived, a grand affair of 'great size and magnificent appearance'[5] – Fatehpur. Father Monserrate lived in Fatehpur for several months and

Figure 7.1   Circumcision festivities for Akbar's three sons, with the newly built city of Fatehpur Sikri in the background. Women in Chagatai Turkish dress dance in celebration and gold is distributed to the poor. Attributed to Dharam Das, c. 1602–03. *Source*: The Cleveland Museum of Art, Public domain.

describes it as a city of spectacle and riches: with its 'Circus [for] elephant fight[s], gladiatorial displays' and polo matches; with its massive reservoir, cooling the breeze that blew over its stone palaces; with its baths and great bazaar, 'filled with an astonishing quantity of every description of merchandise, and with countless people' – and, 'overlooking the whole city', Akbar's large and 'very beautiful' audience hall.

A decade or so before Monserrate arrived, as Akbar supervised the building of his city of victory – a painting shows him talking to a mason while all around men cut stone, saw wood, dig the ground[6] – the emperor had won, once again.

But also, it may be that he was getting bored.

The beginning of Akbar's seventeenth year as padishah (1572–73) includes an odd bit of news. Muzaffar Khan, who, along with Todar Mal, had been trying these past years to bring some coherence to Akbar's finances and check 'embezzlement [by] the slaves of gold',[7] had become the bane of Akbar's nobility. A popular chronogram for the date of his promotion to vizier was '*zaalim*', tyrant.[8] Now, it seems, Muzaffar Khan had fallen foul of the emperor, too. It was not a lapse in financial probity,[9] however, that had upset Akbar but lack of grace when losing at ludo.

Chaupar, or *parcheesi*, an early and more complex form of this dice game, was Akbar's latest obsession. He played it 'with keenness',[10] writes Abul Fazl, which is an understatement. Akbar's chaupar parties were almost as deranged as his musth elephant rides. They could go on for months – up to 200 players compelled to move from game to game, and no one allowed to go home.[11] If Muzaffar Khan 'behaved in a savage . . . manner'[12] during one of these marathons, it is hardly surprising – but the Mughal court was no longer the kind of place in which a crochety Tardi Beg, for example, could grumble freely. Once, Akbar may have greeted a visiting ambassador with louche casualness; he may have run about the roof of his old Agra fort bare-headed for all to see – but that old fort was long gone, and of that old Akbar, too, little trace remained.

This new padishah took protocol – particularly the protocol of deference – very seriously. The previous year, a chieftain who came drunk to court was tied to a horse's tail and paraded in public. Now, Muzaffar Khan was banished on the Haj.

Shortly afterwards, however – and to the great relief, no doubt, of his exhausted nobility – Chenghis Khan of Gujarat died, and Akbar found a new focus for his energies.

Chenghis Khan was not the king of Gujarat. Gujarat had not had a king possessed of any extensive command or worth for some decades. Its last notable ruler, Sultan Bahadur of the Muzaffarid dynasty, died during Humayun's first innings in Hindustan – drowned, possibly killed, while escaping a Portuguese ship, having signed the Treaty of Bassein with the European merchant-conquerors some years previously, by which they gained, among other things, an archipelago of seven islands on India's western coast. Sultan Bahadur's successors have no such historical relevance except in that they were dominated, increasingly, by their nobility. Thus, before Akbar turned his eyes upon it, Gujarat was parcelled out among many chiefs, ruling its various cities and ports in watchful alliance.

Chenghis Khan held some of its richest cities, including Surat and its busy port; Sher Khan Fuladi held Patan, where Bairam Khan had been killed; Sayyid Hamid and Amin Khan Ghori held other regions of north-western Gujarat; and one Itimad Khan, most clever of all, held Ahmedabad, Cambay and a boy named Nannu, scion of the Muzaffarid dynasty. Besides these rulers, some of Akbar's disaffected nobility, too, had ambitions in Gujarat. Most prominently, the Mirzas had allied with Chenghis Khan against Itimad Khan of Ahmedabad and briefly ruled Broach as reward.

Chenghis Khan's demise upset whatever understanding these various ambitious men had had between themselves. Almost immediately, it seems, Sher Khan Fuladi lured young Nannu to himself in Patan and attacked Itimad Khan in Ahmedabad. The Mirzas, whose relations with Chenghis Khan had soured, forcing them to return to Akbar's realm, if not to his fold, now hurried back to grab what they could in Gujarat – and managed to take Champaner and Surat. Meanwhile, for reasons best known to him, Itimad Khan approached the Mirzas – who had so recently fought against him – for an alliance against Sher Khan Fuladi. At this, writes Abul Fazl, 'the market for contention became brisk' – not least because the slippery Mirzas chose to ally with Fuladi instead.

For Akbar – and for his chronicler – the chaos was all to the good. As he had written of Akbar bringing justice to Baz Bahadur's Malwa, so Abul Fazl now muses on how the padishah's 'first thought' when conquering countries was 'to inquire into and sympathise with the condition of the oppressed' – a noble ambition that God, it seems, was more than willing to encourage, for 'He makes a country empty of just rulers', thus giving Akbar the perfect excuse to swoop in.[13]

Who knows, perhaps God was loading the dice in Akbar's favour. In the late summer of 1572, as Gujarat careened in turmoil and Akbar marched west, news arrived that Sultan Sulaiman Karrani of Bengal had died. Not one but two fronts had opened to Akbar, not one but two busy coasts might now be his, and the sun's rays might rise and fall, uninterrupted, across his domain.

At some point in the voluminous *Akbarnama*, Abul Fazl lists the eight principles of world rule. The first is good luck, and Akbar knew not to waste such providential opportunities. He sent word to Munim Khan, stationed in

Jaunpur since the Uzbeks' defeat, to begin an onslaught upon Bengal; himself, the padishah continued west.

His very approach, it seems, scattered Gujarat's warring nobility. Fuladi, besieging Itimad Khan in Ahmedabad with help from the Mirzas, fled at news of Akbar's approach, abandoning both the siege and Nannu, claimant to the Muzaffarid throne, who was found hiding in a wheat field. Itimad Khan, who had already written to Akbar asking for help against his besiegers, came to prostrate himself before his new lord.[14] One by one, the nobility of Gujarat followed, and Akbar, 'mounted in his glory on an elephant', rode upon Ahmedabad, chatting amiably with his new courtiers.[15]

It would have been hard for any man not to start believing in his own destiny.

Among the men who sent their submissions to Akbar during his initial, rather leisurely invasion of Gujarat, was Ibrahim Husain, the best known and most ambitious – and reviled – of the Mirzas, who now enter to play their part in Akbar's story.

The Mirzas, writes one modern historian, were 'troublesome in their own time, and perplexing to posterity'.[16] Indeed, the effort of telling them apart seems hardly worthwhile, the whole lot of them having been painted with the broadest possible brush as the vilest possible traitors to two generations of Mughal emperors.

And yet, the Mirzas had as much claim to imperial destiny as Babur's family. Like Babur and his sons they were descended from Timur, yes, but also, more recently, from another glorious king, Sultan Husain Baiqara of Herat, who had presided over a 'golden age of art, literature, and historical writing'[17] about a century ago. The sultan's heirs in Hindustan had never ceased to chafe, it seems, at a fate that made them subservient to Babur's offspring.

'This was an old failing in the family', writes a historian from the time.[18] Indeed, it was a Mirza who was on guard duty when Sher Shah Suri ambushed the Mughal troops in Chausa – one of Humayun's worst military defeats. A year later, it was a group of brazen Mirzas who switched sides at Kannauj, abandoning Humayun to his second humiliating debacle at the Suri king's hands. And it was the Mirzas, forgiven by Humayun and settled in a comfortable fief by his son, who joined the Uzbek revolt against Akbar with such alacrity.

As for this particular Mirza, Ibrahim Husain who now sent his proposal of peace to Akbar in Ahmedabad – he had even more reason to imagine himself in Akbar's place. Ibrahim was married to Gulrukh Begum, Akbar's cousin and daughter of his uncle Kamran. There is no reason why Ibrahim and Gulrukh might not have wanted to restore the legacy of Humayun's less fortunate brother; no reason why they should have thought that coveting the Hindustani throne was a betrayal of Akbar and not, in fact, a legitimate claim of their own. And there was no reason, therefore, for Akbar to repeat his father's mistakes: he would not hope for loyalty from Ibrahim; he would hunt for his head, instead.

The Mirza's offer of peace was rejected.

Akbar's conquest of Gujarat was equally, even symbiotically, his defeat of the Mirzas, and both victories are significant in many ways. Economically and culturally, the ports of Gujarat opened up whole new vistas for Akbar's empire, in terms of trade and interaction with Europe and the Middle East. Politically, it not only rid Akbar of an endlessly troublesome faction in the family but also strengthened his bond with his Kachhwaha relatives. Eight of this Rajput clan came to Gujarat with Akbar, and many distinguished themselves.[19]

It was also now, at the beginning of his Gujarat campaign, that Akbar turned thirty. He was no longer the boy who put on a crown in the fields of Punjab, inconsolable at the loss of his father and uncertain where his future led. He was no longer, for that matter, the adolescent chafing at the concern and control of his guardians. He had spent over half his life on a throne. He helmed an empire that he was expanding all the way from the Ganga's waters to the Arabian Sea. Always prodigiously strong – there is a record of him punching a man unconscious at thirty-eight as he felled Adham Khan at twenty – Akbar would have been in peak physical condition in Gujarat.

And yet, it is also at about this time that Akbar shows his first fear of his own weakness. Only two years before he set off for Gujarat, Akbar was hunting wild asses in Punjab. The padishah shot thirteen asses in all – each time he got one, the herd ran further away, and Akbar followed. Caught in the chase, the hunter lost track of his companions and of his own thirst, until he found himself all alone, his throat so parched that he could not speak, let alone call out for help. It was now, Abul Fazl writes, that Akbar realized he should 'be more careful in guarding' himself.

The event was important enough, clearly, to deserve a record, and even a painting. In it, Akbar sits upon a cushion under a tree, his matchlock slung on one shoulder, his head tilted at a tired angle. His companions have found him: they are all delighted smiles, one of them rushes forward with a jug of cool water. But Akbar seems not even to see them. He is in a trance, it seems.[20]

What was it that shook Akbar so about being vulnerable and alone – shook him almost into an epiphany, as it appears from his faraway, meditative pose? Perhaps, alone as he had only been once before when he galloped away on the wild Hayran, Akbar realized how powerful he had become – and how powerless he remained, as weak as any man in the face of simple thirst.

This paradox, of an increasingly powerful man shaken by the realization of his innate fragility, would become a propelling force of Akbar's destiny; driving him now, in Gujarat, to the cusp of legend and the brink of insanity.

Surely there is something manic, for example, about Akbar's pursuit of Mirza Ibrahim.

It began as a relatively unhurried march towards Broach, where the Mirza had fled. Akbar even stopped in Cambay en route for his first-ever sight of the sea. The padishah had reached Baroda when he heard that Ibrahim had left Broach and passed within a few kilometres of the imperial camp.

Akbar was incensed at the Mirza's temerity. How dare he come so close to Akbar's army, like a wild ass scampering past a pride of lions, and presume they wouldn't catch him? Akbar leapt on a horse and galloped after Ibrahim that very night.

Badauni says he took only four men with him, leaving word for reinforcements to follow; Abul Fazl says ten, each of whom was allowed no more than two accompanying soldiers. At any rate, it was a small party – much smaller than Ibrahim's 1000 troops[21] – and when, the following day at dusk, they reached the outskirts of a small town called Sarnal, where Ibrahim had camped for the night, it was quite rational if 'the Emperor's followers endeavoured to conceal themselves'.[22]

Their lord, however, was intent on charging in. He would not wait for reinforcements, nor even for darkness to disguise the approach of their small number – only forty-odd men, writes Abul Fazl. A night attack, he declared, was 'a form of deception and fraud'. Instead, standing upon a low hill above Sarnal, Akbar began to put on his armour.

Just then, a gallop of horses: reinforcements had arrived! But Akbar would not have them. 'We'll not suffer them to share in the fight with us.'[23]

Why? They were late, he said.

The unfortunate platoon – which included Raja Bhagwant Das and, for his first prominent role in Mughal chronicles, a young Man Singh – had been on their way to Surat when Akbar recalled them; they had travelled a longer distance than Akbar to get here and arrived not too far behind their emperor. But no. Akbar denounced their delay; if they had so little appetite for battle, why should they have any part in it? The men had to beg to be allowed to fight.

Finally, Akbar relented, and as he rode down the hill with his 200 men, his temper improved. When Man Singh asked to form a vanguard, Akbar agreed laughingly: 'What force have we that we should make a division[?] Today we are all one.'[24]

What sort of battlefield did they have, for that matter? The ground leading to Sarnal was no great plain like Panipat's, allowing for grand clashes of musket and sword. Rather, it was 'broken ground', littered with thorny desert plants.[25] The Mughal horses, wearing armour like their riders and trained to make daredevil charges upon the enemy, were forced, instead, to pick their way through the bushes of thorn with effete caution. It was this infuriatingly slow advance, presumably, that gave Ibrahim time to prepare for the onslaught. The Mirza and his men littered Sarnal's already narrow lanes with their baggage; this, along with a continuing abundance of thorny plants within, scattered Akbar's men – not more than two could ride abreast. Riding through the clutter, with enemies around every corner, many of the Mughal troops died – including Bhagwant Das's brother, 'a very brave young man'[26] called Bhupat.

Akbar might have been reckless and short-tempered, but he wasn't a coward. Having ordered his men into this shambolic onslaught, he led them from the front. With Bhagwant Das by his side, Akbar was riding a bay horse through the town's narrow lanes, seeking Ibrahim, when three horsemen attacked – one the Rajput wounded with a well-aimed spear; the other two advanced on Akbar, who 'received them so valiantly', writes Badauni, 'that they were obliged to make off '.

Surely, there was more than physical strength to this valour; something more than flattery in the 'glory of the Divine radiance' of which Abul Fazl writes, the force of which 'affrighted' Akbar's opponents. He only had 200 men with him, after all, dispersed and distressed. Ibrahim had 1000. The battle was not of force alone, but of will: the Mirza did not continue a fight he might have won; he fled from Sarnal's back gates. The Mughals chased after him until, as night fell 'darker than . . . [his] fate',[27] Akbar recalled his men and declared his triumph.

The rest of Akbar's Gujarat campaign was relatively sedate, as if the fury of his chase after Ibrahim had given it enough momentum to coast on to victory. The Mirzas, meanwhile, regrouped at a safe distance: Ibrahim, his brother Muhammad Husain and their relative Shah Mirza convened in Idar, far to the north. Here, having never managed to sustain an alliance, whether with the Uzbeks or any Gujarati chiefs, the three men fell out with each other, too.[28] Ibrahim decided to march alone upon Agra, no less; while the other two resumed plotting with the Fuladi chiefs of Gujarat.

Akbar, meanwhile, arrived in the port city of Surat, 'thronged with merchants, and . . . full of ships'.[29] The city – with Mirza Ibrahim's wife and children among its population – was held by Ibrahim's men, and Akbar's troops had been camped outside the Surat fort for some time. 'Every hole big enough for a mouse was closed', writes Nizamuddin. Even so, Ibrahim's wife, Kamran's daughter Gulrukh, evidently possessed something of her father's daredevilry. She had escaped Surat with her two small children, a boy and a girl, and fled to the Deccan, pursued by imperial soldiers whom 'that wise woman . . . got away from'.[30]

One of the children, Gulrukh's two-year-old daughter, was captured on the way and brought back to Surat, and to Akbar, who had reached the harbour city. With her was another, less innocent captive – that old rebel Sharafuddin. Ever since his failed insurrection, Sharafuddin, once Akbar's brother-in-law, had been lurking on the borders of Akbar's expanding realm. He had attempted alliances with Chenghis Khan, with the Mirzas, even with the Deccani kingdom of Khandesh – until he fell into the hands of the chieftain of Baglana, a buffer zone between Gujarat and Khandesh, whose ruler had adopted the wise policy of siding with 'whichever of the two is the stronger'.[31] Now, with a third and vastly more powerful force at his door, Baglana's lord offered Akbar his two bargaining chips: Sharafuddin and the child princess.[32]

Sharafuddin was put in chains, and the young girl in Akbar's harem, which wasn't far away. It was routine for the padishah's family to travel with his army; now, the women's tents were pitched by a tank called Gopi Talao, shielded from the firing from Surat's walls by a cover of trees and undulating land. Akbar's first Rajput queen, Harkha Bai, was among them with her son Salim, who now had two brothers. One was Murad, nicknamed 'Pahadi' because he was born upon a hill. Salim and Murad were about three and two years old, respectively – as good an age as any, it seems, to march into their first conquest. Only Daniyal, still an infant, was left behind: he was born in Ajmer to an unnamed mother during the march to Gujarat, and left in the care of Harkha Bai's mother, the queen of Amber. Akbar's own tent, meanwhile, was pitched much closer to the action: cannonballs often landed near it, says Abul Fazl. But what was a little exploding ammunition to the padishah's brave heart?

Akbar's strength and stamina were reaching epic proportions. Strength, stamina – and courage, their alloy – were, of course, the building blocks of a man's reputation in this age; even more so in the court of a conquering monarch. During the siege of Surat, for example, one of Akbar's commanders was wounded in a reckless attack he insisted on making because he had missed Sarnal, that 'manhood-testing place'.[33]

Stories of valour – and attempted valour, usually accompanied by drink – abound in the chronicles. Once, for example, 200 of Humayun's soldiers had charged upon 4000 enemy troops, no less, in a drunken frenzy – and managed to scare them away. Another time, a party of Humayun's clerks and librarians were celebrating his conquest of Champaner when they were inspired by the *Zafarnama*, Timur's biography, recalled through a thick haze of alcohol, to march upon the Deccan then and there.

After Surat fell – it took a little over six weeks – Akbar and his men were enjoying a similar symposium, it seems, regaling each other with tales of martial daring. The talk turned to which of the clans in the imperial army was most brave. Akbar was spoilt for choice in this regard. If the Chagatai descendants of Chinghis Khan were not to be sneezed at, nor were Indian Muslim warriors like the Sayyids of Barha, who would help Akbar rule Gujarat and be described, one day, as the 'bulwark'[34] of his empire. And, of course, there were the Rajputs.

The Rajput's sense of honour as derived from courage in combat held great appeal for the Central Asian warriors with whom they battled and mingled, particularly the Central Asian warrior who was now their emperor. Of one particular Rajput clan in Gujarat, Abul Fazl writes admiringly that they would dismount from their horses mid-battle, lest the horse – or worse, its rider – lose courage and escape at a gallop. On foot, the soldiers had no choice but to meet their fate. In Gujarat, too, the Kachhwaha Rajputs, Akbar's in-laws, had distinguished themselves: at least three of them fought in the absurdly perilous battle of Sarnal, and one of them died in it.

It may have been a Kachhwaha who began to tell the party of a Rajput custom by which two men would run at a *barchha*, a spear with two prongs, so that the blades 'would transfix them and come out at their backs'. Abul Fazl doesn't explain why two men would choose to disembowel themselves in this way – if, as one translation suggests, it was to resolve disputes, it was both drastic and pointless – and Akbar didn't care to ask. Instead, he leapt to his feet, put the 'hilt of his sword against a wall and held the other end near his regal belly'.[35]

A hush fell upon the party – what was Akbar doing? Was it that veil of his again, wonders Abul Fazl, hiding his true intentions; or was he 'weary of . . . worldly success'?[36] Was he, as other, less devoted historians have speculated over time, drunk out of his mind?

No one dared move as Akbar declared he could match any Rajput for suicidal bravado; no one 'had the power to utter a word, nor even to offer any opposition'.[37] No one, that is, except Man Singh. The prince of Amber, nephew of Harkha Bai, was in his early twenties, with nothing of the impressive girth he acquired with age and affluence. A lithe and dark young man, he knocked the sword from Akbar's hand; it cut a bit of the loose skin between the emperor's thumb and forefinger. Furiously, Akbar turned upon Man Singh, pushing him to the ground and falling upon him, his hands tightening around the prince's throat.

The hush was broken: in a painting of the scene, every man is on his feet, gesticulating wildly.[38] One of them, Sayyid Muzaffar, managed to stop Akbar, 'twisting his wounded finger' to make him release Man Singh.[39]

What is one to make of it, such seemingly demented behaviour in the story of a man famed through history for his intelligence and rationality? It wasn't, by any means, a drunken embarrassment to be hidden from the world – Abul-Fazl recounts it in detail; it was painted for Akbar's biography. Perhaps its meaning was only what the words and image declare so transparently: there was no challenge Akbar wouldn't meet, and God save the man who tried to stop him.

For all that he tried to strangle him, Akbar must have been impressed with Man Singh. Soon afterwards, he put the Rajput prince in charge of an expedition to Mewar. Udai Singh, the man who outsourced the defence of Chittorgarh – and, indeed, of Ranthambore – had died, and Akbar hoped that his successor, Rana Pratap, might be persuaded to submit. Gujarat, meanwhile, was parcelled out, once again, to various chiefs, though now they all served the Mughal court – with Akbar's milk brother Aziz keeping an eye on them from Gujarat's capital, Ahmedabad. Akbar returned to Fatehpur.

Shaikh Salim Chishti, whose prayers had delivered Akbar's sons, and whose village, as a result, was engulfed by the grand stone buildings of Akbar's new capital, was there to greet him. There was another shaikh, too, in the welcoming party; a shaikh whose own son, Abul Fazl, would do as much as, if not more than, Akbar's heirs to keep the padishah's name and authority alive over the centuries. Abul Fazl was yet to join Akbar's court, however; his father, Shaikh Mubarak, had come alone – and determined, it seems, to make a mark. Like everyone gathered to welcome Akbar home, Shaikh Mubarak, too, offered congratulations. His compliments, however, were from God: a message from 'the unseen world' as Abul Fazl would write, one day – to say that Akbar would become 'the Peshwa [leader] of the spiritual kingdom'. It was a sign of things to come that Akbar did not brush aside the overblown praise, but rather enjoyed 'this wondrous congratulation . . .'

He may have forgotten about it, though, in the more temporal satisfaction that was soon to come: Mirza Ibrahim's head.

The ambitious Timurid had left Gujarat in a fury, a 'rook on a cleared chessboard . . . plundering and ravaging the towns on his way'.[40] His luck, however, much like Ali Quli's, had run out. He found no support in Rajasthan, was chased and beaten most of his way north, his horse shot down from under him at one point, so Mirza Ibrahim had to escape 'on foot through the mire and blood'.[41] In Punjab, the Mirza was wounded by fishermen while resting by a lake. He was injured, friendless and travelling in the ascetic garb of a qalandar when even his disguise was pierced. He was caught and sent to the governor of Multan, in whose custody he died. It was this governor who brought Ibrahim's head to Akbar's court.

The governor of Multan arrived in Fatehpur on the same day as the governor of Punjab – Husain Quli Khan. For all those dismissive things about fighting chickens that Akbar had once said of him – and, in fact, for all that his father, Wali Beg, had been killed in Bairam Khan's cause – Husain Quli was becoming one of Akbar's best commanders. It was he who had swept Sharafuddin out of Rajasthan, long ago, and it was he, now, who captured Mirza Ibrahim's younger brother, Masud.

The younger Mirza and some 300 of his men were brought and paraded before Akbar, wrapped in animal hide. In a painting of the scene, the prisoners look like they might be performing a pantomime: dressed as cows and camels, deer and cheetahs and monkeys.[42] In fact, of course, it was a much more macabre affair. Badauni describes the men 'with the skins of asses, hogs, and dogs drawn over their faces', a humiliation that would also have been suffocating torture. Abul Fazl says they were all imprisoned afterwards, but Badauni relates that some of them were killed, and with such 'ingenious tortures' that another Mughal chief – and friend of Badauni's – who had brought 100-odd prisoners of his own along, too, promptly released them all.

News of Mirza Ibrahim's bloody and comprehensive defeat had not reached Gujarat, however, or it made no dent on his estranged brother Muhammad Husain's ambitions. This last remaining Mirza of note[43] forged an alliance with two Gujarati powers – Ikhtiyar-ul-Mulk and the Fuladis – and swooped down upon Ahmedabad.

Akbar had left the city to his milk brother Aziz, who raised Ahmedabad's defences before the enemy could enter. Aziz had enough soldiers to battle them, too, but unfortunately, while Akbar could rely on Aziz, the newly appointed governor of Ahmedabad had no such 'confidence in his own men'.[44] Unable to risk an all-out war in fear of desertions on the battlefield, all Aziz could do was send selected men on ineffective skirmishes – one Sultan Khwaja was unhorsed and fell into the city's moat, from which he had to be rescued in a basket. Thereafter, it seems, Aziz realized a better use for the soldier and sent him to Akbar, asking for urgent help.

When Sultan Khwaja came to Akbar with his milk brother's troubles – Shamsuddin Ataka's son, who hunted by Akbar's side in the great Lahore qamargah, who rode in Akbar's howdah against the Uzbek brothers, now besieged by the wretched Mirzas! – Akbar didn't hesitate.

The padishah had not been home three months when he left again. Perhaps he was driven by concern for Aziz, or for his new territories, or simply by rage at his relatives, but driven he certainly was – to a surge of strength and stamina so splendid that it has come to define the very essence of Akbar's conquering spirit.

Abul Fazl has the perfect metaphor for it: Akbar travelled as fast 'as Patience departs from lovers'. Early on a Sunday morning, on 23 August 1573, Akbar mounted a she-camel, bow-necked, 'swifter than an arrow', and galloped west. Just over a week later, he reached Ahmedabad, having travelled a mind-numbing, body-breaking 900 kilometres in nine days.[45]

There were less than thirty men with him, including some who would become his closest friends or most trusted noblemen: Abdur Rahim, the orphaned son of Bairam Khan, not yet eighteen; Raja Birbar, a Brahmin poet recently introduced to Akbar's court. There were men of the Kachhwaha clan, too, though Akbar's brother-in-law, Bhagwant Das, had left a few days earlier so that he might proceed at a more leisurely pace with the harem, and Man Singh was still pursuing Rana Pratap in Mewar. And, in accordance with the Mughal family's obsession with record-keeping, there were paint- ers, for the emperor was not only for acting for the moment but also for the ages.

Good omens, too, accompanied the padishah. Akbar had begun, of late, to hunt for signs – quite literally. He would set a trained cheetah after a deer, declaring that if the predator struck and killed, so would the padishah. He did so now, and the cheetah didn't disappoint.

Some days later, the small group of men was lost in 'a forest full of mud'. Akbar was furious,[46] but it was here that he spotted his second omen: a lion appeared to their left. The men were keen to shoot it; Akbar loved hunting lions and perhaps they hoped a kill would improve his mood. But Akbar refused: it was a Hindustani belief, he said, that a lion to the left was a good sign. They rode on.

It wasn't just omens, but a miracle, too, that paved Akbar's way to his unsuspecting enemy. On 29 August 1573, they were still a day's hard ride from Ahmedabad, but Akbar's men wanted to stop a while in Jhotana, a small fortress the Fuladis had occupied. Akbar didn't see the point of it – to have ridden in such fury for such a small prize? It was the Mirza in Ahmedabad he was after, and the Mirza in Ahmedabad he would have. They were argu- ing when a bullet from Jhotana struck a soldier standing by Akbar's side. The man cried in alarm, but when they checked, they found him unharmed. It was 'the neighbourhood of the holy personality', writes Abul Fazl, that saved him.

A bullet failing to injure its mark was no oddity in these early years of bal- listic technology. Only a few years earlier, in Chittorgarh, a bullet had hit a man standing near Akbar, pierced his armour, but then, cooled by the sweat on his skin, failed to detonate. Then, Abul Fazl attributed the miracle to sci- ence and God, in more or less equal measure; now, the soldier's safekeeping was Akbar's doing alone.

Were people really beginning to believe that Akbar was superhuman? The thought may well have crossed Mirza Muhammad Husain's mind, happily preoccupied with the siege of Ahmedabad, when he heard the padishah had arrived. The Mirza was on a recce along the Sabarmati river when he saw Akbar's scout on the opposite bank. Expecting reinforcements from Fuladi and seeing a fellow Central Asian instead, Muhammad Husain called out across the waters. *Who are you?*

At the scout's reply, he might have rolled his eyes. 'O brother, are you frightening me . . . ?'

No. It really was true, said the scout. Akbar was here. Mirza Muhammad Husain demanded to see elephants, troops or any proof at all, but received the same reply: Akbar had arrived. If the Mirza didn't want to believe it . . .

Muhammad Husain waited no more. He 'hastened to his own camp' and began to array his troops.[47]

Akbar was getting his own men ready, meanwhile; no easy task, when a soldier's pride must be as carefully tended as his sword. Trouble arose over a breastplate; specifically a breastplate that a young warrior called Jaimal found too heavy to use. Akbar offered him some chainmail from his own armoury and gave the heavy breastplate to another soldier called Karan, grandson of Jodhpur's Maldeo who had so troubled Akbar's father in the desert. Karan had come to battle without any armour at all, and would clearly benefit from a breastplate.

It was a neat solution that fell apart, however, when Jaimal's father, Rupsi, discovered the exchange. Rupsi, it now transpired, loved his hefty breastplate almost as much as he hated the house of Maldeo. Enraged, he sent a man to Akbar demanding his armour back. When Akbar refused – 'Your remark is not courteous'[48] – Rupsi threw off his own armour, declaring that he would rather go into battle unprotected than dispossessed. Never to be outdone, Akbar took off his armour, too.

The escalating conflict might have ended with yet another blade upon the royal tummy had Bhagwant Das not intervened, speaking firmly to Rupsi and telling Akbar that the Rajput was high on bhang.

'From there', writes Abul Fazl, relieved, 'he moved forward in proper order.'

'Ya Mu'in!'[49] Akbar's favourite battle cry at this time called upon Moinuddin Chishti of Ajmer, whose dargah Akbar had taken to visiting before and after any important enterprise. This time, too, in his mad rush to Ahmedabad, Akbar had stopped in Ajmer for the Sufi saint's blessing.

God knows, Akbar needed whatever help he could get. He was greatly outnumbered by the foe, whose army included a coalition of Gujaratis and Abyssinians;[50] Afghans under the Fuladis; and, of course, discontented Central Asian followers of the Mirzas. Akbar, meanwhile, had come without the bulk of his army – which could hardly have travelled so fast, and was exhausted, in any case, from the previous year's campaign. Besides, Akbar had planned that Aziz, besieged in Ahmedabad with his troops, would join Akbar in battle. Much like Muhammad Husain, however, Aziz just couldn't believe that Akbar had arrived so quickly – he thought the news was a trick to get him out of the fort, and so he stayed put.

As at Sarnal, Akbar's outnumbered troops were reluctant to wage war; they tried to restrain the padishah 'with stratagem'.[51] Only Bhagwant Das showed any kind of appetite for the venture, discerning three good omens on the way to Ahmedabad: it was a good sign, he said, that Akbar's horse stopped for a moment along the way; that the wind was blowing in the enemy's face; and that flocks of kites and ravens flew alongside Akbar's troops – anticipating a feast of his dead foes.

Whatever their misgivings, when Akbar charged into the Sabarmati's waters, his men were bound to follow. Across the river, Mirza Muhammad Husain's red banners came into view and the padishah gave his troops a quick pep talk: 'Today the measure of [the Mirza's] worthless mettle will be taken.'[52] Akbar was favoured by God. So what if they were few in number? They would stay together, form a 'fist' to smash the Mirza's ranks, lay the foe flat on the ground

Allah-u-Akbar! Ya Mu'in!

But the fist came loose immediately.

The Mirza's first salvo was to hurl firecrackers at the advancing corps. One burst before an elephant and it ran amok. The visor of Akbar's helmet had broken as he crossed the Sabarmati and he had made a good omen out of it, declaring that now 'our field of vision is open for the arrival of good news'.[53] What he saw, instead, was his men scattered wide.

'Standing alone in the battlefield, the emperor called for warriors . . .'[54] – only two men heard him. Some others he could see fighting for their lives. A devil-may-care Kachhwaha who'd come to battle without armour died in front of the padishah's eyes; another soldier fell wounded from his horse. Maldeo's grandson Karan, clad in Rupsi's jealously guarded breastplate, was fighting heroically.

An enemy soldier hit Akbar's horse on the head with his sword. Akbar, steadying the animal by pulling at his mane with one hand, flung a spear with the other. It struck his foe but broke as Akbar was pulling it out; the soldier fled. Another took his place and slashed at Akbar's thigh; a third hurled his blade at him.

As Akbar lost sight of his men, so they began to wonder about him. One of them, Saif Khan, was calling for him, 'Ajmeri! Ajmeri!'[55] – was it an affectionate nickname or a code to disguise the padishah's identity? It was this very Saif who had mourned having missed the 'manhood-testing' at Sarnal. No one would question his valour now: Saif's desperate cries received no reply; instead, enemy swords slashed his face. He died.

It wasn't just his warriors who were falling on the field for the ravens to pick at, a rumour of Akbar's own death had begun to spread. It was a dangerous flow of despair; no battle would hold without its commander. Akbar realized what was happening; he made a charge for the centre, yelling all the while, 'Brave men, come up quickly and dispose of these wretches!'[56] They recognized his voice. All was not ended.

In fact, Akbar's reappearance seems to have given his men a second wind, and his luck to have confounded the enemy. Mirza Muhammad Husain had been fighting all this while, but now he was injured, and soon he was caught. The battle lost one minute was won the next.

Akbar set up a makeshift 'court' – a 'couch . . . at the edge of the battlefield'[57] – and the vanquished Mirza was brought to him. Though wounded in the face, Mirza Muhammad Husain was able to speak coherently, even pleasingly. When Raja Birbar, at Akbar's side, asked who had made him captive, the Mirza replied, 'Ingratitude to His Majesty.'[58]

Akbar had declared he would drink the Mirza's blood to avenge Saif's death; instead, perhaps pleased with his abject reply, he treated him rather kindly, giving him water from his own canteen. The good feeling dissipated, however, when the Mirza's milk brother was brought forward. This was the man who had killed Bhagwant Das's brother Bhupat in the thorny battle of Sarnal. Akbar stabbed him with a spear himself and had him executed then and there.

As blood flowed for blood under the September sky, most of Akbar's troops were heading away to rest. It had been a hard day's fighting. Only 100-odd men stood around the padishah on his couch. It was one of them who, casting a lazy eye upon the horizon, let out a cry of alarm.

Could it be? An army – no, a swarm! – it looked like 5000 men were advancing upon them. Could it be that Aziz was finally convinced of Akbar's arrival and had left the city to join him? No . . . it was the third and last of Mirza Muhammad Husain's coalition, 'the rebel Ikhtiyar-ul-Mulk'.[59]

Once before, in Gujarat, the Mughal troops had been caught unawares by an enemy's delayed arrival. The Fuladis were fighting Aziz, and Badauni explains how Sher Khan Fuladi was held up for 'a whole watch at the latrines', being an avid consumer of opium and 'constipation . . . like a hand-grip' a necessary concomitant of his addiction.

Abul Fazl provides no such colourful explanation for the Fuladis' ally, Ikhtiyar-ul-Mulk's late arrival, though he does offer the superfluous comment that the sight of 5000 men descending upon them in clouds of dust brought '[a]gitation . . . [to] the brows of' Akbar's tired troops. The imperial drummer was so petrified he couldn't make himself play to rally the men; only the threat of a spear in his side made him oblige.

And Akbar? It seems as if he felt something of that lightness of hand he once described, the feeling of having made a good shot. He was filled with 'a wondrous exultation', writes Abul Fazl, 'like a raging tiger who in the exuberance of his youth essays his force and fierceness'. He was born against the odds, after all; the odds could not kill him.

Earlier that morning, Akbar had told his men that God was on his side. Others might call it luck, but there was a magic touch to Akbar's destiny.

Once, it was a stray arrow that pierced Hemu's eye. Now, it was desert thorns that tripped Ikhtiyar-ul-Mulk's horse, sending its rider flying to the ground. He was found by an imperial soldier, who cut off his head.

Ikhtiyar-ul-Mulk's vast army fell into the usual disarray. The panic was so 'disgraceful', in fact, that Nizamuddin says the Mughals were taking arrows from the quivers of their enemies to shoot them with. The man who had caught and killed Ikhtiyar-ul-Mulk arrived with the Gujarati's head 'tucked . . . in his skirt',[60] and threw it at Akbar's feet. Delighted, the padishah ordered all the enemy heads stacked in a tower; over 2000 such trophies, writes Nizamuddin, rose in a fearful monument to victory.

In the chaos of the second assault, Abul Fazl writes that two of Akbar's Rajput generals, Bhagwant Das and Rai Raisingh, persuaded the padishah to execute Mirza Muhammad Husain. Both Nizamuddin and Badauni, however, suggest that Rai Raisingh's men took it upon themselves to kill the Mirza, throwing him off an elephant and stabbing him to death. Perhaps they feared Muhammad Husain's quick tongue would save him, and they were tired of tracking the Mirzas' unrepentant trail.

Whatever the cause of Muhammad Husain's impromptu execution, it had its desired effect. The last surviving Mirza, Shah, left the pages of the narrative 'and became a desert-wandering vagabond'[61] till the end of his days. His Timurid cousins would never trouble Akbar again.

Chapter 8

Talent and Destiny

'The vulgar believe in miracles, but the wise man accepts nothing without adequate proof.'

– Akbar, Happy Sayings, *Ain-i-Akbari*

Gujarat was subdued. There would be bursts of resistance against Mughal rule for years to come, yes. That young prince of Gujarat, Nannu, last seen hiding in a field of wheat, would lead a spirited and tragic fight for his throne. Gulrukh – Ibrahim Mirza's widow, Kamran's daughter, a refugee in the Deccan – would raise her son to stake a claim in Akbar's empire. Never again, however, would the padishah himself have to come hurtling to the western shores of his realm; its revenues would flow into his treasury as surely as the Sabarmati flowed into the Arabian Sea.

There was, in fact, very little hurtling left in Akbar's future. Conquests, many: Bengal would come next, then much of the north and north-west, including Sindh and Kashmir; in his sixties, Akbar would march down to the Deccan and supervise the siege of one last great fort, Asirgarh. Rarely, however, would the padishah – or rather, as Abul Fazl refers to him, the *shahinshah*, the king of kings – lead armies into battle anymore.

Partly this may be because there were many talented men who would lead his armies for him: that old stalwart Munim Khan, of course, but also Abdur Rahim and his guardian Man Singh, Aziz and the fallen Saif's brother Zain. Even the two unpopular accountants, Muzaffar Khan and Todar Mal, and our own Abul Fazl, would prove themselves gifted generals. Akbar could leave much of the work of conquering land to these men, and turn his own energies to the less glamorous work of building an empire.

For this, it was not armies that Akbar needed to overcome but his own nobility – and he did so with a slow-grinding obstinacy that, while not as spectacular as a gallop to Gujarat, was equally stunning in its result: the transformation of a self-willed military aristocracy into a meek, salaried, even worshipful bureaucracy.

But first, he would have to find the man to help him do it.

The pre-monsoon showers of 1574 brought two young men of exceptional talent and widely divergent destinies to Akbar's court. '[W]e were . . . loaves out of the same oven', wrote the first of them, Abdul Qadir Badauni, whose acerbic account of Akbar's reign and personality, written in bitter secrecy, has regaled its readers ever since its publication.[1] The second loaf was Badauni's eternal – he would say infernal – nemesis: Abul Fazl, historian, hagiographer and most devoted of Akbar's courtiers. Unlike Badauni's secret diary, Abul Fazl's account of Akbar, his dynasty and his reign was the most celebrated book of its time, commissioned by the emperor himself, lavishly illustrated and presented as 'the code of regulations of the outer and inner world and the duties of sovereignty and servitude for all mankind from the king to the beggar'.[2] The *Akbarnama* remains the most comprehensive account of Akbar and his times, and its author would pay a great price for such intimate access to his powerful subject's life.

On the face of it, Badauni was the more experienced of the two when they came to Akbar's court. He was older, possibly in his early to mid-thirties; old enough to recall Hemu's siege tactics, and to have witnessed, first-hand, Pir Muhammad's carnage in Malwa. Unlike Abul Fazl, Badauni wasn't applying for his first job.

Most recently, he had been employed by a man of simple-minded bigotry called Husain Khan – nicknamed 'Tukriya' because he had once mistaken a Hindu for a Muslim and risen to greet him. Distraught by his faux pas, Husain Khan, then governor of Lahore,[3] ordered Hindus under his administration to wear a '*tukra*', a piece, of coloured cloth on their sleeves to prevent any further lapses into good manners on his part.

There were few matters on which Husain Khan was not equally inflexible. He believed nuts were intoxicating, for example, and banned them.[4] He spent years of his life in an obsessive campaign to conquer the hill kingdoms north of Punjab and raid their temples, which were, he believed, built with bricks of silver and gold.

Another of his obsessions had been to capture Mirza Ibrahim, who had just escaped the sharp thorns of Sarnal and was on his way to Punjab. Husain Khan and his men, including Badauni, went galloping after him, but it was Husain Quli who reached Ibrahim first. Husain Khan descended upon the battlefield with much fanfare, 'eighty or ninety men, and drums beating', but it was too late: the Mirza had fled the scene.[5] Undeterred, Husain Khan pursued Ibrahim and tracked the Mirza down, wounded and imprisoned in

Multan. When they met, Husain Khan may have derived some solace from the fact that Ibrahim made a great show of his disappointment at not having fallen to Husain Khan's sword. At least then, said Ibrahim, he would have been defeated by a fellow Sunni, 'my co-religionist', and not a Shia like 'Husain Quli . . . alien in religion and sect!'[6]

Ethnic and religious allegiances still united and divided Akbar's nobility, as they had when the Uzbeks joined forces against him, or Munim Khan was brought to tears by slurs against the Chagatais, but these fissures and alliances were also beginning to take unpredictable turns. If two Sunnis shaking their heads over the fact that a Shia prevented the one from hunting the other is odd enough, it is odder still to learn of that very Shia, Husain Quli, defiling a Hindu temple on a brahmin's behalf.

It isn't clear when the brahmin minstrel Mahesh Das joined the imperial court, but he soon became a great favourite of Akbar's. Of the vast number of warlords and officials, feudatory chiefs and zamindars who thronged Akbar's court and fell in and out of his favour, Mahesh Das is one of the very few who never – not once – attracted an imperial reprimand.

Mahesh Das was a 'bhat': 'a class of men', writes P. P. Sinha in his enjoyable biography of the man, 'whom the Persians call badfarosh, "dealers in encomiums"'.[7] If a man trained to sing the praise of kings is popular with kings, that is no surprise, but Mahesh Das's talents seem to have extended beyond flattery. Even Badauni, who calls him Gadai ('Beggar') Brahmadas and deplores the brahmin's proclivity to 'perpetually . . . praise the Hindus' admits that he was a man of 'considerable . . . capacity and genius'. As for Akbar – the padishah almost ran out of encomiums himself when describing Mahesh Das. He was, said Akbar, 'the first among the matchless ones'; knowledgeable and well spoken, he 'charmed the inner circles' and was the centre of any debate, any 'circumference formed by intellectuals'. Best of all, he was 'an affectionate friend and a companion in holy solitude'.[8]

Whatever it was that so attracted the shahinshah to the bard, their friendship has become lore. In hugely popular, apocryphal stories of a clever courtier outwitting his kindly though none-too-bright lord, Mahesh Das appears as Birbal – a corruption of the title Akbar gave him, Birbar, 'great warrior'.

Despite the title, however, when Akbar made Birbar governor of Nagarkot,[9] just before leaving for Gujarat, it was Akbar's commander and governor of neighbouring Punjab, Husain Quli Khan, who went to war against Nagarkot's raja on Birbar's behalf.

As part of their siege of the steeply rising Himalayan fort, the Mughals attacked a temple that stood outside its walls. It was a bloody sack. Badauni describes 'arrows and bullets . . . falling like drops of rain' upon the brahmin priests and holy cows who lived within the shrine. Husain Quli's assault was as much psychological as it was military, it seems, for Badauni relates how many of his soldiers, 'through their zeal and excessive hatred of idolatry . . . filled their shoes full of blood, and threw it on the doors and walls of the temple'. Such was the desecration that 'friends and strangers heap a thousand thousands of curses on the head of Birbar, who reckoned himself a saint among the Hindus' – and in whose name the carnage was committed.[10]

A Shia like Husain Quli Khan, disdained by his Sunni colleagues, running a bloody campaign for a brahmin courtier by assaulting a shrine is not the usual template of bigotry. Instead, it may be telling of the changing affiliations and antagonisms that propelled Akbar's world, the dynamics of which were being transformed by Akbar's policies.

To return, however, to the two men presenting themselves to Akbar in muggy May.

Badauni, who may have come to court because his career seems to have been floundering under Husain Khan, was fond of his employer, and vice versa. Husain Khan gave Badauni a Persian horse worth 500 rupees at their very first meeting, and soon appointed him his sadr – religious judge – administering some of the khan's fiefs. And yet, for all that the two men may have shared both sect and points of view – certainly when it came to righteous suspicion of Hindus – Badauni reveals himself a far more complicated character than his patron. Thus, for example, the future diarist embarked upon a scandalous love affair soon after he was made sadr.

Badauni does not say whether the object of his affection was male or female, only that 'I was captured in the net of desire and lust' and 'committed a terrible . . . impropriety' in – of all places – a shrine. Badauni's beloved's relatives were appalled. A group of them attacked the sadr. One of their swords 'penetrated the bone of my skull, and reached the brain', recalls Badauni, mortified, 'exposing me as a brainless fellow'.

By contrast, Abul Fazl appears innocent of the ways of the world. He was ten years Badauni's junior and describes himself as a shy, bookish man, uninterested in the glamour of court life. 'I was not inclined to do this', he writes, 'and my . . . apprehensions of the social state disturbed my soul, which was inclined to solitude'. It was his elder brother, Faizi, already a poet in Akbar's employ, and his father, Shaikh Mubarak, who pressed the young scholar to show a little more enterprise.

For all his naivete, however, real or assumed, Abul Fazl was as immersed as Badauni in the political and social currents of his time; indeed, his family was almost washed away by them. Briefly, Abul Fazl's father, Shaikh Mubarak, was a Mahdawi; he believed, that is, in a millenarian movement that gathered pace in the tenth century of the Hijri calendar (c. 1494–1592), and held that a final messiah, the last Mahdi, would descend upon the world at the dawn of the second Islamic millennium (1000 AH or 1591–92 CE).[11]

As the great day approached, Mahdawis proliferated, and self-proclaimed Mahdis, too, arose aplenty across Hindustan. While Humayun was still on his long exile, one of these Mahdis, Shaikh Ala'i, created a stir in the Suri court,[12] attracting many, including Shaikh Mubarak, to his fold. Like any belief that promises radical change, the movement of the Mahdawis was inimical to the establishment. Shaikh Ala'i (and Shaikh Mubarak along with him) made powerful enemies.

The most powerful of these was a highly regarded jurist called Maulana Abdullah Ansari, titled Makhdum-ul-Mulk, 'one who is served by the realm'. It was largely by Makhdum-ul-Mulk's doing that Shaikh Ala'i was banished from the Suri court and then died. The death was 'a great triumph' for the court scholars, who followed it with a 'vigorous persecution of all [Shaikh Ala'i's] Mahdawi disciples'.[13]

Among them was the unfortunate Shaikh Mubarak, who would spend the next twenty-odd years entangled in the snares of his 'inveterate enemy'.[14] If Shaikh Mubarak hoped that the fall of the Suri dynasty would also spell the end of its pre-eminent theologian, he was out of luck. Makhdum-ul-Mulk retained his high rank in the early decades of Akbar's reign and continued his persecutions. Indeed, the 'hatred of the court party [against Shaikh Mubarak] rose to such a height'[15] at this time that Abul Fazl's father, having already lost his position in court and his grants of land, also almost lost his life.

Badauni was no friend of Abul Fazl's or his family's, but he was, like many, a Mahdawi, and no admirer of the court ulema, whom he regarded as being more invested in power than in theology. Of Makhdum-ul-Mulk, for example, he writes that the supposed scholar looked upon his books 'as bricks'.[16] Badauni tells the story of Shaikh Mubarak's troubles with sympathy, therefore, writing that this was a time 'when it was customary to get hold of, and kill such as tried to introduce innovations in religious matters'.

Thus, Makhdum-ul-Mulk – along with another increasingly powerful cleric called Shaikh Abdun Nabi – sent policemen to arrest Shaikh Mubarak. The scholar was hiding with his young sons, so the police broke the 'pulpit in his prayer room'. Terrified, the shaikh appealed to Salim Chishti, but the Sufi saint had yet to acquire any influence over Akbar. He could only advise Shaikh Mubarak to leave Agra. Eventually, it was Akbar's milk brother and friend Aziz who intervened and saved the shaikh and his family.

For the moment, the shaikh and his sons were safe, but they lived on tenterhooks. Sometime later, Shaikh Mubarak's elder son, Faizi, was summoned to Chittorgarh – 'carried off'[17] by an aggressive contingent of soldiers. It wasn't until he came face to face with the emperor that Faizi knew whether he was being punished for his father's beliefs or rewarded for his increasingly popular poetry.

Fortunately, it was Faizi's poetry that had caught Akbar's eye. Faizi and his father must have breathed a sigh of relief; neither could have known how much their fortunes were about to change.

For all that his court ulema may have been hostile to innovation, Akbar was not; nor, for that matter, was his realm. This was a time of religious, social and political fermentation – beliefs and communities coalescing and breaking apart like so many amoebas evolving out of their single cells, while Akbar's empire (and his court) grew more complex and diverse with every annexation and every appointment. '[I]n those days', as Badauni puts it, 'the chattels of learning had considerable currency' – so it was fitting that his interview at court took the form of a debate. 'The Emperor made me dispute with sages', he writes, '. . . and was himself the arbiter'.

Abul Fazl, meanwhile, brought along a commentary on the *ayatul kursi*, a verse from the Quran popularly recited to ward off danger. No performative disputes for this shy twenty-three-year-old; just the handing over of his composition, and love at first sight. 'Love for that holy personality', he would later write, 'took possession of my heart'.

Akbar's own first impressions of these two applicants are unrecorded. He would have had many things on his mind: just a few weeks after Badauni's and Abul Fazl's appearances in court, Akbar left Fatehpur for a conquest of the east. One may wonder why, then, he was spending time conducting job interviews. The answer may lie in the padishah's other preoccupation at this time: he was planning an overhaul of his administration.

Running a government, then as now, is expensive business,[18] and sixteenth-century Hindustani governments had two broad methods of generating revenue. One was loot. So, for example, Jouher describes Humayun's conquest of Champaner and the subsequent discovery of its treasures under a giant bath. Its water was drained and the treasure 'was immediately divided among the army, by filling the shield of each person with materials in proportion to his rank'.[19] Shields full of gold from secret hordes have an undeniable romance, but they do not make for long-term economic plans. Another, far more stable source of revenue was hidden in plain sight: not loot from fortresses but tax on economic activity, of which the most important, at this time, was agriculture.

It was already a decade or so since Akbar began a long struggle to ensure an uninterrupted and transparent flow of revenue from the fertile fields of Hindustan to the imperial treasury. Just now, for example, when he visited Ajmer, as usual, before heading east, Akbar ordered that any farmers whose crops were damaged by the marching of his troops be indemnified. This would become 'a rule in all [Akbar's] campaigns', writes Nizamuddin, with imperial inspectors sometimes heading into the fields with 'bags of money' to settle any claims as they arose, and thus 'obviate any interference with the revenue collections'.

Keeping farmers happy was important.[20] If Akbar wanted agriculture to thrive, to bring more and more land under cultivation, he would have to ensure the contentment of his cultivators – but that, alone, wasn't enough. Much of Akbar's empire was held in fief, after all, by various chiefs of varying honesty. These fief-holders were responsible for collecting and remitting taxes to the centre, but they did so – if they did so – on the basis of outdated land records and inaccurate assessments of their worth. One of the great projects of Akbar's rule, therefore, was an extensive reassessment of cultivated land. This was easier said than done – fief-holders would hardly appreciate or encourage reassessments that increased their tax obligations to the imperial treasury. It was to deal with such resistance that Akbar began to toy with the idea of turning all his realm into imperial '*khalsa*' land – to be administered by the crown, that is – and of turning his revenue-collecting fief-holders into salaried officers, '*mansabdars*'.

Bureaucracies were creeping upon the world. The Chinese already had an entrance exam for their administrators.[21] In both Central Asia and Hindustan, meanwhile, a slow but certain shift in 'political structure' had been ongoing for some time, as a modern historian argues, its command moving from 'aristocratic lineages to . . . kings and men of lesser social standing who had been "trained" by the monarch'. A time was coming, that is, when it was not so much a man's noble ancestry, '*asl va nasab*', that gave him worth or power, but rather his education and training, his '*tarbiyat*'.[22]

Perhaps this explains why Akbar sat and scrutinized the opinions and intelligence of men like Badauni and Abul Fazl with such a close eye – not only because they were seeking their fortunes in his court, but equally because he sought a future for his realm in their talents.

But first, he sought Bihar and Bengal.

Sulaiman Karrani, the Afghan sultan of Bihar and Bengal, died on the eve of Akbar's march into Gujarat. Ever since, various men had made grabs for his throne; none of them had gained unchallenged control of the east, and all of them had weakened – if not entirely undone – the careful balance of military strength and diplomatic subservience that had kept Sulaiman Karrani safe from the Mughals.

First, Sulaiman's eldest son and successor frittered away his inheritance by disparaging his nobility and was murdered by his cousin. The cousin wasn't long on the throne either – he was soon dispatched by a nobleman called Lodi. Lodi had great influence over the Afghans of the east, and he decreed that

Sulaiman's younger son, Daud, be crowned sultan. One eastern Afghan, however, did not want Lodi speaking for him: Gujar Khan, 'the sword of the country',[23] found himself a grandson of Sulaiman's and set up his own rule under the grandson's aegis. Daud, meanwhile, became increasingly suspicious of the man who'd made him king. A kingmaker, after all, can crown more than one head.

It was an ideal opportunity for the Mughals to exacerbate suspicions between the Afghans, divide their ambitions and swallow their land. There were three contending powers in Bengal and Bihar: Daud, Lodi and Gujar Khan, and Akbar's man in Jaunpur, Munim Khan, tried hard to sow dissension between them. Unfortunately, his intrigues had the opposite effect. In the winter of 1573, news arrived that Gujar Khan had mediated a peace between Lodi and Daud.

Had the Afghans remained united, Munim Khan might have had to return to Jaunpur with little achieved. But the star of the Afghans in the east was fading. The young Sultan Daud 'was a dissolute scamp', writes Nizamuddin, 'and knew nothing of the business of governing'. He was particularly ignorant of the principle of trust. Now, as Lodi began to negotiate with the Mughals to compel their retreat, Daud suspected that he was, in fact, brokering a deal to his own advantage. Thus, for no reason at all, Daud had his best adviser killed. With Lodi perished Daud's chances; the Mughals were soon on his tail.

The suspicious sultan fled to Patna and barricaded himself in the city, while Munim Khan began a long siege.

It was for Patna, as the monsoon of 1574 set in, that Akbar set sail.

The rain-swollen waters of the Yamuna were filled with 'wonderfully fashioned boats'.[24] Each had an animal-shaped prow, some had gardens on board, others carried the emperor's 'equipments and establishments',[25] from armour and drums to carpets and kitchenware – even two favourite elephants, Balsundar and Suman, each with his own suite and two she-elephants for company.

Akbar's ship, writes Badauni, had a prow shaped like a crocodile, and it was with the fearsome ease of that amphibious beast that the emperor navigated his way to Patna – disembarking to hunt every day, 'searching into science and poetry' every night, riding the river's high waters as if they were just another musth elephant.[26] The same could not be said of his retinue.

While the bulk of Akbar's army marched alongside, on the riverbank, many of his courtiers, servants and nobility were travelling by boat, too, and they were terrified. The monsoon is no time to sail.

All the 'tumult of the waves', writes Abul Fazl, of the day on which Akbar set sail, all 'the force of the wind, the rush of the . . . rain, the roar of the thunder, and the flashing of . . . lightning produced a strange appearance'.

The storms did not subside; indeed, they got worse, and ships sank regularly. On one particularly bad day, eleven boats sank into the river, like so many pebbles flung to their fate. Another time, a sinking ship took two imperial cheetahs with it. There was a day when the storm was so strong that many men disembarked in alarm, preferring to walk rather than follow those unfortunate animals. Akbar, of course, 'went on by boat with . . . cheerful heart'. What was a little rain? When they crossed from the Yamuna into the Ganga, he led 500 of his elephants into its raging waters.

Only one drowned.

A lost animal here, a handful of broken ships there, these were no hurdles. Akbar looked, as the ambitious must, on the bright side. Wading into the Ganga with his elephants, Akbar watched a 'large fish' emerge from the river. Was it a Gangetic dolphin? Perhaps; more importantly, for Akbar it was a good omen. Another day, out on his daily hunt, he made one of his auguries by cheetah – this time, however, the deer escaped the first predator, though it was 'eager . . . [and] swift as the wind'. A second cheetah was unleashed; this one broke the deer's neck. No matter, said Akbar. It only meant that Daud would escape Akbar once, but fall to his generals later.

It happened exactly so.

The siege of Patna had begun in the winter of 1573. When Akbar arrived, on 4 August 1574, it had been going on for at least eight months. Partly this was because the Mughals had focused their forces on Patna, while the city was supplied with provisions from Hajipur, across the river.

Akbar expanded the siege to two fronts, Patna and Hajipur, fought it on two levels, strategic and psychological, and won it in two days. This is what happened.

By Akbar's orders, Munim Khan arranged an intimidating display of fireworks to greet him, filling the air with smoke and thunder, turning it as 'dark as the fortunes of the enemies . . . The horrific noise wound its way into the brains of the darkened foe', Abul Fazl writes, 'and their gall-bladders became as water'. Indeed, his 'liver-less soul upset', Daud prayed for peace the very next day. Akbar refused. Like a cheetah toying with its prey, he offered his luckless enemy three choices: one-to-one combat between Akbar and Daud, between their nominees or between their elephants.

Meanwhile, Akbar also sent 3000 men on a night attack upon Hajipur. This was no covert operation executed in dark secrecy. As Badauni describes it, the 3000 soldiers were all cavalry, and they were sent out 'fully equipped . . . in boats with such ornamentation and display, that at the sight of it the eye was rejoiced'. Not, of course, the eyes watching from Hajipur. The enemy garrison 'fell into the whirlpool of anxiety', writes Abul Fazl; Hajipur fell that very night and the boats returned to Akbar, loaded with enemy heads. Akbar sent the grisly trophies to Daud, who was 'plunged into dismay' at the sight and 'set his mind upon flight'.[27] Thus, on 6 August, only two days after the shahinshah's dramatic entrance into the fray, Daud fled the city, 'in a swift boat' from a wicket gate, leaving a stampede in his wake. The Afghans could not leave fast enough; many jumped off the city's walls, its moat filled up with men and animals; others leaped into the river and drowned.[28]

The next day, Akbar mounted his mighty Balsundar and rode into yet another city in yet another outpost of Hindustan that was now his own.

Daud would lead the Mughals a merry dance for a while yet; it was only in mid-1576, two years after his escape from Patna, that his head would roll at Akbar's feet. But Daud was no longer the point. He was defeated as all who stood in Akbar's path were defeated – eventually, comprehensively, and, as it was beginning to seem, miraculously.

The emperor was on his way back west within a week of Patna's fall. Munim Khan, his old ataliq, a venerable and remarkably fit eighty-years-old,[29] was to lead the pursuit of Daud and the conquest of Bengal. With him went Todar Mal, one of the brightest talents in Akbar's court. Todar Mal was back, recently, from sorting out the revenues of newly conquered Gujarat, but his skills were hardly restricted to accounting; he would also prove himself one of Akbar's best generals.

Akbar, meanwhile, sailed to Jaunpur, where his harem had camped while the emperor was in Patna, and decided to spend a few weeks there. It was a good base from which to keep an eye on the goings-on further east. As Akbar held court at Jaunpur or toured the neighbourhood, news of his presence must have spread. Curious men and women may have come to see if it was true, all that they had heard of him. That he could ride mad elephants with ease, gallop as fast as the wind and vanquish rival kings with his mere presence. There must be something special about a man who had held on to the famously slippery throne of Hindustan for almost twenty years. For over half a century – from 1517, when Ibrahim Lodi was crowned, through the entire Suri dynasty and Akbar's forebears – no one had reigned as long.

Akbar had done what other men could not. How much further might his powers extend? One day, in Jaunpur, a delegation of farmers came to the emperor. The rains had stopped before they should have; the farmers feared a famine. They begged Akbar to pray for rain.

Was Akbar surprised, maybe even a little embarrassed by their pleas? From the way Abul Fazl tells it, Akbar was no stranger to miracles, but Abul Fazl's portrait of the emperor as born to near-divine fate and fortune was far in the future still – it would be another fifteen years before he began to write the *Akbarnama*. Had Hamida told her son he made her skin glow so bright it blinded her brother, Muazzam?

When Akbar's commander Saif Khan died in the battle against Muhammad Husain Mirza outside Ahmedabad, did his mother tell the grieving emperor how he had brought about the life now sacrificed in his service? The story goes that Saif's father, desiring sons and begetting daughters, had threatened to divorce his wife if she had another girl. The poor woman was walking through the Kabul citadel to ask Hamida's permission to abort the child in her belly, when she came across Akbar, a toddler then. The prince divined her sadness, it seems, and prophesied a son. And lo, Saif was born.

Were these stories commonly told, intimate anecdotes remembered and recounted at family gatherings – or were they the result of Abul Fazl's trawling through the suggestible memories of fond relatives and retainers? Even if Akbar – like boys across cultures and times – had grown up with an idea, howsoever faint, of himself as divinely ordained, the 'miracles' of his childhood were really blessings. The many visions of light before he was born, the unexpected (and verbose) pronouncements from his infant tongue, the toddler's prophecy were all gifts from God, much like the happy shortage of just kings in Akbar's neighbourhood.

This was different: the farmers that stood before him were asking him to intervene with heaven, to demand God's favours, to act beyond the bounds of normal human agency. Akbar hesitated.

Why should he force his prayers upon God? It was hardly appropriate, or necessary, to explain to the All-Knowing what His devotees needed. Abul Fazl bolsters the point with a line of verse: 'Wilt thou teach God the path of mercy?' Perhaps Akbar was a little appalled.

Akbar was still talking when it began to rain. It rained for a week, the farmers' 'fields . . . became verdant', and their emperor . . . if he had not thought so yet, did he think so now? Who, in his place, would not have wondered whether the shahinshah of Gujarat and Bengal and everything in between, the harbinger of sons, of light, of rain, was gifted with a special destiny?

Chapter 9

Doubt

'Akbar, a king like Alexander, attained his every wish.'

– Abu'l Fazl, *The History of Akbar*, vol. 6

There was a new confidence in Akbar when he returned to Fatehpur from Patna. In the first few months of 1575, he did two things that would not only cement the foundations of his own reign but create a blueprint for rule that would endure centuries after Akbar's demise.

First, after years of hedging by his nobility, Akbar finally pushed through his administrative reforms – every bit of land in the realm would belong to the crown, there would be no more fiefs, and every bit of farmed land would be remeasured – not with the customary rope, but with bamboo rods, for greater accuracy.[1] As for the fief-holders, they were mansabdars now, with ranks and responsibilities, for which they would be paid a salary. Thus, a man might hold a rank between 10 and 5000, the number indicating how many cavalry-men he was obliged to provide the emperor when called upon to do so, and his salary calculated on how much it would cost to maintain so many men and horses – and, of course, the mansabdar himself.

Second, Akbar began to host weekly theological debates in his newly built Ibadat Khana, a 'house of worship' to which the emperor invited clerics, scholars and believers of various (for the moment, only Muslim) sects for night-long debates of increasing acrimony.

It is hard to say which of the two decisions was more controversial, though both were born of ideas whose time had come.

It was now, writes the modern historian Ali Anooshahr, in the sixteenth and seventeenth centuries, that the Ottoman, Safavid and Mughal empires all moved from 'the war band . . . to a bureaucratic absolutist "state"'.[2] Presumably, this was at least partly because there was only so far an empire could run on shields full of hidden treasure shared between warlords. It also indicated, however, a new focus on the monarch of this evolving state as the source of its legitimacy and authority. This was, as many historians have argued, the logic and the genius of the mansabdari system. Warlords like the Uzbeks or the Mirzas drew sustenance from the strength of their own arms and that of their clans; a mansabdar owed his salary, his authority, and therefore his loyalty, to the shahinshah.

It would be a long while, of course, before these newly minted mansabdars – and particularly the higher-ranking noblemen, '*amirs*', among them – came to accept Akbar's new design. Resentments would fester, battles would erupt and the turmoil would be such that even Muhammad Hakim, Akbar's half-brother, safely retreated to Kabul these past many years, would sniff another opportunity in Hindustan.

If Akbar anticipated any of this in 1575, when he announced his reforms, he did not let it worry him unduly. In fact, having decided to bring his nobility to heel and their revenue into his own treasury, Akbar opened up a second front, too – he would also take on his clergy.

If the shahinshah was the symbolic core of the Mughal bureaucracy as it was now emerging, Akbar also occupied the literal centre of his Ibadat Khana. The building does not stand any longer, but the descriptions are clear. It was a large hall with four wings, each assigned to a particular group of men: amirs, philosophers, sayyids and Sufis. Akbar's own seat was at the very centre of the hall, from where he watched them all, and 'tested them company by company'[3] – until he formulated his own creed.

It was also at this time that the man whom you might call Akbar's high priest re-entered his life. At his first shy meeting with the emperor, Abul Fazl had been invited to travel east with him. The young man had made his excuses. For all his claims about being invaded by love for the shahinshah, the reclusive scholar may have been quietly horrified at the idea of travelling so far away from home with a boisterous military camp. Abul Fazl had hurried back to his father's house, while Akbar 'gave rein to his river-drinking crocodile'[4] and sailed away to Patna.

Afterwards, Abul Fazl may have regretted not accepting the emperor's invitation; or perhaps it was his family that was dismayed by such a wilfully missed opportunity. At any rate, he was back at court: armed with excuses (he couldn't have travelled without his father's permission); flattery (he'd had visions of Akbar's victory); and yet another essay on yet another set of verses from the Quran (of which Badauni observes cattily, 'people said it was written by his father').

Walking through the grand mosque in Fatehpur, Abul Fazl saw the emperor arrive, in the distance. Not daring to approach, he bowed from where he stood. And . . . could it be? Akbar saw him, recognized him! Thrilled, Abul Fazl rushed forward. The rest is history.

More than once, in the *Akbarnama*, Abul Fazl portrays himself as a shy and lonely character dragged into the material world despite himself. When he arrived in Fatehpur for the second time, Abul Fazl says he had no friends in the city, that 'there was no kind person to console me'. Yet, he continues piteously, '[m]y youth would not allow me to ask for assistance'.[5] What pulled him out of his shell was the all-powerful emperor, his near-divine muse. 'What portion can a bewildered, headless and footless mote have in the beams of the world-lighting Sun? It can only be tossed about in the wind', he wrote in his preface to the *Akbarnama*.

Others saw Abul Fazl differently. The authors of the *Maathir-ul-Umara*, a who's who of the Mughal nobility compiled in the eighteenth century,[6] describe a gregarious, generous man. He kept a lavish table, for example, with 22 *seers* (about 20 kg) of food served every day; in the first and last military expedition of his life, he had 1000 dishes cooked for every meal, mostly to be distributed. Abul Fazl would never dismiss an employee, the *Maathir-ul-Umara* goes on, nor ever fine or otherwise punish anyone, no matter how poorly they performed. Every year, he would burn his books of account (to eliminate all debts, presumably) and give all his clothes to his staff.[7] The reticent bookworm, if at all he ever existed, must have blossomed in the warmth of Akbar's patronage.

But success does not guarantee popularity. Badauni's pen is never so acidic as when he describes his 'officious . . . openly faithless', colleague, 'continually studying the Emperor's whims, a flatterer beyond all bounds'. It was by such 'time-serving qualities', writes Badauni, that Abul Fazl raced through the ranks, while – 'poor I'! – Badauni 'could not manage to advance myself'.[8] Even Badauni suggests, however, that it wasn't only the usual currying for favour and promotion that animated Abul Fazl. The young scholar came to court not so much to make his own fortune but to destroy the ulema that had persecuted his family. 'He is the man', writes Badauni, 'that set the world in flames'.

Whether or not Abul Fazl really daydreamed of setting alight an old world order as he walked the streets of Fatehpur, clutching his essay and hoping to catch the emperor's eye, there was a great speed, certainly, with which the court ulema lost favour after his appointment in Akbar's service – the speed, one might say, of a vengeful blade.

The idea of Akbar's rare, possibly unique vision of harmony between religious communities – *sulh-i kul*, or peace for all – is so deeply ingrained in the popular imagination that it has produced its own corollary, a fraught religious terrain 'before and after Akbar'. Thus, for example, R. C. Majumdar has argued that, 'With the sole exception of Akbar, who sought to conciliate the Hindus by removing some of the glaring evils to which they were subjected, almost all the other Mughul Emperors were notorious for their religious bigotry.'[9] The idea of such Akbarid exceptionalism is as logically and historically untenable, however, as the idea of any one nation out of all others having a manifest destiny. No man, let alone a society, can exist in absolute terms – least of all a man who lived as long and varied a life as Akbar did. There was a 'before Akbar' to Akbar's own self, in fact, as the emperor confessed quite cheerfully.

One of the sections in Abul Fazl's *Ain-i-Akbari* is a compendium of Akbar's most quotable quotes titled, in translation, 'The Happy Sayings of His Majesty'.[10] If the title evokes an unfortunate vision of fixed smiles around North Korean dictators, the sayings themselves are often disarmingly frank. Thus, Akbar recalls the religious zeal of his youth with regret: 'Formerly I persecuted men into conformity with my faith and deemed it Islam.' With age and learning, he continues, 'I was overwhelmed with shame.'

He was also overwhelmed, it seems, with a febrile yearning. In another of his Happy Sayings, Akbar sounds decidedly miserable:

> Although I am the master of so vast a kingdom, and all the appliances of government are to my hand, yet since true greatness consists in doing the will of God, my mind is not at ease in this diversity of sects and creeds, and my heart is oppressed by this outward pomp of circumstance; with what satisfaction can I undertake the conquest of empire? How I wish for the coming of some pious man, who will resolve the distractions of my heart.

A king's duty was God's will, after all; or, as Akbar put it, 'Divine worship in monarchs consists in their justice and good administration.' But with such a multiplicity of gods in his realm, how was a ruler to know he wasn't in thrall to the Devil by mistake?

Akbar returned from Bengal and became as obsessed with prayer as he had been with conquest. Badauni describes him sitting alone on 'a large flat stone of an old building' near his palace, his head bent to his chest, absorbed in contemplation. Sometimes, he spent 'whole nights in praising God . . . pronouncing Ya huwa and Ya hadi . . . full of reverence for Him, who is the true Giver'.

While Akbar sought after Truth, what of his subjects? It is hard to get a proper sense of religious feeling across the many diverse societies that comprised Akbar's growing empire; what impact religion had, great or little, on people's everyday lives. It is equally hard, however, to escape the sense that religion

– whether as ritual or as a way of imagining a just world – was a quotidian and compelling force.

It was during the sixteenth century, for example, that Tulsidas wrote the Ramcharitmanas and Guru Arjan Dev compiled the Adi Granth[11] – some indication of the sheer variety of ideas, religious and social, that were in ferment, even in competition, at the time. These two monumental texts both offered ideas and ideals of truth and justice that would not have agreed with each other in every point. Thus, for example, B. B. Majumdar describes how Tulsidas

> states with evident regret that the Sudras now impart knowledge to the Brahmanas, take the sacred thread and accept reprehensible gifts . . . This was certainly a fling at the popularity of Ravidas the shoe-maker, Dharna the Jat, Sena the barber and other religious leaders belonging to non-Brahmana castes,

some of whom were prominent Bhakti saints.[12] Sikhism, on the other hand, the tenets of which Guru Arjan Dev first compiled in the Adi Granth, was influenced by the Bhakti movement; indeed, the Adi Granth contains verses by several Bhakti saints. Evidently, this evolving faith ruffled some feathers; complaints about the Adi Granth seem to have reached Akbar, at which Guru Arjan Dev sent him the book. The emperor, having heard some excerpts, declared, 'Excepting love and devotion to God I so far find neither praise nor blame of any one in this Granth. It is a volume worthy of reverence.'[13]

Poets, philosophers and saints might argue, emperors might adjudicate, but what of the everyday Hindustanis who practised what they preached? It might be almost impossible to imagine any of these lives were it not for the wonderful autobiography of a Jain trader and poet called Banarasidas.[14] In a lucid, honest and often very funny account of his adventures (beautifully translated by Rohini Chowdhury), Banarasidas includes his struggles with ritual and faith. In his youth, writes Banarasi, he fell for a sanyasi's get-rich-quick scheme and bought a mantra that he was to recite every day for a year, after which, every day, a gold coin would appear at his door for the rest of his life. 'For an entire year, every day', writes Banarasidas, 'With firm and unwavering belief, / In the solitude and secrecy of the privy / Banarasi, the blockhead, recited the mantra . . .' A year later, he opened his front door. No immediate glitter caught his eye. Poor Banarasi 'examined the ground carefully' – no doubt growing more annoyed with every desperate scrutiny of the soil and shadows. 'He found no dinar anywhere.'

It was a blow, but it did not end Banarasi's quest. The young man would go on to experiment with Saivism, then return to his own Jain faith, but never to find the spiritual satisfaction he sought. 'The performance of rituals no longer held any joy for him', writes the merchant of himself, 'But he could not appreciate the spiritual aspects either. / Banarasi's condition became similar to / That of a camel's fart, which hangs between earth and air.' Eventually, Banarasidas gave up on all forms of worship and ritual, veering full tilt into heresy instead, so much so that he would even eat the food left in offering to the gods.

So, it seems, a man could journey from superstition to scepticism as freely as Banarasidas travelled from Jaunpur to Agra for his trade.[15] That is not to say, however, that religious belief imposed no constraints on how people were allowed to live.

Thus, Badauni tells the tragic tale of an inter-religious (and adulterous) love affair. Romance, it seems, was the otherwise sardonic Badauni's Achilles heel – himself not above canoodling in a dargah, he couldn't resist a good love story, whether between Ali Quli and that beautiful rake, Shahim Beg, or, now, between Sayyid Musa and the beguiling Mohini.

Some five years before Akbar began his debates in the Ibadat Khana, at about the time that Akbar's Rajput queen was pregnant with Salim, a young sayyid nobleman from Kalpi called Musa arrived in Agra to pay his respects to the increasingly powerful padishah. Musa was making his way through the city when he caught a glimpse of a beautiful face at a high window. It was Mohini he had seen; she was a goldsmith's wife, and he was ensnared in 'the lasso of her pure glance'.

Fortunately for his heart, less so for his future, Musa's feelings were returned. The lovers knew they were treading dangerous ground and so, for two and a half years, they were 'content with a glance now and then from afar'. But patience is not the strong suit of wildly beating hearts. One night, Musa took his life in his hands and broke into Mohini's house, climbing up to her room 'like a rope-dancer' and finding his own home in her arms. The next morning, Mohini left home with her lover, 'despising fair fame and reputation', writes Badauni with admiration, '. . . as the moonlight with the moon'. Soon, however, as her relatives gathered in protest and Musa's life came under threat, Mohini returned home. She told her family that she had been spirited away to an enchanted land. 'The silly Hindus believed this beautiful deception', says Badauni, though evidently not without large grains of salt, for they kept Mohini 'in a ring of iron serpents' from now on, shut away 'in an upper room' under lock and key.

In the time-honoured manner of lovers separated from their beloveds, Musa went mad. Mohini, unable to bear the thought of her suitor's grief, escaped once again – and once again, the lovers were caught and parted. This time, the police was involved, and Musa was sent to jail where, from longing, he grew as 'thin as a new moon'.

Again – a third time – the lovers tried. A man called Qazi Jamal, a Hindi poet possessed of a good horse and strong nerves, helped them. He carried Mohini away on his 'charger, head-tossing like the . . . steed of Fate . . .

wind-footed and prancing', racing along the banks of the Yamuna with half of Agra watching.

Mohini's relatives were chasing behind, and many of Agra's citizens 'who were spectators of the scene [were shouting] in front' – and yet, the young girl might have made her escape if the steed of fate had not caught its feet in the mud. Mohini threw herself off the horse and told the poet to escape – *tell Musa I tried!*

The news of this third failure broke the wretched Musa. He died. It would have to be, of course, that his bier passed by the goldsmith's house. Standing at the very window, perhaps, from which she had once exchanged flirtatious glances with a stranger, Mohini watched the funeral procession. When Musa's still form was just below, she threw herself down, breaking the chains that bound her in the process. They found her weeping at his grave.

What could the family do? They let her be, 'forgave her delinquencies'. Mohini converted to Islam and died.

'Forgive me!' Badauni writes in conclusion. 'The language of love carried the reins of my pen irresistibly out of . . . my control.'

What is one to make of this story, except, of course, that Musa and Mohini might have suffered no differently in the Agra of the twenty-first century? It was as they died in forbidden love that Akbar had his first son with his Hindu wife, but Badauni draws no contrast between the two facts. Perhaps there is no contrast to be drawn: an emperor's bride was not of one faith or another, she was a queen. And yet, it is Badauni, too, who often cavils at the great influence that Akbar's Hindu wives had on him – as, for example, in the case of the brahmin accused of blasphemy.

Both Badauni and Abul Fazl are personally involved in the story, so it must have occurred after Akbar's return from Bengal, when both men were in his employ. Here is what happened.[16]

A *qazi*, or judge, in Mathura, who had been collecting building material for a mosque, accused a brahmin of taking some of it and using it to build a temple instead. In the argument that followed, the brahmin poured salt on the injury caused by his alleged theft by abusing the Prophet Muhammad – a sacrilege confirmed by Abul Fazl, who was sent to Mathura to investigate.

The case came before Shaikh Abdun Nabi.

Abdun Nabi had joined Makhdum-ul-Mulk in persecuting Abul Fazl's family and had risen to the highest judicial rank in the realm. He was Akbar's sadr – his chief justice – who not only adjudicated legal matters but also distributed pensions and grants of land to holy men. Akbar was both fond and respectful of his sadr. Badauni describes the emperor rising 'to adjust the Shaikh's slippers when he took his leave', and Akbar sent his eldest son, Salim, to Abdun Nabi's school. The shaikh had great influence on the emperor, and great power, too, but he wasn't very popular.

It may not be surprising if Abul Fazl, knowing how Abdun Nabi and men like him had conspired against his father, is less than admiring of the sadr. Describing how Akbar gave Abdun Nabi his high post, Abul Fazl mutters the aside that the shaikh 'decked out his shop with hypocrisy'. Badauni, too, has little good to say about the judge – partly because of how Abdun Nabi dealt with his powers over grants of land to religious men.

It began well enough, writes Badauni, being dependent himself on such charitable *madad-ma'ash* grants and always appreciative of generosity – but things were soon 'reversed'. As he would do with agricultural land, Akbar ordered a comprehensive reappraisal of all madad-ma'ash grants in his realm, putting the fate of countless men in Abdun Nabi's hands. The shaikh did not take to this exponential increase in his powers with humility. Badauni describes him surrounded by petitioners, many of whom had already had to bribe his clerk, 'or make presents to his chamberlains, doorkeepers, and sweepers'. Even then, it was difficult to get your voice heard and imperative to beg. Some even died in the heat of the throng; while Abdun Nabi sat unconcerned on his 'throne of pride', sometimes washing his hands and feet, and making sure to splash the dirty water 'on the head and face and garments' of the men around him – many of whom were powerful chiefs but, having come to plead a case, 'bore all this, and condescended to fawn on him, and flatter and toady him to his heart's content'.

Akbar didn't seem to notice. No other emperor, writes Badauni, had ever given such 'absolute power' to his sadr. The blaspheming brahmin of Mathura would change all that.[17]

The brahmin's guilt was undisputed, it seems; it was his punishment that divided the court. Some favoured death; others suggested a less drastic penalty, such as 'public exposure and fine'; while a third party, 'the ladies of the royal household', pressed the emperor to release the man. From 'regard to the Shaikh', writes Badauni, 'the King would not give his consent'. The case dragged on until Shaikh Abdun Nabi came to Akbar and asked for leave to execute the culprit. Akbar seems to have given him the same excuse he gave his queens. It was the sadr, he said, who was 'responsible for carrying into execution the sentence of the law' – why had he come to Akbar?

Perhaps Abdun Nabi was so used to the emperor's esteem that he mistook his indecision for deference. The brahmin was killed. And Akbar was furious.

As Badauni tells it, the 'ladies within and the Hindus without' stirred the pot of Akbar's fury, until the emperor summoned a meeting of scholars, jurists and divines around the great tank at Fatehpur, the Anup Talao. Badauni was among them and was eventually ordered to speak. 'When ninety and nine opinions are in favour of a sentence of death', Akbar asked him, 'and a hundredth in favour of acquittal, do you think it right that the muftis should act upon the latter. What is your opinion?' Badauni replied that the law advised against punishment 'where there was any doubt'. He added, however, that Abdun Nabi may have had compelling reasons to act as he did. Did he do it, perhaps, 'for the sake of expediency'? If Badauni was trying to strike a balance that would offend nobody, he did not please Akbar. The emperor's 'hair stood on end', writes Badauni, 'like that of a roused lion'. People around him whispered for Badauni to shut up. Then, Akbar himself looked at him and said, 'You are not at all right.'

Badauni bowed low and stepped back, silently vowing never to attend such meetings again.

Akbar's fury did not have any immediate consequence on Abdun Nabi's career. Perhaps the shaikh brushed it from his mind, telling himself that Akbar would soon find a conquest to distract him. But Akbar did not forget,[18] and if he thought of marching into new territory, it was that of his clergy.

'A general proclamation was issued', writes Abul Fazl, inviting the intelligentsia of Fatehpur, whether from scholarly circles or the common public, to descend upon the 'delightful precincts' of the Ibadat Khana every Thursday night, for debates that carried on till dawn. It was not always that Akbar sat at the centre, with his debaters in carefully demarcated spaces. In fact, Badauni describes Akbar going from group to group, listening and talking, giving money and lending books. It is a congenial scene, and Badauni approved of it, writing that 'all kinds of instructive and useful topics' were discussed in the Ibadat Khana's collegial atmosphere. Too soon, however, the discussion had degenerated into dispute.

First, there was the question of precedence: it was to placate egos that the hall was separated into its four wings, each reserved for one category of discussant, with Akbar at their centre. Then, of course, there was the question not so much of having discussions as of winning arguments, and this was not so easily resolved. Badauni describes one particularly agitated night, when the 'vein of the neck of the Ulama . . . swelled up, and a horrid noise and confusion ensued'. Annoyed, Akbar told Badauni to let him know, henceforth, if anyone spoke improperly in the hall; he would have them removed. 'If I carried out this order', Badauni muttered under his breath, 'most of the Ulama would have to leave.' Akbar asked him to speak up, and laughed at his wit, but he wasn't amused.[19]

Soon enough, it appears, the unruly theologians were evicted and the weekly discussions were closed, for Abul Fazl writes of them being resumed some three years later. It wasn't, however, that Akbar had hit upon a scheme for ensuring calm and reasonable discussion; in fact, he seems to have decided to raise their pitch. In 1575, only Muslims of various stripes were invited into the Ibadat Khana. When the hall reopened in the autumn of 1578, it was flooded with every faith and philosophy in the land. 'Sufi, philosopher, orator, jurist, Sunni, Shia, Brahman, Jati, Siura, Carbak [Charvaka, sceptic], Nazarene, Jew, Sabi [Sabian], Zoroastrian, and others enjoyed exquisite pleasure', writes Abul Fazl cheerfully, as Akbar sat upon a 'lofty pulpit' listening to his guests, who 'opened out [their secrets] without fear of hostile seekers after battle'.

Badauni paints a less rosy picture. It wasn't debate that occurred in the Ibadat Khana, but war. 'The learned men used to draw the sword of the tongue on the battle-field of mutual contradiction and opposition, and the antagonism of the sects reached such a pitch that they would call one another fools and heretics.' Former friends became bitter foes in their desperation to impress the emperor, as, for example, Makhdum-ul-Mulk and Abdun Nabi, once joined in their persecution of Mahdawis, now hissing and clawing at each other aboard their sinking ship. Makhdum-ul-Mulk went so far as to write a whole treatise condemning Abdun Nabi for the various death sentences he handed out to suspected blasphemers, adding, for good measure, that the shaikh was 'undutiful towards his father, and . . . afflicted with hemorrhoids'. Abdun Nabi, writes Badauni, replied that his colleague 'was a fool'.

All this unseemly drama gave 'persons of novel and whimsical opinions' the perfect opportunity to mislead Akbar into their various heterodox swamps, writes Badauni. Already, as he sees it, Akbar was far too indulgent of a Shia scholar, Mulla Muhammad of Yazd, and of his brahmin bard Birbar – 'that bastard!' Already, Akbar was too readily influenced by three newly arrived brothers, Sunni refugees from Shia Iran – Hakim Abul Fath, Hakim Humam and Hakim Nuruddin. The first and eldest of them, a charming and well-spoken man, was able to accommodate 'every change in the religious ideas of His Majesty, or even went in advance of them', so that he was soon Akbar's 'most intimate friend'. Already, that is, Akbar had been far too welcoming of far too many kinds of men; now, they were joined by 'sages of various religions and sects', each favoured with Akbar's attention.

Now, there was the brahmin Debi, pulled up in a *charpai*, a cot, to the emperor's bedroom balcony, to explain ideas like the transmigration of souls; the brahmin Purushottam whom Akbar commissioned to invent Sanskrit names for 'all things in existence'. Now, there was a Sufi called Shaikh Tajuddin similarly suspended 'in a blanket' to recount his 'obscenities and follies',[20] and, though Badauni doesn't mention them, there were charismatic Jain and Parsi priests.

And now, there was, Abul Fazl.

In the four-odd years since Badauni and Abul Fazl arrived in Akbar's court, Abul Fazl's career had progressed much faster, and certainly more happily, than Badauni's.

Badauni was employed in Akbar's increasingly active translation department, and he was good at his work. His first book was the *Singhasan Battisi*,
'a series of thirty-two tales about Rajah Bikramajit king of Malwa'. Badauni
was commanded to begin work immediately – a 'learned Brahman was
appointed to interpret the book for me' – and present a page that very day. He
managed, and Akbar approved. When the book was done, it was 'graciously
accepted, and placed in the Library'. However, as the unfamiliar – and, in
Badauni's eyes, unfit – texts followed one after the other, the translator began
to lose heart. In the *Atharban* (Atharva Veda), Badauni was pleased to discover Islamic elements – 'I found that a Hindu under certain circumstances
may eat cow-flesh; and also that Hindus bury their dead, but do not burn
them.' The Ramayana, he thought, might be compared to 'the Shahnama, and
the stories of Amir Hamzah'. But the Mahabharata? '[P]uerile absurdities!'
cried Badauni. 'But such is my fate, to be employed on such works.'

The trouble wasn't only that Badauni couldn't accept his fate but that his
talent wouldn't let him escape it. Many, many years later, he was trying for an
appointment in the Ajmer dargah, but Akbar was loath to let his translator go.
'[W]henever I give him anything to translate', the emperor said, 'he always
writes what is very pleasing to me, I do not wish that he should be separated
from me'. Badauni was working on some more 'Hindu lies', this time the
Bahr ul-Asmar ('Sea of Tales', possibly the *Rajatarangini*) and Akbar summoned him to his bedroom to tell him some of its stories. All night long,
Badauni regaled the emperor, like Akbar's own Scheherazade. Afterwards,
Akbar ordered him to finish the work and gave him 10,000 *tankahs* and a
horse. None of this did anything to alleviate Badauni's gloom – he only hoped
he would finish in two or three months and then die.[21]

Abul Fazl, on the other hand – the shy student who only wanted to bury
himself in his books – was having a whale of a time. His happiness, and
Akbar's growing affection for him, derived greatly – as Badauni saw it – from
Abul Fazl's eager embrace of radical or heretical ideas, and a corresponding
willingness to bait the old guard – poor Makhdum-ul-Mulk, his father's one-
time nemesis, among them. Abul Fazl did not hesitate 'in putting them to
shame', writes Badauni, 'at which the Emperor was pleased'.

Baited and battered, it seems these high-ranking scholars sent Abul Fazl
a pleading message, 'Why are you always falling foul of us?' Abul Fazl's
answer was as cryptic as he was unmoved. 'The fact of the matter', he is
said to have said, is that 'I am the servant of a mere mortal, and not of an
eggplant'.

It may be he meant that, unlike an eggplant which fruits all year long,
a mortal must one day die,[22] and that Abul Fazl was taking advantage
of a temporary turn of events in his favour. Badauni, who reports this
story, had little sympathy for the 'imbecile old men' thus rebuffed by his

colleague. Badauni's grouse was not with conservative Muslim scholars being challenged – he was a Mahdawi too, after all, like Shaikh Mubarak. What troubled Badauni was Abul Fazl's wilful acceptance of heretical and blasphemous creeds. Once, in fact, 'in the early days of these discussions', Badauni had a private argument with Abul Fazl, asking why he was so willing to challenge the truths of Islam. In the end, it seems, Abul Fazl only said, 'I wish to wander for a few days in the vale of infidelity for sport', and walked away, smiling.

For Badauni, Abul Fazl was the cynical manipulator playing with the mind of an emperor 'who was possessed of an excellent disposition . . . but very ignorant' and 'used to the company of infidels and base persons', thus throwing him 'into perplexity, till doubt was heaped upon doubt'.

Doubt is the bane of the believer, but was it, for Akbar, the very horse that took him hunting for the Truth? Abul Fazl acknowledges that the Ibadat Khana made many people very unhappy, particularly those who 'were disgraced and disappeared into obscurity' – and this was so, he writes, because Akbar favoured debates based on 'reason', not 'blind tradition'. Reason and the audacity to question, these were the weapons of Akbar's new conquest, and Abul Fazl was his arms-bearer. For all the insults heaped upon the courtier by his fellows at the time – a popular pun on his name was 'Fazlah', garbage[23] – for all the accusations of flattery that have followed him through the centuries, it was Abul Fazl who articulated one of the foundational principles of Akbar's rule, and indeed a defining tenet of the distant future. 'They do not know', he wrote of the hapless men floundering in the waves of ideas washing across the Ibadat Khana, 'that much of acquired learning is subject to doubt and scepticism'.[24]

There is little that exists in the modern world, from its politics to its medicine, that does not owe itself to this truth.

The 1570s were not quite modern times, of course. Doubt may have flourished in the curious emperor's court, allowing him access to a wealth of learning and giving him a weapon by which to clip the wings of his powerful clergy, but doubt is a double-edged sword. Scepticism is the antidote to blind belief but also to absolute power – and if Akbar wanted to reduce the authority of his ulema, he desired no such bounds to his own.

Indeed, Abul Fazl's very rational precept regarding doubt goes hand-in-hand with a code of mystic belief: the debating scholars, as he wrote, 'think that knowledge is only to be had in schools. They do not know that much of acquired learning is subject to doubt and scepticism.' All knowledge can bear examination, that is; but knowledge is not the same as revelation. Thus, Abul Fazl declares in his very next sentence: 'It is clear that a pure heart can be enlightened without book learning . . .'[25]

At the very time, therefore, that religious debate raged in Fatehpur, a new kind of faith began to develop across the realm in the superhuman powers of the enlightened emperor himself.

No one can doubt that Akbar was lucky. It was a chance arrow that blinded Hemu and allowed Akbar the Delhi throne; it was an accident that tripped Ikhtiyar-ul-Mulk's horse and saved the exhausted Mughals from a second battle outside Ahmedabad; and it must have been good fortune that made it rain just as that delegation of farmers pleaded with Akbar in Jaunpur.

Soon after, in March 1575, the Mughal generals that Akbar left behind in Patna had chased the Afghans, Daud and Gujar Khan, all the way to Tukaroi, in Orissa. The Mughal side, far from home in an unfamiliar land, was rife with dissension and indecision, yet Munim Khan managed to rally them to a fight. A battle began, but the Mughal men had little appetite for Gujar Khan's elephants, charging at them bedecked with 'black yak-tails and the skins of . . . animals',[26] presenting an even more fearsome sight than usual. Then, one of the best Mughal generals, Khan Alam, was knocked to the ground and killed by the Afghans. Munim, meanwhile, charging into battle in his eighties, came face to face with Gujar Khan but was unable to find his sword. With impressively quick thinking and strength, the octogenarian fought off the Afghan with his whip, but only just escaped. Wounded on his neck, head and face, Munim Khan was carried away from the battlefield, barely conscious. The Mughals had lost two generals, one after the other; how long would it be before they lost heart? Todar Mal yelled at a man who came with news of Khan Alam and Munim, 'Don't prate, and don't say such things'.

The battle 'hung in the balance between the Rajah and Daud' – until the news came. Another 'arrow from the quiver of fate' had found its mark. It had struck Gujar Khan and killed him. Daud heard the news and fled. A miraculous victory for Akbar's army, once again.

Could it be that such consistent luck went to Akbar's head; or is it possible that his soldiers, his courtiers, his subjects began to believe there was something truly exceptional about their emperor, that he was blessed? Perhaps a bit of both, and its result was clear: 'Akbar, of all the Mughal Emperors', writes the modern historian Harbans Mukhia, '. . . became the embodiment of many miraculous powers'.[27]

A few months after the Battle of Tukaroi, another contingent of Mughals and Afghans was battling in the east. A Mughal soldier fell unconscious in the battlefield and would, no doubt, have died, except that a vision of Akbar came to him, riding a 'steed of fortune . . . equipped for battle, and bringing the good news of victory'. The apparition lifted the soldier 'from the dust' and sent him back into the fray.[28]

Another Mughal soldier, Peshrau Khan, imprisoned and sentenced to die by a powerful Bihari zamindar, was taken by a 'scoundrel' to meet his end. At the moment of his execution, however, Peshrau Khan began to meditate on Akbar – and lo! 'however much I tried, my arm refused to act [against you]', the executioner exclaimed. A second executioner, too, was unable to harm the supernaturally protected Mughal, who managed to escape and return to court, where he told his tale.

Not everyone embraced the idea of Akbar's miraculous powers with equal enthusiasm. No man can be a hero to his harem, after all. In May 1577, half a year or so after the Peshrau Khan affair, Abul Fazl describes Akbar the 'loving lord bent in meditation' by his elder son's bed, prophesying the end of seven-year-old Salim's fever. The astrologers agreed with their emperor, as did the fortune-tellers, but the ladies of the harem were not quite as firm of faith. They did not want predictions, they wanted 'skilful physicians' to tell them what was wrong with the boy; without a diagnosis, 'the ladies . . . and the servants in general were not reassured'.

Salim recovered, however, and Akbar was unfazed. Cures and visions, prophesies and miracles tumbled one after the other over the following months, with all the speed of the emperor chasing an enemy.

In the very month of Salim's illness, Akbar gave 'medical remedies, and . . . spiritual medicines' to a poisoned courtier; later that summer, the emperor used his 'Messiah-like breath' to perform an eye operation on his cheetah-keeper; and in October that year, he fed a wild deer from his own hand, while onlookers gazed in amazement.[29] This was nothing, however, to the miracle that awaited in November, when Akbar saved the whole of his empire from the baleful influence of a comet, the 'blessing of the holy personality' keeping its curse at bay.

In mid-December that year, Sadiq Khan was among the Mughal generals leading a punitive expedition against the raja of Orchha. It wasn't long ago that Sadiq Khan had been punished himself – he had lost one of Akbar's elephants to the Ganga's waters during the march to Patna. Furious – and rather unjustly so, given how many imperial animals drowned thanks to his own madcap navigation of the rivers to Bihar – Akbar had confiscated Sadiq Khan's estate and banished him to Sindh, with orders not to return without a replacement for the deceased beast. It was many months and the gift of 100 elephants later that Sadiq Khan was able to win his way back into favour.

Now, hacking through a jungle to confront Orchha's raja, it looked like Sadiq Khan might be in trouble again. Two hundred Rajputs in the Mughal army had already been killed, the battle was getting out of hand. Desperate, Sadiq Khan conjured an image of Akbar in his mind and made one last charge. 'Suddenly', the victorious khan would later tell the court, the emperor's 'standards appeared, and [his] glorious figure', too. Of course, the Mughals won.

The next year, in January 1578, Akbar was camped in a village in Punjab, lecturing his gathered nobility on the virtues of vegetarianism. He had stopped eating meat on Fridays – the holiest day of the Muslim week – and he hoped that others, though 'wolfish' in their habits, would follow his lead. '[H]ail to the lofty perception which keeps sovereignty shoulder to shoulder with saintship . . . !' Abul Fazl cries out. Badauni was less impressed.

In fact, Akbar's changing diet was among the many pieces of evidence that Badauni uses to allege the emperor's apostasy from Islam, laying much of the blame for it on his Hindu wives, whom Akbar would join in their rituals,[30] and under whose influence he had repudiated beef, onions and garlic, along with 'men who wore beards'.

For all that Akbar was glad to experiment with Hindu – indeed any – ritual and philosophy, he does not seem to have been rejecting Islam, certainly not in the absolute terms that Badauni alleges. Thus, for example, the first big miracle of 1578 was that of a hermit reciting the azaan.

Eighteen-odd months earlier, in mid-1576, Man Singh had led the Mughal army against Rana Pratap of Mewar at the famous battle of Haldighati.

Much is often made of the great rivalry between the Rana of Mewar and the Emperor of Hindustan, both equally stubborn in their will for victory. 'Single-handed . . . did he withstand the combined efforts of the empire', writes Colonel James Tod of Rana Pratap's long and romantic resistance, '. . . flying from rock to rock, feeding his family from the fruits of his native hills, and rearing the nursling hero Amra [his son], amidst savage beasts and scarce less savage men, a fit heir to his prowess and revenge'.[31]

It is true that the rana was determined not to submit to the Mughal, and ruthless in his pursuit of independence. Until Chittorgarh was regained, Rana Pratap declared, Mewar would forsake every luxury: its nobility would eat from plates of leaf, not silver and gold; its men would not shave; the great *naqqara* drums would follow the troops, not lead them. Peasants, he said, would no longer cultivate their fields, so no aspiring conqueror would gain as much as a grain of wheat from his land. 'The silence of the desert prevailed in the plains', writes Tod, 'grass had usurped the place of the waving corn; the highways were choked with the thorny babul, and beasts of prey made their abode in the habitations of his subjects'. In addition to such 'patriotic severity', Rana Pratap sent out regular plundering missions to destroy any trade travelling between the plains and the ports of Gujarat.

It was a resistance that continued to the very end of the rana's life, and one that Akbar never stopped trying to break – and yet, if there was a personal rivalry between Rana Pratap and his foe, one could argue that it was not so much with Akbar, whom the rana never met, but with Akbar's young Rajput general, Man Singh.

In the spring of 1573, some three years before Haldighati and only weeks after Man Singh stopped Akbar from stabbing himself in the stomach, the emperor had sent the young Rajput prince to try and extract submission from Mewar. Man Singh was back in Fatehpur by the summer, having met the rana but with little success. Again, in September, after the great battle for Ahmedabad, Akbar sent Bhagwant Das, Man Singh's father, to Mewar. Bhagwant Das returned within the month, writes Abul Fazl, bringing the rana's young son, Amar Singh, as guarantor of his father's fealty, along with a flattering message: for now, the rana 'presented his petition through the Rajah [Bhagwant Das] . . . When his desolate heart should become soothed by the lapse of time, he too would come and do homage in person.'

Abul Fazl's dry narration – of diplomatic missions making their slow progress – is a far cry from the tales of unbending pride that fill the histories of Mewar as James Tod tells them.[32] This, then, is how Tod relates the encounter between the Rajputs of Mewar and those of Amber.

Man Singh did, indeed, arrive at Rana Pratap's door, but the rana would not eat with him. He sent little Amar Singh instead, and when Man Singh protested, he sent cold regrets, saying that 'he could not eat with a Rajput who gave his sister to a Turk, and who probably ate with him'.[33]

Raja Man Singh, no less proud than his host, got up from his meal and on to his horse. Rana Pratap came out, it seems, as Man Singh was about to leave. The prince of Amber turned to the rana of Mewar and declared, 'If I do not humble your pride, my name is not Man.'

Man Singh would have been in his very early twenties; Rana Pratap was ten-odd years his senior, and amused, perhaps, by the challenge. The rana replied that 'he should always be happy to meet him' – and a less restrained voice from among the chiefs of Mewar called out that Man Singh should 'not forget to bring his "Phupha"' – his paternal aunt's husband, that is, Akbar – when he visited next.

The ground where Man Singh's untouched meal had been laid out was 'deemed impure' as, indeed, was his very presence: the ground was washed in water from the Ganga, and the chiefs 'bathed and changed their vestments'.

The next time they met, it would not be to exchange barbs, but to war.

Abul Fazl and the bards of Mewar are not the only ones who speak of Man Singh and Rana Pratap. There is also Man Singh's own historian, Amrit Rai, author of a ballad-biography called the *Mancharita*. Amrit Rai prefaces his account of the battle of Haldighati with a scene in which Akbar offers paan to a gathering of his generals, asking for volunteers to battle Rana Pratap. It is Man Singh, writes Allison Busch in a lovely essay, who 'accepts the challenge'. The offering of paan, Busch continues, like the gift of a robe of honour, 'symbolized the incorporation of the vassal into the body politic'.[34]

As Man Singh was shunned by Rana Pratap, who would not eat with him, so he became one with Akbar by eating the proffered paan.

And so, on 18 June 1576, the battle began.

Haldighati is a mountain pass in Udaipur, which had been Mewar's base ever since the loss of Chittorgarh. When the Mughals fought Mewar at Chittor, it was Mewar's rana – Udai Singh – who was absent and the Mughal padishah who led his men. This time, the situation was reversed: Rana Pratap leading the charge against a Mughal general, Man Singh.

Man Singh had not brought his phupha along, but he had, perhaps, brought the fury of his humiliation at the taunt. 'The price of life was low, that of honour high', writes Abul Fazl. At dawn, when battle began, 'Shiva arrives on the scene to augment his skull garland', in Amrit Rai's account, 'and Kali dances in the midst of the carnage'.

It is Badauni, however, who provides an account shorn of metaphor. He was there, having insisted on coming – hoping to escape another translation job, perhaps – declaring his desire to 'dye these black mustachios and beard in blood through loyalty to your Majesty's person'. There was no dearth of gore. And several times, it looked as if the Mughals were done for.

At the very start, the rana's Afghan commander, Hakim Sur, demolished the Mughal vanguard. These men, along with some eighty-odd skirmishers called 'chickens of the front line' – 'became hopelessly mixed up together', writes Badauni, in the thorny, uneven ground and the 'twistings of the road'. They 'sustained a complete defeat'. Next, the Mughal left wing, mainly Rajputs, began to fall apart. Rana Pratap came 'charg[ing] out of the pass, and . . . broke through the centre'. A division of Shaikhzadas from Sikri 'all fled at once', followed by Badauni's own battalion.

'Livers grew hot, cries resounded', writes Abul Fazl, and to those watching it seemed that Mewar would win. Then, all of a sudden, the tide began to turn. Badauni gives some of the credit to an unnamed elephant driver, who fought the rana's legendary elephant, Ram Prasad, an animal Akbar had long coveted. The Mughal mahout led an imperial elephant at Ram Prasad, and 'the two kept charging at one another, until by chance an arrow reached a mortal place in the driver of the Rana's elephant, so that the shock . . . threw him to the ground'.

Rana Pratap began to retreat.

Man Singh, meanwhile, had taken the place of his own mahout, and 'exhibited such intrepidity as surpasses all imagination'. His company of Rajputs, too, got a second wind. Badauni, who had no love lost for his Rajput comrades-in-arms, writes that they 'performed such exploits as were a perfect model'. Indeed, he goes on, Man Singh's leadership exemplified a poet's line: 'A Hindu wields the sword of Islam.'[35]

Abul Fazl tells a different story. According to him, it was at the arrival of the imperial rearguard, and their loud broadcasting of the news that Akbar himself had come to the battlefield, that the enemy, so far 'more and more predominant, lost heart'.

Both historians agree, however, that the Mughal army was too exhausted to pursue its narrowly defeated enemy. It was noon on a summer's day in the desert; Badauni was not exaggerating when he said that it was so hot that 'the very brain boiled in the cranium'. The Mughal troops retreated to Gogunda town nearby, worried about possible night attacks by Mewar, and trying to recover their strength on a diet of meat and mangoes. The latter, eaten 'in default of bread', made many soldiers ill, and besides, writes Badauni, ever the critic, this particular variety of mango, 'for sweetness and flavor [was] . . . not up to much'.

Akbar, it seems, was not entirely pleased by what he heard of the battle. The emperor sent a man to examine the battlefield – upon which, in Amrit Rai's description, 'Severed limbs are likened to fish swimming in a pool of blood'[36] – and though he was 'satisfied on the whole' by whatever evidence he procured on the nature of the fight, he was unhappy that his army hadn't chased after Rana Pratap.[37]

He may even have found the rana's escape slightly suspicious. Two years later, in 1578, the Mughals were still pursuing the lord of Mewar, as they would until the day he died. They found and besieged him in Kumbhalgarh fort, but now a new commander called Shahbaz Khan arrived. Shahbaz Khan took command of the siege – which he could hardly have done without Akbar's blessing – and sent Man Singh and Bhagwant Das away, just in case 'their feelings as landholders', as Abul Fazl puts it delicately, were hampering the Rajputs' mission.

And so to the miracle of the azaan.

Kumbhalgarh is a grand old fortress, sprawling over more than 650 acres. In one of its nooks, there lived a hermit who had acquired some fame, and people 'always sought blessing from his lofty spirit'. Now, however, his words came as a rude shock. At dawn, a few days before the Mughals attacked, the hermit climbed to the top of Rana Pratap's temple and 'sounded the azan', the Muslim call to prayer, predicting an imperial victory. When the startled rana asked him what he was up to, the hermit said he had had a vision of a Mughal triumph. The rana 'was enraged and put him to death', Abul Fazl reports.

Indeed, the Mughals did win Kumbhalgarh – and Udaipur, too, the following day. It was a good showing, and Akbar would have been pleased; as pleased as he was with the hermit's 'Divine boon'.

There was little that Akbar did not see a divine hand in these days. Only a week or so after the fall of Kumbhalgarh, one of Akbar's elephants, Pundarik, drowned while crossing a river. Akbar rejoiced because loss of property meant an increase of life – a happy reading of the accident that Sadiq Khan, hauled up for letting an imperial elephant drown in the Ganga, might have rolled his eyes at.

It wasn't just good omens and prophesies that fell to Akbar like blessings from above. A greater gift was in store for him, and a greater shift in his own understanding of himself. Akbar was still touring Punjab when Pundarik met his end. Soon afterwards, a sudden burst of rain troubled the imperial camp.

'Wilt thou teach God the path of mercy?' Four years ago, in August 1574, Akbar had been reluctant, even a little shocked, perhaps, when farmers asked him to make it rain. Something fundamental had changed since then. In April 1578, as the storm thundered and his soldiers 'were distressed and complained', Akbar did not hesitate. He took a mirror and breathed upon it, then he put it in a fire. The clouds obeyed his command: the rainfall stopped.

Chapter 10

A Lamp for the Dark World

'I see in 990 two conjunctions,
I see the sign of Mahdi and that of Antichrist;
Either politics or religion must change,
I clearly see the hidden secret.'

– Abdul Qadir Badauni, *Muntakhab-ut-Tawarikh*

In 1578, when Akbar stopped the rain, the world was only two years away from the last decade of the Islamic millennium; the last Mahdi must already be walking the earth. Akbar, apparently, decided it was him.

So much of a person's character and destiny is woven with gossamer thread; a translucent, finely connected tapestry of instinct and belief, chance and determination, only parts of which are ever clearly visible in any particular light. One part, then, of Akbar's messianic impulse was that such claims were quite common. As Azfar Moin has argued in his account of what he calls 'sacred sovereignty . . . practiced by Muslim dynasts in early modern India and Iran', Akbar's 'critics considered his spiritual pretensions to be far from original'. Shah Ismail, first of the Persian Safavids, had done very much the same. It might seem counter-intuitive to modern readers, writes Moin, to imagine 'Muslim kings transmuting into saints and messiahs, venerated by courtiers and worshipped by soldiers', such blasphemy going against the caricatured idea of Muslim rulers being rigidly orthodox. In fact, Moin argues, '"heretical" conceptions of sacred authority attracted Muslim monarchs more than "orthodox" notions of Islam'.[1]

It's not hard to understand why: no emperor would baulk at being worshipped. If Akbar became 'inclined to claim the dignity of a prophet', or, as Badauni mutters darkly, 'perhaps I should say, the dignity of something else',[2] he was also reinforcing his authority vis-à-vis his reluctant mansabdars. The miracles that he was increasingly willing to perform, the accounts of visions and apparitions that he did nothing to discourage, these were, perhaps, the 'symbolic acts' that J. F. Richards refers to in his classic essay on Akbar's formulation of imperial authority, acts by which Akbar created a 'metaphor of the Emperor's person as an embodiment of the Empire'.[3]

Look at it from another angle, however, and Akbar was not only asserting imperial authority but also abiding by the imperial duty of care. It may not be a coincidence that the emperor's first two rain-related miracles came at the behest of farmers and soldiers. 'Perhaps the most frequently used pair of terms in Mughal historical literature is "soldiers and peasantry"', writes Harbans Mukhia, 'whose care redeems the state' – and it may be a legacy of this state that soldiers and peasantry, *jawan* and *kisan*, remain a fulcrum of modern Indian political discourse. Indeed, writes Mukhia, in Abul Fazl's construction of his beloved monarch's authority, 'The king's absolute power . . . gets circumscribed by the responsibility to establish absolute peace among his subjects through the practice of non-discrimination, and to bring about tranquillity and prosperity through paternalistic care' – to perform, in fact, a miracle more difficult than changing the weather.[4]

Still, one cannot argue that Akbar's idea of himself as a messiah evolved from a blueprint, nor that it was a well-planned coup against his nobility on behalf of his subjects. There is nothing to suggest that the emperor was merely using the contemporary anticipation of the last Mahdi for his own ends; nothing to suggest that he did not truly believe in the prophecy and in himself – and nothing to suggest that he was an utter lunatic for doing so.

From the wonders that had come, and the spectacles that were to follow, it is tempting to deduce delusions of grandeur at the very least. Few modern readers will imagine Akbar feeding wild deer without also recalling the much-vaunted affinity of contemporary megalomaniacs with their pets. But this was the sixteenth century and 'it would not do', writes Moin, 'to dismiss the emperor's behavior as pathological'. In this particular time and place, after all, 'there existed no sharp social distinctions between being absorbed in divinity and being neurotically engrossed in oneself'. Akbar may have nurtured doubt, but only as a way of reaching certainty.

On the one hand, he could think about messiahs and divinities with some degree of sardonic distance. In one of his Happy Sayings on the subject, Akbar sounds quite wry: 'In Hindustan no one has ever set himself up as a prophet. The reason is that pretensions to divinity have superseded it.'[5] On the other hand, the man who sat on a rock all night long, head bent in prayer, wanted to believe; the emperor who rode musth elephants and gathered pious men to find the will of God had not given up the search for Truth. He had only found it in himself.

When a man like Badauni, therefore, railed in his writings against Akbar's pretensions to prophethood – or worse – he did not accuse the emperor of being either cynical or insane. 'If Akbar's transgressions followed a certain cultural logic', writes Moin, 'so did the accusations against him'. Badauni answered in Akbar's own coin. The emperor was not the Mahdi, no; nor was he mad. Akbar was the Antichrist.

It is a lot for a man to hold in his head, all these ideas and instincts, arguments and aspirations sparking in his brain. No wonder Akbar fainted.

It happened only days after he stopped the rain in Punjab. Remembering, perhaps, his last visit to the region, the emperor had ordered another grand qamargah hunt. While he camped near Bhera, his nobility formed a huge circle and drove in hordes of prey for Akbar to kill. But when the qamargah was ready, Akbar did not mount his horse and ride in joyfully with his cheetahs and spears, his lassos and guns. Instead, he had a seizure.[6]

Akbar was possessed 'by a sublime joy', writes Abul Fazl.[6] Badauni is more forthright: 'a strange state and strong frenzy came upon the Emperor, and an extraordinary change was manifested in his manner'. It may have been an epileptic fit; it may have been a holy trance; and it was altogether unprecedented.

When Akbar recovered, he cancelled the hunt. There would be no spilling of blood today. Instead of prey, Akbar had ascetics and the poor gathered around him while he sat under a fruit tree and gave out gold. He also ordered a building and garden made at the spot; and, for himself, a haircut. It was now he declared why he'd grown his hair in the first place, 'from sympathy with the natives of India'. Was it not time for others to adopt his style? The emperor shortened his 'long and beautiful' locks, and many courtiers followed suit, on the spot.[7]

News of the strange scene spread quickly.

Two years earlier, two young noblemen had crashed into each other during a game of polo; one fell to the ground and began to bleed. Akbar was part of the game, too, but entirely unharmed by the accident. Still, he only had to dismount to check on the injured player for 'cries and lamentations' to arise among the spectators and for 'strife-mongers [to take] advantage of the opportunity'.[8] Badauni suggests that the emperor himself didn't realize how dangerous the situation was until an older courtier grabbed his reins and said, 'My Lord, what are you doing here? Go away!' The courtier's anxiety stemmed, presumably, from a fear that rumours might arise that Akbar, too, had been unhorsed and injured. Back in the palace, Akbar sent urgent assurances of his well-being across his realm, particularly to its frontiers, 'so that the panic was stayed'.[9]

If the emperor toppled, that is, so might his empire. And what if, as had now happened, Akbar went into an inexplicable trance? Would his empire collapse in an equal frenzy?

The news was particularly agitating in the newly conquered east, writes Badauni, as 'strange rumours and wonderful lies became current in the mouths of the common people'. There were even insurrections, although 'quickly quelled'.

This time, however, no messengers went hurtling in all directions with reassurances. Instead, there was more and more news of Akbar's grand gestures and growing eccentricities, all of which followed, at ever grander scale, a pattern of symbolic actions that proclaimed the emperor's care for his subjects, authority over his officers, and, of course, his growing saintliness, if not divinity.

Soon after his epiphanic haircut, Akbar ordered a spectacle that managed to combine all three 'visions' of himself in one. The great tank in Fatehpur, the Anup Talao, was to be filled to the brim with coins. One may gauge the scale of the enterprise by the fact that it was only half-completed when Raja Todar Mal reported that 170 million *dams*[10] had already been poured into the massive tank. It took months to fill it all the way up. Finally, on 5 October 1578, Akbar inaugurated the distribution of the money. First, there was a prayer. Then, picking out 'one by one a mohar, a rupee, and a dam', the emperor handed them to selected mansabdars, Abul Fazl among them. They were to take the coins as an 'amulet', Akbar lectured, and make a 'vow' to give to the poor themselves.[11] It wasn't money he was handing out, but a duty – and a sacrament.

A little over two months later, Sultan Khwaja – who was once pulled up from the moat outside Ahmedabad in a basket – arrived in court. He had been appointed leader of a Haj caravan, escorting pilgrims to Mecca, and was back with Arabian horses and tales of Akbar's wonders.

One night, said Sultan Khwaja, as their ship sailed west in the dark, a boy fell 'from the . . . deck into deep water'. It was impossible to see him in the pitch black, but his cries were all too clearly heard. Not knowing what else to do, Sultan Khwaja 'made a vow to the world's lord', and sent some sailors in a dhow to look for the boy. Still, there was no sign of him for a long time, and the khwaja 'was sunk in sorrow'. He should have had more faith in his vow. At midnight the boy was found.

'Everyone', writes Abul Fazl, 'put a ring of servitude to the emperor in his ear'.[12] It isn't clear if he means the courtiers gathered around Akbar, listening to Sultan Khwaja's tale, or the pilgrims and sailors aboard his ship. The idea of a ring of devotion, however, was crystal clear: it was a symbol of enslavement, in this case of spiritual enslavement, to a saint or a pir.[13]

Some six months later, on a Friday in June 1579, Akbar climbed up to the pulpit in the mosque at Fatehpur and delivered the sermon. The *khutba* was always read in the name of the sovereign, of course – *khutba-u-sikka*, sermon and coin, were twin markers of sovereignty, in fact – but never by him.

Akbar, however, had learnt that not only the Prophet but also the four Abbasid Caliphs, and Akbar's own ancestors, Timur and Ulugh Beg, had preached their own sermons, and was keen to try it. As Nizamuddin, most dispassionate of Akbar's chroniclers, writes, 'His Majesty therefore felt it to be his duty to carry into practice . . . the custom observed by the Khalifas and Imams.'[14] Badauni is less circumspect: Akbar read the khutba because 'he held it to be an insufferable burden to be subordinate to any one'.

'[T]he pulpit was honoured by the [emperor's] sky-touching feet', writes Abul Fazl, and Akbar was well aware, it seems, that he was stepping into terrain as unknown and dangerous as the forests of the east or the deserts of the west, into the well-guarded realm, in fact, of his court clergy.

Fittingly enough, given the family's embittered history with Makhdum-ul-Mulk and his coterie, it was Abul Fazl's brother, Faizi, who had composed a poem for Akbar to recite in the mosque. According to Badauni, however, the emperor could not read it. Akbar 'stammered and trembled . . . [and] came quickly down', held up by others, having only managed to read three verses of Faizi's elaborate composition.

Still, it may be that Akbar had made his point. The last of the verses he read was: 'Exalted is His Majesty, Allah-u-Akbar!'[15]

Whether or not the emperor intended a play on words, their ambiguity was not lost on his critics. Was Akbar merely repeating the Muslim piety, 'God is great', or was he trying to suggest – and they would not put it past him – that Akbar was God?

Some years earlier, Akbar had proposed engraving the phrase on his seal and his coins, but one of his courtiers had advised against it, precisely because of the possible misunderstanding. He had offered, instead, '*Lazikrullahi Akbaru*' – 'To remember God is the greatest thing' – less pithy, yes, but less ambiguous too.[16] Akbar had grumbled that surely no reasonable person would distort his meaning so, but let the matter rest. More recently, according to Badauni, Akbar had come up with a new 'formula': There is no God but God, and Akbar is His representative – so close to the Islamic assertion of faith in God and His Prophet as to cause 'commotions'. Akbar had withdrawn his order. Now, wrote Badauni, only 'a few people in the harem' would use the phrase. Later, a poet and wit called Mulla Sheri would put the whole matter into a couplet:

The king this year has laid claim to be a Prophet, after the lapse of a year, please God, he will become God![17]

It wasn't very long, in fact, before Akbar followed his detractors' fears to their logical conclusion and declared himself the religious head of his empire.

In September 1579, only two months after Faizi composed a poem for Akbar's khutba, his father Shaikh Mubarak drafted what has come to be called the 'Infallibility Decree'. Technically, the document was a '*mahzar*', an opinion or a petition, declaring that the court ulema, having given the matter much thought, had decided that a just ruler ('*sultan-i-adil*') was 'higher in the eyes of God' than the most learned of His devout scholars, a '*mujtahid*' considered wise enough to interpret Islamic law. Akbar, besides, was 'a most just, a most wise, and a most God-fearing king' and therefore, the ulema went on, Akbar should have the final say in any future disputes between scholars and jurists of Islam in his realm. Not only that, the ulema vowed to 'be bound' by any new orders that Akbar issued; refusal – as befits Akbar's straddling of two realms – would invite both 'damnation in the world to come', and 'loss of property and religious privileges in this'.[18]

In effect, it was an utter rout. Abul Fazl has Akbar offering coy refusals while the ulema falls 'to entreaty', but surely the real reluctance was on the side of the clerics. Among them were poor Abdun Nabi and Makhdum-ul-Mulk, now wretched in the shadow of Shaikh Mubarak's increasing heft. All of them, writes Badauni, 'signed it against their will'; except, of course, Shaikh Mubarak, who even added an eager postscript to his signature, saying that 'he most willingly signed his name; for this was a matter to which for several years he had been anxiously looking forward'.

It wasn't just the meaning of the mahzar that would have troubled the ulema, but also its language. Shaikh Mubarak had proclaimed Akbar 'the imam of the time and the mujtahid of the age'. As Wheeler M. Thackston explains it in his translation of the *Akbarnama*, 'imam' would refer to the Shiite belief in successive descendants of the Prophet Muhammad sent to earth to lead the Muslim world; while 'mujtahid', an interpreter of Islamic law, was an office considered unnecessary by Sunni jurisprudence, which favoured precedence over interpretation. In assuming these titles, therefore, Akbar was '[a]pparently determined to offend everyone' – both Shias and Sunnis would consider his claim controversial, if not downright heretical.[19]

Iqtidar Alam Khan[20] argues for a rather different interpretation of the mahzar's meaning. Is it not a little odd, he asks, that Abul Fazl, whose own father drafted the mahzar, doesn't include a copy of it in the *Akbarnama*? We have it via Badauni. Abul Fazl only provides a summary, and a misleading summary at that, 'creat[ing] the impression that the mahzar declared the king's role to be that of an arbitrator' between quarrelling jurists, whereas, in fact, it proposed Akbar as the 'sole head of the orthodox Muslims of India'[21] – it did not mean to offend them but to bring them into the ambit of Akbar's authority.

Why would Abul Fazl downplay the mahzar's meaning? Possibly, writes Iqtidar Alam Khan, because it gave Akbar paramount religious authority over his Muslim subjects alone, 'and not . . . the whole world'. For Abul Fazl, whose entire narrative presents Akbar as a universal king, the petition's limited scope would have been 'rather embarrassing'.

Indeed, Abul Fazl's ambitions for his emperor were boundless. Fairly early in the *Akbarnama*, the historian offers a quick summary of Akbar's ancestors, tracing them all the way back to Adam. This is not just fanciful padding. 'Very deliberately', in fact, writes Harbans Mukhia, Abul Fazl's genealogy 'seeks to construct an alternative teleology of universal history' – a whole new way of understanding the story of humankind, that is – 'in which Akbar . . . would not be contained within the frame of a sect of humanity, i.e. Islam . . . heir not to Muhammad and the caliphs, but to Adam himself, the first human being, and thus the ruler of all humanity'.[22] For those who might argue that even Adam is particular to Semitic traditions, Abul Fazl may have an answer when he describes the Jain Tirthankaras as the 'twenty-four Adams' of the faith, the first of whom 'was Adinath, also called Raghunath'.[23]

Such happy incorporation of the many sects, religions and ethnicities of Hindustan in Akbar's embrace is the very foundation of the *Akbarnama*, though not original to it. The very idea of a 'sultan', in fact, as Richard Eaton argues, was that of a 'universal ruler', 'above all ethnic groups and religious communities'. It was an idea that grew over centuries in the Muslim world, following various historical developments, including the decline of the Abbasid Caliphate in Baghdad, that precipitated a split between religious and temporal power. Religious authority still vested in the caliph; but for the many sultans across the world who gave him their spiritual allegiance, managing increasingly diverse populations was the greater concern. Thus, Eaton continues, 'long before Renaissance or Enlightenment thinkers in Europe', scholars in Iran and Central Asia were propounding the separation of church and state. A twelfth-century Persian historian, Ibn Balkhi, for example, proposed this succinct tenet for temporal kingship: 'There is no kingdom without an army, no army without wealth, no wealth without material prosperity, and no material prosperity without justice.'[24]

Seen in this light, the mahzar went against the grain of both contemporary ideas of rulership and Akbar's own eventual vision of his authority. It was an evolving vision, however; there was a decade to go, at least, before Abul Fazl began putting it into words in the *Akbarnama*. For now, Akbar and his new friends were still experimenting.

For now, in Iqtidar Alam Khan's words, the mahzar was not an assertion of universal authority, nor even of universal religious authority, but rather 'the final and . . . most blatant of Akbar's measures to placate and win over orthodox Muslim opinion in India', which he had been wooing ever since the Uzbek revolt some fifteen years ago. And, as such, it was 'a debacle'.

Far from placating anyone, the document created a loud and immediate controversy. Even Abul Fazl acknowledges the explosion of criticism: Akbar hated Islam, had adopted Shia beliefs, had become a brahmin, wanted to be God Himself – 'the stupid denizens of the demon-haunted land of ignorance indulge[d] in foolish talk', 'every faction went about in the streets of ignorance . . . spreading calumnies', on 'every side there arose the dust of commotion'.

But what basis did these '[a]ssemblies of wickedness' and slander have, asks Abul Fazl. Take the matter of disdaining Islam or Muhammad: it was crystal clear that Akbar honoured the Prophet's family – why else would he excuse, indeed forbid, the sayyids in his court, the Prophet's descendants, from prostrating before him?

That the emperor had embraced Shiism was equally ludicrous! It might be, yes, that many Persians – many of them Shia – held high positions in court, but Central Asians were promoted too – were such honours 'hidden from . . . bigoted eyes' or wilfully ignored? To say that Akbar has turned 'to the Brahman religion' because he 'received Hindu sages into his intimacy, and increased . . . the rank of Hindus' – Abul Fazl could only shake his head in despair.

Badauni may have been among those making this last charge. Years later, he would write of the 'accursed Birbar' that the brahmin poet was trying to convince Akbar to worship the sun, and 'fire, water, stones, and trees, and all natural objects, even down to cows and their dung'; to start wearing caste markings and the 'Brahmanical thread'.

But it was absurd, Abul Fazl protested, an 'improper notion' with no foundation except that Akbar treated Hindus well 'for the good of the country'. And why not? The emperor 'was not only kind to them but an avid admirer of their civilisation'.[25]

As for the 'misfortunate ignobles . . . no more than beasts lurking in their nests' who alleged that Akbar was claiming the place of God's messenger – or even of God! – to them, Abul Fazl quotes Akbar's own response: 'Good God! How can it enter the minds of the ignorant that a created being mired in nature could claim divinity?'[26]

And yet, it is not for nothing that Abul Fazl is one of the world's most influential writers, the creator of one of the world's most iconic portraits of a ruler. The very words he uses for the ignobles' accusation also justify Akbar's claim. These men, writes the historian, 'lurking in their nests by night and stomping about blinded by daylight accused the world lord, whose lineage became more illustrious with each succeeding generation, of claiming divinity . . .'[27]

Adam is not the only ancestor of note in Akbar's genealogy. There is also Alanqoa's union with pure light, after all. Akbar was a Niru'un; his glory would, of course, blind those accustomed to the darkness of their own unexamined traditions. Metaphors of light fill the *Akbarnama*, in fact, and not by accident; his superhuman origins are part of Akbar's claim to superhuman authority.

But the story of Alanqoa does not end with light alone. It merges, in fact, with the story – and the claim – of Akbar's increasingly illustrious lineage. One of the many Mongol kings who descended from Alanqoa, writes Abul Fazl, had twin sons, Qabul and Qachulay, and the younger of them, Qachulay, had two dreams. In one, three stars rose to the left of his elder brother Qabul, and a fourth from Qabul's neck. In the second, seven stars rose from Qachulay's own neck, followed by an eighth of stunning brightness. Astrologers were consulted, and all agreed on the meaning of the dreams: both brothers would have illustrious sons, but at different times – Qabul after four generations and Qachulay after eight. This prompted their father to bequeath them both his rule. Qabul would occupy the throne while Qachulay wielded administrative and military power.

Traditionally, later astrologers identified Qabul's fourth star with Chinghis Khan, and Qachulay's eighth with Timur – the two brothers engendered two clans, in fact, Chingizid and Timurid, both of which were joined in Babur, born of a Chingizid mother and Timurid father.

It is not for this fortuitous mixing of royal blood, however, that Abul Fazl tells the story; he has far grander claims to make. Learned astrologers may have seen Timur's bright fortune in Qachulay's eighth star, but Abul Fazl's own interpretation of the facts indicates that its 'resplendent light' could only mean the 'holy personality of . . . [Akbar] the King of Kings who hath by the light of his Being illumined the terrene and terrestrials'. Thus, as Corinne Lefèvre argues in an enlightening essay on the link between Qachulay's dreams and Akbar's reality, Abul Fazl uses 'genealogy . . . in support of the exceptional status now claimed by the emperor and, consequently, of his divine right to rule'.[28]

It would be a while before either Akbar or his historian made their claims explicit. However, it may be no coincidence that now, at about the same time that Abul Fazl's father, Shaikh Mubarak, drafted his mahzar, he 'also suggested . . . that Akbar embodied *farr*, the pre-Islamic Iranian concept of a divinely bestowed charismatic essence'.[29] Or, as Abul Fazl would write one day, summoning all the rhetorical force of a clear truth told in simple terms: Akbar was 'a lamp for the dark world'.[30]

On 7 September 1579, a week after the Infallibility Decree had been signed and proclaimed, and possibly as a result of the furore it created, Akbar left Fatehpur for Ajmer, once again. It had long been his habit to visit Shaikh Moinuddin Chishti's dargah before and after any great enterprise and yet, though Akbar had won as great a victory against his jurists as against any

Uzbek or Mirza, Abul Fazl insists that this time the emperor travelled reluctantly. The blessings of Ajmer's Chishti saint had been integral to Akbar's rule these past decades, but now he only went as a way of 'calming the public' – all those 'ignobles' stomping in protest, no doubt.[31]

En route, the emperor was met by a far more agreeable gathering of his subjects. They wanted to tell Akbar the story of a traveller who was going past 'a dreadful forest' nearby when he ran into a hungry lion that 'rose up to destroy his life'. Terrified, the man drew a circle around himself and 'called upon the name of the world's lord'. At Akbar's name, the lion stopped in its tracks. The traveller lived to tell his tale.[32]

Did Akbar wonder, as he heard the story and promised never to hunt a lion again – adding, modestly and pragmatically, 'If the tale be true'[33] – did he wonder why he worried about clerics and mansabdars grumbling and gossiping in the bazaars of Fatehpur when the faith of his people grew stronger by the day? It was on this trip to Ajmer, at any rate, that he ordered Abdun Nabi and Makhdum-ul-Mulk into exile.

The two men must have seen it coming. Two years earlier, in December 1577, Akbar had dissolved the powers of his sadr, Abdun Nabi, and distributed his judicial duties across multiple offices in the various provinces of Hindustan. The emperor was tactful about it, explaining that the job was 'larger than one person can control',[34] but tactically, Akbar had done to Abdun Nabi and his ulema what he did to his warlords: curtailed their independence and made what power he left them dependent on his own.

Unlike the warlords, moreover, neither Abdun Nabi nor Makhdum-ul-Mulk seems to have been able to gather support to fight Akbar. Abdun Nabi's arrogant disbursal of grants, spraying used water on his petitioners' faces, could not have endeared him to them. Of Makhdum-ul-Mulk, Badauni writes that his greed was such that he would transfer his property to his wife at the end of every year, to avoid paying the compulsory Islamic tax, zakat, and 'practised some other tricks of which even the Israelites would have been ashamed'. As for his piety, Badauni tells of a convoluted argument that Makhdum-ul-Mulk had come up with to avoid the Haj. To go to Mecca, he said, would mean traversing Shia Iran or suffering the heresy of a Portuguese passport stamped with 'pictures of Mary and Jesus (peace be upon Him!)'. Therefore, the Haj became sinful, and its avoidance a virtue.

One can imagine Badauni and others chortling at the fate that banished the two old men on this very pilgrimage, but it is hard not to feel a little pity for them – once so powerful that people trembled at their names, now scrabbling for relevance. Ever since they felt the emperor's favour turn cold, the jurists had been struggling to please him. Makhdum-ul-Mulk, who would have had Shaikh Mubarak executed for blasphemy; Abdun Nabi, who once scolded the emperor for using saffron during a birthday ceremony – throwing his stick at

Akbar in anger![35] – were now willing to say anything to gratify the emperor's irreverent spirit. They would even, writes Badauni, suggest that the Quran was a forgery, throw 'doubts on the authority of prophets and Imams', utterly deny 'the existence of demons and angels', but it did them no good.

They 'knew nothing of science and had nothing but . . . long tongue[s]', writes Abul Fazl, enjoying his revenge. The two men protested their banishment as vigorously – or piteously – as they could, but Akbar treated them as good doctors must when they make their patients, 'willing or unwilling, swallow bitter drugs'. Like it or not, the maulanas were off to Mecca.

On 10 December 1579, Akbar was back from Ajmer, holding court in Fatehpur and sparing not a thought, presumably, for the empty spaces where his wretched clerics must once have stood. It might have been now that Akbar uttered another of his Happy Sayings, dismissing the Devil as 'an old-world notion'. 'Who', he asked, 'has the power to oppose the will of God?'

It was only four years earlier that Akbar had prayed on a hard stone outside this very palace, wishing for a pious man to resolve his fears about taking the wrong path. True greatness consists in doing the will of God, he had said, but what if he was following the Devil's way by mistake? Now, it may be that Akbar had decided to frame the matter in ontological terms rather than moral or ethical ones. That is to say: if, as his question presumes, the will of God is an irresistible force that cannot be challenged – well then, whatever path he was on must be the way of God.

It was no longer musth elephants the emperor was riding, looking for signs of divine approval – he was astride his entire realm, goads in hand, driving it forward. Like it or not.

Only one month later, the empire bucked.

On 19 January 1580, the feast of Bakrid, when Muslims commemorate the unquestioning submission of Ibrahim to his ineffable deity, Akbar's officers in Bengal mutinied against their lord.

Chapter 11

A House of Turbulence

'Tyranny is unlawful in everyone, especially in a sovereign who is the guardian of the world.'

– Akbar, Happy Sayings, *Ain-i-Akbari*

It was five years earlier, when Akbar returned from Patna and inaugurated his Ibadat Khana, pushed through his mansabdari reforms, and began to look for the Truth, that his uncle Sulaiman of Badakhshan arrived in Fatehpur, mouth agape at the splendour of his nephew's realm. If Babur's sons had failed to grasp the destiny he left for them, his grandson had fulfilled his dream. The parade of gaily decorated elephants and bejewelled cheetahs proclaimed a well-justified pride in what he had achieved. Babur, after all, had only assumed the title of padishah; Akbar was the real thing.[1] Under his watch, beleaguered Timurids did not flee north across the Indus to lick their wounds in Kabul and squabble over its possession; they came south, instead, seeking the aid and refuge of the emperor of Hindustan.

Sulaiman had lost his kingdom. Or, as some might say, he had lost the kingdom of his redoubtable queen, Haram Begum. Annette Beveridge writes that Sulaiman 'held Badakhshan so long as Haram's watchful eye was on him, and lost it at her death'[2] – two clauses that hold a book's worth of adventure between them. Sulaiman's life, over the past years, had been a relentless mix of power politics and soap opera.

After Kamran's defeat, exile and death, his cousin Sulaiman had developed a fondness for Khanim, one of Kamran's widows. That he dared entertain such a thought while married to Haram is testament to his Timurid blood, but he had underestimated his wife. Haram had 'anticipated matters', writes Abul Fazl, and married Khanim off to her son, Ibrahim.[3]

197

It is no surprise that the two women were possessed by 'evil thoughts' for each other thereafter. Things got worse after Ibrahim died in battle. For the rest of her life, his mother would dress in dark blue, the Central Asian colour of mourning, but her grief did not spark a reconciliation with Ibrahim's widow. Instead, Haram began to taunt Khanim, hoping that she would run away to her father's home. Khanim was made of stern stuff, however; besides, she had a young son, Shahrukh, whom she was raising to change her fortune one day. Thus, writes Abul Fazl, Khanim 'treated those cutting reproaches as if she heard them not. But she [did indulge] in . . . thoughts of revenge.' It wasn't long before her daydreams took form. First at seven, then at fifteen, Shahrukh was the fulcrum of rebellions by Sulaiman's and Haram's chiefs. 'Haram was a clever woman', however, writes Nizamuddin, 'she kept a sharp watch over Shah Rukh, and prevented any outbreak'.[4] The rebellions did not succeed.

But now, Haram had died and Shahrukh, though still in his teens,[5] had begun such a vigorous assault on Sulaiman's territories that his widowed grandfather had fled to Akbar in Fatehpur.

Akbar had greeted his embittered uncle cheerfully, and, at a banquet in his honour, promised to send Husain Quli, Akbar's governor in Punjab, to get Badakhshan back for him.

Sulaiman, old and alone, dazzled by unfamiliar customs and luxury, may have comforted himself, later that night, with visions of going back home. Sadly, it was not to be. It wasn't ten days after Sulaiman found refuge in Fatehpur that another old Central Asian chief, Munim Khan, died in Bengal and the former lord of Badakhshan found his small ambitions drowned in the vast turmoil of empire.

Somehow, ageing and injured, Munim Khan had managed to keep both Bengal and – equally difficult – the Mughal commanders under control. Akbar's indulgent ataliq was in his eighties now, but more energetic than his army, it seems – all that the Mughal chiefs thought about was 'taking their ease', according to Abul Fazl. Still, Munim had managed to keep them chasing after the Afghans across Bengal and – after that bloody battle in Tukaroi – negotiated a truce with the slippery Daud.

Some of Munim's zest for conquest may have derived from the presence, in his neighbourhood, of Akbar's disgraced accountant and sore loser at chaupar, Muzaffar Khan. It was this very Muzaffar Khan who had superseded Munim, his old patron, and replaced him as vakil of the realm. Since then, however, Muzaffar Khan had fallen foul of Akbar on several occasions. When forbidden his love for a man, Muzaffar had declared himself a dervish; for protesting those endless rounds of chaupar, he was exiled. His response to Akbar's mansabdari ideas had been grudging at best; soon afterwards, he had spoken out of turn just before the emperor set sail for Patna, for which offence Muzaffar Khan was expelled from the expedition.

In short, Muzaffar Khan had not had the smoothest of career graphs, but he had found something of a second wind in the east.

Here, working independently of Akbar's 'official' conquest of Bengal and Bihar, which was headed by Munim, Muzaffar Khan had made great efforts to regain Akbar's favour, including a valiant if unsuccessful bid for Rohtas fort, and an impressive victory against an Afghan army in Bihar, for which Akbar gave him Hajipur.

Munim Khan, unhappy with the sudden return to favour of his erstwhile underling, wanted Muzaffar gone, but Akbar was pleased with his accountant's performance on the battlefield and ordered him to remain. Muzaffar Khan settled down to feast on the fruits of his success. He 'came to Hajipur', writes Abul Fazl, 'and spread the carpet of enjoyment' – little knowing how the rug would be snatched from under his feet.

Munim, meanwhile, settled in Gaur, the old capital of Bengal, at the very time that the city was afflicted by a plague. '*Az Gaur ba gor*' is how Nizamuddin describes the devastation – from Gaur to the grave. His officers begged to leave the city for the newer capital, Tanda, but Munim wouldn't budge. Maybe he knew something the others did not: though corpses were being chucked out of Gaur into the river outside, Munim remained immune to 'that typhoon of plague'.[6] It was only when he did finally move to Tanda that Munim caught 'a little illness'.[7]

Munim Khan had lived a long life. Perhaps, in these last ten days of it he remembered how Humayun had come chasing after him as he tried to abandon the destitute padishah; perhaps he remembered sitting mid-river with Ali Quli Shaibani, shedding nostalgic tears for Humayun's death. Perhaps he remembered letting Akbar skip school to fly his pigeons and was amazed, one last time, at what a formidable man that restless boy had become. Or perhaps it was not Akbar's childhood Munim recalled, but his own – the crisp air and orchards of Kabul, as he breathed his last mouthfuls of rain-moist air by a river in Bengal.

On 27 October 1575, Munim Khan died. Two weeks later, the news of his death arrived in Fatehpur along with reports that Daud had reneged on his truce; there was 'great uneasiness' in the imperial army, its commanders were 'disgusted with the country',[8] and some were even spreading 'unpleasing reports' about Akbar.[9]

This was the very year in which Akbar initiated his Ibadat Khana debates, so it isn't hard to guess what the rumours might have been. Akbar may even have confirmed them by sending his Shia commander Husain Quli to replace Munim – and thus, incidentally, dashed his own uncle Sulaiman's hopes of having the general escort him back to Badakhshan in triumph.[10]

When Husain Quli reached the east, its disgruntled and leaderless army had already abandoned their Bengali conquests – the old capital cities of Gaur and Tanda among them – and were in Bhagalpur, halfway back to Patna. The Central Asian Sunni chiefs were not happy to see their new Shia commander, mistrustful and prone to 'chatter foolishly'[11] about him. To sweeten the deal, perhaps, Akbar also sent 'boats laden with money and goods'. These arrived along with a man who would become even more unpopular than Husain Quli among the Central Asians in Bengal: the new lord of Hajipur, Muzaffar Khan.

Muzaffar Khan was now one of four broad power centres among the Mughals in Bihar and Bengal. The others were Todar Mal, a clan of Central Asian warlords called the Qaqshals, and their unpopular new governor, Husain Quli. Somehow these commanders managed to cobble together a working coalition. On 12 July 1576, just over three weeks after the fiercely fought battle of Haldighati, another Mughal army fought another ferocious enemy – and defeated Daud in a battle so bloody that streams of gore 'carried away heads like polo-balls'.[12] Daud was taken prisoner and seemed on the verge of getting a lucky truce once again. When Husain Quli asked why he had reneged on his pact with the Mughals, Daud replied cheekily that the old pact was with Munim; would Husain Quli like to make a new one?

Besides charm, Daud possessed good looks, too. Husain Quli 'did not wish to kill him, for he was a very handsome man', writes Badauni. It was the other commanders – having already suffered the result of trusting the fallen sultan, perhaps – who persuaded him to do so. For all that Daud had failed to keep his father's throne, he showed himself capable of a noble death. When he asked for water, writes Badauni, an unkind Mughal soldier brought it to him in his slipper. Defeated but dignified, Daud refused, and Husain Quli gave him his own canteen. When the time for his execution came, the sultan was as unwilling to part with his head as with his pride: the Mughal men 'took two chops at his neck without success', writes Badauni, before 'they succeeded in killing him'.

So fell the Bengal sultanate. Its last sultan's head was 'stuffed . . . with straw, and anointed . . . with perfumes', and given to one Sayyid Abdullah Khan, to take to Akbar.

The messenger and his prize arrived just in time. Daud had been creating such a ruckus that Akbar had decided to go east once again, but had only just left Fatehpur when he had one of his new visions: news of victory would soon arrive. Indeed, he was still on the outskirts of Agra when Abdullah Khan came bearing Daud's head, and, in an indignity that the dead sultan couldn't prevent, threw it into a shed.

Akbar was delighted at news of Daud's defeat. As a reward, he had such quantities of gold poured into Abdullah Khan's lap, the messenger couldn't pick it all up.

The Anup Talao overflowing with coins, the messenger's lap heaped with gold – Akbar had come a long way from the young ruler whose attendants scrambled for 17 rupees in an echoing treasury. It was only a little before Abdullah Khan that Badauni, too, had arrived bearing news from a battlefield – in his case, Haldighati – and he presents a scene of Akbar disbursing largesse that is the spitting image, if not the genesis, of the stereotypical oriental despot and his pots of gold. 'The Emperor was exceedingly pleased', writes Badauni, both at news of the battle and because Badauni had brought Rana Pratap's grand elephant, Ram Prasad, along with him. To reward the messenger, Akbar reached into 'a heap of Ashrafis (which in those days, just like a heap in a treasury, used always to be laid before him)' and gave him ninety-six gold coins.[13]

For all the magnificent display of excess, Akbar's munificence was neither profligate nor unplanned. Almost as frequent as battles in the *Akbarnama* are scenes of Akbar in consultation with the men who calculated his revenues, planned the assessments of his lands, and, in sum, turned conquest to profit. As Abul Fazl would put it, 'the care of property, and the increase of finances are, in the code of princes, a choice form of . . . Divine worship'.

Besides, all the early Mughals had a near-obsessive interest in order and categorization, and Akbar's organizational bent of mind, as revealed in the *Ain-i-Akbari*, was as impressive as his physical courage. Abul Fazl records that Akbar had at least four categories of accountants and twelve of treasurers (nine for cash, three for gems and jewels). The heaps of *ashrafis* that Badauni describes were petty cash, 'gold and silver for the needy', who might 'have their wants relieved without delay'. In addition, Akbar's court also contained 10 million copper dams kept in coarse cloth bags holding 1000 dams each, and one amir who carried a 'purse' with 'a large sum of money' – presumably for sudden exigencies.[14]

Best known of Akbar's financial advisers was Todar Mal, a 'far-sighted and incorruptible man, who understood the secrets of administration',[15] as Abul Fazl describes him, and equally adept at war. More recently, a diwan of Munim Khan's, Shah Mansur, jobless after Munim's demise, had caught Akbar's eye and been appointed his vizier. In early September 1577, these two men were joined by Muzaffar Khan. Three years after he was expelled from the Patna expedition, two years after he was rewarded with Hajipur, and a year or so after Daud's perfumed head arrived in Fatehpur, Muzaffar Khan finally returned to Akbar's court, bringing a lavish tribute of 400,000 rupees. Akbar welcomed the reformed grump and appointed him head of his administration, with Todar Mal and Shah Mansur as his deputies. This time around, Muzaffar Khan must have behaved himself, for an even greater increase in power would follow within eighteen months.

On 22 December 1578, just days after Khwaja Sultan returned from the Haj with his story of the miraculous rescue of the boy who fell overboard, Husain

Quli died in the east. It does not appear as if Akbar regretted his demise, for all that Husain Quli had been an effective and uncomplaining general all these years. It may be that Husain Quli was tiring of doing his duty, or that he was impatient for more. According to Abul Fazl, he had even killed Daud's mother so that the loot he had seized from the Afghans 'might remain concealed'. It was twelve years since Akbar had galloped to Malwa to retrieve his due from Adham Khan, but clearly his commanders still liked to try and keep their earnings for themselves.

Some three months later, in March 1579, Akbar made Muzaffar Khan his governor in the east. A whole new set of commanders – or, more accurately, officials – went with him, including the refugee from Shia Iran, Hakim Abul Fath, whom Badauni accuses of pandering to Akbar's heresies and thus becoming his best friend. But that was not all. Not only did Akbar send a most finicky accountant, Muzaffar Khan, to govern the battle-weary, loot-hungry chiefs of Bengal, not only did he send a most provocative thinker, Abul Fath, who often went 'in advance of' Akbar's own heresies, to plague them, he also issued an imperial order: the amirs in Bengal should not presume to 'exceed'[16] their new governor's command.

It was not for the warlords of Bengal, however, to succumb, like Abdun Nabi and Makhdum-ul-Mulk, to a decree. By the spring of the following year, Muzaffar Khan's unwilling new subordinates had killed him.

It would be an understatement to say that Akbar's pet mansabdari reforms were unpopular. His milk brother Aziz, the only man who had been allowed to hunt with Akbar in that first, grand qamargah in Lahore, who had ridden in Akbar's howdah in the battle against the Uzbek brothers, who was the son of Shamsuddin and Jiji, the quasi-parents that had cared for the emperor when he was an infant howling in the dark – his milk brother and closest friend, that is – hated the reforms.

In October 1575, the year that Akbar inaugurated both his Ibadat Khana and his new administration, the emperor invited Aziz to court, planning to put him in charge of branding his mansabdars' horses. Branding, or '*dagh*', was as much a part of the mansabdari plan as the appropriation of semi-independent fiefs. Unlike the warlords of old, whose loyalty to monarchs like Humayun was calculated with one eye firmly on political advantage and material gain, mansabdars would be ranked and paid according to the number of soldiers and horses they maintained, and would be expected to produce them on order, not inclination. To prevent any possible, and predictable, corruption of the system – soldiers and horses paraded on hire, basically – Akbar had reintroduced the system of dagh, devised by Alauddin Khilji and used more recently by Sher Shah Suri, by which his mansabdars' horses would be branded and therefore easily, and uniquely, identified.

Akbar would have known, of course, that warlords would not like being forced to give account of their armies, and so he called Aziz, his oldest friend, to help him. Perhaps he imagined that Aziz would gallop east from Ahmedabad as eagerly as Akbar had once galloped to Aziz's aid. If so, Aziz's reaction to Akbar's offer came as a rude shock.

Aziz used such 'language about . . . branding', writes Abul Fazl, that even 'men of ordinary prudence would not use' – let alone trusted friends. Badauni says that the conversation was more widely condemnatory of Akbar's policies: 'Everything that [Aziz] knew about these things he mentioned with unqualified disapprobation.' Furious, Akbar demoted his friend, banned him from court and put him under house arrest. Others whose corruption was revealed by branding (those who 'collected gold instead of troops',[17] that is) were banished to Bengal for Munim Khan to deal with – in the very month, as it happens, that Munim Khan died.

It was three years – in October 1578 – before Aziz was released, and another sixteen before the two friends were properly reconciled, but not once, in all that time, did Akbar hesitate to go ahead with his plans, even if he admitted they weren't perfect.

Badauni writes with disgust of fief-holders who, before Akbar's reforms, only 'amassed wealth' and had little interest in looking after their soldiers and peasants, and who, after the mansabdari system came into effect, would dress their servants in soldiers' clothes for the sake of their salary, while 'dust fell into the platter of the helpless soldier'. These new systems were amenable to other kinds of fraud, too. All kinds of people, 'tradespeople, weavers and cotton cleaners, carpenters, and green-grocers, both Hindu and Musalman', seeing an opportunity for a quick buck, 'borrowed horses, got them branded, and were appointed to a command'. Having pocketed a salary, the men faded from view: 'a few days afterwards no trace was to be found of the imaginary horse and the visionary saddle'. Akbar was well aware of this latter fraud, writes Badauni, but chose to let it slide, saying, 'With my eyes thus open I must give these men pay, that they may have something to live on.'

It wasn't the case, however, that mansabdari at these lower ranks was a kind of imperial charity; in fact, it was a whole reimagination of the idea of imperial service. Any man, theoretically, could become a mansabdar, whether or not he had the advantage of ethnic or clan affiliation; whether or not, indeed, he had any military experience. Ranks ranged from 10 to 5000, and only talent – in principle – decided if a man travelled up (or down) these grades. Abul Fazl, for example, came to court with an essay, not a sword; he was appointed to the branding department, as Badauni records, and 'worked so strenuously at the *dagh-u-mahalli* business, that he managed . . . to raise himself to a mansab of two thousand'.[18]

For anyone of a large mass of people – soldiers, scholars, painters, refugees – looking for a government job, mansabdari would have been a relatively transparent and effective system of employment. For the warlords, on the other hand, whose aspiration was to rule not serve, Akbar's reforms would have appeared like an assault on their pride. And that was partly the point: for mansabdari to work, Akbar would have to effect a fundamental shift in how his nobility conceived of their honour, 'from personal, lineage, or sectarian pride – that of the "free" warrior chief – to a more impersonal, imperial pride – that of the "slave" warrior-administrator'.[19]

This was easier said than done, and Akbar wasn't always very tactful about it. It has even been argued that Abul Fazl's bristling censure of 'the wicked ways of Transoxiana', to accompany Akbar's stern discouragement of his nobility's homosexual love affairs, was part of a 'very public campaign . . . in which [Akbar] juxtaposed his patriarchal and heterosexual model of north Indian male virtue against the corrupt practices of central Asian outsiders'.[20] Indeed, Central Asian chiefs in Hindustan were becoming outsiders to what they might have regarded as their own. By 1580, as Iqtidar Alam Khan has shown, the percentage of Central Asian chiefs in Akbar's court had shrunk to hardly a quarter, having comprised over half at the beginning of his reign.[21]

No wonder, then, that they were on edge. It was in 1580, in fact, that the chiefs of the east rebelled, led by a proud and deeply unhappy clan of Central Asians called the Qaqshals.

Eight years earlier, when Akbar was marching to Gujarat in 1572, trouble broke out in his camp between Baba Khan Qaqshal and a famously hot-tempered Punjabi called Shahbaz Khan (who would, some years later, take Kumbhalgarh from Rana Pratap).

The Qaqshals had long been with the Mughals in Hindustan; it was a Qaqshal, Majnun Khan, who had introduced Bihari Mal, Akbar's father-in-law, to the young padishah after the Kachhwaha chief negotiated his surrender of Narnaul. In the 1570s, most of the Qaqshals were in the east with Munim Khan, but some of them had been separated from their tribe and enlisted in Akbar's Gujarat expedition. This transfer was part of a larger policy of dispersing clans across the realm, to prevent the kind of accumulation of forces that had allowed the Uzbeks their rebellion. It was soon after the Uzbeks were defeated, in fact, that Akbar broke up the ataka khail, his foster father's increasingly powerful family, posting the various uncles, brothers and nephews out of Punjab. Only Aziz, Akbar's favourite, was allowed to remain in his fief.[22]

Akbar was right: much as a union of workers is a greater threat to a corporation than one disgruntled employee, a clan with shared interests could exert far more pressure on the imperial centre than a lone rebel. Now, for

example, rumours of the quarrel between Baba Khan Qaqshal and Shahbaz
Khan reached the east and caused an uproar. Some 'idle talkers and liars',
writes Abul Fazl, had exaggerated news of the fight and its consequences;
it was rumoured that Baba Khan and the other Qaqshals in the camp had
killed Shahbaz Khan and joined the Mirzas' rebellion. In retaliation, Akbar
had ordered all the Qaqshals in the east to be arrested. The eastern Qaqshals
panicked and abandoned Munim Khan, and Akbar might have found himself
fighting revolts on two fronts had the Qaqshals in Gujarat not sent a reassuring letter to their kin in the east, who returned to Munim Khan amid an
exchange of '[v]arious courtesies'.

In 1580, the conciliatory Munim was long gone. Instead, there was Muzaffar Khan.

Whether as accountant or as governor, Muzaffar Khan lacked the genial-
ity of spirit that is so necessary to lead men – if not to browbeat and command them. Instead, writes Abul Fazl, 'the forehead of his heart [was] full
of wrinkles'. Badauni tells the story of one Khalidi Khan, a noble 'of great
importance', positively begging to be excused from branding. The venerable
khan was imprisoned and bastinadoed at Muzaffar's command.

The governor's new deputies in Bihar were equally harsh '[in] matters of
reviews and drills and of branding . . . and in their blindness [they] neglected
tact and the acceptance of excuses', and his officials, it seems, were particularly incompetent or corrupt. Baba Khan Qaqshal, the man who had
quarrelled with Shahbaz Khan en route to Gujarat, complained that he had
paid 70,000 rupees 'in presents, and not one hundred horsemen have had the
branding effected, and the condition of the other fief-holders of this province
is still worse'.[23]

'*Bulgakh-khana*' is what the Mughals called Bengal, a 'house of turbulence'. It was a land, writes Abul Fazl, where the climate 'favour[s] the base,
[so that] the dust of dissension is always rising', and at this time, the eastern
chiefs were already nursing deep suspicions of Akbar and grudges against his
treasury. News would have come filtering in of their strange emperor wanting
to read the khutba, having convulsions on a hunt, encouraging newfangled
ideas in his palace, while his representatives ransacked and humiliated his
chiefs. Akbar's court may have been a 'garden of concord', as Abul Fazl
chirrups, but still '[b]ase minded people cast suspicions [on the emperor] and
fabricated . . . disturbance'.

It wasn't just foolish or arrogant, therefore, but positively hare-brained of
Muzaffar Khan to choose this moment to reduce military stipends. Worse, he
did so retrospectively. The army's salaries had been raised by 200 per cent
in Bengal and 150 per cent in Bihar; Muzaffar brought them down to 150
per cent and 120 per cent respectively, and began demanding money back. It
was in this tense atmosphere, rife with resentment and rumour, that a spark

fell into the eastern powder keg: a Qaqshal called Roshan Beg, newly arrived in the Bulgakh-khana from Kabul – the court of Akbar's half-brother, Mirza Muhammad Hakim.

It may seem that Akbar had forgotten all about Hakim, now in his late twenties and holding fast to Kabul ever since he made his ill-advised adolescent advance on Lahore fourteen years earlier and fled at the mere thought of Akbar's approach. But Akbar was not the kind of man to forget a possible threat, no matter now remote: he kept a watchful eye on goings-on between Kabul and Hindustan. Thus, as Roshan Beg Qaqshal greeted his kinsmen in Bengal, an imperial *farman*, order, arrived for Muzaffar Khan: have the Kabuli arrested.

If the idea was to keep the visiting Qaqshal under observation, Muzaffar Khan could have interpreted the order accordingly. As Badauni tells it, however, the governor took to the task with ham-fisted and mean-spirited zeal. He rode out to arrest Roshan Beg himself; then, waving his farman in Baba Khan Qaqshal's face, ordered the respected leader of the clan to cut his kinsman's head off. At this, writes Nizamuddin, all the Qaqshals in Bengal 'trembled together, and resolved upon mutiny'.[24]

The Bengal rebellion had begun.

News of the storm arrived in Fatehpur in late February 1580, and it is telling of how volatile Akbar's court was at this time that, by March, several of his courtiers were plotting to join the Bengalis. They were promptly executed. Back in the east, however, the revolt gathered force by the day, while Muzaffar Khan fumbled and hesitated.

Neither would the governor 'himself arrange the troops' for battle nor let his officers do so. When, finally, he did send an army against the mutineers, the battle was a shambles. Khwaja Shamsuddin, leading the imperial troops, saw his men 'going over to the enemy from every side' and his fellow commanders deserting in a steady stream. When an officer and friend came towards the khwaja, 'I thought that he would help me', he said, 'but the faithless . . . fellow hit me with a spear, and I fell and was nearly dead'.[25]

The leaders who remained loyal, meanwhile, were hardly serving the imperial cause any better. These were Akbar's newly recruited talent, and '[it] need hardly be said', writes Badauni's acid pen, 'that by Hakim Abu-l-Fath, who was a bottle-man rather than a battle-man, and by Patr Das, who was a Hindu writer, no great signs of valour would be likely to be shown in this line'. Muzaffar Khan barricaded himself in the Tanda fort ('four old walls and nothing more')[26] and began to woo the rebels with belated generosity. But '[w]hat profit comes of good nature and liberality at an improper time . . .?', asks Abul Fazl wisely. The most the furious warlords would do is allow their hated governor a choice: join them, or leave for Mecca. Muzaffar Khan chose exile.

As part of the deal, he also released an old prisoner. Sharafuddin, the emperor's former brother-in-law, languishing in chains ever since he was handed over to Akbar in Gujarat, was blessed with many lives and a stubborn spirit. A string of failed alliances had landed him in Akbar's dungeons, but when Sharafuddin walked out of Tanda a free man, he promptly joined the Qaqshals.

Whether at the tireless old rebel's suggestion, or from their own unabated resentment, it was on the day after Sharafuddin's release that the mutineers broke their promise to Muzaffar Khan. Instead of letting the governor go, they stormed Tanda and began to plunder. Muzaffar Khan, out to save money till the end, managed to sink eight chests full of gold in a nearby lake. But his luck had run dry. Sharafuddin found the chests, took the gold and replaced it with stones. Muzaffar Khan, meanwhile, was imprisoned, along with Abul Fath and Rai Patr Das. These two, regardless of Badauni's low opinion of them, had the wits to escape. Or perhaps the rebels weren't watching over them with much care; it was Muzaffar Khan they were after. The irascible accountant, so happy these past few years in the glow of Akbar's favour, had shown as much skill in battle as with his ledgers, but none, in the end, for governance. He was so hated that the rebels put him through 'all sorts of tortures', writes Badauni, as they killed him.

On 22 May, four months after the Qaqshals began their revolt and a month after they killed Akbar's governor, the chiefs of Bengal held a grand assembly, at which they gave themselves titles and land – and a new king. They read the khutba in Mirza Muhammad Hakim's name.

A terrible 'Divine wrath', writes Abul Fazl, descended upon the rebels' party. A great storm 'scattered' their tent, flinging their carpets 'into the mire' as the 'wretches . . . crept away'. For all the loyal indignation of his scribe, however, Akbar may have taken the matter far more in his stride. In fact, he had anticipated it. When news of the rebellion first arrived, the emperor had declared that he would not hurry east to suppress it. The rebels' 'audacity . . . is being backed . . . by the ruler of Kabul', he had said. 'It is not unlikely that flatterers may bring that light-headed, evil-thinking one into [Hindustan].' Akbar decided to wait and watch, and he was proven right.

Even now, when he received news of the rebels' proclamation, Akbar acted in no haste. For all the unrest among sections of his nobility, for all the unhappiness of his critics, Akbar's talent for conquest and organization had given him a vast and largely stable realm. He was thirty-eight years old and had ruled a quarter-century; no longer the young monarch who galloped after Adham Khan, after Ali Quli and Bahadur, after the Mirzas, a furious whirlwind establishing his authority by sweeping away any affront to it. Now, he could have other men do the job for him.

Three weeks after the mutineers' assembly, on 9 June 1580, Akbar met Aziz. His milk brother had been in the doghouse for half a decade, ever since he damned Akbar's reforms in 1575, but there were few men that Akbar could trust more than him. A 'river of milk' bound them, as the emperor would say,[27] excusing Aziz's sharp tongue and the fact that he never quite learnt to speak to his old friend as he ought to an emperor. Now, Aziz was restored to great favour: titled Khan Azam – the greatest khan – given command of an imperial army and the highest mansabdari rank, 5000 – and sent to quell the east.

Aziz was not the only man whom Akbar could rely on. His Persian courtiers remained broadly loyal to the emperor.[28] Even more so, the Hindustanis (not only Rajputs, but also Todar Mal and Indian Muslims such as the quarrelsome Punjabi Shahbaz Khan, for example), whom Akbar had cultivated over the years, had little sympathy with his disenchanted, disenfranchised Central Asian chiefs, and 'as a body sided with the King'.[29] Aziz was one of three senior commanders, therefore, that Akbar sent east; the other two were Todar Mal and Shahbaz Khan. All were true to their emperor, but all were also men of great pride, with little love lost for each other. As the campaign progressed, the imperial commanders were as much at loggerheads with each other as with the rebels. As Abul Fazl puts it, Shahbaz Khan 'looked at himself in the mirror, liked what he saw, and fell prey to arrogance'; Aziz was 'disgusted' at such preening self-importance; while Todar Mal 'threw in the towel'.[30]

Luckily, the rebels were similarly divided. It was one of Sharafuddin's new-found allies, for example, who finally ended his mutinous career. According to Abul Fazl, Sharafuddin acquired a dangerous rival in Masum Kabuli; both wanted to lead the rebellion and 'each lay in ambush for the other'. This unproductive state of affairs ended when Masum Kabuli bribed his competitor's young male love to poison Sharafuddin's opium.

Many others among the mutineers, if not actively plotting against each other, were far less committed to their cause than the imperial troops seem to have been. Soon after arriving in the east, for example, Todar Mal noticed that his colleague in the finance department, Shah Mansur, was demanding taxes from Bengal even while the rebellion raged. The raja complained to the emperor, who put his over-scrupulous vizier in prison. Promptly, many deserters in Bengal returned to the imperial fold.

Such reneging on the revolution was not taken lightly by the rebel commanders. Abul Fazl describes one of them, called Arab, killing a lapsed mutineer and drinking 'some of his blood'. And yet, no matter how terrifying these warlords, they had begun to lose their authority. Foremost among them was Baba Khan Qaqshal, the acknowledged leader of the whole enterprise, who had developed a terrible case of gangrene: 'every day he put two [seers] of flesh into the wound to feed the maggots',[31] while blaming his disgusting fate on his breach of loyalty.

The Bengal rebellion was losing some of its steam, therefore, when, in late December 1580, Akbar's half-brother Mirza Muhammad Hakim sent two successive contingents, one led by a man considered to be the very 'sword of his army', into Hindustan.

Once again, Akbar kept his cool; though Abul Fazl, in his aggravation, can hardly control his metaphors. What could Hakim be thinking? 'Little did he know that a trickle of water is useless against a raging fire, and scratching is not an effective treatment against chronic haemorrhoids.'[32] Indeed, Akbar's men in Punjab – led by yet another of his most trusted generals, Man Singh – made quick work of Hakim's troops. His crack swordsman was wounded and died.

Then, in January 1581, exactly one year after the Qaqshals mutinied, news arrived that Mirza Hakim had ridden into Hindustan himself. Until now, Akbar had insisted he wouldn't make hasty decisions about Hakim's incursions. 'A son can be acquired', he would say, 'but how can a brother be obtained?'[33]

By crossing the Indus, however, his brother had crossed a line that Akbar could not ignore. Two weeks later, on 6 February 1581, Akbar rode out of Fatehpur to war, as his father had done so often before, against his own.

Chapter 12

Brotherhood of Man

'He also had this bad habit: while one of his questions was being answered, he would suddenly, and before there had been time to deal with it, ask another. He had not the patience to hear one explanation at a time but in his eagerness for knowledge, tried to learn everything at once, like a hungry man trying to swallow his food at a single gulp.'

— The Jesuit Fathers, *Akbar and the Jesuits*

That Humayun's brothers loom as large in history as the padishah himself while Akbar's brother is entirely forgotten says as much about the two emperors as it does about how history is written. As Munis Faruqui points out in his aptly titled essay, 'The Forgotten Prince', three currents of historiography have come together to sink Muhammad Hakim in the dull waters of obscurity.

First, there was Akbar's propaganda, via Abul Fazl, characterizing his half-brother as a 'dim-witted, self-serving, and cowardly but obdurate political gadfly'; followed by colonial writings in which Hakim appears as a 'narrow-minded Muslim bigot . . . a foil against which to better appreciate Akbar's tolerance'; and finally, the unfortunate mirza's 'multiple identities as a Kabul-based, orthodox-Muslim, Persian-speaking, ethnic-Turk' made of him an ungainly square peg in the round hole of nationalist narratives written in the twentieth century.[1]

And yet, as Faruqui demonstrates, Hakim posed a serious challenge to Akbar while he lived, and did so far more cleverly than he is given credit for. In brief, while Akbar embodied the ideal man become all-powerful emperor, exercising his God-given right to rule for the betterment of his people, Hakim adopted the persona of the adventurer – and not of just any adventurer but of the most adventurous man in the two brothers' family, their grandfather Babur.

'Like Babur', writes Faruqui, Hakim, 'actively embraced a rough-and-ready Turkish-steppe identity'. In equal parts ghazi, Islamic warrior, and avid gardener; as much a 'bold risk-taker' (marching upon Lahore in the 1560s while on the run from Sulaiman and Haram) as a generous companion, 'carousing with friends . . . in the hills above Kabul'. The most critical play in this competition of personas between Akbar and Hakim, however, was how 'the Mirza emulated Babur in his patronage of the Naqshbandi sufi tariqah'.

After his mother was murdered, when Hakim was still a child, the prince had grown increasingly close to Khwaja Hasan Naqshbandi, and through him to his highly orthodox Sufi order, which not only served to give Hakim's Kabul a clear identity as 'a bastion of Naqshbandi and orthodox-Sunni Islam' but also bolstered the prince economically and politically – with its extensive landholdings, for example, or by providing a basis for alliance between Hakim and the increasingly powerful Uzbek ruler to his north, Abdullah Khan of Turan, also a follower of the Naqshbandis.

Given this context, Akbar's embrace of the Chishtis takes on a whole new dimension. The Chishtis, as Faruqui points out, 'were a quintessentially Indian Sufi order with few or no ties to either Afghanistan or Central Asia' – but a definite and popular presence in Punjab 'where Akbar needed all the support he could get to checkmate Mirza Hakim's longstanding territorial claims'.[2] How consciously or not such decisions were made is difficult to say, of course. It is possible that the Naqshbandi order appealed emotionally to Hakim as much as it did strategically – he was an orphaned child, after all, when Khwaja Hasan first came to him. The Chishtis' 'eclectic and accommodating religious and spiritual practices', meanwhile, would certainly have struck a chord with Akbar's own curious and inventive soul.

The fact of the matter is also, however, that in many public aspects of their lives, the brothers played out a public rivalry. Thus, if Hakim adopted Babur, then Akbar exerted his claim on their father, Humayun. Humayun's beautiful tomb, which remains a landmark in Delhi, was built for exactly that purpose: to indicate 'the new center of an imperial Mughal geography now in Hindustan and under Akbar's control'. Akbar didn't just build the tomb. As Faruqui notes, the emperor made several 'highly publicized visits to [it] . . . between the 1560s and early 1580s' – between the Uzbek and Bengal revolts that is – and 'each of these visits . . . occurred against a backdrop of heightened tensions or actual strife with the Mirza [Hakim]'. Hakim, meanwhile, played his politics in a different coin, quite literally: he banned Akbar's currency from Kabul in favour of the traditional 'shahrukhi' coinage used by Babur and Humayun, as a way of contrasting his own 'loyalty to Central Asian political traditions with Akbar's neglect'. During and after the Uzbek disturbances in the 1560s, writes Faruqui, Hakim offered Kabul as 'a safe haven for Akbar's enemies', positioning himself as the protector of defeated refugees returning home, and also as a king in the style they remembered with such nostalgia, not an absolute monarch but 'a *primus inter pares* – or first among equals'. Akbar – 'the greater' – had never had much use for this old model. Thus, when the emperor marched out of Fatehpur in February to teach Hakim a lesson, he had seven groups of high-ranking mansabdars – or amirs – leading the various battalions of his army. This was to symbolize and sustain a protocol that Akbar had invented soon after he promulgated his mansabdari reforms in 1575. By the emperor's orders, seven groups of amirs were assigned seven watches – each group to guard the emperor for a full twenty-four hours once a week. For anyone watching to see if their stubborn emperor was having second thoughts about his style of rule for fear of Hakim's appeal to the outraged warlords in the east, the message was clear. Akbar's nobility stood in his service; they should not dream of stepping into his shoes.

A year had passed since news of the Bengal insurrection reached his court, and although Akbar had spared neither resources nor men in crushing the rebellion, he had shown no sign of undoing the policies and actions that led to it: the consolidation of political and financial power in the emperor's hands, the expansion of his social, moral, even religious authority, and the increasing diversity of his court and his beliefs. In fact, news of Bengal had arrived in the very month that a much-anticipated set of fresh debaters reached Akbar's controversial Ibadat Khana. These were three Jesuit priests – a sensitive, self-flagellating Rudolf Aquaviva, his mind inclined towards martyrdom; the more genial Antonio Monserrate, who later wrote an account of their journey; and Francis Henriquez, a Persian convert and interpreter for his colleagues. The three men travelled from Goa to the Mughal court at Akbar's express invitation, with a clear mission: to convert the emperor to Christianity.

They had some reason to believe they might succeed. 'Royal converts were not unknown in the Indies', writes a colonial historian. Kings in the Maldives and Sri Lanka had become Christian, 'and a near relation of the King of Bijapur had been baptized at Goa shortly after Father Rudolf's arrival from Europe'.[3] The Fathers made the long and difficult journey to Fatehpur in optimism, therefore, as Monserrate describes it, even if they were occasionally downcast to observe the 'wild and savage cries' of Muharram, or the no less 'degraded' celebrations of Holi. As they travelled along the western coast, from Goa to Gujarat, ever north via the forested inclines of the Satpuras, across the clear waters of the Narmada ('the fish and turtles, and even the smallest pebbles, can be counted') and past the royal ruins of Mandu, the priests shook their heads at the 'carelessness' of the Muslim rulers of these lands, who may have destroyed some temples, but 'allowed sacrifices to be publicly performed, incense to be offered, oil and perfumes to be poured out, the ground to be sprinkled with flowers, and wreaths to be hung up, wherever . . . any fragment of an idol is to be found'. Worse, many of the temples were now replaced by the shrines of equally 'wicked and worthless Musalmans'.[4] The Fathers couldn't help having a little weep at this state of affairs, but cheered up in Gwalior, where they took the city's famous Jain statues, carved on the walls below the Gwalior fort, for Jesus Christ and his disciples. Indeed, wrote Father Monserrate, he knew for a fact that 'three hundred years ago this district [Gwalior] was inhabited by Christians, who were, alas, defeated in various battles by the Musalmans, and so effectively crushed that all memory of Christianity has perished from the minds of men'.

The Fathers hoped to revive that past glory, and their confidence was bolstered when they met another priest, Francis Julian Pereira, in Fatehpur. Pereira told them that Akbar was on the very brink of conversion, that he believed in Christ's miracles, that he had paintings of Christ, Mary and Moses, alongside Muhammad, in his dining hall.[5] It only needed one last little nudge for the world's most powerful monarch to join the Fathers', and their nation's, faith.

What a coup that would have been! But Pereira was wrong, and the Fathers failed – as did the two missions that followed in their wake. What they did succeed in doing, however, and with Akbar's active encouragement, was to rankle his conservative courtiers and ulema more than ever before.

The best-known example of the Jesuits in furious debate with Muslim theologians is the 'Fire Test', recounted by several chroniclers of the time, from Badauni to Father Monserrate himself.

Each tells it in his own way. In Badauni's version, it began when one Shaikh Qutubuddin, brought to court at Akbar's orders and set to debate the Jesuits, invited them to undertake a trial by fire with him. 'The Shaikh pulled one of the Christian priests by the coat, and said to him, "Come on, in the name of God!"' Whichever of them practised the true faith would escape the flames unscathed. The priests were too scared to accept, writes Badauni, and the shaikh was soon after exiled to Sindh.[6]

Abul Fazl, on the other hand, writes that it was Padre Rudolf, a 'Nazarene [sage] . . . singular for his understanding and ability', who dared the 'untruthful bigots' that he was debating to walk into a roaring fire with him, each holding their holy books, leaving the rest to God. 'The liverless and black-hearted fellows wavered', Abul Fazl concludes mercilessly, 'and in reply to the challenge had recourse to . . . wrangling'.[7]

Finally, there is Monserrate's version. According to this, the most detailed of the three tellings, the Fathers had launched a full-scale attack on the 'haughty pride' of the Prophet Muhammad. At this, the Muslims proposed a trial by fire; a proposal that Akbar seconded with some enthusiasm – he 'urged the same course upon the priests' – but the Jesuits refused. Annoyed, Akbar got up and left.

Monserrate is quick to add that they did not refuse from cowardice. On the contrary, Rudolf 'eagerly sought' any opportunity to martyr himself.[8] It wasn't that he didn't want to enter the fire, it's just that 'he was in doubt as to its rightness at present'.

Soon after, in a private conference with a clearly disappointed emperor, Rudolf gathered his wits and declared that he and his companions would gladly enter 'not one but a thousand pyres' – and they didn't even care if they burned alive in them. Why just fire, he went on, carried away by his own eloquence, 'Trusting in divine aid, we have no fear of elephants, lions, panthers, leopards, precipices, crosses, stripes, and all manner of tortures.' Let the flames be lit!

But then, Rudolf introduced a caveat into the matter. He would gladly walk into fire and burn – or not – but he would not admit it as a test. They were all three sinners, he said, of himself and his colleagues; how could they presume that God wanted to save them? Besides, when even Christ had refused to trouble God for miracles, how dare the Fathers?

At this, Akbar replied that he hadn't invited the Fathers all this way from Goa just to roast them alive. All he wanted, he said, was to enlist them in tricking a 'religious preceptor' (possibly the Shaikh Qutubuddin of Badauni's story). Rudolf refused, declaring primly that, as priests, they were neither allowed to 'kill a man . . . [nor] make any attempts to bring about a man's execution'.

Akbar insisted: 'I do not wish you to undergo the ordeal; I only desire that you should say you will'.

But no. 'We cannot do even that, O King.'

What if Akbar made the challenge on the Fathers' behalf? They need not implicate themselves in a lie, only remain silent through it. But again, Rudolf refused, declaring he would announce his dissent loudly should Akbar do any such thing.

Thus, it appears, Akbar's fire fizzled out under the wet blanket of the padre's piety, but the stories remain, and they cast a most revealing light upon the emperor. Azfar Moin, who analyses these three narratives of the Fire Test in some detail, suggests that Akbar's alleged enthusiasm for the trial reveals, or underlines, two core facets of the emperor's personality: '[his] fondness for "hands on" knowledge and [for] public spectacle'. Just as he enjoyed the battle of the sanyasis, long ago, on the banks of the lake in Kurukshetra, so, now, he delighted in the equally gladiatorial combat between 'learned men of all stripes . . . [competing] with each other in an arena specially built for this purpose'.[9]

More than one writer has described the emperor's sheer physicality – the punch to Adham Khan's face or the leaping on to musth elephants, of course, but also less dramatic activity. Father Monserrate, for example, describes the emperor joining his workmen to quarry stone for one of his many building projects; or visiting workshops he'd built for various artisans – goldsmiths and gunsmiths, painters and weavers – to relax 'his mind with watching . . . their work'. Later Jesuit priests would describe the emperor as 'deeply emersed in state affairs' one moment and 'the next . . . shearing camels, hewing stones, cutting wood, or hammering iron, and doing all with as much diligence as though engaged in his own particular vocation'.[10]

Akbar enjoyed all kinds of arts, crafts and technologies. His 'household', writes Abul Fazl, included 'over one hundred offices and workshops each resembling a city, or rather a little kingdom'.[11] It was in these workshops – *karkhanas* – that Akbar promoted carpet-weaving, for example, with such

Figure 12.1   This beautiful portrait of a lion may be an early work by Ustad Mansur, who went on to become one of the luminaries of Jahangir's atelier. Dated c. 1585. The Alice and Nasli Heeramaneck Collection, Gift of Alice Heeramaneck, 1985. *Source*: The Metropolitan Museum of Art, Public domain.

success that Indian carpets surpassed their Persian counterparts in quality. 'His Majesty has such an eye for the finer things', wrote a contemporary writer on Akbar's interest in textiles, 'that he has introduced [lit. invented] silken clothes, brocade, tapestry and carpets of silk, and brocade in India, and instructed highly skilled masters in the art, so that the work in India is now much better than the work of Persia and Europe'.[12] The gold and silver minted in his realm were of such high quality that some suspected 'witchcraft or alchemy'.[13] Akbar's patronage of painting is splendidly clear from the profusion of art produced during his reign (of those in his court who disapproved of painting, Akbar said, 'such men I dislike'[14]). He loved music, too. Abul Fazl describes how an orchestra of drums, trumpets, horns and cymbals would play at midnight and dawn in Akbar's court, culminating in seven kinds of melodies – many composed by Akbar himself, who was also, it seems, a dab hand at the naqqara, kettledrum – followed by a 'reading of beautiful sentences and poems'.[15] The emperor's *khushbu-khana*, in which the Jesuits lived for a few days, contained jars upon jars of 'ointments, perfumes and . . . scented water'.[16] Akbar was 'very fond of perfume', writes Abul Fazl; the scent of amber or aloe, flowers and incense filled his court, and the emperor himself dabbled in inventing 'mixtures'.[17]

Dabbling, tinkering and inventing were among Akbar's great pleasures. Abul Fazl, of course, is glad to ascribe any innovation in the realm to Akbar's genius, but this is not only, or always, flattery. Irfan Habib examines some of these claims in an essay and finds some of them quite legitimate: that Akbar first had the idea of using *khus*, vetiver, frames to cool the air, for example, or that he discovered the use of saltpetre to cool water.[18]

The Ibadat Khana debates, in this light, were a kind of tinkering, too: a physical manifestation, a playing out of belief. The Jesuits were invited, as Azfar Moin writes, 'to embody and perform their faith for [Akbar's] pleasure' and a Fire Test would fit perfectly in the performative and participative – not to mention deadly – atmosphere of Akbar's court, with the added advantage of ridding the emperor of yet another inconvenient shaikh, of course.

The early 1580s were a do-or-die moment not only for Akbar's warlords but also for his clergy. Sometime in the first half of 1580, as the Bengal revolt gathered pace, Akbar's qazi in Jaunpur issued a fatwa 'insisting on the duty of taking the field and rebelling against the Emperor'.[19] Oddly enough, this qazi, Maulana Muhammad Yazd, was one of Akbar's favoured interlocuters: not too long before he was posted to Jaunpur, the maulana was being pulled up to the emperor's bedroom balcony for theological chats. Evidently, relations between the emperor and the scholar had grown sour. Badauni suggests the resentment may have been financial: Akbar was reassessing land grants to

Figure 12.2   Akbar in his Ibadat Khana with Jesuit priests in attendance, among others.
Akbar's theological debates are as closely associated with his personality as his mad rides on musth elephants – and were often as dangerous. Attributed to Narsingh, c. 1603–05.
Source: Wikimedia Commons, Public domain.

religious individuals and organizations just as he was reassessing his empire's agricultural revenue.

Akbar took the maulana's fatwa as seriously as he took the eastern insurrection. In June 1580, at the same time that Akbar sent Aziz, Todar Mal and Shahbaz Khan to Bihar and Bengal, the emperor sent another contingent of soldiers to Jaunpur, with orders to arrest the qazi. Abul Fazl is discreet about the affair, only accusing the maulana of 'foolish talk and . . . strife-mongering', because of which Akbar ordered him brought to court. As fate would have it, his boat 'sank in the waves' of the river en route. Badauni, however, declares that the drowning of Muhammad Yazd was no accident. Akbar, he writes, had ordered that the maulana be 'made away with'.

The qazi of Jaunpur was not the only Muslim scholar or priest who lost his life or his position during this time: Akbar charged through their ranks as he had once galloped through the deep waters of the Ravi in Lahore. '[O]ne by one', writes Badauni, 'he sent all the Mullas, against whom he had any suspicions of dissatisfaction, to the closet of annihilation'. Mir Muizzulmulk, who, too, had been talking foolishly in Jaunpur, drowned with Muhammad Yazd; the qazi of Bengal followed soon after. Others, more fortunate, he separated from each other 'like dishevelled thread' – just as he had dispersed the ataka khail from Punjab and should have dispersed the Qaqshals. 'A large number of Shaikhs and Faqirs were also sent to . . . Qandahar', writes Badauni, 'where they were exchanged for horses' – that is, sold as slaves.[20]

A marked man might try and escape his fate with flattery, though with little guarantee of success. Badauni tells the story of a petrified Haji Ibrahim cooking up a forged manuscript filled with predictions of how the coming caliph would have many wives and be clean-shaven – much like Akbar – and 'includ[ing] many other peculiarities of the Emperor'. At first, it seemed as if the trick was working, but Haji Ibrahim went too far when he began making fun of Abul Fazl and Hakim Abul Fath. Akbar packed him off to jail in Ranthambore, where he died.

Bengal was in flames, his ulema in revolt, but Akbar was doing little, it seems, to soothe the suspicions of either his warlords or his court scholars. Not only had he invited the Jesuit Fathers and encouraged 'so many wretches of Hindus and Hinduizing Musalmans' to argue irreverently in his court, Akbar had even begun to make grand displays of his heresies. Thus, Akbar began the twenty-fifth year of his reign, in March 1580, with a grand and public prostration before the sun and fire, and ordered that the court 'rise up respectfully' when the evening's lamps and candles were lit.[21]

This lighting of lamps would become an elaborate affair. As Abul Fazl describes it, every day, before sunset, Akbar would take off all his ornaments, thus 'lay[ing] aside the splendor of royalty, and bring[ing] his external appearance in harmony with his heart'. Attendants would bring in twelve white candles on twelve candlesticks of silver and gold – some of them so tall that you needed a ladder to reach the wicks – and a singer, holding a candle, would sing 'a variety of delightful airs to the praise of God'. The whole ceremony began and ended with prayers for the continuation of Akbar's reign, while *diyas*, oil lamps, were lit all around the palace and outside it. Besides the candles and diyas, there was also a seemingly sacred fire-pot called the Agingir, lit from a stone heated by the sun itself, and preserved the whole year round, to be used by lamplighters, torch bearers and cooks.[22]

Akbar's 'fire-worship' was hardly the end of his provocations. Another day, Akbar entered his audience hall, 'his forehead marked like a Hindu . . . [with] jewelled strings tied on his wrists by Brahmans, by way of a blessing'. He was celebrating Rakhi; wearing these protective threads would become quite the fashion in Akbar's court.[23]

As the years went by, Akbar would try out many other sacred and protective rituals. 'The list of such reports is long', writes Azfar Moin. By the time Akbar was done, he had worn the Parsi kusti as well as the Hindu rakhi; he had 'memorized one thousand and one names of the Sun in Sanskrit; he had . . . matched the color of his clothes to the planet of the day; he had practiced rites of "fire worship" in Brahmanical and Zoroastrian style; he had modified his diet according to tantric principles . . . '

The hands-on emperor was putting himself in the hands of his true Maker, whoever He might be; trusting Him to take Akbar's side against his mortal enemies.

'Make your preparations, Father, for a long journey', said Akbar to Monserrate before he began to march towards his impudent half-brother Muhammad Hakim, 'for you are going with me'.[24]

And it is good that he did: the Jesuit's awestruck eyes reveal, far more than Abul Fazl ever can for all he tries, the sheer majesty of the emperor of Hindustan at this time. Even if Akbar 'thought as much of [Hakim] as an eagle of a mosquito', as Monserrate claims, he marched with all the pomp at his disposal. It began modestly enough, with a small camp, including Akbar's two older boys, Salim and Murad, some of his wives and older daughters, even Akbar's mother, Hamida, for the first two days – the ladies and their maids riding camels, under white sunshades. Every night, Akbar's own white tent was pitched on a well-chosen spot, and around him, in strict hierarchy and following an unchanging map, the tents of his sons and nobility, and several urdu bazaars,[25] filled with 'all sorts of merchandise, so that these bazaars seem to belong to some wealthy city instead of to a camp'. A great flame atop a tall mast spread its light over the tents and beyond, guiding anyone who had fallen behind.

Every day, as more of his mansabdars and their troops joined him, the camp expanded, until 'it soon seemed to hide the earth', writes Monserrate, sprawling out over more than two kilometres, 'covering the fields and filling the woods'. Should a wild animal find itself embroiled in the mass of marching feet, it could not break through. 'Even the birds', the Jesuit continues, 'wearied by trying to fly out of danger, and terrified by the shouts of the soldiers, fall down exhausted to the earth'.

By the end of it, according to the Father, there were 500 elephants, 50,000 horsemen and an 'almost countless' infantry: Mongols and Persians, Turks and Uzbeks, Baluchis and Pathans, Hindus and Muslims, each with their own fighting styles. Rajputs would ride into battle 'on little ponies hardly as big as donkeys', writes Monserrate, dismount on the battlefield 'and await the attack of the enemy armed with short spears . . . and light shields'. Baluchis rode camels[26] and used bows and arrows; while Hindustanis had turned elephants into terrifying war machines. They might dash a soldier to the ground and trample him: 'They do not cease from crushing their wretched victims till they are ground and smashed to pieces', the Father explains. They might toss others 'into mid-air, so that they are killed by the fall', or they might 'split [a man] in twain by placing a foot on one of their victim's legs, seizing the other leg with their trunk and tearing it forcibly upwards'. ('They can even be taught to dance', concludes Monserrate blithely.[27])

The Persians and Central Asians were no less deadly. They were 'most dangerous', writes the priest, when 'flying in headlong riot'. It might seem as if the soldiers were caught in a frenzy of speed, but as they galloped past, they could turn around 'on their horses . . . [and] fling their javelins with such deadly aim that they can transfix the eye of an enemy'.

Father Monserrate does not mention them, but the infantry would also have included an elite corps of *bandukchis*, matchlock-men, Akbar foremost among them. Guns were not only increasingly important to any serious arsenal, they were also one of Akbar's passions. Abul Fazl reports in the *Ain-i-Akbari* that the emperor even invented new kinds of guns: one that could fire seventeen barrels with a single shot, another that could be taken apart and reassembled. Hindustan, writes Abul Fazl, had more guns for 'securing the government' than any empire except Turkey, the acknowledged leader in the field. And each one of these matchlocks, as Abul Fazl tells it, was tested by Akbar himself, in a long and rigorous process by which guns arrived at the emperor's chambers in the harem, marked with the source of the iron used to make them, the place of their making, the workman who made them and on what date. The guns went back and forth between the workshop and the harem many times. At the third trial, when a gun was fully made but undecorated, it was called '*sada*', plain, and sent to the harem with five bullets; of which Akbar fired four and returned the fifth, with orders for the colour of the gun's barrel and stock, gold inlay and enamel. Once ten guns were '*rangin*', coloured, this way, Akbar had their mouths and butts inlaid with gold, tried them one last time, and sent them to the armoury.

Akbar had 105 '*khasa*', select, guns for his own use – as, indeed, he had khasa weapons of all kinds, from swords to spears, daggers to bows, each with a name and a rank. His khasa guns, divided into seven groups of fifteen each, were always kept ready – Akbar used one from each group every day of the week – alongside another 101 guns kept in the harem, also rotated in this obsessive-compulsive manner.

Monserrate may not have met the bandukchis, but he did note a less lethal group of men, with far less lethal equipment, marching behind the emperor. These were surveyors, not soldiers, carrying 10-foot rods with which they measured 'each day's march'. In front of Akbar were drummers and trumpeters, though his journey was not accompanied by music. Only one drummer played at a time, writes the Father, '[sounding] his drum at short intervals, perhaps at every tenth pace, with a slow and dignified rhythm'.

On went Akbar, day by day, hunting with his beloved cheetahs, reaffirming friendships and alliances with 'petty kings' along the way. He took a leisurely three and a half months from Fatehpur to the banks of the Indus, when once he had covered a comparable distance to Ahmedabad in nine days. And yet, for all his unhurried calm, the grave and solemn cadence at which he marched, Akbar was not as unruffled by his brother's threat as he seemed.

It was on his way north that Akbar arrested Shah Mansur, the stickler who'd wanted to tax the rioting Bengali soldiers, and had him executed on suspicion of treason.

Briefly, this is the sorry tale: soon after Akbar's Rajput commander Man Singh's men had repelled Mirza Hakim's troops from Punjab and killed his star swordsman, Shadman, Man Singh sent word that he had found a letter from Hakim's secretary to Shah Mansur in Shadman's bags. Such letters were a common trick – they were meant to fall into the wrong hands and create disharmony and suspicion in the enemy ranks. Therefore, Akbar dismissed the news. Soon after, however, an old servant of Hakim's arrived in Akbar's camp and made a beeline for Shah Mansur, choosing him as his intermediary to the emperor. At this dubious coincidence, Akbar had his accountant arrested. A few days later, the chief of his camp police came to Akbar with another set of letters detailing a plot by which Shah Mansur's troops – stationed in Punjab – were to join Hakim's army. Now, writes Abul Fazl, Akbar's 'wrath . . . blazed forth'.

Akbar's anger was no joke. His usual expression was 'tranquil, serene and open', writes Monserrate, but 'when he is angry, [full] of awful majesty'. Once, on this very trip, when a man took a shortcut in obeying Akbar's orders, the emperor had him tied to an inflated leather tube and flung into the Indus, to be 'carried hither and thither in the middle of the river at the mercy of the current'. The poor man was taken out and eventually pardoned – Akbar was 'easily excited to anger, but soon cools down', as the Father noted. Until he did, however, the emperor's fury was not easily faced, and it is no wonder that when Akbar, enraged, accused him of treason, Shah Mansur 'blathered in reply'.[28]

Whatever excuses the accountant stammered out, they did him no good. Shah Mansur was 'hung . . . on a tree'.[29]

No one mourned his passing.

Of the legions of men who fill the annals of his reign, Akbar's accountants are the most unpopular. Perhaps this is a good indication of how rigorously Akbar enforced his revenue reforms, but it was bad luck for the officials involved. Of his three best-known money managers, only Todar Mal died a natural death. Muzaffar Khan was tortured and killed by the Bengal rebels; Shah Mansur was hanged – and, here too, Akbar's amirs may not have been entirely innocent of his death.[30]

According to Abul Fazl, there was 'great rejoicing in the camp' when Shah Mansur died. Worse, it is possible that many of the cold hearts celebrating Shah Mansur's demise had conspired to bring it about. Those incriminating letters that provoked Akbar's fury would turn out to be forgeries.

Historians suspect various noblemen – including Shah Mansur's colleague, Todar Mal – of masterminding the plot, though it is generally agreed that the conspiracy was a wide-ranging collaboration. 'Most, nay all, of the Amirs, who had received many annoyances from Shah Mansur, were longing for his fall', writes Badauni. 'With one consent they exerted themselves to secure his execution.' Badauni himself had no sympathy for the poor vizier, writing balefully that Shah Mansur's 'numerous oppressions . . . formed the halter round his neck, and may it remain clinging there till the day of Resurrection'.

Only Akbar regretted it. Abul Fazl quotes the emperor saying that 'the thread of accounting dropped from the hand' after Shah Mansur's execution. It wasn't only selfish concerns that upset Akbar; it was the injustice that he, sultan-i-adil, provider of justice to his people, had inflicted on his terrified accountant. Badauni writes that Akbar regretted his death and was 'very much grieved' when he discovered the forgeries on account of which he had had Shah Mansur executed.

At the time, however, marching ever closer towards Kabul and the inevitable confrontation with his half-brother, Akbar was willing to let the threads of accountancy slip, as long as the reins of his own destiny remained firmly in his grasp. He was taking no chances.

On 24 May 1581, Akbar camped on the banks of the Indus river. It may have occurred to him that, within the last fifty years, both his father and grandfather had stood on the other side of these blue waters, calculating their chances of conquering Hindustan. He may have remembered sitting with Humayun in the light of a setting moon as his father blessed him with his breath. But now, Akbar was no adventurer, no exiled king seeking his fortune; he was master of a vast realm, sending word to his little brother, who clung to precarious independence in the family's old seat: surrender, or be swallowed whole.

Having camped outside Lahore for about twenty days that spring, '[shooting] arrows at an imaginary target', Muhammad Hakim had fled at news of Akbar's approach. From Kabul, in July, he sent replies to Akbar's stern messages, filled with apologies. Akbar was unconvinced. Hakim should have submitted in person, or sent one of his sons, or Khwaja Hasan Naqshbandi – now Hakim's brother-in-law – to submit on his behalf. In fact, anticipating such half-hearted surrender, Akbar had already sent out an army under Man Singh and the eleven-year-old Prince Murad with orders to march – but slowly – upon Kabul. Akbar himself had waited a long while to cross the Indus, 'lest by the crossing of the army things would go beyond the prospect of peace' – but had taken the plunge ten days before Hakim's unconvincing apologies arrived. Now, he summoned a council of twenty amirs, telling them to draft a reply and bring it to him the next day.[31]

Just as Akbar's own stand across the Indus had changed, so had the composition of his nobility. Many of his amirs were Indian now and had already travelled too far into unknown land. And none of them, writes Abul Fazl, wanted to go to Kabul – some from 'dread of a cold country', others from 'love for India'; some even 'influenced by good will towards [Hakim]'. With the exception of Abul Fazl's stubborn voice – 'I had not white hair and long beard', he declares – the amirs agreed that Akbar should forgive Hakim, so that they might turn back around and quickly go home.

Abul Fazl's little sermon on how it was 'proper to finish the work which is nearly completed' did not go down well with the others. '[T]hey were angry', he writes, 'and consulted together with evil intentions'. One of them advised Abul Fazl to make himself more amenable, 'especially with those who are powerful in the state' – suggesting, clearly, that Akbar's favour was not enough to ensure a successful career; there were other powerful men who could make life difficult for an intransigent colleague. Abul Fazl agreed to a compromise: he would not offer his opinion in court unless he was asked for it.

The next day, as it happens, Abul Fazl was unwell; he does not say so, but he might have developed one of those nervous aches that afflict a person anticipating a tense day at work. The amirs went to court free of worry and declared themselves unanimously in favour of forgiving Mirza Hakim and forgetting about marching into Kabul. When Akbar asked about the absent Abul Fazl's view, one of them, most 'shameless', replied, 'He too agrees with this opinion.'

In his Ibadat Khana, Akbar may have encouraged every kind of opinion, but when faced with an enemy, he was still the same man who had raced after Mirza Ibrahim in Sarnal and made latecomers beg to join the thorn-ridden battle. Akbar was furious at his peacenik amirs, and quite inclined to gallop away as he had done then. '[T]he officers are afraid of the cold', he declared, quite correctly – many of them were Hindustani, they had never known a winter – 'I'll leave them all behind'.

Abul Fazl reappeared in court the next day, and wondered why the atmosphere was so tense. 'Traces of anger [still] shone from the emperor's brow', he writes.[32] When Akbar summoned him and began an interrogation, the wretched man – he had only been a mansabdar for about five years – 'fell into despondency, and came into a condition which may no evil-doer fall into'.[33] Abul Fazl was in a terrible state, but no matter how he protested his innocence, Akbar was unrelenting. It wasn't six months since he had lost trust in another of his chosen men (Shah Mansur, as Abul Fazl writes, became vizier without the recommendation of courtiers, and without experience). Would the emperor now re-examine his trust in another of his hand-picked talents? One by one, Akbar summoned the amirs to confirm what Abul Fazl had said at the meeting, and one by one they 'took the same road of impudent assertion'.

'I almost lost my mind',[34] Abul Fazl remembers. He, too, may have recalled Shah Mansur's body hanging from a tree. Finally – thankfully! – one of the amirs, unnamed but memorably described as a man with nothing to fear, having 'too many enemies to ever rise to any prominence',[35] came to the scribe's defence. Akbar, already moved to sympathy by Abul Fazl's distracted state, closed the investigation and marched on.

It was exactly this kind of dissension and backbiting among Akbar's men that Mirza Hakim and his advisers were relying upon. 'The Turanis and Persians who are in the imperial army will join us without fighting', was their calculation, according to Abul Fazl, 'and the brave Rajputs and gallant Afghans will end their days.' Any remaining Hindustanis would find themselves prisoners of Kabul.[36]

'No! No!' Abul Fazl cannot refute such 'hallucinations' hotly enough. Hakim attempted to lure away the Central Asian chiefs in Man Singh and Murad's vanguard, with letters that proposed 'acting in concert'. But, for all that the lord of Kabul may have been right about the pride of Akbar's nobility and the vortex of bitter rivalries in his court, he had underestimated the structural unity of his army. No commander in the vanguard deserted. One of them even killed the messenger who brought him Hakim's invitation to do so.

'In fine', as Abul Fazl puts it, 'the Kabulis were dumbfounded by the might of the victorious troops'. Twice, on the 1st and 2nd of August 1581, Hakim attacked the Mughal vanguard, hoping for desertions and collapse, and suffered, instead, a resounding defeat.

Five days later, Akbar and his reluctant amirs, along with the victorious Man Singh and Murad, were camped on the outskirts of Kabul city, as 'Turk and Tajik came in droves to catch a glimpse of the emperor';[37] some of them remembering, perhaps, the child once dangled from the walls of Kabul fort, the boy who raced dogs through its courtyards, and the prince who left with his father almost thirty years ago, and was now, amazingly, the king of kings come back home.

Akbar did not allow himself prolonged nostalgia. Once, when he was evading his tutors in this very city, his father had worried if he would acquire the discipline a ruler needs. What is growing up except a losing battle against responsibility? Akbar went into Kabul and 'remembered the places which he had seen in [his] boyhood', describing them so exactly to his amirs that Abul Fazl offers a round of applause to Akbar's 'intelligence and memory'. But he did not linger.

It would have been irresponsible to do so. Every day that Akbar spent in Kabul was driving Hakim to increasing desperation. Having been defeated on the battlefield by Man Singh and Murad, his eleven-year-old nephew, Hakim had fled a 100-odd kilometres north, to Ghorband, from where he played his trump card. He sent word that should Akbar try to arrest him, he would 'become . . . a Qalandar' and wander off into 'retirement'. This, in itself, was not much of a threat; the sting was in its tail. Hakim added that his wandering would not be directionless. It would take him to Turan.

Turan, along with Iran and Akbar's Hindustan, was one of three neighbouring and competing powers, each keeping a close eye for opportunities to expand its borders. Kabul – the kingdom, not just the city – was a critical buffer between Turan and Hindustan, and it would have been quite the coup for Turan's clever and ambitious Uzbek ruler, Abdullah, to give refuge to Kabul's exiled king and Akbar's estranged brother. Akbar couldn't risk it. He sent reassurances of his forgiveness to Hakim, who replied with fulsome apologies, professing 'his own want of wisdom . . . and his shame'.

The very next day, on 14 August, only a week after he had come, Akbar left Kabul so that Hakim might return to the city with whatever dignity remained to him. Arresting, or even executing his brother, as some in Akbar's court had advised, would have served no useful end; Hakim was crushed already.

So was any real remaining opposition to Akbar.

Chapter 13

Bring Me My Flute!

'And so those who were before in favour now fell out of favour, and those who were before out of favour came into favour, those who had been near became afar, and those who had been afar became near. Praise be to Him! who ruleth absolutely in his kingdom as it pleaseth Him. And the common people with as little sense as brute beasts repeated continually nothing but "Allah Akbar".'

– Abdul Qadir Badauni, *Muntakhab-ut-Tawarikh*

At the end of November 1581, Akbar returned to Fatehpur in triumph. His 'great officers [and] loyal servants' lined both sides of the road for several kilometres out of the city, as their emperor rode in upon a 'heaven-like' elephant, heralded by drums and musicians, accompanied by his sons and his amirs. His people, too, had come out in crowds for a glimpse of their glorious monarch and were 'gathered in astonishment on the roofs and at the doors'. There was even a rebel called Bahadur, from Bengal, awaiting Akbar's arrival. He was brought out 'with chains on his neck, and stocks on his feet', and executed.[1]

The Bengal rebellion wasn't over; it would simmer for a long while yet. Its originators, the Qaqshals, would only return to the imperial fold in the spring of 1584, some two years from now,[2] and disturbances in the east would continue until the very end of Akbar's reign. To the west, too, there would be outbreaks of unrest in Gujarat, both from discontented mansabdars and a Gujarati prince, Muzaffar Shah, the suppression of whose stubborn ambition earned Abdur Rahim the title of Khan-Khanan.[3] There would be another kind of rebellion against Akbar's empire, more scattered but as sustained as the resistance in Bengal or Gujarat. 'By one count', writes Michael Fisher, 'there were 144 armed revolts by landholders during Akbar's reign

227

that were large enough to be recorded by his central administration; additionally, lesser conflicts were frequent, particularly after each harvest.'⁴ One of these landholders, Abdullah 'Dulha' Bhatti, remains a folk hero in Punjab. It was not just his warlords, then, who were unhappy at losing their independent, unaccounted wealth, the zamindars of Hindustan – 'warrior-aristocrats' as Fisher describes them – were equally reluctant to pay their taxes.

There would be further conquests, too. Northwards and west, from Srinagar to Sindh, east, all the way to Cuttack, 'at the end of the country and on the seashore'.⁵ In the last years of his life, Akbar would even descend upon the Deccan and begin the campaign that would eventually consume his dynasty.

In some ways, then, the second quarter-century of Akbar's reign followed the pattern of the first: a steady, unrelenting expansion of the realm, a clear focus on the generation of wealth and an equally resolute suppression of any opposition to the emperor. In other ways, however, Akbar's second innings has a palpably different quality to it.

In March 1582, for example, four months after his triumphant return from Kabul, Akbar sent out 'for all sorts of troops of singers and musicians both Hindu and Persian, and dancers, both men and women by thousands of thousands'⁶ and celebrated Nauroz – a Zoroastrian festival that inaugurates the spring and the Persian new year. Akbar would use it to mark the start of every year of his reign. He had at least two good reasons to choose Nauroz as the festival of his rule: one, he inherited Humayun's throne in February, shortly before this March festival. And two, Nauroz heralds the spring equinox, one of two days in the year on which the sun is aligned with the earth's equator – in much the same way as light (of the sun, of fire, of the blaze in Alanqoa's womb) was explicitly aligned with Akbar and his descendants' imperial image.

'A special grace', Akbar declared in one of his Happy Sayings, 'proceeds from the sun in favour of kings, and for this reason they pray and consider it a worship of the Almighty; but the short-sighted are thereby scandalised.'⁷ Whatever little hesitation Akbar might have had about scandalizing men – by reading the khutba, debating religions, wearing rakhis – that hesitation had been magicked away, much like the rain clouds that Akbar once dispersed with his breath. As Abul Fazl puts it, Akbar had long wanted to celebrate Nauroz but had refrained on account of the 'general ignorance' in his court, and courtiers 'enchained in bigotry'. But now, in 1582, now that Akbar had ruled an astonishing twenty-six years and vanquished every challenge thrown at him, from the sudden death of his father to the control of his regents, the resentments of his warlords and clergy to the ambitions of his brother; now, with rebels in retreat, Hakim chastised, and critical maulanas exiled, 'everything reached perfection'⁸ – and no one would dare tell the emperor what he might or might not do. 'I'll drink no coffee, bring me wine!' goes one of Akbar's most carefree lines of verse. 'I'll play no harp – bring me my flute!'[9] At thirty-nine, the emperor could, at last, rule with a free hand.

A measure of the untrammelled extent of Akbar's authority was taken the very next month, when the unfortunate Makhdum-ul-Mulk and Abdun Nabi tried to cut short their reluctant pilgrimage to Mecca.

In April 1582, Akbar rode out of Fatehpur to greet a caravan of his female relatives. Chief among them was his aunt Gulbadan, yet to write her wonderful memoir, along with Salima, Bairam Khan's widow and then Akbar's wife, and even Askari's widow Sultan Begum, who had taken such tender care of her hostage nephew in Qandahar. It was seven years since Akbar had met them: the ladies had left Fatehpur in 1575, were stranded in Gujarat awhile and sailed for Mecca in 1578.[10] They were back in Hindustan after three and a half years and many adventures, including a shipwreck in Aden. Akbar and his realm had changed a great deal since the ladies had last met him. When they left Fatehpur, for example, Abdun Nabi was a powerful sadr; on their return, the poor man, along with Makhdum-ul-Mulk, sought to smuggle himself back to the capital under their protection.

It was news of the Bengal rebellion that had tempted the two scholars to come home; news of its failure reached them too late. When they landed in Gujarat, hoping to hear that the nightmare of Akbar's reign was over, they learnt of his victory instead. Akbar, too, learnt of their unauthorized return and sent men to arrest them ('in such a manner that the ladies should not know of it', writes Abul Fazl). Makhdum-ul-Mulk was so terrified, it seems, that he died en route, in Ahmedabad.[11] Abdun Nabi, possibly braced by angry resentment against a man who had once treated him with such deference, summoned the courage to appear at court, and even spoke a few rude words to the emperor, at which, according to Badauni, Akbar hit him in the face. 'Why don't you strike with a knife?' the old shaikh responded bitterly.

Akbar, unabashed, demanded an account of the 7000 rupees he had given the shaikh before sending him to Mecca, then put him in prison, under Todar Mal's charge. It was here, locked up 'like a defaulting tax-gatherer' that the erstwhile sadr of Hindustan, the highest judge in all the land, met his end: 'one night', writes Badauni, 'a mob strangled him, and he went to God'.[12]

If Akbar's free hand had only been occupied in swatting his opponents, the story of his life would be far less engaging than it is. It is true enough that Akbar was more than a little autocratic, even megalomaniacal. It required a person of such enlarged ego to straddle the realm and assert his authority as he did – it is Akbar, after all, not Babur, who created the empire that bears his dynasty's name. But if that is all that he had been, the kind of despot in whom power and ruthless ambition feed upon each other towards no better end than exalting the ruler and enriching his friends, then Akbar might not have survived as much more than one of history's many Caligulas; madmen with the capacity to exert limitless authority towards the narrowest goals. Even a cursory reading of Akbar's life, however, reveals a man whose energies extended far beyond self-interest; he was driven towards the accumulation of power and territory, yes, but equally towards the welfare of the increasingly vast population over whom he held sway.

Even Badauni admits, with some disgust, that the 'common people' loved their lord, repeating his double-edged slogan, 'Allah-u-Akbar', like so many 'brute beasts'. They had reason for their affection.

More than one of the Jesuits who spent time in Akbar's court noted the stark contrast in his treatment of nobleman and commoner. 'To prevent the great nobles becoming insolent through the unchallenged enjoyment of power', writes Father Monserrate, Akbar would summon 'those whom he learns to have become enriched by the revenues of their provinces, and gives them many imperious commands, as though they were his slaves – commands, moreover, obedience to which ill suits their exalted rank and dignity'.[13] Akbar's amirs were to be kept in check by many means, that is, logistical and psychological. At the same time, the priest notes Akbar's great affability with his people. 'It is hard to exaggerate how accessible he makes himself to all who wish audience of him', he writes. Public audiences were a daily affair, and Akbar would be 'pleasant-spoken . . . rather than severe toward all who come to speak with him', adopting a manner that had a 'remarkable' effect, in Monserrate's opinion, 'in attaching to him the minds of his subjects'.

A little over a decade later, Father Xavier led the third and last Jesuit mission to Akbar's court and observed two equally telling scenes. In one, a vassal king came to Akbar to pay tribute, performing every manner of obeisance, bowing to the ground, touching the emperor's feet, and offering grand presents, from jewelled daggers and goblets to horses and camels dressed 'in green and crimson velvet'. All of this Akbar acknowledged with no more than placing 'his hand on his vassal's neck'.[14] The emperor was far more animated, by contrast, when some young women arrived at his court, having prayed in his name for children, or for a child's health, and now, their wishes fulfilled, bringing Akbar 'offerings, as to a saint, which, though they may be of little worth, are willingly received and highly valued by him'.[15]

It was clear to the Fathers, by this time, that Akbar wasn't interested in converting to Christianity so much as he wanted to be 'esteemed as a God, or some great Prophet', and the priests could do as little about it as Badauni. For a great number of his subjects, Akbar was clearly a saint-king, performing miracles and 'healing the sick with the water with which he washes his feet'.[16] It wasn't the case, however, as both the Fathers and Badauni suggest, that

Akbar was mesmerizing the credulous masses with miracles. Sometime in 1580, when the Bengal rebellion was raging and two years after the emperor had gone into a trance before a qamargah hunt, Akbar had another of his epiphanies. It happened as he was eating.

Akbar's 'lofty' mind and disposition was such, of course, that Abul Fazl would like us to know that 'the question "What dinner has been prepared today?" never passes over his tongue'.[17] From the historian's own detailed, sometimes mouth-watering, account of the imperial kitchen and its recipes, it is clear that Abul Fazl himself wasn't immune to the pleasures of a good meal.

Akbar ate only once a day, at no fixed time; he began his meal with milk or curd and ended with a prayer, and he became increasingly fond of vegetarian fare over the years. 'From my earliest years', said the emperor in one of his Happy Sayings, 'whenever I ordered animal food to be cooked for me, I found it rather tasteless and cared little for it'.[18] However, for all that Akbar was not interested in food and had ascetic taste, the one meal that did come to him every day was anything but frugal.

A 100-odd dishes would arrive in a grand procession of gold, silver and copper dishes, prepared by chefs 'from all countries', cooked with water from the Yamuna and Chenab rivers, mixed with rainwater and a few drops from the Ganga.[19] Abul Fazl classifies the cuisine into three broad types. Sufiana – devoid of meat – might include *zard birinj* (rice cooked with sugar, ghee, almonds, pistachios, raisins, ginger, saffron and cinnamon), *khichri* (rice and moong daal, cooked in ghee), halwa or green *saag* ('one of the most pleasant dishes' made of leafy vegetables). If it wasn't one of Akbar's vegetarian days, the rice might also be cooked with meat, to make *qabuli, pulao, halim,* or an extravagant dish called *bugra*, made of meat, flour, ghee, gram, sugar, vinegar, onions, carrots, beets, turnips, spinach, fennel, saffron, ginger, cloves, cardamom, cumin, cinnamon and round pepper. Finally, there was meat cooked on its own, with spices, from kebabs to a whole sheep, or a deboned fowl stuffed with minced meat, eggs, ghee, onions, coriander, ginger, saffron and pepper to make a delicious *musamman*.

Then, of course, there was an endless variety of pickles and chutneys – of mango, lemon, turnip or carrot, apple, peach or raisins, cucumber, bamboo, brinjal or mustard – along with curd and green salads, ginger, limes and bread, on which last Abul Fazl speaks for the subcontinent when he says that a *chapatti* 'tastes very well when served hot'.[20]

It was on one such day, writes Nizamuddin, 'when His Majesty was taking his dinner, it occurred to his mind that probably the eyes of some hungry one had fallen upon the food; how, therefore, could he eat it while the hungry were debarred from it?' From that day on, he ordered that he would only eat after a portion of his meal had been distributed to the poor.[21]

Again, in July 1582, some three months after Akbar first celebrated Nau-roz, he institutionalized two occasions for annual charity, on his lunar and solar birthdays.

It began with yet another omen. At midday on 30 July 1582, one embank-ment of the artificial lake above Fatehpur collapsed. The lake, two miles long and half a mile wide, not only provided water to the city but also 'when the sun gets low in the sky . . . a cool and pleasant breeze'.[22] Unsurprisingly, it was a popular spot for picnics, people gathering for games of parcheesi, chess and cards; even Akbar coming by 'on holidays, [to refresh] himself with its many beauties'.[23] It is lucky, then, that when the great lake's waters burst, only one man, a cheetah-keeper called Madadi, died in the flood. Many were injured, however, and the gushing waters even swept away houses.

It was a sign of divine displeasure with 'this business of recreation' on the lakeside, said Akbar. In atonement, he ordered his court – or possibly his empire, Abul Fazl doesn't specify – to forgo meat on the 30th of every month, and, to further demonstrate that he had heard and heeded God's advice, he announced that he would, henceforth, be weighed on his solar and lunar birthdays against twelve and eight kinds of goods, respectively, ranging from gold and silk to ghee and salt, plants and grain to sweets and incense, all of it to be given away.[24]

By contrast, Akbar had introduced the system of escheat in 1575, by which the crown inherited an amir's estate on his demise. The first of Akbar's noble-men to suffer such posthumous appropriation of his wealth was Munim Khan: when the aged Chagatai died in the winter of 1575, everything he owned 'reverted' to the state. His wife, it seems, was left without even the means to pay for the rituals of mourning.[25] Similarly, when poor Makhdum-ul-Mulk died of fright upon his arrest in Gujarat, Akbar took every last penny of his accumulated treasures. The avaricious old man had hidden gold in his own tomb, writes Badauni; 'boxes full of ingots of gold were discovered . . . where he had caused them to be buried as corpses'. The once-powerful cleric's sons, Badauni continues, not without satisfaction, fell into 'the most abject poverty' when Akbar took their inheritance.[26]

Akbar was taking, quite literally, from the rich, and he was giving to the poor. However, just as Akbar's concern for his subjects was not restricted to miracles like making it rain or healing the sick, so it was not confined to the disbursement of charity. He wanted both to better the lives of individual sup-plicants and improve the very system in which they lived.

Thus, when Akbar celebrated Nauroz for the first time in 1582, he not only had the palace decorated with gold-embroidered cloth and 'varieties of jewels', ordered his amirs to organize parties, present their emperor with offerings, and had the 'lock . . . taken off' the imperial treasury and money distributed to the poor, he also conducted a brainstorming session for the bet-terment of his realm.[27]

Abul Fazl lists the suggestions that were made. Akbar's milk brother Aziz, for example, said that no one except the emperor should be allowed to order an execution. Quite possibly, the outspoken amir was making a subtle reference to how he had been under a cloud, just two years earlier, when Akbar appeared to disapprove of Aziz executing a mansabdar. Back in favour after his successes against the rebels in Bengal, Aziz may have been trying to convey his submission to his friend and emperor as well as his blunt manner allowed. Akbar's son Salim, on the verge of his teens, declared that no one under twelve be allowed to marry, an idea he may have received from his father, whose Happy Sayings include a clear disapproval of child marriage. The others, too, would have hoped to please, even flatter, Akbar, as instinctively as executives hope to please and flatter their CEOs. If, then, his amirs were trying to match Akbar's own inclinations, it is worth noting how many of their suggestions concerned the public good. Todar Mal wanted to regularize charity, suggesting a new law that mandated the empire's rich to 'have a care of the empty-handed'. Qasim Khan wanted more *serais*, travellers' inns, and Abul Fath a hospital. Faizi, Abul Fazl's brother and Akbar's favourite poet, hoped that 'experienced and sympathetic persons might be appointed' to fix the prices of goods across markets.[28]

It is worth noting, too, that Akbar's very first order of business, after Nauroz, was to introduce a series of land and revenue reforms, as formulated by the lone surviving member of his triumvirate of accountants – Todar Mal. As much as these new measures aimed to increase cultivation, and thus imperial revenue, they were clearly informed by concern for the cultivators, too. There were twelve ordinances in all, the first of which regularized rent and taxes, and imposed fines on collectors who took more than was due. 'Consideration should be shown in the exaction of dues', read the third ordinance; an increase in cultivated land was to be encouraged and 'destitute farmers' assisted with loans. Tax collectors were also to appoint 'trustworthy and rightly-acting' clerks, instead of the usual 'corrupt' fellows who worked 'in collusion with the village head man, and . . . oppressed the peasantry'. Currency was to be regularized, farmers were to get receipts, and surveyors and their scribes to receive fixed salaries. Thus, as one of the ordinances concluded, 'the country might soon be cultivated, the peasantry satisfied, and the treasury replenished'.[29]

The relief of his subjects was not a passing fancy of Akbar's. According to Abul Fazl, his very first orders as a newly crowned thirteen-year-old included the 'remission of taxes'. It is more than possible, of course, that the historian is inventing this legislation; no taxpayer at the time would have known, or cared, about an adolescent putting on a crown in the fields of Kalanaur. Indeed, Abul Fazl, who never lets his ideals drown his facts, admits that 'for some time [the rebate] was not carried into effect'.[30] The point of mentioning the order, articulated or not, executed or not, wasn't to record history so much as to underline an intention. The happiness and prosperity of his subjects, that is, was the first principle of Akbar's reign.

It wasn't long, in fact, before Akbar did abolish some taxes. In the eighth and ninth years of his rule, between 1563 and 1564, he got rid of a tax levied on pilgrims, and then, more famously, the jizya. It wasn't very long since Akbar had married Harkha Bai, in the early months of 1562. His first Rajput and Hindu queen, or her clan, may well have influenced his decision to rescind these 'Hindu' taxes – both the pilgrim tax and the jizya applied to non-Muslims in the realm.[31]

It may also be, of course, that the chronology is as much coincidence as cause. The historians J. S. Hoyland and S. N. Banerjee, writing about Akbar's interest in religious discourse, relate how he visited the third Sikh Guru, Amar Das, 'dined with him, and received a dress of honour'. Afterwards, some brahmins in Akbar's court complained of how Sikhism – a new religion and one of many reformist movements to have developed across India, often in reaction to Brahminism – was creating social upheavals.[32]

Brahmins were, as they remain, a dominant social and cultural force in sixteenth-century Hindustan. The Jain poet Banarasidas relates a wonderfully telling anecdote of the great reverence that brahmins were accorded. Once, writes Banarasi, he was travelling through a forest with two men when they were accosted by the chief, *chaudhari*, of a gang of thieves. Thinking on their feet, Banarasi and his friends pretended to be brahmins – they chanted *shlokas*, fashioned *janeus* out of yarn, put *tilaks* of mud on their foreheads and thus made their escape. Indeed, the chaudhari escorted them to safety himself, saying, 'Revered pandits, / Come with me, let me show you the way out of this forest.'[33]

Much like his court ulema, then, the brahmins in Akbar's court guarded their authority. The modern historian Pushpa Prasad tells of how brahmins 'jealous' of Akbar's admiration for a Jain *acharya*, teacher, called Vijayasen Suri spread a rumour that Jains were atheists.[34]

As Akbar would do with the Jains, so, now, he did with the Sikhs: he arranged a debate, to which Guru Amar Das sent Jetha to argue against brahmin scholars. Jetha, who would be the fourth Guru, Ram Das, and whose celebrated hymns comprise a significant proportion of the Sikh holy book, the Guru Granth Sahib, ended his argument with a suitably poetic flourish: 'The Brahmans claim to be equal to God. The Guru maketh no such boast, for he knoweth that he is God's slave.'

Akbar was pleased by the young Sikh's rhetorical skill but advised Jetha to visit Haridwar and placate the Hindus. He also promised that Jetha and his party would not have to pay the pilgrim tax. 'This', write Hoyland and Banerjee, 'probably resulted in the total remission of the pilgrim tax . . . [in] 1563'.[35]

Abul Fazl, meanwhile, has Akbar abolishing the pilgrim tax with heroic flourish. The emperor was out lion-hunting near Mathura, had levelled 'five with the dust by arrow and bullets' and taken a sixth alive (there were 'a thousand wonderings', writes the historian). Mathura may not have lions any longer, but it remains, as it was, a pilgrimage site; so Akbar decided to mix 'worship with pleasure' by remitting the pilgrimage tax, declaring that no matter how misguided a sect might be, 'to put a stumbling block in [their] way' to worship was 'not doing the will of God'.

The story of the jizya is even more complicated.

'Who can estimate the amount thereof?' Abul Fazl exclaims, heralding its removal in 1564. But what was money to a man creating a new world order? Historically, by Abul Fazl's explanation, the tax was collected for three reasons: to aid in the 'contempt and destruction of opposite factions'; for 'political purposes'; and for material gain. Akbar's remission of the tax invited ideological and financial resistance, therefore, but the emperor persisted despite 'the disapproval of statesmen, and of the great revenue, and of much chatter on the part of the ignorant'. Akbar, on the other hand, heir to Adam and ruler of all men, was a unifier; his personality and policies had ensured that 'those who belong to other religions have, like those of one mind and one religion, bound up the waist of devotion', and no longer 'cherished mortal enmity' against the throne. Given all this, and the prosperity of the empire besides, how could any 'just and discriminating mind apply itself to collecting this tax'?

Having penned his eloquent paean to his emperor's 'abundant good-will' and 'sublime decree', Abul Fazl may have been too embarrassed to record that in 1575, a little over ten years after removing it, Akbar brought the jizya right back.

Iqtidar Alam Khan has argued that both the remittance and the resumption of the jizya had clear political reasons.[36] In 1564, Akbar was recruiting Rajputs to his court. It was also in this year of the jizya's abolition, however, that the first of his Uzbek warlords began to sow insurrectionist oats in Malwa; the very next year the Uzbek rebellion broke out in full force. In the course of battling Ali Quli and Bahadur, Akbar seems to have tweaked his larger political paradigm.

Now the emperor felt compelled to prove his Islamic credentials to his restless Central Asian warlords and his newly recruited Indian Muslim courtiers and commanders. Thus, the massacre of civilians in Chittorgarh and the characterization of its conquest as a victory over 'infidels'.[37] And thus, too, the re-imposition of the jizya in 1575.

Abul Fazl doesn't mention this complete about-face, but it may be that Badauni is alluding to it when he writes of how Akbar ordered Makhdum-ul-Mulk and Abdun Nabi 'to decide the amount of tax to be levied on Hindus'.

It was not, however, a very long-lived order, disappearing as quickly, writes Badauni, as 'a reflection on the water'. To put it in Iqtidar Alam Khan's words, the 1570s ended with 'a sudden collapse of the policy' Akbar had espoused over the last decade and more: in 1579, Makhdum-ul-Mulk and Abdun Nabi lost their jobs; soon after, the jizya was removed once and for all.[38]

In 1580, Abul Fazl writes that Akbar rescinded some 'taxes'. He does not specify what these were, but he does bring a narrative verisimilitude to the affair by connecting the dots with Akbar's original attempt at abolishing taxes upon his accession – which the young emperor's 'veil' and his underlings' 'avarice' had rendered ineffective. Even if he doesn't record the exact facts, then, the historian does convey an essence of the truth: in the 1580s, the tide of Akbar's rule had turned.

It was in the 1580s, too, that Akbar began to remit taxes for reasons of economic, not social, justice. First in 1585, then in 1586, 1588 and 1590, the prices of crops fell across the empire – a result of increased agricultural production under Akbar's new policies. Thanks to this deflation, however, farmers were unable to pay taxes on their produce. Each time, Akbar remitted their taxes, once by over 190 million rupees. Such remittances were consistent with a policy of making the calculation, collection and distribution of the empire's revenue more efficient and more just.

In late 1582, after the brainstorming during Nauroz, Akbar implemented Faizi's suggestion and put various amirs in charge of keeping an eye on the prices of essential commodities. The list of these commodities is both eclectic and illuminating, covering, as it seems to, the needs of a broad swathe of society, from the soldier's home to the commander's mansion. Akbar's milk brother Zain, for example, was put in charge of oil, and one Ghazi Khan Badakhshi in charge of salt – essential items by any reckoning – while the ill-tempered Shahbaz Khan, who quarrelled with Baba Qaqshal in Gujarat and with Aziz in Bengal, watched over the prices of brocade, and Hakim Abul Fath, the Persian émigré (fonder of bottles than battles as Badauni once put it), had charge of opiates. The list went on, spanning elephants and horses, grain and weapons, medicine, sheep and goats as well as silver and gold, books as well as perfumes – and in Abul Fazl's special charge, woollens.

It was in 1582, too, that Akbar invited a man called Amir Fathullah Shirazi to his court. A man of many and varied talents, from astrology to mechanics,[39] and capable, equally, of 'accompanying the emperor on hunting parties, with a rifle on his shoulder, and a powder keg in his waistband',[40] Fathullah may have mirrored something of Akbar's own physical and intellectual adventurism, and he became one of the stars of Akbar's court.

He also became a good friend of Abul Fazl's, who wrote of Fathullah that 'If the books of antiquity should be lost, the Amir will restore them'.[41] This was high praise coming from a man who had, in fact, restored a book himself. Once, it seems, a rare manuscript half burnt by fire came to Abul Fazl. The scholar took on the challenge, 'cut away the burnt portions, pasted new paper to each page, and then commenced to restore the missing halves of each line, in which attempt, after many thoughtful perusals, he succeeded'. When, later, an undamaged copy of the book was found, Abul Fazl's restored version 'presented so many points of extraordinary coincidence, that his friends were not a little astonished at the thoroughness with which [he] had worked himself into the style and mode of thinking of a difficult author'.[42]

Abul Fazl and Amir Fathullah were not only similar in their intellectual rigour, they were also alike in how they narrated the destiny of their emperor. The early pages of the *Akbarnama* include three horoscopes of its subject – one by Maulana Chand, who was there at Akbar's birth, keeping a close eye on Hamida's contractions; another by Jyotik Rai, based on Indian calculations, as opposed to the maulana's Greek ones; and a third by Fathullah.

It is Fathullah's reading that appears to aim, much like the *Akbarnama*, to project the emperor's life as ordained. Thus, Fathullah found that Akbar's marital alliances with 'the ruling families of India' were fated by the stars, as was the 'depart[ure]' of Humayun when Akbar reached 'the years of discretion'. He even discovered that the emperor's brother (who else but poor Mirza Hakim) would 'be of no account alongside [Akbar's] glory'.

Much like the miracles and genealogies that fill the *Akbarnama*, such a 'forecast' – it could not have been made sooner than 1583, when Fathullah arrived in Akbar's court – reinforces the idea of the predetermined perfection of the emperor's rule. And if, again, Akbar had been content with such flattering portraits alone, his life might have provided little more than a study of pre-modern propaganda. In fact, Fathullah is not remembered for his horoscope as much as for overhauling the empire's revenue and administration.

In 1585, together with Akbar's brother-in-law, Bhagwant Das, Fathullah Shirazi proposed twenty reforms, mostly for the assessment of agricultural land and the welfare of its farmers and soldiers. Among these: tax collectors were to give receipts and credit any excess payment to the next year; the collectors' own pay was to be reviewed and their expenses to be granted; soldiers were not to lose their pay if their horses died – the mansabdari salary being paid according to how many horses a man could bring to battle – instead, the salary was to be transferred to the new horse even if there was delay in branding it.

It is no wonder, then, that Badauni reports how every evening, 'a most terrible crowd' of needy Hindus and Muslims, men and women, healthy and sick, gathered below Akbar's balcony, waiting for their lord, their benefactor, their God to appear. And every evening, when Akbar appeared, 'the whole crowd prostrated themselves'. There was even a cult that grew around this ritual viewing – this darshan – of the emperor. Darshaniyas would come to 'feast their eyes'[43] on Akbar when he made his first public appearance every morning.

A few years previously, Badauni notes how 'low and mean fellows' had hailed Akbar as the *sahib-i-zaman*, lord of the world, who 'would remove all differences of opinion among the seventy-two sects of Islam and the Hindus'. Maulanas had dropped broad hints about 'the promised appearance of the Mahdi'. Now it was '[c]heating, thieving Brahmans', writes a disgusted Badauni, who 'told the Emperor that he was an incarnation, like Ram,

Figure 13.1   A Jain ascetic walking along a riverbank. Several charismatic Jain priests were among Akbar's favoured interlocutors. Siddhi Chandra, a Jain monk in Akbar's court, wrote, 'There is not a single art, not a single branch of knowledge, not a single act of boldness and strength which is not attempted by young Akbar' – and compared him to the son of Kaushalya, that is, to Rama. Attributed to Basavana, c. 1600. *Source*: The Cleveland Museum of Art, Public domain.

Krishna, and other infidel kings', brought into the world to fulfil a prediction by which 'a great conqueror would rise up in India, who would honour Brahmans and cows, and govern the earth with justice'.[44] This story has survived the ages, though in somewhat more vengeful form. The historian A. L. Srivastava remembers his father telling it to him: a hermit called Mukand Brahmachari undertook a penance in Prayag 'so that he might be born a powerful Kshatriya king and exterminate Islam from India'.[45] Some error in his prayer – or a play of the gods – produced a mixed result: the determined hermit was reborn, yes, but as a Muslim himself: the emperor Akbar.

Like the Hindu reborn a Muslim, Akbar was acquiring new lives as he lived, in the customs, the legends and cultures of his people. The emperor who had once proclaimed the victory of Islam in Chittorgarh was hailed as Hindupati, 'Lord of the Hindus', by a contemporary poet called Holrai.[46] Siddhi Chandra, a Jain monk in Akbar's court, wrote, 'There is not a single art, not a single branch of knowledge, not a single act of boldness and strength which is not attempted by young Akbar' – and compared him to the son of Kaushalya, that is, to Rama.[47] Amrit Rai, writing his ballad-biography of Man Singh, the *Mancharita*, in the early 1580s, describes Akbar as a '*cagattā cakkavai*', a Chagatai Chakravartin, a wonderful amalgamation of Mongol and Hindu king. Akbar had 'rescued dharma, virtue, and generosity from drowning, as Varaha rescued the earth', he goes on. In the poet's free-flowing imagination, however, Akbar is not only an avatar of Vishnu, like Varaha – or Rama and Krishna as others in his court declared their emperor to be. In fact, as with Chagatai and Chakravartin, Amrit Rai manages a poetic union between Akbar and Vishnu himself, such that 'The goddess Lakshmi shares her time between Vishnu's embrace / and nestling at Akbar's breast.'[48]

It might appear from the preceding pages that Akbar was binding his people to him with equal parts justice, generosity and miracles, while terrifying and pauperizing his nobility into obedience. Akbar's understanding and deployment of his own authority was far more complex, however. Yes, his amirs were greatly more subservient than the cantankerous warlords who had blithely deserted Akbar's father on the banks of the Ganga in Kannauj, or risen in rebellion against Akbar himself, but it was not their deference alone that the emperor desired – it was also their devotion.

The year 1582, or 990 in the Hijri calendar, was significant in more ways than one: politically, of course, in that it ended the dreams of Mirza Muhammad Hakim, and thus the last viable threat to Akbar's throne, but also historically, in that it began the final decade of the first Islamic millennium, and astrologically, in that it witnessed a rare conjunction of Saturn and Jupiter – a conjunction, or *qiran*, that was itself a millennial event and had last occurred at about the time of the beginning of Islam. Such rare conjunctions of planets had long been used by conquerors and emperors to mark their own reigns as equally unique, even world-changing. Timur, for example, had titled himself Sahib Qiran, Lord of the Conjunction, as would Akbar's grandson, Shahjahan. Akbar, characteristically, went a step ahead of both.

Just as Akbar celebrated Mirza Hakim's defeat with Nauroz, he celebrated the qiran, notes Azfar Moin, by issuing a new coin stamped with the word *'alfi'* ('millennium') and commissioning a new history, *Tarikh-i-Alfi*, of the past 1000 years. It is significant that this history begins with the death of the Prophet Muhammad, not his birth, which would have been the more conventional and appropriate choice. Instead, by beginning 'with the end of a sacred being, an embodied absence', Moin argues that the history 'set up an expectation of a new beginning and a new being, i.e., a new cycle of time'.[49] This new beginning is, in fact, the book's punchline: it '[ends] with the reign of Akbar, [so] one can surmise that it was the Mughal emperor who had filled this absence and fulfilled this expectation by inaugurating the new millennium'. For anyone who missed the hint, the *tarikh's* authors also declared Akbar 'the Renewer of the Second Millennium (*Mujaddid-i Alf-i Thani)*'.[50]

Mujaddid, Mujtahid, Mahdi; a brahmachari reborn, Vishnu's avatar, Chagatai Chakravartin: it followed that an emperor of such destiny – prophesied and political – should have a special category of men in his service; not subjects, not mansabdars, but disciples.

'And they sacrificed their wealth, and life, reputation, and religion', Badauni sighs, 'to their friendship for the Emperor'. These were the four pledges made by new recruits to what is popularly known as Akbar's *din-i-ilahi*, his 'divine faith'. Having made their vows, the faithful would bow low to the emperor – now their spiritual master, or pir – putting their heads to his feet. He would raise them up, place a turban upon their heads, with a miniature portrait of himself pinned upon it, and give them an image of the sun.

Like every one of Akbar's major innovations, this, too, faced its share of resistance. Akbar had begun experimenting with taking on disciples before 1582. Abul Fazl, evidently a gatekeeper of the faith, describes himself discouraging a man called Fath Dost, whom he did not trust, from joining it. Akbar allowed it, however, declaring that 'becoming a disciple of this supplicant to God is a test of men, and brings out their internal qualities'. True enough: no sooner was Fath Dost inducted to the faith than he met the fate Abul Fazl felt he deserved. He was murdered during a drinking party.

It was after 1582, however, after Mirza Hakim's defeat, when, in Munis Faruqui's words, Akbar could afford to '[throw] all caution to the wind, abandoning even the slightest pretence of being an orthodox-minded Sunni-Muslim ruler',[51] that the emperor began initiating mansabdars as devotees in a systematic, though not always successful, way.

Not everyone, it seems, was as eager as Fath Dost to join Akbar's cult. Badauni describes a scene between the emperor, Birbar and two unwilling recruits, Qutubuddin Muhammad Khan and the Punjabi Shahbaz Khan. Both 'staunchly resisted', writes Badauni. Qutubuddin warned Akbar that his court would become a scandal, a laughing stock across the Islamic world. 'What would the kings of the West say, such as the Sultan of Constantinople, if they heard all this?'

Sardonically, Akbar asked whether the khan had come 'on a secret mission from Constantinople', or would he like to immigrate and 'become an honoured subject there'. The other reluctant convert, Shahbaz Khan, known for his temper, got 'excited' at this, and Birbar – 'that hellish dog' – took the opportunity to take a dig at Islam.

'Affairs became rather unpleasant', writes Badauni, as one can well imagine, with Shahbaz threatening to kill Birbar, and Akbar wishing he could beat the khan's furious mouth 'with a slipper full of filth!'

Akbar would be piqued, naturally, at having his spiritual overlordship rebuffed, but he never forced it upon anyone. Badauni himself declined to acknowledge Akbar as his pir, and while he says that the emperor 'used frequently to allude' to this fact, he was not punished for his refusal in any way except by such, possibly tart, remarks. Indeed, Badauni writes that while 'shameless and ill-starred wretches' instigated Akbar to do more to popularize his cult, Akbar replied that 'confidence in him as a leader was a matter of time, and good counsel, and did not require the sword'. He would not compel devotion, nor would he bribe it, even if Badauni believed that had Akbar only 'spent a little money', he'd have caught many more disciples in 'his devilish nets'.

It wasn't only Badauni who refused to be thus entangled. Raja Todar Mal remained devoted to his idols until the end of his days – once, having lost them on a march, he stopped eating – which may account for why Abul Fazl often balances praise for the warrior-accountant with disappointed comments on his 'bigotry'. Akbar, too, may have made the kind of allusions Badauni complains about to Todar Mal's recalcitrance: the emperor's grandson, Shahjahan, remembered how Akbar 'complained of the raja's independence, vanity, and bigoted adherence to Hinduism'.[52] Bhagwant Das and Man Singh, too, are said to have declined Akbar's invitation, though somewhat less dramatically than Qutubuddin or Shahbaz, with Man Singh declaring that he would convert from Hinduism to Islam on the emperor's command, but knew of no religion other than these two.[53]

Amir Fathullah Shirazi, for whom Akbar had such fond respect, would not entertain his new faith, so much so that even Badauni, though decrying Fathullah as a 'worldly office-hunter, and . . . worshipper of mammon' acknowledges his 'bluff honesty'. Akbar was keen, according to Badauni, to have Fathullah join him in his critical examination of Islam. Once, the emperor tried to tempt the mechanically talented amir to participate in a debate on various scientifically impossible miracles attributed to the Prophet Muhammad, glancing at him every so often 'because he wanted him to say something', but Fathullah did not oblige: he 'looked straight ahead of himself, and did not utter a syllable'. Indeed, far from joining Akbar, either in his irreverence or his new religion, Fathullah, a 'staunch Shiah', would offer his own prayers in court, 'with the greatest composure . . . a thing which no one else would have dared to do'.[54]

But was it a religion at all that Akbar was propounding? 'Since the early nineteenth century', writes J. F. Richards, 'generations of historians, in sorting out the various rituals and beliefs of Akbar, have tried to determine influences and filiation – whether Zoroastrian, Sufi, Nath Yogi, or Brahmanical . . . A general tendency has been to treat the "Divine Faith" as a bizarre concoction of Akbar's fertile intellect.' Richards, however, following the work of S. A. A. Rizvi, argues that Akbar did not seek to invent a religion, but rather a system of discipleship to himself – or, in the words of Munis Faruqui, a 'religiously eclectic imperial cult', a *silsilah-i muridan*, 'circle of disciples', rather than a din-i-ilahi, divine faith.[55]

'In Rizvi's view', writes Richards, 'discipleship represented a major effort to create an exceptionally loyal and reliable cadre of nobles' – a clever and necessary invention, and a logical extension of the mansabdari system, by which Akbar's disparate nobility, Khurasani to Khatri, might overcome their many differences to share a 'solemn commitment to an Emperor who had reached the highest degree of purity, knowledge and ontological status possible for a mortal'.

So, in 1582, Akbar was unchallenged, and began to become unchallengeable, a god to his people, a glue to bind his amirs. And yet, it was in this year of unleashed possibility that Akbar began, also, to confront the pitfalls of middle age.

In October 1582, days before his first solar weighing and fortieth birthday, Akbar caught a stomach bug. At first, the emperor left it to God to heal him. When, eventually, he let some doctors in, they argued endlessly over treatments – the prescription of laxatives being a sticking point between followers of Greek and Indian medicine. Abul Fazl 'much upset . . . got into the fray', chivvying them along to make up their minds. 'How can such inappropriate argument help a delicate patient?'[56] It was over a month before the emperor was fully cured. The public 'rejoiced' – and yet, the prolonged illness strikes a faint note of foreboding in an otherwise rousing symphony.

Chapter 14

The Lonely Immortal

'When I came to India I was much attracted by the elephants, and I thought that the use of their extraordinary strength was a prognostication of my universal ascendency.'

– Akbar, Happy Sayings, *Ain-i-Akbari*

One of Akbar's many acts of public charity was to establish 'two places for feeding poor Hindus and Musalmans' and a third for feeding yogis. It was with this third group that Akbar once celebrated Shivratri, eating and drinking with some of the principal ascetics, who predicted that the emperor would 'live three or four times as long as ordinary men'.[1]

'Fawning court doctors, wisely enough, found proofs of the longevity of the Emperor', Badauni continues; they even hailed the beginning of a new age, in which the 'original longevity of mankind' – there were books that said that men once lived 1000 years – 'would again commence'. Even now, ascetics in Tibet and China could live as long as two centuries.

Death – and its avoidance – was becoming one of Akbar's obsessions. The emperor who had ridden musth elephants across bobbing and sliding pontoon bridges, gambling on God's opinion with his life, now began to practise ascetic disciplines that might help him put off his own demise – celibacy and a vegetarian diet among them.[2] Even when death came, as death must, Akbar would not cease to exist: he shaved the crown of his head, from which 'he believed that the soul of perfect beings' escaped when they died, making a sound like thunder, which 'the dying man may look upon as a proof of his happiness and salvation from sin, and as a sign that his soul . . . will pass into the body of some grand and mighty king'.[3]

Badauni, always a little disparaging of what he thought of as Akbar's susceptibility to outrageous ideas, writes that the emperor 'fully believed' all that he was told about his longevity. If that is so, if Akbar was convinced by, say, Fathullah Shirazi's forecast that he would live over 120 years, he was also determined, it seems, to fill every unforgiving minute of his long life with frenetic activity.

In October 1583, a few months after Fathullah arrived in his court and a year or so before he celebrated Shivratri with the yogis, Akbar sketched out a plan of action for the months (not years) to come. First, he would go east and 'found a great city' in Prayag, it being 'regarded by the people of India with much reverence', stay awhile and calm the region. Next, he would travel south and conquer the Deccan, 'which was longing for a just ruler', ride on towards Turan, to deal with his brother Hakim once and for all, and sort out matters between his ageing uncle Sulaiman and Sulaiman's grandson Shahrukh, still feuding over Badakhshan. And thus, come full circle, Akbar would recover 'the land of his ancestors'.[4]

Akbar announced these plans in the month of his forty-first birthday. If Fathullah's calculations were to be believed, he was barely one-third of the way through his life, and if Akbar meant to conquer his ancestral Samarqand that very year, one wonders what he had planned for the decades that remained to him.

In fact, however, Akbar was closer to the end of his life than to the beginning. He had a little over twenty years left, and while, in the early 1580s, the emperor was at the very height of his power, showing every sign of blazing through the second quarter of his reign as he had through the first, a sense of ending runs through the annals of these years, as death begins to haunt the emperor: not only the fear of his own, but the actual, accumulating demise of the people who filled his world – his enemies, including Rana Pratap and, in Kabul, Mirza Hakim; his friends, from Todar Mal to Fathullah and Birbar, and, most tragically, his children.

Once, for Akbar to have an idea was to execute it: whether to gallop after Adham Khan in Malwa or set sail in the monsoon after Daud. Now, somehow, though Akbar was stronger than ever before, his plans were more fallible. Thus, of his three stated ambitions for 1583–84, his twenty-eighth year on the throne – a city in Prayag, the conquest of the Deccan and the recovery of Samarqand – Akbar only managed one. Barely four weeks after announcing his plans, Akbar did, indeed, arrive in Prayag, 'that place of worship',[5] and establish the city known as Illahbas, 'God's abode'. It would be almost two decades, however, in the very last years of his life, before Akbar descended upon the Deccan. As for any hope of banging Sulaiman and Shahrukh's heads together and marching upon Samarqand, that was easier said than done.

When, in 1575, Sulaiman's hopes of regaining Badakhshan from Shahrukh with Akbar's help were stymied by Munim Khan's demise in Bengal, and the diversion of imperial troops to the east, the disappointed widower had begged leave to go on the Haj. Pilgrimage, however, was the last thing on the homesick warlord's mind: instead of Mecca, he went to Persia. Some four years later, having wrangled troops from the Persian shah, Sulaiman arrived in Kabul, seeking help from Akbar's half-brother this time. This was in 1579, when troubles in Bengal were brewing, and Hakim thought he might enlist the aid of his 'old and experienced'[6] uncle to exacerbate discontent in Hindustan. Sulaiman was too experienced to allow any such foolhardy meddling with Akbar's realm, however, and persuaded his nephew to march with him to Badakhshan instead.

Akbar wasn't pleased with the alliance. It was one thing for Sulaiman to ask Akbar for aid, entirely another to ally with Hakim. The emperor, too, was about to send troops to Badakhshan – to help Shahrukh, this time – when news of a truce between grandfather and grandson arrived.

The truce did not hold. It was such an abject failure, in fact, that far from establishing a peaceful joint command, the two squabbling lords of Badakhshan lost their kingdom to neighbouring Turan. Sulaiman and Shahrukh were ejected from the family seat, and, one by one, they would both seek shelter in Hindustan. Shahrukh came in 1584 and joined Akbar's court; Sulaiman, older and less willing to give up hope of his throne, arrived two years later, a vagabond in his old age, forced to retire his ambitions. He would spend three years in Lahore, where he died, aged seventy-seven. It is likely that the old warlord's last years, if comfortable, were tinged with an ache for home. Not for Sulaiman the global ambitions of his ancestors and relatives: the farthest he had ever ventured for conquest of his own was Kabul. He died, writes Abul Fazl, having spent his last days, 'in repose and enjoyment', but also, one imagines, in fretful melancholy.

The monarch of Turan, who took Badakhshan from under Sulaiman's and Shahrukh's stubborn noses, was called Abdullah Khan. The Uzbek ruler shared Akbar's appetite for expansion, and when Abdullah Khan took Badakhshan in 1584, Mirza Hakim wrote to Akbar in a panic, worried that the Uzbek ruler would swoop further east. The chastised lord of Kabul did not have to suffer his anxiety very long: the next year, in July 1585, Hakim died.

Abul Fazl hints that it was as much destiny as drink that did him in – any opponent of Akbar's was fated to a bad end, and the 'death of this young man is a fresh instance of it'. He may well be right, in that Hakim gave up the fight. He was barely in his thirties, but he had lived a battle-worn life: his mother keeping a bloodstained grip on Kabul for her child; Sulaiman and Haram making repeated bids for his throne; his own daring but ill-planned assaults on Lahore; and his hunger for a fortune as great as his brother's – all come to nothing, now, as he lived out his days at Akbar's pleasure. If all the joy that remained to Hakim was in his drink, it is no surprise.

Akbar may or may not have mourned his half-brother's death, but he did react to it. Abdullah of Turan was not a man to forgo the temptation of an unoccupied Kabul, and there were rumours that the Kabuli chiefs, too, were planning to ally with Turan, using Hakim's young children in their negotiations. Akbar sent Man Singh from Punjab to Kabul, and the emperor himself left Fatehpur within three weeks of Hakim's death, marching north to Lahore.

Man Singh arrived just in time to stop Hakim's Uncle Faridun – the 'leprous spot' who once urged the prince to invade Hindustan – from smuggling Hakim's two sons off to Turan. Instead, Man Singh bundled the boys and Faridun to Rawalpindi, where Akbar met them, took the young princes in his care, and put Faridun in prison.

Kabul was safe, but with the province still divided in its loyalties, the time was not right, clearly, to march against the powerful monarch of Turan. Having arrived in Punjab, however, Akbar would stay on. With his hapless nobility in tow, the emperor settled in Lahore.

The city had many attractions. Father Monserrate describes it as 'second to none, either in Asia or in Europe, with regard to size, population, and wealth'. Every kind of imported merchandise was available and every kind of 'art or craft useful to human life' was practised; the Father was particularly delighted with the perfumes, whose 'scent in the early morning is most delicious', filling Lahore's covered bazaar. The city was rich in its people too: 'Most of the citizens are wealthy Brachmanae and Hindus of every caste, especially Casmirini' – these last were often bakers, and the scent of their bread, too, must have wafted through the air.[7]

Such allurements may have reconciled Akbar's amirs to their new home; for Akbar, meanwhile, the great advantage of Lahore was that, from here, he could keep an eye on both Kabul and Turan, and supervise conquests to the north and north-west – which he would do for the next fourteen-odd years, from 1585 to 1598.[8] The great city of Fatehpur, not even fifteen years old, was abandoned.

Akbar never returned to his splendid capital. Ralph Fitch, an Englishman who travelled to Hindustan in the 1580s, describes Agra and Fatehpur as equally 'great cities, either of them much greater than London and very populous', and the 40-odd kilometres between them busy with 'a market of victuals and other things, as full as though a man were still in a towne'. Barely a quarter-century later, another Englishman called William Finch found Fatehpur 'all ruinate, lying like a waste desart, and very dangerous to pass through in the night, the buildings lying waste without inhabitants'.[9] Why did Akbar allow Fatehpur to fall to ruin? There are many theories, but it isn't clear.

It may be, as Munis Faruqui argues, that Akbar no longer needed Fatehpur as a symbol of his alliance with the Chishtis after Mirza Hakim's downfall.[10] It may be, as J. F. Richards has written, that even cities were becoming subordinate to Akbar's own authority – the imperial 'capital', whether Agra or Delhi, Fatehpur or Lahore – was where the emperor was.[11] It may be, too, that Akbar's push into the northern frontiers of his realm took up a lot of time. When he finally made his way back south, he would be preoccupied with matters of succession and troubles with his sons – and in no mood, perhaps, for all the spring-cleaning Fatehpur would have required after a decade and a half of his absence.

Whatever his reasons may have been, Fatehpur was forgotten, as were any plans of marching on Samarqand. Instead, Akbar sent expeditions to Kashmir and Swat, led by Bhagwant Das and Zain Khan – brother of the Saif who had died trying to prove his manhood in the battle for Ahmedabad. Both conquests were successful, in the end, but they would bring Akbar two great losses in their wake – the one of a friendship, the other of a friend.

Both campaigns left on the same day, 20 December 1585, and two months later, news arrived that Bhagwant Das and his officers, having marched into the bitter cold, across bad roads, through rain and snow, had negotiated a truce with the king of Kashmir, Yusuf Shah Chak. The shivering Mughal men – many of them Rajputs who would never have seen snow before – were in no state to offer battle, but Yusuf Shah, not having expected them to attempt an invasion at all through such difficult clime and country, offered to submit and return with them to Akbar's court. To this, Akbar offered no objection, but he insisted that his men march all the way through the valley and make it theirs before they returned. The officers were as reluctant to obey as the Kashmiris were unwilling to let them advance any further. Yusuf's son, Yaqub, met the Mughals with an army, and the two sides came to yet another settlement. Kashmir would offer Akbar the homage of khutba-u-sikka – the sermon to be read and coins to be minted in his name – along with revenue from its saffron, silk and game.

Again, word came to Akbar, in Punjab. Once, at the merest whisper of such reluctance to fight, Akbar would have leaped upon a horse and raced north to shame his men and shock his enemy. But now, as unhappily as his army had marched into the mountains, Akbar let them return. At the end of March 1586, on the last day of Nauroz, Bhagwant Das arrived in court, a submissive Yusuf Shah in tow – and Akbar put the Kashmiri king in jail.

It wasn't Akbar's usual policy to depose a conquered king who offered submission. The Rajput lords continued to rule their ancestral lands, as Sultan Daud might have in Bengal if he hadn't broken his truce with Munim Khan. 'Dignity is the maintenance of one's station' is one of Akbar's Happy

Sayings.[12] Some years later, when Man Singh plundered an Oriya king called Ram Chand, the emperor 'who appreciates dignities' made Man Singh apologize. Why, then, would he show such disregard, both for Yusuf Shah's station and for the pride of his own amir and brother-in-law, Bhagwant Das, and the pledge he had made to the Kashmiri king?

Abul Fazl declares he did it on the bidding of his advisers, though it goes against the very grain of his narrative to have the divinely inspired Akbar acting by command of an anonymous council. (Although it has been argued that the grain of Abul Fazl's narrative is exactly this, that Akbar is right no matter what. As Peter Hardy puts it memorably: 'Whatever Akbar is, is for the best; whatever Akbar does is for the best; but the best is what, from moment to moment, Akbar is and does.' Akbar's actions do not follow precepts, that is, they are principles in themselves.)[13]

Even if there were good reasons behind Akbar's order to arrest the Kashmiri king to whom Bhagwant Das had promised safe passage, the Rajput did not approve of them. Twice in the following weeks, Bhagwant Das had fits of 'madness'.[14]

First, when he was given command of Kabul, he proclaimed 'improper desires', writes Abul Fazl, without elaboration. The modern historian Afzal Husain suggests that Bhagwant Das may have demanded guarantees for his authority in Kabul, to avoid the dishonour of having his word broken on his behalf again.[15] If so, no such promise was forthcoming; instead, Akbar cancelled the Rajput's appointment. Bhagwant Das apologized, was reappointed, but '[became] mad' once again after crossing the Indus. He was brought back to the fortress of Attock where, while a doctor took his pulse, the overwrought Rajput tried to stab himself.

Again, Abul Fazl offers no explanation except insanity. While it is true enough that, for Abul Fazl, anyone who cannot see the perfect rightness of all Akbar's actions qualifies 'for admission to the Mughal equivalent of a psychiatric hospital with maximum security',[16] there was a strain of mental illness that ran in Bhagwant Das's family. Two of his children, including Akbar's daughter-in-law, would also try, and succeed in, killing themselves. It may have been manic depression that drove Bhagwant Das's hand to his dagger, but the Rajput had reason for his unhappiness. Badauni, more plain-spoken, as always, writes that Akbar had broken his amir's pledge, and Bhagwant Das was willing to end his life 'to save his . . . sense of honour'.

Akbar had grieved his Rajput kin, but the emperor, too, was grieving. It was only a few weeks before Bhagwant Das's return from Kashmir that Akbar received news of Birbar's death.

Twice Akbar had saved Birbar's life. Once, in 1583, when Birbar fell off his horse during a polo match, Akbar healed him with 'his holy breathings'.

A year later, a mad elephant ran at Birbar during an animal fight and Akbar came charging between the two on his horse. It was the emperor's usual courage, of course, but also 'his . . . especial kindness' for the brahmin poet.[17]

What was it that so attracted Akbar to Birbar? Why did he risk his own life for him, or build palaces for him in Fatehpur – an honour not accorded any other mansabdar?

Birbar was a talented poet. P. P. Sinha quotes some lovely verses by him in his biography of Akbar's friend.[18] This, for example, would have appealed to Akbar's mind as much as to his ear:

Toote par eekh taaki mistri gud kand karo taake le prasad dev-devin chadaaiye
Phuti ke kapaas par raakhat hai aalam ki vaake hot vastra kahan lo ginaaiye
Sade jab san taake svet ban kaagaz ke taapar Quran-o-Puranh-u likhaaiye
Kahe kavi Braham suno Akbar Badshah, toote-phoote sade taako ya bidhi saraahiye

When cane is crushed we get sugar whereof to make sweets for the gods
When cotton flowers burst we get clothes whereof to cover our shame
When the jute plant rots we get the paper whereon
    the Quran and Puranas are written
'Hear O Akbar Shah,' says the poet Braham, 'so the
    broken of the world may be reformed'

Sinha also offers some examples of the apocryphal wit for which Birbar is renowned in popular culture. What decays when cooked and thrives when burnt? A brick.

Akbar was not averse to a good joke. Father Monserrate describes the emperor as friendly and accessible, but liable to become morose, for which condition he organized all kinds of entertainment, from polo matches, boxing bouts and pigeon-flying to 'concerts, dances, conjurer's tricks, and the jokes of his jesters, of whom he makes much'. He was as unselfconscious in his merriment as he was in his anger. 'When he laughs', writes the priest, 'his face becomes almost distorted'.

Abul Fazl describes a scene from one of Akbar's early elephant hunts that had Akbar and his men in splits. A man called Shah Fakhruddin was thrown off his horse by a wild she-elephant. When the other hunters arrived to his rescue, Fakhruddin 'in his confusion, lost his head and put his finger on his mouth as a sign to them to be silent'. The memory of the dazed man's desperate 'Shh!' to keep a dangerous beast at bay was a 'source of amusement' for a long time, writes Abul Fazl – Akbar must have remembered and retold it decades later, still chuckling perhaps, for his scribe to write the story.

For all his sense of humour, it isn't clear whether Akbar approved of frivolous behaviour by his mansabdars. 'A king should not be familiar in mirth and amusement with his courtiers' was one of Akbar's Happy Sayings, in fact. The *Akbarnama* includes a passing mention of a man called Jafar Beg who was imprisoned alongside Muzaffar Khan during the upheavals in Bengal. Unlike the poor governor, Jafar Beg managed to escape by virtue of his wit, 'joking and making light of the situation'. This was apt, Abul Fazl implies: Jafar Beg had been exiled to Bengal for making unseemly jokes in court.[19]

Birbar, by contrast, is among the few men who never suffered a rebuke from Akbar. Only once is there even a hint of Birbar getting into trouble with the emperor. Badauni tells of how Akbar, in one of his many social innovations, had instructed the prostitutes of Fatehpur to name any amir who visited and 'seduced' them, so the emperor might have the wretched man punished. Birbar's was one of the names the women gave up. The poet was distraught; he threatened to give up life in court and wander the streets as a yogi. And far from punishing him, Akbar mollified his friend.

They influenced each other, too. Birbar made no objection, for example, to joining Akbar's circle of disciples; while both Akbar and his mother Hamida began to patronize Vaishnavism and a well-known philosopher of the school called Vithalnath thanks to Birbar's interest in the sect.[20]

Perhaps there is no point seeking reasons for Akbar's affection; or perhaps the friendship between the emperor and the poet had the same foundation as any lasting relationship. Trust.

Akbar was greatly accessible to his people, as Father Monserrate noted, and he made his court open to diverse talent, as his Uzbek and Central Asian warlords complained. But his trust was less easy to obtain and impossible to regain.

There is a clear example in Badauni's own life. Though the disillusioned scholar bemoans his failure to rise in court – poor I! – and blames it on his inability to flatter as Abul Fazl could, there is enough evidence in his own writing to suggest that Badauni was faring fairly well until he lost Akbar's trust. He had pleased the emperor with his enthusiasm for war in Haldighati; his dulcet tones had gained him the post of *imam*, leading prayers at the mosque; and his various translations had been well received. But Badauni was a restless soul. First, he wanted to go on the Haj, but Abdun Nabi wouldn't allow it because Badauni had a mother to take care of. Sometime later, he lost a son, a shock that further undermined his commitment to his job. Eventually, Badauni took five months off, but stayed away a full year. When he returned, Akbar had lost interest in him. 'Even to this day although a period of eighteen years has elapsed since that event, and eighteen thousand worlds have passed away', wrote Badauni, he had no 'chance of confirming myself in [the emperor's] favour'.

With Birbar, on the other hand, it was, as Badauni puts it, 'a case of "Thy flesh is my flesh, and thy blood my blood"'. How it must have plagued Akbar, then, to know that it was he who sent his friend to his death. And yet, at the time, it was an honour Birbar craved.

In February 1586, at about the time that Bhagwant Das was ready to return from Kashmir, Zain Khan sent a request for reinforcements. He was far west of the valley, fighting the Afghans of Swat and Bajaur and, after twenty-three battles, Zain wrote to say that his men were 'somewhat worn out'.[21]

Immediately, Abul Fazl volunteered for the job. He wanted, he writes, to 'shut the mouths of . . . envious persons' who were being snide, presumably, about his lack of military experience. Debating theology in the evenings might well please Akbar and win promotions, but a man was still only a man with a sword in his hand. It may have been for similar reasons that Birbar, too, made an aggressive bid for the job. Such was the fervour of both men that Akbar cast lots to choose between them. Birbar won.

Hakim Abul Fath – bottle-man not battle-man, last seen escaping the rebels in Bengal – went along too. It could not have been a worse pairing: neither Birbar nor Abul Fath had shown any great skill for battle, and, besides, they despised each other.

'On the march there were daily, improper expressions used to one another', writes Abul Fazl about their unhappy journey. Things only got worse when they reached Zain's camp. Not only did Birbar not get along with Abul Fath, he disliked Zain, too. All along the way, it seems, he muttered in disgust at his situation, 'It looks as if my fortune has been inverted that I should have to traverse hill and plain with the Hakim, for the support of [Zain Khan]. When shall the things end?'[22]

They ended as badly as they had begun. At the very first meeting between the three men, the 'Rajah and the Hakim came from hard language to mutual abuse'. Then, maybe tired of haranguing each other, they joined forces against Zain, who had made a misguided effort to bring peace and proffer a plan. Zain wanted part of the army, now strengthened with reinforcements, to march on to further conquest, and part to stay behind to guard his acquisitions. But no, Birbar and Abul Fath insisted they must all march: 'The orders were to attack the country, not to guard it.'

Akbar's amirs, bound by oaths and devotion to their emperor, were at loggerheads with each other; more fearful of Akbar's disapproval, it seems, than of making bad decisions in an alien land. Thus, Abul Fazl writes that while Zain knew that the newcomers had completely misjudged the dangers of marching jauntily, flanks unguarded, into hostile ravines, he gave in when they insisted because he knew how close Abul Fath and Birbar were to Akbar, and was afraid they would complain about him. Birbar and Abul Fath, meanwhile, were equally afraid 'that they should be disgraced' if they did not act precisely as Akbar had commanded.

On 12 February 1586, therefore, the squabbling generals set off on their 'unsuitable march'. They had some initial victories, but then the Afghans got behind them and attacked. Having, somehow, defended his flank, Zain went to Birbar's tent that evening and made a last-ditch appeal to reason: the Afghans had occupied all the heights nearby; the road ahead would only take the Mughals into deeper defiles. The best they could make of this bad situation was to remain where they were and try to defuse the Afghan onslaught.

Again, the two inexperienced commanders 'stuck to their own opinions'. Four days later, the Mughals were marching once more; Birbar and Abul Fath in front, Zain fighting off Afghans in the rear. It was thus that Zain discovered only too late that his two colleagues had called a halt in a defile, vulnerable to assaults from a height further on. It was already late, Afghans were 'pressing on them from behind', so Zain Khan did the best he could: he ordered a vanguard to march ahead and take over the tactical height, while he turned back to keep the encroaching Afghans at bay.

Chaos fell upon the Mughal camp as he left. The vanguard's resumption of its march confused everyone, more and more Afghans began to attack from all sides, and the Mughal troops rushed ahead pell-mell, not knowing they were going into even lower ground. It was to this scene of stampede and panic – 'elephants, horses and men . . . mixed up' – that Zain returned.

He had escaped the Afghans when they took a break to count their plunder. Night had fallen when Zain rode back into the main camp, and in the anxious dark, some Mughal soldiers mistook their commander's arrival for a fresh attack by the enemy: 'Foolish babblers called out that the Afghans are coming after us!'

Fortunately, the rumour was quickly quashed, but the cold night was spent in fear. Dawn brought no relief. Instead, Afghans appeared on the heights around them, 'like ants and locusts, from all sides of the mountains'.[23] The Mughal soldiers were like fish in a bowl to their enemy, who 'showered . . . stones and arrows [upon them] like rain'.[24]

It was a debacle; the worst defeat that the Mughals had sustained under Akbar's ever-victorious reign. Historians of the time estimate that between 500 and 8000 men were killed.[25] But the emperor counted only one man's death. Birbar did not survive the massacre.

Akbar was devastated. For two days and nights after news of the disaster arrived, Akbar wouldn't eat or drink; it was his mother, Hamida, who finally made him. His 'heart turned away from everything', writes Abul Fazl. Akbar himself wrote to Abdur Rahim, telling him of the tragedy. '[T]he memory of the pleasures of his lofty company has become very bitter', said Akbar's letter, 'and this sudden calamity has greatly afflicted my heart'.[26]

A rare example of Akbar's Hindi poetry is a deeply moving couplet for his friend: '*Deen dekhi sab din, ek na dinho dusah dukh, / So ab ham kan din, kachhahun nahin rakhio Birbal.*' (He gave the needy all he had, gave no one ever sorrow / But now that too he's given me, Birbar kept nothing for his own.)[27]

So upset was Akbar, according to Badauni, that he wouldn't let the two surviving generals, Zain Khan and Abul Fath, into his sight. To those who did gather around him, the emperor mourned the fact that Birbar's body had not been brought back and burned according to the rites the brahmin would have liked. His courtiers tried to comfort him, saying the corpse would be purified by the sun.[28]

Akbar never recovered from the loss of his friend. Years later, when an imposter claiming to be Birbar appeared in Nagarkot, Akbar clutched at the possibility, imagining that Birbar had stayed away all this time, embarrassed by his defeat.

Within weeks of the massacre, Todar Mal had led a vengeful, victorious campaign into Swat and Bajaur. By autumn of that year, another Mughal general called Qasim Khan had led a contingent of troops into Srinagar. Akbar's soldiers had scaled the mountains of the north as they had taken the ports of the west and the rivers of the east. The emperor's gains piled up, unstoppably. But now, in the wake of Bhagwant Das's wounded pride and Birbar's death, so did his losses.

Two years or so later, in 1589, Akbar lost five of his most trusted and talented mansabdars. The first to go was Tansen, the great singer whom Akbar had poached from Panna decades ago. His death, said Akbar, 'was the annihilation of melody', and he ordered a fitting tribute.[29] All Akbar's musicians sang and played along Tansen's funeral march. Then, in summer that year, while Akbar was touring his newly conquered territories in Kashmir, the talented astrologer, engineer and staunch Shia, Amir Fathullah Shirazi, succumbed to mismanaged treatment by a doctor. It was only six years since Fathullah joined Akbar's court and, though he had refused to join the emperor's cult, he had become one of his most valued friends and advisers, so much so that Akbar said he would have given all his treasure to ransom Fathullah, and considered 'that precious jewel [bought] cheap'.[30]

Akbar was on his way back from Kashmir, still mourning his friend's passing, when Hakim Abul Fath – finally forgiven his failure to protect Birbar – fell ill with violent diarrhoea. The camp came to a halt, doctors were called, but the hakim died. Only three months later, in November 1589, Akbar suffered another dual loss when Todar Mal and Bhagwant Das died within days of each other.

Todar Mal had written to Akbar two months earlier, requesting retirement; he wanted, he said, to spend his 'old age and sickness' by the Ganga 'remembering God'.[31] Akbar agreed, then quickly rescinded his decision. It was Todar Mal who had chased after Sultan Daud with Munim Khan; Todar Mal ('upon whose tactics, bravery, and loyalty the army depended'[32]) who fought the Bengal rebels with Aziz and Shahbaz Khan. It was Todar Mal, too, who had managed so much of Akbar's agricultural and revenue reform – with enough success, evidently, to merit celebratory elegies from an aggrieved nobility. Badauni records an anonymous wit who wrote, 'Todar Mal was he, whose tyranny had oppressed the world, / When he went to Hell, people became merry.'[33] A court poet from Orchha, Keshava Das, recipient of Birbar's patronage, composed a similarly disparaging assessment of Todar Mal versus his patron: '*Todarmal tum mitra mare, sab hi sukh socho / More hit Varvir bina, tuk deenani rocho*' (Todarmal died, everyone slept peacefully / But in the absence of my friend Birbal, the poverty-stricken wept bitterly).[34] Akbar needed Todar Mal, the man who had so long combined his military and administrative genius towards the expansion and management of the realm, so he wrote to him that 'no worship of God was equal to the soothing of the oppressed', and asked him to withdraw his resignation.[35]

Todar Mal had already set out for Haridwar when Akbar's message arrived. Dutifully, he returned to Lahore, where he died on 8 November. Bhagwant Das was among those at Todar Mal's funeral and fell ill upon his return. He, too, was gone by the 14th of the month.

When, at the end of this year of loss, Akbar's horse stumbled during a hunt while chasing a hyena, flinging the emperor face first into stony ground, it is perhaps no wonder that Akbar's thoughts turned to his own demise: he had an epiphany that he would leave the world as empty-handed as he'd arrived. It was only nine days previously that two great doctors of Hindustan, Narain Misra and Bhim Nath, had died. This was read as an omen: Akbar would never need doctors again. But the truth of his omens, like the health of his friends, was proving increasingly unreliable.

The emperor was pushing fifty, and while he wasn't yet old, he was certainly ageing. Akbar was marching back to Lahore when the hunting accident happened. He had spent most of the year touring Kashmir and Kabul, and refused to halt his journey now, even if he had to proceed in a litter instead of on a horse. In January 1590, the camp crossed the Indus and Akbar must have been showing signs of fatigue; Abul Fazl reports that his mother, Hamida, asked the emperor to stop and rest awhile. Rest! Akbar was a man who killed lions single-handed and cured men with his breath. He ignored his mother's fretting. Instead, the emperor decided to amuse himself upon a musth elephant.

As Akbar had khasa guns, so he had khasa elephants, 101 of them – each with at least three 'wives', and a special diet of sugar, ghee, milk and rice with chillies and cloves. The emperor himself was the mahout, and he would 'put his foot on [their] tusks, and mount them, even when they are in the rutting season, and [astonish] experienced people'.[36]

In January 1590, two years short of his fiftieth birthday, Akbar began to mount an elephant with all his usual flair – and fell down.

Never before, in the annals, had the emperor failed to control an elephant, barefooted astride its neck, with his sharp goads and his mad will; never had Akbar not overpowered his favourite animal, no matter how enraged. His fall was shocking enough to engender all kinds of rumours; violence broke out in the more faraway outposts of the realm and 'many remote parganas were plundered'.[37]

Again – as much to staunch the rumours as to assuage his pride, perhaps – Akbar did not halt. He treated himself by letting blood and marched on. Only days later, the emperor ordered an elephant parade, feeding each one with his hands, as if to tell the world – or was it himself? – that the Niru'un who ruled Hindustan was neither weakened nor scared.

The fact is, however, that no matter his incontestable wealth and power, Akbar could no longer command the strength and reckless self-confidence of his youth. And it wasn't only the inevitable decay of age that was beginning to hamper his stride, it was also the weight of his responsibilities.

One of the many minor keys that sounds in the overwhelming symphony of information, opinion and symbol that comprises the *Akbarnama* is Akbar's desire to see the snow. It would have reminded him of his childhood. When Akbar left Kabul with his father, he was twelve years old, and he first returned to the city in 1581, just shy of forty. At the time, however, his half-brother Hakim was threatening to ally with Abdullah of Turan, so Akbar spent only a few days in what had once been home. Again, in 1589, before his accidents with horse and elephant, Akbar had visited Kabul at greater leisure. This time, he had hoped to show the 'active young men' in his service some snowfall, have them 'tread the ice', thinking that his Hindustani mansabdars 'might enjoy this'.

Perhaps, in Akbar's freewheeling boyhood, the prince had skated on Kabul's frozen waters, bombarded his tutors and ataliq with snowballs. This time, however, it was Abdullah of Turan himself who was becoming restive at the thought of Akbar so close to his border, and Akbar left before the snow arrived. Three years later, in the month of his fiftieth birthday, October 1592, then again in 1597, Akbar was in Kashmir, hoping to see the winter in his new pleasure retreat, if not in his old home. Both times, however, the emperor realized that his men were not enjoying the cold as he wanted them to, and abandoned his plans.[38]

'Students well versed in European history seldom . . . realize', writes Vincent A. Smith, '. . . that the empire of Akbar during the last quarter of the sixteenth century undoubtedly was the most powerful in the world, and that its sovereign was immeasurably the richest monarch on the face of the earth'.[39] And yet, the richest, most powerful of monarchs – whose proximity caused tremors in Turan, whom the new young king of Persia called 'shah-baba', king-father – would never be free to throw a snowball again.

It wasn't just his friends, or the ability to do as he pleased, that Akbar was losing as he grew in stature and age; he would soon experience the most difficult loss of all – that of his children.

So much is written about Akbar's relationship with his sons and grandsons, particularly his heir Salim, that it is easy to forget the emperor had daughters and granddaughters, too. And he loved them deeply.

Two of Akbar's daughters died in infancy, and both times, writes Abul Fazl, their father's grief exceeded 'the mould of description'. Akbar, in sorrow, 'withdrew his heart from everything'. When, in December 1584, Akbar had a daughter who survived, Abul Fazl hails her as 'a night-gleaming jewel of fortune'. Salim, in his wonderful memoir, the *Jahangirnama*, puts it in less lofty terms. His younger sister, Aram Banu, was Akbar's '*ladli*', his darling, and 'greatly inclined to volatility and sharpness'. She was spoilt silly, that is. 'My father loved her so much', writes Salim, 'that he politely tolerated her acts of rudeness, and in his blessed sight . . . she did not seem so bad. He often said to me, "Baba, for my sake, after I'm gone, treat this sister of yours . . . as I do. Tolerate her coquettishness and overlook her rudeness and impudence."'[40]

For Salim's own daughters, too, the emperor had a special fondness. His first grandchild was a girl born to Man Bai – Salim's first wife and daughter of Bhagwant Das. Akbar was thrilled, writes Abul Fazl; he held a grand party in Hamida's house, with 'gifts, and . . . largesse' – even though such celebrations were 'contrary to the usage of contemporaries'. Three years later, in 1589, Salim had another daughter and Akbar another celebration – once again, 'contrary to the custom of contemporaries'.

Abul Fazl does not clarify what was unusual about celebrating a child's birth – in fact, a girl's birth – but it isn't hard to guess. Sons, of course, were – and remain – valued across cultures; Akbar himself had prayed for an heir. But valuing sons is not quite the same as scorning daughters – 'The result of karma' as the Jain poet Banarasidas describes his younger sister.[41] Akbar's own feelings about women were quite different from the notions he encountered in Hindustan, most intimately with his new Rajput allies and kin – and the two ways of seeing were often intermingled, often uncomfortably, in the emperor's mind.

It was with a bemused mix of wonderment and horror, for example, that Akbar noted the custom of *sati* among his Rajput nobility. 'It is a strange commentary on the magnanimity of men', he said, in one of his more sardonic Sayings, 'that they should seek their deliverance through the self-sacrifice of their wives'.[42] In one of his discourses in the Ibadat Khana, Akbar had marvelled at how widows walked into their husband's pyres, remarking to his Jesuit interlocuters that the custom might have made sense in a monogamous tradition, like theirs, but that it was truly 'extraordinary . . . that it occurs among those of the Brahman religion' who had several wives. These women, he went on, were 'neglected and unappreciated and spend their days [unfruitfully] in the privy chamber of chastity, yet in spite of such bitterness of life they are flaming torches of love . . .'[43]

Akbar – and his descendants – never quite made peace with the idea of widows being burnt alive. The Mughal administration would not ban the custom, but it would keep a close eye on it to prevent unwilling satis.[44] Once, famously, Akbar himself saved a widowed queen being forced upon the pyre by her son, Udai Singh. When Akbar heard the news, he rode out of his palace so fast, according to Abul Fazl, that his guard couldn't keep up with him, and panic and rumours spread in his wake. Furious, Akbar spared Udai Singh's life but had him imprisoned. Another time, less dramatically, he talked a widowed queen of Panna out of immolating herself, convincing 'her to refrain . . . on account of the tender age of her children'.[45]

Akbar's relations with the women in his own family are marked with both tenderness – as for the volatile Aram Banu – and deep respect, as for his own widowed mother, Hamida, various aunts, including Gulbadan, and milk mothers like Jiji Anaka. The eldest prince, Salim, even writes that Akbar undertook that staggering nine-day dash to Aziz's rescue in Ahmedabad 'because of the distress of Jiji Anaka', Aziz's mother.[46] And yet, in these relations, too, the emperor who doubted everything yet believed himself near-divine was not without his contradictions.

Akbar talked pityingly, for example, about the wives of Rajputs trapped 'in the privy chamber of chastity' – and certainly there is no indication that his own mother and mamas, aunts, wives and daughters were similarly confined. In fact, the opposite: Gulbadan's long journey to Mecca and back is only one example of the royal women travelling. Akbar's stepmother and Humayun's eldest wife, Haji Begum, had also made the pilgrimage, before returning to supervise the building of her husband's magnificent tomb. His mother, Hamida Banu, was as peripatetic as Akbar himself; the *Akbarnama* is littered with instances of her travels across her son's empire.

Many of these women enjoyed a great deal of power, too. When Akbar went chasing after Mirza Hakim for the last time, for example, he had two governors keeping watch over Bengal and Gujarat. 'The King's mother', writes Father Monserrate, 'was to be superior to both of these, and was to have charge of the province of . . . Delinum'.

It was from knowing the kind of influence the harem exercised on Akbar that poor Makhdum-ul-Mulk and Abdun Nabi had tried to smuggle themselves back to Hindustan under Gulbadan's skirts. Indeed, Babur and his descendants shared a deep-seated love and respect for their older female relatives. The historian and recent biographer of Babur, Stephen Dale, writes of how Babur would kneel to acknowledge older women in his family.[47] Similarly, Abul Fazl writes of Akbar and his mother, Hamida Banu: 'everything that lady says is granted by the emperor'.[48]

And yet, a change was creeping upon Akbar's harem, as it had crept upon every power centre in his realm, from the Uzbek warlords to the disgruntled ulema. Akbar might not refuse his mother anything, for example, but he had not hesitated in imprisoning her brother.

Muazzam, the young man who had played detective in Persia and recovered Humayun's rubies, had done little to distinguish himself thereafter. Eccentric, unreliable and increasingly violent, Hamida's brother had been exiled in exasperation by Humayun and Bairam Khan both, but Akbar gave him another chance. Sometime in 1564, however, Muazzam murdered his wife. The girl's mother had suspected he might do some such thing and had pleaded with Akbar to rescue her daughter, but the emperor arrived too late. All he could do was have Muazzam imprisoned in the dungeons of Gwalior, where he died.

'Relatives are like scorpions in the harm they do', writes Badauni in his account of the affair, and Akbar might have agreed. Muazzam had been by Hamida's side all through that terrible journey she made as a fifteen-year-old, thirsty and pregnant in a desert full of enemies; he had been with her on her Persian exile. It isn't impossible to imagine that she asked for mercy on his behalf. If she did, Akbar was not swayed.

Many years later, in 1582, the year of Akbar's triumphant return from Kabul and his first Nauroz, Abul Fazl does, in fact, write of Hamida asking Akbar to forgive one of his less-than-loyal Bengal nobles: the man was a close friend of the family and Hamida wanted him restored to favour.

Akbar agreed. And yet, while he wouldn't refuse his mother's wishes, there was no reason why the emperor shouldn't get his own way despite them. Three months after the chieftain was restored to favour, he was on his way home from court at around midnight when 'an armed troop fell upon him . . . and cut him in pieces'.[49] Despite 'much investigation and close inquiry', writes Abul Fazl, poker-faced, 'the affair was not cleared up'. Nothing came to light; except, of course, that yet another enemy of the emperor's had died.

Clearly, Akbar would not let his mother interfere in his government, any more than he would the Qaqshals. The curb on his harem's powers was not quite the same, however, as the taming of Akbar's warlords. Timurid women had long played active political roles: Babur describes his grandmother as his best adviser, and there is a painting that depicts his sister, Khanzada, sitting in council with Babur and his chiefs. Akbar, too, would accept advice and help from his female relatives – and learn Hindu rituals from his Rajput wives – but something was changing.

'He gives very great care and attention to the education of the princesses', writes Father Monserrate, 'who are kept rigorously secluded from the sight of men'. Thus, the Fathers were made to stand by the Anup Talao when they arrived, so that Akbar's harem might observe them without being seen. The scene captures something of Akbar's increasingly ambiguous relationship with his women. His daughters were to be educated and prepared to engage in public life, and yet, they were to be kept hidden from it.

If Akbar was surprised, even distressed, by what he saw of Rajput women's exclusion from the world in which their men thrived, he was also influenced by what Harbans Mukhia calls 'the Rajputs' normative placement of high value of honour in their women's bodies, manifest in the performance of *sati* and *jauhar*'.[50] Mukhia notes that Babur's memoirs 'hardly ever' make reference to female 'chastity'; that Gulbadan's memoirs abound with unveiled princesses who 'rode horses, went on hunt (*shikar*), practised archery and went out on picnics'. Indeed, Babur's sister Khanzada Begum, having been married under duress to his great enemy, Shaibani Khan, returned to her brother when the khan was killed and was welcomed with joy. She married again and became an honoured matriarch, the Padishah Begum of the family – certainly no harbinger of shame upon it.[51]

'It is in Akbar's time', Ruby Lal argues, 'that a clearly demarcated "sacred incarcerated" sphere emerges as the space of the Mughal domestic'. Quite literally so. Earlier, 'harem' was only a collective noun to describe the women – wives, relatives and attendants – in a household; now it was a place, a 'fixed realm',[52] as Lal writes, '"sacred and hidden" – a sanctum sanctorum'.[53]

Abul Fazl describes how Akbar 'made a large enclosure with fine buildings inside, where he reposes'. Five thousand women – queens, princesses, attendants – lived in these palaces and apartments, guarded by layer upon layer of security: female soldiers, then a guard of *kwajasaras*, eunuchs; separate troops of Rajputs, amirs and *ahadis*, elite soldiers – not to mention the porters at the gates.[54] It was, as Mukhia describes it, 'a fortress-like institution', unprecedented in the dynasty. Such, in fact, was Akbar's growing 'obsession with female chastity' that even the names of the royal women 'begin to get omitted' from official chronicles. Hamida herself is only ever 'named' by her title, Maryam Makani, in the *Akbarnama*; many others must make do with 'cupola of chastity', Abul Fazl's favourite shorthand for noblewoman.

Akbar's relationship with his harem – like Akbar's relationship with his nobility, his friends and his God – was complicated; his 'attitudes towards sexuality . . . an ensemble of paradoxes'.[55]

For all that he felt compelled to lock them up in luxury, Akbar was deeply attached to, even dependent on, many of the women in his harem, particularly his mother. Once, impatient for Hamida to join him in enjoying the delights of Kashmir, Akbar wrote her a lovely couplet: 'The pilgrim may go to the K'aaba to perform the haj / O God! May the K'aaba come towards us!'[56] Years later, Akbar borrowed a painting of the Madonna from visiting Jesuits because he wanted to show it to his wives and daughters.[57] The Fathers were worried they might never see their painting again, but Akbar returned it, only to ask for it one more time. Hamida wanted to see it, the emperor explained, and 'although his mother was a very old lady, she expected, not unnaturally, all the indulgence and attention which was due to her position'. Similarly, the well of Akbar's affection for his aunts and daughters was deep – Rajput notions of honour might stop Akbar from naming his brides, but they would not stop him celebrating the birth of a girl.

Its waters ran cold, however, when it came to his sons, Salim, Murad and Daniyal.

When Father Monserrate arrived in Fatehpur, Akbar made the priest a teacher to some of the young boys in court, including the emperor's own middle son, Murad. Monserrate remembers the prince, who would have been about ten years old, as extraordinarily well behaved; indeed, 'so submissive that he sometimes did not even dare to raise his eyes to his teacher's face when he was reproving him'.

It goes against expectation, such meekness from a boy of such privilege, and certainly from a son of Akbar's – who, at that age, was running his tutors to distraction with his camels and pigeons. It was precisely because Murad was Akbar's son, however, that he was so obedient.

Akbar loved his sons. Salim he always called 'Shaikhu ji', since the boy was born by Shaikh Salim Chishti's prayers; Murad was better known as 'Pahari jiu',[58] because he was born atop a hill. The emperor took a keen interest in his children's education, too; Monserrate writes that Akbar would ask Murad to recite his new learnings to him every day. For all the affection of the nicknames and the attention that he gave them, Akbar was also often strict and impatient with his boys. 'For the King's nature was such', remembers Monserrate, 'that, though he loved his children very dearly, he used to give them orders rather roughly . . . and he sometimes punished them with blows as well as with harsh words'. Worse – and ironically, given his own misspent schooldays – Akbar had given the prince's new teacher leave 'to punish his pupils if they committed any offence'. Knowing the authority that Monserrate held, Murad was 'in the utmost dread of him'. When, instead of beating him, the priest spoke kindly to the boy, Murad and both his brothers 'became the closest friends of the Fathers'.

Monserrate returned the affection of his young charges. Of Murad, he wrote that the 'young prince was an ideal pupil as regards natural ability, good conduct and intellectual capacity. In all these respects it would have been hard to find any Christian youth, let alone a prince, surpassing him.' There is something of a proud father's delight in the Jesuit's words, further exaggerated in his account of Murad's battle with his uncle, Mirza Muhammad Hakim.

It was Murad, together with Man Singh, who had led the Mughal troops against Mirza Hakim in 1581, and helped obliterate his uncle's hopes of ever challenging Akbar again. While Abul Fazl praises Murad's courage in battling alongside Man Singh, Monserrate credits his pupil with winning the battle almost single-handedly – rallying his reluctant troops, spear in hand, declaring he would take on the enemy alone if he had to. 'Seeing the prince's boyish courage (for he was only twelve years old), and hearing his brave words, the troops were overcome with shame, and rallied round him.' It may have been to his kindly tutor that Murad came with excited stories of his first-ever battle, knowing that Monserrate would lend him an indulgent ear. Akbar would not have been as doting; he said so himself once, in a critical appraisal of his neighbour Abdullah of Turan's parenting skills. The Uzbek king, he said, 'from excess of affection could not give [his son] paternal counsel', instead, he offered him 'the advices of a mother'.[59] Salim, Murad and Daniyal – each a potential heir to Akbar's throne – should expect no such mollycoddling from the emperor.

There is no record of Humayun treating Akbar with similar harshness, but then, at twelve, Akbar feared Hemu's bellowing elephants, not his father's harsh tongue or heavy hand. Bairam Khan, Akbar's Khan Baba and father figure, may have tried exerting some authority over the young padishah, but Akbar had dismissed him by the time he was eighteen. Shamsuddin Ataka, his foster father, was murdered two years later. Perhaps Akbar never quite learnt what a relationship between adult sons and their fathers could be. Or, perhaps, having spent so long building and managing his empire, the herald of a new age, Akbar was strict so that his sons would not fritter away their legacy. If so, it was terribly ironic that all three – Daniyal, Murad and Salim – took to drink like bears to honey, and that two of them did, in fact, squander what their father gave them – not his empire, but their lives.

The first to go was Murad.

The three Jesuit priests who arrived in Fatehpur in 1580 with such fond hope of Akbar's imminent conversion left in 1582. They were sadder, wiser men. Akbar had no intention of converting, it was clear; instead, he had begun propounding his own wretched cult.[60] Besides, Father Monserrate had come to a sharp conclusion about Akbar's free-flowing debates and willingness to consider all religions as equally worthy – and to the heart, in fact, of the brittle tension that underpins any modern multicultural society. 'He cared little', wrote the priest, 'that in allowing everyone to follow his own religion he was in reality violating all religions'.

Figure 14.1   Prince Murad with one of his wives. Once, Murad seemed the most promising of Akbar's three sons, and he was the apple of his Jesuit tutor's eye. Badauni decried his arrogance, writing that Murad boasted 'of being a ripe grape when he was not yet even an unripe grape'. But Murad never met the potential he might have had, dying before he was thirty, a grape that never ripened but only fell off the vine. Attributed to Manohar, c. 1597. *Source*: Freer Gallery of Art, National Museum of Asian Art, Public domain.

So, the Fathers left – Rudolf to achieve his dream of martyrdom in Goa, and Monserrate to be imprisoned in Yemen, where he wrote his fond account of their improbable attempt to convert the emperor of Hindustan.

This was not, however, the end of Jesuit missions to Akbar's court. The priests were as stubborn as the emperor. Thus, some fifteen-odd years after Father Monserrate left Fatehpur, a third mission, this one led by Father Hierosme Xavier Navarrois,[61] was on its way to Akbar in Lahore. The priests were crossing Gujarat when they met Murad.

Now in his mid-twenties, the middle prince was heading south as the Fathers went north; he was off to battle the Deccan on Akbar's orders. Murad had lost none of his affection for Jesuit priests; he greeted them warmly and invited them for a private chat, 'asking them many curious questions . . . if there was snow or ice in Portugal, and whether bears, hares, and other wild animals were to be found there'. Before leaving, the prince insisted on giving the Fathers a gift of money. He made an impressive exit, too, vaulting from one elephant upon another, the second 'a larger one, which seemed like a tower'.[62]

And yet, this third mission of Jesuit Fathers was not half as impressed with Murad as Monserrate had been. The prince was 'by nature mild, kind, liberal, and good-tempered', they agreed, but he listened only to the 'youthful retainers by whom he was surrounded', his 'actions were not of the wisest', his 'sole pleasure was in the chase, in love-making, and in running hither and thither'.

It has been speculated, not least by contemporary (and competitive) Europeans from other nations, that the Jesuits in the Mughal court were not driven by missionary zeal alone; that they were, in fact, political agents of the Portuguese – if not spies, then certainly charged with helping to safeguard the Portuguese monopoly over trade in the Arabian Sea, which had become, as a modern historian puts it, a 'Portuguese lake'.[63] Their opinion of Murad, then, would have been keenly observed, especially since the prince, in heading to the Deccan, was also coming dangerously close to Goa. Its Portuguese viceroy would have liked to know if the prince would be a useful ally or a potential threat.

Badauni's assessment of the prince backs that of the Fathers – that he wasn't up to much. Murad boasted 'of being a ripe grape when he was not yet even an unripe grape', he writes, describing Murad's behaviour during his first independent charge some years previously.

In 1591, Akbar had sent his middle son to Malwa, with particular instructions to bring the rebellious raja of Orchha, Madhukar, back into the imperial fold. Murad had not wanted to go, it seems, declaring to Akbar that he would rather remain by his father's side, if only as his ewer-bearer. Besides, he feared he would be slandered by his 'enemies' while he was away. Foremost among these foes – if we are to believe one of Badauni's most unsavoury tales about the imperial family – was none other than Murad's elder brother, Salim.

Shortly before sending Murad to Malwa, Akbar had fallen ill and accused Salim of trying to poison him. In 1591, the year after his two falls from his horse and elephant, Akbar was forty-nine years old, and Salim twenty-two. Relations between father and son had been deteriorating, it appears, for a while – not unlikely because the prince had embarked upon his long and spectacular drinking addiction some years ago. (Between the ages of eighteen, when he first tasted wine, and about thirty, when he began to fall ill from it, Salim had progressed to drinking 'twenty phials of double-distilled spirits, fourteen during the day and the rest at night'.[64] These spirits were no joke. Abul Fazl writes of such '*dutasha*' (twice-burned) alcohol, 'It is very strong. If you wet your hands with it and hold them near the fire, the spirit will burn in flames of different colours without injuring the hands.'[65])

It seems a stretch to deduce murderous intent from a drinking habit, but Badauni insists it was so. Akbar, ill and delirious, cried out, 'Baba Shaikhu ji, since all this Sultanate will devolve on thee, why Hast thou made this attack on me: To take away my life there was no need of injustice, I would have given it to thee, if thou hadst asked me.'

As Akbar's health deteriorated and his suspicions grew, Badauni writes that Salim put his men to spy on Murad – with the intent, clearly, of keeping his brother away from the throne, should it fall vacant all of a sudden.

When Akbar recovered, he decided to put some distance between the brothers, and also, possibly, to give Murad a chance to prove his abilities. If the reams of advice that Akbar bestowed on his son before sending him off to Malwa is anything to go by, Akbar wanted Murad to succeed. 'Let not difference of religion interfere with policy'; 'If apologies be made, accept them'; 'Do not make ease your rule'; '. . . live so that the crowds of foreigners be not distressed. Especially see to it that merchants have a good opinion of you for their report carries far'; 'Expect from every one service according to his ability'; 'Secure the affection of the contented hermits and of the matted-haired and barefooted'; 'Apply yourself to sympathise with the soldier'; 'Do not lose sight of an old servant'; 'Choose a good companion and be not offended at his truthful speech'.[66] Murad was to represent the emperor, to rule in his stead and with his tenets; to prepare, perhaps, to step into his shoes.

Murad welcomed his father's advice. Abul Fazl, who was sent to explain Akbar's instructions to Murad, and emphasize how their physical separation was, in fact, a 'spiritual union' between father and son, reports a 'confidential meeting' between the two men, at which Murad 'uttered pleasing words' that 'delighted' Akbar.[67] Some sources indicate that Murad's flattering queries ranged from which days he should fast on to how he should 'regulate his time of sleep' – and, in a possibly arch aspersion on his brother, how he should 'check drunkenness among his followers'.[68]

Was Murad glad, on the whole, for a chance to hold his own, independent court far from the emperor's critical gaze? He may have been quite pleased with the pennant and kettledrum, the regal standard and marching music that accompanied his journey, announcing the splendour of his rank and mission. Perhaps he nursed the hope that reports of his successes would flow to Akbar, composed in superlatives as if by his old Jesuit tutor, and bring a proud smile to his father's face.

Murad's campaign in Malwa was energetic; he showed no slackness in carrying out Akbar's commands. He had been sent to bring Raja Madhukar to heel, so when the raja hesitated in coming to pay homage to the newly arrived prince, Murad went chasing after him.

Badauni, when criticizing Murad's arrogance, adds the caveat that the prince, in his 'over-weaning pride . . . imitated his illustrious Father'. There was certainly a hint of Akbar's reckless impatience in Murad's pursuit of Raja Madhukar. Abul Fazl, also critical, writes that Murad embarked on his chase 'without regard to his [own] rank', and one wonders how the historian could write the words without blushing, given how often and how glowingly he describes Akbar flouting exactly such objections from his worried chiefs.

At any rate, Murad's quick chase had its effect: before you knew it, the prince and his men had sacked the raja's home and Madhukar had fled.

News of his son's bravado did, indeed, reach Akbar; however, he was anything but pleased. Akbar was no longer the young padishah ridding his empire of rebels, and Raja Madhukar was not a discontented warlord. Murad had been too aggressive, Akbar said; the prince had broken agreements between the raja and the crown, he had 'without orders attacked the landowner'. Murad must fall back immediately, or Akbar would send an army against his own son.

Akbar knew how to delegate. He could not have built his empire without letting men like Todar Mal, Muzaffar Khan, Man Singh, Aziz Koka and Abdur Rahim do their jobs without too much interference. All of these men had displeased Akbar at one point or another; often they had been barred from court for their sins but never threatened in the mortifying way that Akbar now threatened Murad.

Is it any wonder that when Father Xavier met the prince some three years later, he was more interested in hunting and lovemaking than impressing Akbar with a successful Deccan campaign? And little wonder, for that matter, that the Deccan campaign was a disaster.

The rich and unyielding sultanates of Bijapur, Ahmednagar and, further south, Golconda would become, a bit like Samarqand, a holy grail and a graveyard of Mughal ambition in the subcontinent. Murad was not the last general to fail at conquering these lands; nor was he the first.

It was almost a decade since Akbar had made his first serious foray to the south. In 1586, he sent his milk brother Aziz and Shihabuddin – the man who had once been Maham Anaka's deputy – to lead a joint campaign into the Deccan. Instead, however, the two men almost went to war with each other. Aziz had managed to keep his cool in the face of Shahbaz Khan's provocations in Bengal, but Shihabuddin – Maham Anaka's trusted friend and colleague, and a possible conspirator in the murder of Aziz's father, Shamsuddin Ataka – was a different matter. For six months, writes Nizamuddin, the Mughal armies were inactive because Aziz refused to work with Shihabuddin. Finally, 'matters reached such a pitch' that Shihabuddin abandoned the mission and left for home, at which Aziz lost his previous lassitude and began to march – not to the Deccan but after his colleague. A 'dire calamity was upon the point of falling upon the royal army', writes Nizamuddin; it was narrowly averted.

Akbar and Aziz's relations had mended somewhat after Aziz helped secure Bengal, but Aziz's temper and tongue were still as sharp. Badauni tells of how, when Aziz returned from Bengal to Fatehpur in the early 1580s, Akbar's koka launched into another tirade against Akbar's policies and his new friends – including Abul Fazl and Birbar – carrying 'his speech to [such] wonderful excesses . . . that he became the common talk of high and low'. He left the court in high dudgeon 'on pretext of letting his beard grow' – shorthand, presumably, for practising his religion, not Akbar's. Eventually, Akbar wrote to him, asking, 'Is your beard not yet grown that you do not come?' Aziz sent 'a long and rude letter in reply, which made an impression on the Emperor's mind'.[69]

Akbar did not, however, arrest his friend; Aziz went and exiled himself. In 1593, seven-odd years after the debacle with Shihabuddin, Aziz 'put his children and his wives and treasures into a boat'[70] and sailed off to Mecca. From there, it seems, he wrote another letter, declaring that 'it would be only fit . . . to take this body to the Sacred dust of Mecca' in preference to having it buried 'in the same place . . . [as] the infidels of Hindustan who are the creatures of the king's bounties and favours'.[71]

Akbar had already lost so many friends and advisers, he was loath to lose another. He did not hold Aziz's outburst and departure against him, only wrote to his milk brother 'reproaching him for distressing his mother [Jiji Anaka] and himself by going off without leave and exposing his family to the dangers of the ocean'.[72] The emperor was sure that Aziz would be back soon, and sure enough, his friend returned in 1594. It was an emotional reunion.

'From exceeding love, tears fell from [Akbar's] eyes', writes Abul Fazl. As for Aziz, he'd had a terrible time in Mecca, so much so that he gave up all thought of his beard and joined Akbar's circle of disciples.

It took him twenty years – ever since Aziz first condemned Akbar's mansabdari reforms – but the emperor had managed to win his friend over.

In the Deccan, meanwhile, dissension grew increasingly rife. Murad had only just reached the empire's southern borders, in 1595, when rumours of his 'hauteur'[73] began to drift to Akbar in Lahore. The prince was meant to work with Abdur Rahim, Bairam's orphaned son, now an accomplished general, who had so distinguished himself in Gujarat a decade ago that he had been given his father's old rank and made Khan-Khanan in 1584. Perhaps Murad resented the favour that Akbar showed Abdur Rahim, or perhaps he just didn't like him – and 'tale-bearers and interested persons', of whom there was no lack in the Mughal ranks, 'widened the breach'.[74]

Murad showed no interest in working with the vastly more experienced amir. Abdur Rahim had to race after the prince when Murad decided to march upon Ahmednagar without waiting for him; and even then, Murad wouldn't meet him. '[D]isgusted', Abdur Rahim went on strike.[75]

Somehow, in the winter of 1596, the squabbling Mughals managed to besiege Ahmednagar, guarded by its redoubtable queen, Chand Bibi. The siege, writes Abul Fazl, was 'a tedious affair'. For once, the historian is guilty of understatement. The Mughals' onslaught was an embarrassment. After two months of a listless siege, in February 1596, Murad's men managed to make a breach in the fort walls – and then, remembering what had happened with the delayed second fuse in Chittorgarh, refused to charge in.

Meanwhile, and in stark contrast, Ferishta writes of how Chand Bibi 'appeared with a veil on her head . . . [and] caused guns to be brought to bear on the assailants, and stones to be hurled on them'. At night, while the Mughals dilly-dallied, 'she stood by the workmen, and caused the breach to be filled up nine feet before daylight with wood, stones, and earth, and dead carcasses'.[76]

Two days after the breach was made, Murad had lost his strategic advantage and left. He had a face-saving truce and a great deal of booty, but Ahmednagar remained free. By the following year, the three great Deccani kingdoms, Ahmednagar, Bijapur and Golconda, had formed an alliance against the Mughals. This time, it was Abdur Rahim, with Sulaiman's grandson Shahrukh, who led the troops. He barely avoided defeat; worse, he managed to alienate the Mughals' only Deccani ally, Khandesh – Abdur Rahim's troops plundered the king of Khandesh's camp when he died fighting on the Mughal side.

The next year, 1598, began with news that Abdur Rahim had given up on the whole affair and gone home.

Akbar was fed up. He sent messengers to tick Abdur Rahim off and bring Murad to court. Murad wouldn't come. It was Abdur Rahim who arrived, instead, and he was followed, within two days, by Qilij Khan.

The previous year, Akbar had sent his youngest son, Daniyal, to govern Allahabad, and Qilij Khan was to advise and assist him. Daniyal was much more amiable than the imperious Murad. Salim describes him with affection, as a good-looking young man of poetic temperament, fond of composing Hindi verse. This was not enough, evidently, to win him loyal courtiers – or maybe neither Murad nor Daniyal wanted to be watched over by their father's appointees. At any rate, Qilij Khan was 'somewhat displeased' with Daniyal, much like Abdur Rahim with Murad, and had abandoned him.[77]

Akbar, meanwhile, was having no better luck with the one prince who remained under his own charge – his eldest, the boon of his prayers, Salim. In January of this very year, 1598, news had arrived that Abdullah of Turan had died. For fourteen years, Akbar and Abdullah had kept covetous eyes on each other's kingdoms – and it was to Akbar, of course, that fate handed its winning card. In the potential instability that followed the death of any monarch, the Mughals might well swoop in upon Samarqand as they had upon Gujarat and Bengal.

Akbar wanted to send Salim off immediately. The eldest prince was made of more stubborn stuff than his brothers, however, and he would not go haring off on his father's command as they had. Or, as Abul Fazl puts it, the 'pleasure-loving youth . . . could not wean his heart from India'.

Some of Akbar's amirs proposed to go in Salim's place, but Akbar was reluctant to let them: 'Now that Turan is a seat of turmoil, how does an expedition there agree with our humanity?' he declared with rhetorical flourish, having seemingly forgotten all about the divinely ordained civilizing missions that had won him other neighbouring kingdoms.

Maybe Akbar wanted someone from the family to go and claim the family seat. If Salim refused, the emperor 'would send whichever one of [his other sons] showed an inclination for the task', he said. But how was he to send them if they wouldn't show him their faces?

Abul Fazl describes how Akbar had taken to reserving one day a week for various kinds of inspections: horses on Sundays, camels, cows and mules on Mondays, and soldiers on Tuesdays. Wednesdays and Thursdays were reserved for financial and judicial matters, Fridays he spent with the harem, and Saturdays mustering his beloved elephants.[78] The whole empire, it seems, was paraded before Akbar; only his sons would not appear. Murad made excuses for not coming to court. Daniyal, less brazen than his elder siblings, agreed to return, without actually returning.

By November that year, a wasted eleven months after Abdullah died, Akbar had realized that if he wanted the great city of Samarqand, the city that Babur had so hoped to rule, he would have to go and get it himself. Once again, Akbar made a plan. He would leave Punjab, find Murad in the south and give him a piece of his mind, and, having conquered the Deccan, return to take Turan.

Once again, however, as was so often the case now with so many of Akbar's plans, it was not to be. The emperor had travelled from Lahore to Agra by the end of the year, all set to give Murad more lectures on kingship, but then, uncharacteristically, he stopped. Something about Murad's and Daniyal's refusal to come to court was troubling him; Akbar was 'uneasy', writes Abul Fazl, and wanted 'to reflect'.

It was the historian who found himself continuing the journey in the emperor's stead.

On 5 January 1599, Abul Fazl left Agra to fetch Murad, or at least make the prince listen to Shahrukh, one of the few commanders who still remained in the Deccan with him. Murad, meanwhile, panicked at the news of the historian's coming and decided to march back to Ahmednagar. This would give him an excuse, at least, 'a reason for not going' to Agra.[79]

The prince was not well. A year or so ago, his nine-year-old son Rustam had died; the final straw, it seems, on the load of Murad's troubles. It was almost a decade since the prince had left Akbar's court, armed with his father's books and advice, and he had achieved nothing – winning neither Akbar's admiration nor the Mughal amirs' loyalty. When his son died, Murad 'set himself down to drink'.[80]

He got up a year later, at news of Abul Fazl's imminent arrival, but in no state to march. It may be that his ill health was not the result of drink and disappointment alone. Muzaffar Alam and Sanjay Subrahmanyam suggest that the Portuguese might have had a hand in it, the viceroy in Goa hoping to 'increase internal dissensions in the Mughal camp, and draw their attention away from projects of conquest'[81] – projects that were bringing them uncomfortably close to Portuguese territory. If so, Murad's fate is doubly tragic: the prince mourning his son and bereft of companions could not bring himself to admit defeat to his father, while the political patrons of the Father who had loved the timid boy plotted against him.

Murad did not reach Ahmednagar. He had an epileptic fit on the way and died a week later, not yet thirty years old, a grape that never ripened but only fell off the vine.

Abul Fazl, who had galloped hard to try and reach the dying prince but failed, sent the news to Akbar. No one – not even Salim – had the courage or the heart to read the whole message aloud to the emperor. It was many days later, when his mother rode down from Lahore to tell him, that Akbar learnt his Pahari jiu had died.

Chapter 15

Bad Blood

'The Lord of the world . . . was searching for some individual among the sons of men that he might hold fitting converse with . . . Though he made much search, he did not find anyone. The evangelists of the inner world, and the informants of the external, all announced that a person who could hold converse with the cream of existences must be born from himself, and that he should be urgent in begging a son from God.'

– Abul Fazl, prefatory remarks to the birth of Salim, *Akbarnama*

In 1600, Banarasidas was fourteen years old, living in Jaunpur, and falling in love with all the 'yearning of a Sufi fakir' – stealing gemstone dust from his father's jewellery business to buy his beloved 'paan and sweetmeats'.[1] The young Jain was very far, it might seem, from the turmoil of empire. Little did he know that the unravelling of Akbar's family was to reach his very door.

It was in 1600 that Akbar went to the Deccan himself, and Salim took advantage of his father's absence to run away to Allahabad and declare himself 'shah'. The last of the rebellions against Akbar was to be led by his own son.

Now, barely 100 kilometres east of Allahabad, the governor of Jaunpur, Nuram Khan, had received an imperial farman. Salim planned to go hunting near Jaunpur and Nuram Khan was not to allow it on any account. Hunting was as often a euphemism for war as Mecca was for exile, a show of force meant to intimidate. Nuram Khan prepared for battle and siege.

'All roads leading to and from Jaunpur were blocked', Banarasidas recalls. 'Boats were no longer allowed to stop at the ghats along the Gomti / All bridges and gateways into the city were closed.' There were guards everywhere, 'And artillery set up on the walls and ramparts of the city'; Nuram Khan stockpiled provisions of every kind: grain, clothing, water,

271

armour, saddles, guns, and, of course, 'Much wine, and many kinds of weapons'.

As the city filled up with soldiers and their armaments, it emptied of residents, who 'ran away in all directions'. Banarasidas's father was part of a delegation of jewellers who went to Nuram Khan, asking if they, too, should leave. Nuram Khan had little solace for them. 'Listen O merchants', he said to them, 'You are wondering whether to stay or go. / My own end is before me. / What solution can I give you?'

For the rest of Akbar's life and reign, from 1600 to 1605, the empire, like Nuram Khan and the jewellers, would hang in precarious balance, between an ageing, anguished and often very angry emperor and his stubborn son.

A painting from about this time shows Salim, goblet in hand, lounging in a tent, one arm resting on the back of an attendant who offers him a golden plate – containing a snack, perhaps, to go with his drink, or possibly the opium he used, increasingly, as a substitute for alcohol.[2] Musicians, a man holding a book, another a sword and a pageboy fanning the prince comprise the rest of his court. At first glance, there is something louche about the scene – the informality of Salim's pose, the crowding of pleasures, the fact that his sword is swaddled in cloth, unprepared for conquest or battle. And yet, for all the ease and luxury that emanates from it, the painting also conveys a compelling intensity of purpose. Despite the clear signs of indulgence, there is nothing unkempt about Salim's appearance – he is both well dressed and well formed, the dark patches at his armpits, showing through his sheer muslin shirt, may be oil-based perfume, but they also communicate brawn. For all that his arm lies loose and familiar on his attendant's back, Salim's eyes are sharp and focused, and his face is deadly serious.

It was with such serious intent that Salim had begun to eye his father's throne. Between 1598 and 1599, the two years before he decamped to Allahabad, Salim had shown little enthusiasm for military campaigns. Instead, he had fired his first salvo at an enemy closer to home: Abul Fazl. The historian was 'always making snide remarks' about the prince, Salim would write in his autobiography.[3] Naturally, then, Salim was keen to rid the court of Abul Fazl's influence, and he did, indeed, manage to create a rift between Akbar and one of his last remaining friends.

Abul Fazl writes an extensive and overwrought account of the affair without revealing any precise details – only that he was too busy to attend 'upon the Prince-Royal' so that the 'anger of that hot-tempered one blazed forth'. Abul Fazl was so upset, he even offered a Fire Test to prove his innocence – 'I and my accuser [to] enter the furnace' – but even this did not reconcile the emperor with his favourite scribe.[4]

Historians have speculated that Salim discovered a chink in the armour of Abul Fazl's devotion to Akbar in the writer's conflicting loyalty to his own father.

Shaikh Mubarak may have flattered Akbar, but he was also a man of strong opinions, it seems. Badauni writes, for example, of Shaikh Mubarak giving Akbar 'a lecture on his extravagant expenditure'. On another occasion, Akbar sent all his best musicians, including Tansen, to the shaikh so that 'he might tell him what they were worth'. Shaikh Mubarak was unimpressed. 'He said to Miyan Tansin: "I have heard that you can sing a bit." At last he compared his singing to the noise of beasts, and allowed it no superiority over it.'[5]

The opinionated Shaikh Mubarak had composed a commentary on the Quran before his demise and, having neglected to mention Akbar in it, had caused the emperor some offence. Now, it seems, Abul Fazl had forty clerks employed in making copies of the book – which he liked to send off to neighbouring courts – and Salim may have used this to suggest that Abul Fazl was neither as sceptical of Islam nor as faithful a disciple of Akbar's as he pretended to be.[6]

It was '[i]n consequence of . . . intrigues', at any rate, that Akbar sent Abul Fazl away, in early 1600, with the ostensible purpose of bringing Murad back home. It must have been like exile to the scribe; he had not left the emperor's side for any length of time ever since he had joined Akbar's court a quarter century ago. To make matters worse, his mission began with failure: Abul Fazl arrived at almost the very moment of the prince's death. It was not Murad he would send home but only his remains. And yet, for all the bad blood that sent him south and all the bad luck of this beginning, Abul Fazl would run a better campaign in the Deccan than any of Akbar's sons or amirs.

The writer with no experience of military command, and so long embarrassed by the fact,[7] had a knack, it seems, for war. When he reached Murad's camp, the officers were anxious, fearing the kind of mutiny that had occurred when Munim Khan died in Bengal and imperial authority broke down. Murad had been marching towards Ahmednagar, but his men wanted to retreat. Abul Fazl, stubborn in his loyalty to Akbar's orders – 'my eyes were full of light from the fortune of the Shahinshah' – argued against them. They did not listen; in fact, 'many got angry and went off', he says.

Unfazed, the historian marched onwards anyway, with a small army of 3000 cavalry. He managed to persuade Shahrukh to join him and ordered his own son, posted in Daulatabad, to come to his aid. A Mughal troop was besieged by Deccanis nearby, eating their own horses while the 'horses ate the reed thatching of the houses', and Abul Fazl was determined to relieve them. He marched out in heavy rain and was able to disperse the Deccanis. One cannot but cheer when Abul Fazl writes that the enemy 'lost heart on hearing that . . . the writer had arrived'.

By the end of the year, Abul Fazl was nearing the gates of Ahmednagar and had begun secret negotiations with Chand Bibi, its queen.[8] Daniyal – marching south to replace Murad – sent urgent messages telling the scribe to slow down. 'Your energy is impressed upon everyone', wrote the prince, clearly worried about what impression it would make if Akbar's biographer made a greater success of the Deccan campaign than his son. 'Your desire is to take Ahmadnagar before we arrive, but you must restrain yourself . . . After this, there will be no delay on the road.'[9]

Daniyal had indeed been dawdling on the way; so much so that Akbar had followed after his son to hurry him along. Abul Fazl, it seems, turned away from Ahmednagar to greet the emperor – and to attempt an even trickier negotiation than with Chand Bibi.

Far from making any significant inroads into the Deccan, the Mughals had managed to alienate the one Deccani kingdom that did offer them fealty. Khandesh, being the northernmost of the Deccani sultanates, was most vulnerable to Mughal assault and had long made peace with the fact, and with Akbar. Three years previously, in 1597, the ruler of Khandesh, Raja Ali Khan, had even joined the Mughals in a battle against a Deccani coalition. Unfortunately, Raja Ali Khan was killed in the battle, and worse, the Mughal troops, having lost sight of the fallen king, assumed that he had deserted them and looted his camp.

Abul Fazl may have written about the impossibility of knowing the truth of a battle – 'Every one relates it differently' – but Raja Ali Khan's son and successor, Bahadur, was not half as philosophical about what he would have seen, quite rightly, as a betrayal of his father by the untrusting Mughals.

So when Daniyal marched into Khandesh, Bahadur declined to come and greet him. Abul Fazl tried to negotiate with the new king but had no luck. Bahadur had shut himself up in the towering fortress of Asirgarh, and he would have no further truck with the Mughal empire, no matter if it was breathing down his neck.

It was from this failed meeting that Abul Fazl rode on to greet Akbar. The emperor had missed his scribe, it seems; he greeted him with a cordial verse: 'Serene be the night and pleasant the moonshine / That I may talk with thee on every subject.'[10]

There was much to talk about. Murad's death, of course, Salim's unwillingness to go to war, Daniyal's lack of enterprise. Or perhaps Akbar did not linger on the subject of his sons. Perhaps he was happy to be out on a campaign again, after such a long time, amid soldiers and bellowing elephants, with yet another grand fortress to conquer.

'Old soldiers, and men who had travelled into distant lands – men who had seen the fortresses of Iran and Turan, of Rum, Europe, and of the whole habitable world, had never beheld the equal of this.'[11] Asirgarh – massive, monstrous, built in three stages upon a high hill, its walls often indistinguishable from the rocks – would be the final test of Akbar's fortune in war, and one of the glories of Abul Fazl's brief military career.

Of course, at fifty-eight, Akbar would not be standing in the smoke and blaze of a siege, shooting the enemy down with his guns. He had travelled with a full court, including the latest mission of Jesuit Fathers, his harem and grandchildren, among them Salim's eldest boy and the emperor's favourite, Khusro. The emperor settled 25 kilometres south of Asirgarh, in a town called Burhanpur, which would become the Mughals' Dakkan ka Darwaza, their headquarters in the Deccan. From here, Akbar would contribute to the war effort with prayer and prophecy.

Akbar 'engaged in special acts of devotion, and took to repeating the Great Name', writes Abul Fazl, whose duty it was to send the emperor halwa after each such session. Over the long months in which Abul Fazl and his colleagues undertook the siege of Asirgarh, Akbar spent long hours calling to God. He was following a custom, writes Henry Beveridge, in which the names of God or verses from the Quran are repeated, 'perfumes are burnt and sweetmeats are distributed' – possibly the Sufi meditational practice called *zikr*.[12]

Once before, on Akbar's return from his riverine conquest of Bengal, Badauni described him absorbed in such meditation, on a rock outside his palace in Fatehpur. Then, perhaps, Akbar was looking for a 'true' path, one God from all the multitudes of faiths around him in whom to believe. Almost thirty years later, why would the emperor return to the customs of his youth the devotions that, according to Badauni, he had long abandoned?

Akbar's successes had made him proverbial while he lived. 'Scarcely ever did he engage in an enterprise which he did not bring to a successful conclusion', wrote a Jesuit, 'so that "as fortunate as Echebar" became a common saying throughout the East'.[13] The emperor would have been quite sure of God's help against the rock-solid walls of Asirgarh, or against Ahmednagar and Chand Bibi. In fact, as the siege dragged on without success, Akbar had taken to repeating a comforting prophecy: 'This fort will be taken.'[14] Abul Fazl sounds less impressed with the mantra than he might once have been. In fact, in a startling detour from his usual faith in the emperor's divine destiny, Abul Fazl comes close to suggesting that the Mughal army's slow progress against Asirgarh was partly Akbar's fault. It was this prophecy of his that was making the men lazy as 'many accepting the soothing words continued to slumber'.

Not so the writer.

In November 1600, eight months after escorting Akbar to Burhanpur, Abul Fazl set out on a 'dark and rainy night' to scale one of Asirgarh's many battlements. So far, the Mughal forces had managed no assault on the fortress, no breach of its walls; their only success had been to occupy a neighbouring hill, which offered a better view of and line of fire to Asirgarh. Abul Fazl, however, had learnt of a secret path up the hill, to the fort walls. Few in the army were as enthused as the writer by the prospect of a midnight scouting expedition into heavily guarded enemy terrain. 'However much I tried the men would not give their minds to the subject', Abul Fazl complains. They had reason for their reluctance. Another contemporary historian writes that defensive firing from the fort was so relentless 'that in the dark nights . . . no man dared to raise his head, and a demon even would not move about'.[15] But Abul Fazl was undaunted. He wrested command of the expedition and sent two contingents into the night, following close behind himself.

Their scout lost his way, Asirgarh opened fire, but still, in 'the heat of the battle, and the rain of cannonballs, at dawn I mounted the scaling ladder'. The writer had managed to breach one of Asirgarh's three encircling walls. The enemy retreated. Soon afterwards, Bahadur sent an ambassador to Akbar, following meekly behind, and surrendered.

Bahadur should not have lost. The fortress had 'such abundance of stores, such numbers of guns, so many defenders', writes Abul Fazl – its occupants should have been able to tire out any besieging force, even Akbar's.

One of the emperor's new mansabdars, Jani Beg, the former ruler of Sindh who had lost his kingdom to Akbar's army some years previously, was now a lonely drinker in Akbar's court. Jani Beg had surveyed the towering black walls of Asirgarh with some feeling, it seems, and declared that 'if Asir had been his, he would have held it for a hundred years'.[16]

Asirgarh's generals seemed to feel the same. Their king, Bahadur, might have gone to Akbar's camp, but they would not surrender the fort until they got a letter from him telling them to do so. The siege continued.

Eventually, after 'pressure was put on him',[17] Bahadur agreed to write a letter of surrender to his generals – one Abyssinian and several Portuguese. His command was not well received. According to a Jesuit Father's report of the event, Asirgarh's Abyssinian general gave a rousing speech against the surrender, then strangled himself.[18] Despite its fallen king, Asirgarh might have remained firm against the Mughal troops.

But what was rock, what were guns, what was abundant grain or endless resolve in the face of Akbar's blessed luck? The fortress was struck by a plague.

Jani Beg of Sindh, watching sullenly from the sidelines, may have shaken his head in disbelief. It was a plague, too, that had brought about his defeat – another of Akbar's miracles by which only the besieged Sindhis succumbed to a great sickness, not the Mughals. Akbar wasn't surprised when he heard the news. 'The True Artist [God] made an old woman the means of the health of a tribe', he said, 'if He made this servant, who sits upon a lofty seat of rule, a source of good, what is there to cause surprise?' The emperor was referring to a story from the time of his ancestor Chinghis Khan. The khan's army was in Georgia, and Georgia was overrun by a plague. 'On the first day there was fever. On the second the teeth loosened. On the third the cup of life became full.' Meanwhile, an old woman in the town was less concerned by the sickness than by the fear that she would not live to put henna on her daughter – that is, get her married. Sure enough, the old woman fell ill. On the second day, her teeth loosening, she began 'putting henna on her darling', wetting it with her spit. The next day, she prepared to die but recovered instead. She had stumbled upon a cure for the plague – and a source of great profit for the precursors of the pharmaceutical industry. 'Henna became the value of pearls, and the merchants made great profits.'[19]

There was no such woman now to save Asirgarh. Some 25,000 people died of the sickness, and Asirgarh's generals, battling disease on the one hand and the psychological disadvantage of a fallen king on the other, could no longer hold out. Asirgarh fell. 'I myself sat at the gate', writes Abul Fazl, 'and in four days 34,000 persons came out with their families and goods'.

Once again, a 'glorious victory adorned the face of fortune' – if, however, for the last time.[20]

Akbar had continued, throughout, to recite God's name. Ahmednagar had fallen a few months previously, soon after Chand Bibi – 'that choice lady', in Abul Fazl's admiring words – was murdered by her own insecure nobility. Now Asirgarh was Akbar's.

God had listened, as He always did. Or had He? Was it for military success, at all, that Akbar was praying?

It was during the siege of Asirgarh that news arrived of Salim's rebellion. The prince had made a failed attempt at raiding Agra's treasury, then sailed east, commandeered 3 million rupees from Bihar and installed himself on a throne in Allahabad. In two years, Akbar had lost two sons – one to alcohol, the other to mutiny. When, in February 1601, some two months after Asirgarh's fall, Daniyal arrived in Burhanpur with news of a moderately successful campaign in Ahmednagar, Akbar was so pleased to see him that he 'took the prince in his arms and involuntarily danced'.[21]

Is this what Akbar had prayed for, to have at least one of his sons alive and well disposed? That Nauroz, Daniyal held great feasts and gifted his father precious gems, but it was the 'jewel of [his] sincerity', writes Abul Fazl, that had greater value in Akbar's eyes. Indeed, the emperor was keen, it seems, to share his power and his pleasures with his only dutiful son. Khandesh was renamed 'Dandesh' after him, and Daniyal received, besides, an award of 200,000 *mohurs*, gold coins.

Two months later, in April 1601, Akbar decided to return to Agra. This was partly his amirs' doing. Once, only two decades ago, Akbar had marched to Punjab after his half-brother Hakim died – and stayed on for fourteen years. His amirs would not risk having their lives and households disrupted once again. Thus, Abul Fazl writes that while Ahmednagar had fallen, the Deccani resistance was only just beginning – 'things went somewhat backward' – but much of this was kept from the emperor. Even without news of the reverses, Akbar was keen to march all the way to Golconda, but his amirs 'increased their intrigues'.

Akbar was persuaded to return, but he wasn't going to rush the journey. The emperor wanted to spend more time with Daniyal; he thought they might go elephant-hunting on the way. As it happens, however, news of the emperor's departure sparked insurgencies across the Deccan – the beginning of a resistance to Mughal rule that would continue for over a century. As he had so often given up the sight of snow, the skid of ice under his feet, Akbar gave up the few days of pleasure he had planned with his son. He sent Daniyal back to Burhanpur to bring things under control[22] – and continued north alone.

It would have been irresponsible not to. Besides, Akbar had an insurrection to handle too, that of his own flesh and blood.

In 1602, the forty-seventh year of Akbar's reign and the sixtieth of his life, news arrived that Shah Abbas of Persia had made a bid for Balkh – the province that once, long ago, Humayun, his brothers and their cousin Sulaiman of Badakhshan had pledged to conquer as a first step towards Samarqand. Shah Abbas was unsuccessful, and the political turmoil in Turan, meanwhile, settled under the rule of Baqi Khan, nephew of its recently deceased Sultan Abdullah. Both Shah Abbas and Baqi Khan were doing what Akbar had asked Salim to do over two years ago. But Salim was very far from reclaiming the city of his ancestors; instead, in 1602, he marched towards Agra, against his own father.

It wasn't a particularly impressive attempted coup. Having travelled from Allahabad to Etawah with, by some accounts, an army of 30,000 men, Salim turned tail at a stern message from Akbar, telling the prince to proceed alone or be prepared for consequences.

The prolonged war of attrition between Akbar and his eldest son might fill a book on its own. Salim was the son Akbar had most keenly desired; every story of the prince's life begins with an account of Akbar's ceaseless prayers for a child and of how Shaikh Salim Chishti promised him three boys.[23] Abul Fazl makes no secret of Akbar's joy at Salim's birth: 'Delight suffused the brain of the age.' Salim was all that Akbar had ever asked of God. A decade and a half after Salim was born, Father Monserrate described him as the son 'whom [Akbar] loved best of all'[24] – but the years to come would drive wedge after irretrievable wedge between father and son. The most damaging of these would be Akbar's increasing affection – even preference – for Salim's son, Khusro.

Father Xavier of the third Jesuit mission offers a lovely little glimpse of Akbar doting on his grandson. When the mission arrived in 1595, Akbar showed the Fathers some paintings of Jesus and Mary that their predecessor Rudolf had given him. On seeing the paintings, the Fathers fell to their knees, at which seven-year-old Khusro 'also knelt down, and clasped his hands together. This greatly pleased the King, who turned with a smile to his son the Prince, and father of the child, and said, "Look at your son."'[25]

The previous year, in 1594, when Salim was twenty-five, Akbar raised him to the rank of 10,000, with cavalry from Bengal and Lahore, while Khusro 'who though small in years was great in wisdom' – he was all of six – got a mansab of 5000 and Orissa in fief. Khusro's maternal uncle, Man Singh, now among the highest-ranking, most powerful men in Akbar's court, was made his ataliq – his guardian. In 1602, the year that Salim marched to Etawah, Khusro acquired another powerful backer when he married Akbar's milk brother Aziz's daughter. Between them, his uncle and his father-in-law would lobby for Akbar's favourite grandson to pass over his own father to the throne.

A tense, often tragic endgame had begun to play itself out between the various contenders for Akbar's empire – and most tragically of all, its first casualty was Abul Fazl.

Akbar was perfection for his historian. As Harbans Mukhia explains it, the idea of *insan-i-kamil*, a 'perfect man', was developed by a philosopher called Ibn al-Arabi to describe a 'millenary appearance on earth at God's command. Muhammad, for Ibn al-Arabi, was the exemplary Perfect Man; Akbar was for Abul Fazl'.[26] There is a mirrored perfection, too, in Abul Fazl's unshakeable devotion to his lord. Sent away from his desk to the Deccan, the historian was as committed to winning battles for Akbar as he had been to composing his life in praise. Salim might have thought he was rid of the scribe, but Abul Fazl rose, instead, 'from rank to rank of confidence and intimacy'.[27]

Salim, meanwhile, was falling further from grace by the day: 'As the ways of the prince were displeasing to [Akbar] and he continually went counter to his father's wishes, his father's neglect of him was increasing daily.' So writes Inayatullah, who completed the *Akbarnama* after Abul Fazl's demise. Inayatullah is clearly biased against Salim, but the facts indicate that he wasn't far off the mark.[28] It was in 1602 that Salim made his tentative march towards Agra, and in 1602 that Akbar raised Abul Fazl to the rank of 5000, sent him 'a swift special horse' for Nauroz and 50,000 rupees for his campaigns. Soon afterwards, he also sent him a farman: Akbar needed his friend and adviser back in court.

Back in Allahabad from his failed coup, Salim heard the news with apprehension. Abul Fazl, he would write some years later, was forever disparaging him. It is said that the writer had taken to calling Salim the 'King of Allahabad',[29] no doubt the kind of snide remark that so annoyed the prince. Salim was convinced that Abul Fazl must be 'prevented from reaching [the emperor]', and he makes no bones about how he planned to stop the meeting: Abul Fazl would have to die.[30]

Salim sent a message to Bir Singh Bundela – son of Raja Madhukar of Orchha whom Murad had once attempted to chastise. Salim, more clever than his brother, had made friends with the discontented Bundelas. Now, Bir Singh was to 'waylay the miscreant [Abul Fazl] and dispatch him to nonexistence', writes Salim, 'in return for which he could expect great rewards from me'.

It happened exactly so. On 12 August 1602, Abul Fazl was almost exactly halfway between Orchha and Agra, riding past a village called Antri in Bundela territory, when Bir Singh and his men fell upon him. It wasn't, strictly speaking, an ambush: the writer had advance warning of the trap, but insisted on riding into it. As the Bundela king galloped towards him, the leader of Abul Fazl's escort, Gadai Khan Afghan, tried to make him escape. Again, Abul Fazl refused, dismissing every argument, preferring death to the disgrace of fleeing from an 'unwashed thief'. What would Akbar think of him if he did otherwise?

'My gracious sovereign has raised me from the rank of a student to the lofty position of an amir, a vizier, and a general. On this day, if I act contrary to [his] opinion of me, by what name shall I be called among men . . .[?]'[31] In vain did Gadai Khan tell the historian that it was perfectly acceptable to flee a battle and fight another day; in vain did the Afghan grab the writer's reins and try to turn his horse around. The 'brave man urged on his steed', writes Inayatullah, and rode straight at 'a spear thrust in the breast'.

Inayatullah may have based his account of the murder on the memoirs of Asad Beg, a long-time employee of Abul Fazl's. Asad Beg had been left behind by the writer when Abul Fazl rode into Bundelkhand; it was he whom Akbar summoned, afterwards, for details of his friend's death. Asad Beg was not a witness to the scene, and may have more reason even than Inayatullah to embellish his master's final moments in melodrama, but his account contains a detail or two to suggest that, for all the nobility of his dash into harm's way, Abul Fazl did, in the end, make a last-ditch, instinctive bid for life.

Asad Beg, too, writes that one of Abul Fazl's men tried to lead him away, and it seems the writer had turned around, because it was in the back, not the chest, that a Bundela spear struck him, so hard that it 'came out through his breast'.[32] Now – and who can blame him? – Abul Fazl tried to escape; he was riding his horse across a stream, when horse and rider both fell. One of his Abyssinian guards, Jaffar, pulled Abul Fazl out from under his horse and tried to lead him away. But Abul Fazl, speared through his chest and, most likely, injured from the fall, could not walk. He collapsed.

Just then, Bir Singh and his men approached. Jaffar left his lord and hid behind a tree. He watched as the Bundela chief took the historian's head upon his lap, wiping the mud and sweat off his face with chilling gentleness. Abul Fazl opened his eyes. 'The all-conquering lord has sent for you courteously', said Bir Singh. It is what Salim had titled himself in Allahabad: world-conqueror, Jahangir. From Asad Beg's telling, it seems that Bir Singh planned to take Abul Fazl alive – though this hardly matches Salim's own explicit orders for his assassination.

But Abul Fazl had negotiated with Chand Bibi and climbed the walls of Asirgarh; he had argued with the most powerful scholars in Akbar's realm and written a prodigious history of his reign; he had ensured his family's rise and avenged himself on their enemies – he would not succumb to the hired assassin of a dissolute, pleasure-loving prince who gave himself grand names. Abul Fazl 'began to abuse [Bir Singh] angrily', writes Asad Beg. The Bundela king let the proud writer's head fall back to the ground; he got up and walked away. In his wake, one of his men cut off Abul Fazl's head.

Some say that when Salim received this grisly prize, he flung it into the toilet.

Akbar was flying pigeons in Agra fort when he heard what had happened. For over half a century, ever since he escaped his tutors to play with his birds, Akbar had delighted in pigeons trained to swoop or be still at his call. He called it '*ishq-baazi*', it was his love.

Father Monserrate tells of how Akbar's palaces had separate dwellings for the emperor, his queens, his sons and his pigeons. The priest was as enthralled as the emperor by these trained birds. 'It will seem little short of miraculous', he writes, 'when I affirm that when sent out, they dance, turn somersaults all together in the air, fly in orderly rhythm, and return to their starting point, all at the sound of a whistle. They are bidden to perch on the roof, to conceal themselves within their nesting-places, or to dart out of them again; and they do everything just as they are told.' It wasn't only tricks that pigeons were good for. The *Ain-i-Akbari* records that some had peculiar calls, some distinctive struts, and, of course, some were '*rath*' pigeons that could deliver messages.

Akbar had 'khasa' pigeons, naturally – 500 out of his collection of 20,000 were specially chosen by the emperor. They came in many beautiful colours: *chini* (porcelain blue), *surmai* (dark grey), *kishmishi* (dark brown), *halwai* (light brown), *shaftalu* (peach), *kaghazi* (paper-yellow). His favourite was Mohana, given to him by Aziz, and Mohana's various progeny – Askhi, Parizad, Almas and more – filled Akbar's dovecotes.[33]

One or more of them may have been flying about this August noon, as Akbar stood on his roof, 'admiring [their] wonderful movements'. His mind was full of their flap and call when one of his amirs came up and told him the news.

Akbar, says an eyewitness, fainted where he stood.

Some six-odd years before, Akbar had had another of his accidents, this time during a deer fight. One of the contending stags attacked the emperor, butting him with his antlers, and managed to gore one of his testicles. It was Abul Fazl who tended to him, applying balm to his wound over the long and anxious weeks of his recovery until, after a month and twenty-two days, Akbar finally bathed.[34]

No metaphor, even of Abul Fazl's devising, could have better captured the intimacy between the two men. This was how much Akbar, who would not let poor Jouher see him naked, who would stab himself to prove his courage, trusted his historian. Akbar 'never forgave [Salim]' for the murder of his friend, writes Inayatullah, and for the rest of his life, the emperor would send out vengeful expeditions against the raja of Bundelkhand. He 'thirsted', in Asad Beg's words, 'for the blood of that wretch'. It was a thirst he never managed to slake.

Chapter 16

A Mighty Death

'Bid the druggist close his shop,
I've tried his drugs a thousand times.'

– Akbarnama

Three years remained between Abul Fazl's death and Akbar's own. They were crowded with incident, like the previous forty-seven years of Akbar's reign, or, in fact, the previous sixty years of his life. But now, it was no longer soaring tales of conquest that filled the annals, no longer the coming of the Mahdi that preoccupied Akbar. The drama had become decidedly domestic.

There is a famous portrait of Salim holding a painting of his aged father.[1] Akbar's son was notoriously finicky about accuracy in the art he patronized. The Akbar in Salim's hands is an old man. His moustache is as much of a wisp as it was when Akbar was a boy-king. His face is lined, and the skin at his throat hangs loose. For all that the yogis and doctors and astrologers had said, Akbar was nearing his end. The man who had made such wide-ranging plans for his empire, its people and its religions, its administration and its finances, now had to make a final decision: who would helm the empire after him?

In 1577, when Salim was about eight years old, Murad seven and Daniyal five, Akbar had given his sons mansabdari ranks. These ranks, 6000 for Daniyal, 7000 for Murad and 10,000 for the eldest, Salim, were higher than anything his officials could aspire to – the highest rank for an amir was fixed at 5000 – but the very induction of the princes into the mansabdari fold made one thing very clear: as Akbar's warlords would no longer be allowed independent fiefs, neither would his sons. This was a radical departure from the 'unspoken rule' of Mughal succession – as Munis Faruqui demonstrates brilliantly in *The Princes of the Mughal Empire* – '. . . that every son had an equal share in his father's patrimony and all males within a ruling group had the right to succeed to the throne'.[2] It was the rule, for example, that Babur followed when he left Hindustan to Humayun and Kabul to Kamran. It was the rule that Akbar's half-brother, Hakim, had recourse to in keeping an independent hold over Kabul and even, as Faruqui argues elsewhere, in his bids for Lahore. It was Kamran, from Kabul, who had governed Punjab during Humayun's first stint on the Hindustani throne, and 'Hakim probably saw control over the Punjab as his birthright'.[3]

Akbar, who had witnessed from the womb what chaos could result from competing fraternal ambitions, who had spent much of his adult life fighting warlords bent on independent rule, who had managed, besides, to create an overarching bureaucracy and philosophy – mansabdari and sulh-i kul, peace for all – to manage a vast empire, from Kabul to Orissa, as if it were one land –this Akbar wasn't going to break the whole thing down just to please his sons. Nor, however, would he simply declare the eldest his heir – Akbar had flouted almost every tradition he inherited, but to break this last custom of his forefathers may have been the line he could not cross. Or it may be that the idea of primogeniture was far too arbitrary for Akbar's rational mind.

So it came down to this: one of his sons would have to prove himself better than the others, more deserving of the throne. Over the generations, the result of this policy is 'best summed up', writes Faruqui, 'by the terse Persian phrase: *ya takht, ya takhta* (either throne or funeral bier)'.[4] For Akbar and his immediate descendants, it caused immense dysfunction and heartbreak. Akbar, who loved so much to work with his hands, had been his whole life a potter at the wheel, creating a mould for Hindustan – of administrative coherence amidst ethnic and religious diversity – that would survive for centuries. But no man can mould his own children; none of his sons were as he wanted them to be.

So much so, in fact, that Akbar began to look beyond them. 'There can be no doubt', writes Faruqui, 'that Akbar was working to make the next succession a more competitive one'.[5] The emperor 'loved grandchildren more than sons', according to Abul Fazl, and he was particularly fond of Salim's eldest boy, Khusro.[6] It was to Khusro, one of the most intriguing and tragic characters in the Mughal annals, that Akbar gave a high mansab when he was still a child, a decision 'fully intended to under-cut Salim'.[7]

The emperor had forgotten, however, that he was not the sole arbiter of the future of his dynasty. There was also his harem. It had long been customary for elder Mughal women to maintain an equilibrium between warring brothers and sons. Hindal's mother had once ticked off her son for not treating his elder brother as a father; Khanzada had negotiated between Humayun, Askari and Kamran. So, now, Hamida pleaded for peace between Akbar and Salim.

'She was devoted to the young Prince', say the Jesuits, 'and fearing that he would be vanquished in an encounter with a veteran warrior like the King, she tried her utmost to turn the latter from his purpose'.[8]

Her arguments must have been persuasive. Akbar agreed to a truce. It was another of the women who went to bring Salim home: his aunt Salima, Akbar's cousin and wife, once married to Bairam Khan and a woman of renowned intelligence. 'She possessed all good qualities', Salim would write of her years later, with gratitude.[9]

Salim and Salima returned to Agra in April 1603. Hamida came out to meet him, 'soothed the prince's terrified soul' and took him to Akbar.[10] To all appearances, father and son were reconciled. Akbar even put his own turban on Salim's head. But such goodwill between the men, if it existed at all, did not last long. Akbar had not forgotten Abul Fazl. It was soon after Salim's arrival that Abul Fazl's son came to court; Akbar condoled with him and gave him a special shawl – a pashmina, which Akbar called '*parm-narm*', so-so-soft. As for Salim, the prince may have grown accustomed to his own rule over the past two years. To be back in court, subordinate to the emperor, does not seem to have suited him. Six months later, Akbar gave Salim a mission against Mewar but the prince went back to Allahabad instead – to the satisfaction, it seems, of both parties.

There are so few moments of rest in the *Akbarnama*, so much conquest and debate, so much travel and diplomacy, that it is easy to forget that Akbar was a bookworm. It had long been Akbar's custom, and his great pleasure, '[a]fter the lights had been lit . . . to sit in a great hall', as the Jesuits describe it, 'surrounded by numerous people whose duty it was to read books to him, or narrate stories'.[11] After these daily readings, Akbar would make a mark on the page where the reader had stopped and reward him with gold or silver coins.[12]

Akbar was famously illiterate – or, more likely, dyslexic, as modern historians suggest. It isn't that he could not read or write: according to Annemarie Schimmel, there even exists 'one small note written by [Akbar] in clear Arabic letters'. Besides, at the time, Akbar's inability to read or write 'testifie[d] to Akbar's greatness, not to any deficiency'. He wasn't illiterate, he was '*ummi*', just as the Prophet Muhammad was ummi, a term that, 'in the tradition of Islamic mysticism, has come to mean an inspired mystic'[13] and fit very neatly, therefore, with Akbar's, and his friends' and flatterers', idea of the emperor as a messiah.

Unlettered, dyslexic or divine, Akbar's appetite for literature was as boundless as his curiosity about faith.[14] Many of the books that were read out to him were commissioned by the emperor himself, often from his busy translation department working on Hindi, Greek, Arabic and Persian literature. And if Akbar could not read, he could certainly absorb; it was his most disgruntled translator Badauni who wrote, with no intention to flatter, that the emperor 'by a peculiar acquisitiveness and a talent for selection, by no means common, had made his own all that can be seen and read in books'.[15]

These days, however, the emperor's evenings had become less convivial. In fact, Asad Beg writes that Akbar had begun to 'retire for a long interval' after his evening prayers.[16] Perhaps he tired more easily as he aged, and needed a nap. Or perhaps he did not find peace in other people's stories anymore; wanting, instead, to be alone and piece together the memory of his children when they were yet unshattered by their foibles. His servants and courtiers had grown accustomed to Akbar's absence at this time of day and would 'disperse' in the evenings, only returning when they 'expected His Majesty to re-appear'.

One particular evening, however, sometime in the summer of 1604, Akbar was unusually keen to hold court. It was Asad Beg, in fact, who caused this spurt of enthusiasm. He had just returned from a diplomatic mission to Bijapur and escorted a Bijapuri princess to Daniyal, who was to marry her as part of a largely unsuccessful Mughal attempt to build marital alliances in the Deccan.

Akbar, eager to hear all the news, arrived in court and found it deserted. To add insult to injury, a 'luckless lamplighter [was] coiled up like a snake', fast asleep, near the throne. In a fury, Akbar had the man thrown off a tower; the lamplighter was 'dashed into a thousand pieces'.

Maybe it wasn't nostalgia that occupied Akbar's evenings; maybe it was fury. For a half-century, Akbar had nurtured an empire: growing it from the fields of Kalanaur to the Arabian Sea and the Bay of Bengal, across the Himalayan snows and the Vindhyan plateaus. Could he not have hoped, at the end of his days, for a suitable heir, just one son who wasn't greedy for wine or impatient for power?

Like a wounded beast slashing at anything that moves, Akbar hurled invective at the mansabdars who now scurried into court. Among them was Khwaja Amiruddin, whose turn it was to keep the watch. After 'abusing and disgracing him', Akbar ordered him to leave 'instantly . . . and join the Prince's camp'. (Presumably, he meant Salim, and to suggest that only the riff-raff from among his mansabdars had allied with the prince in Allahabad.) Daulat Khan, also on guard duty, was 'disgraced and dishonoured'; then came Ram Das's turn. But Akbar's temper was cooling: Ram Das 'was not so severely punished'.

Akbar sat down on his throne, and Asad Beg approached, trembling. In fact, the interview went better than he might have feared. Akbar's anger dissolved quickly, and Asad had so many stories to tell: not least that of the Bijapuri elephant that had grown accustomed to a daily drink. Asad Beg, escorting the animal to Akbar as a gift from the Deccani kingdom, had to supply its needs from crates of expensive Portuguese wine.

Asad Beg had brought other gifts from Bijapur too, including a pipe, lighter and pouch of tobacco. The pipe was 'beautifully dried and coloured, both ends being adorned with jewels and enamel', its oval mouthpiece made of cornelian. The lighter was 'golden . . . as a proper accompaniment'. And the tobacco – a Portuguese import and never before seen in court – was of the best quality, said Asad, having arranged the whole kit 'on a silver tray'.

Akbar's curiosity was aroused. Even more than the novelty of tobacco, he may have enjoyed the brief but energetic debate that followed the lighting of the pipe. The emperor, always keen to try his hand at things, took a few puffs, but his doctor, 'in great trouble' by his side, stopped him. Aziz, once again the emperor's companion on his adventures, had a go. Aziz summoned his own 'druggist', too, who had heard about this 'new invention . . . and [said that] the European doctors had written much in its praise'.

At this, Asad turned to Akbar's doctor and pooh-poohed his fears. 'The Europeans are not so foolish as not to know all about it', he said, 'there are wise men among them who seldom err or commit mistakes'. Besides, the doctor shouldn't dismiss the leaf without trying it. Akbar's doctor was a cultural conservative, however. 'We do not want to follow the Europeans, and adopt a custom, which is not sanctioned by our own wise men, without trial', he replied.

But weren't all customs once new, asked Asad Beg.

Akbar, listening, was impressed with Asad's rhetoric, and praised him to Aziz: 'Did you hear how wisely Asad spoke? Truly, we must not reject a thing that has been adopted by the wise men of other nations merely because we cannot find it in our books; or how shall we progress?'

His doctor tried to argue, but Akbar wouldn't let him. Instead, he called for an opinion from one of the Jesuits still lingering in his court. The priest had many good things to say about tobacco, 'but no one could persuade the physician'. Still, Asad Beg admits, 'he was a good physician' – and, as regards smoking, well ahead of his time.

Tobacco was soon, and predictably, flying off the shelves in Hindustan. Akbar never took to it, though, even if he may have remembered it fondly as one of the last subjects of debate in his court. There would have been little time, in the months following Asad Beg's return from Bijapur, for the eclectic, intellectual argument that Akbar so enjoyed.

By the monsoon of 1604, news of Salim's increasing high-handedness was flowing into Agra, and Akbar decided to sail east. He would go to war, if need be, to bring the prince under control. It was raining once again, as it had been when Akbar last set sail to conquer the east, but this time, the air was not as full of good omens. In fact, Akbar's boat got stuck in the sand; then heavy rain prevented his departure; and, finally, he heard that his mother Hamida was unwell. Akbar returned to Agra from the riverbank.

He sat by her bed and 'spoke to her several times but got no reply'. Akbar couldn't bear it, writes Inayatullah; he 'was helpless' – the greatest emperor alive unable to speak to his mother one last time. He 'sate down in solitude' and cried.

Thus it was that, once again, Salim's grandmother saved the prince from his father's wrath. On 29 August 1604, Hamida Banu Begum, Humayun's reluctant bride, who glowed with divine light during her pregnancy, and must have glowed as much with pride at her son's remarkable life, died in bed, unconscious. Akbar shaved every last bit of hair on his head and face, removed his turban and 'donned the garb of woe'.[17] That very evening, however, he ordered that the rest of his court might remove their mourning clothes. It was Dussehra the next day, and Akbar didn't want to stop the celebrations. What difference would it make if his court continued to mourn, anyway? Akbar had lost one parent when he was a boy, the other, now, in his old age, and no matter who joined him to grieve his mother's death, Akbar would be alone.

Salim joined him.

It may be that the prince understood his father's loss and shared his grief for the woman who had loved them both so deeply; and it may be, too, that Hamida had given him one last opportunity to make amends – or even, more bluntly, to get on Akbar's right side. Later on, he would write that it was 'through that very act I became emperor'.[18] Salim abandoned his rebel throne in Allahabad and came to Agra with condolences.

Akbar greeted the prince warmly in public, but afterwards, in private, the dam of his anger burst and overflowed. Akbar may have hit Salim, he certainly yelled at him, while the prince stood meek, head bowed. For some days, Akbar even had the prince locked up in a makeshift rehabilitation pro-gramme, to wean him off alcohol, until Salim's sisters pleaded for him and he was let out.

Akbar may have been furious with Salim, but he was 'especially hopeless about Prince Daniyal'.[19]

It was soon after news of Abul Fazl's death that word arrived of Daniyal drinking again. Ever since, panicked, it appears, at the thought of losing another son to alcohol, Akbar had sent scolding letters and emissaries to Burhanpur, one after another – including a doctor and a childhood nurse 'not afraid to speak strongly' to the prince – by turns denouncing his 'perverted career', pleading with him to have pity on his own life and come home. But Daniyal would not return.[20]

Finally, in desperation, Akbar sent an order banning anyone from supply-ing the prince with drink. This cold turkey regime did no good; in fact, it killed Daniyal. The prince asked his friends to smuggle him wine any way they could: in animal entrails, in gun barrels. It was not alcohol, therefore, that poisoned Daniyal, but rust from the barrel of his favourite musket, improvised into a decanter.

In March 1605, after forty days of agony, Akbar's youngest son died. The good-looking young man, fond of poetry and hunting, was evidently much loved. The women of his harem were heartbroken and furious at his demise. Daniyal need not have died: he had fathered a son only the previous year and still managed to keep the fast of Ramzan. He was not so weak, that is, not entirely enslaved to wine as yet. If only his friends had not indulged him. They were all arrested, nine in all, including a gunman, two eunuchs and a barber; and the women had them all killed 'by sticks and stones, clods and kicks'.[21]

According to Inayatullah, when the news reached Akbar, 'there was no upset in his disposition'. Daniyal's harem might scream or weep in grief and anger, but what could Akbar do or feel? God had given him three sons, and now, no matter how Akbar fought to save them, He was taking them away, one by one. Akbar had looked for signs from the divine most of his ruling life; what did he think of God's actions now, His wilful murder of Akbar's heirs?

It was over forty years since Akbar went on his mad ride on musth Hawai, racing across the Yamuna, pitching and rolling upon a bridge made of boats, offering God His vengeance while Shamsuddin Ataka threw off his turban and Agra's citizens wondered if their emperor had 'some drunken-ness in the brain'.[22]

If Akbar had displeased God, then God would take Akbar's life.

Now, on the banks of that very river, Akbar asked for God's opinion one last time. He arranged an elephant fight – no ordinary entertainment, but a duel tense with undercurrents. The two fighting elephants belonged to Salim and his son Khusro, the grandson Akbar favoured so highly that, at under eighteen, he held a rank of 10,000, a drum and his own standard. It was only the previous year, in 1604, that Khusro's mother Man Bai – Salim's first wife, Bhagwant Das's daughter and Harkha Bai's niece – had overdosed on opium, unable to bear the constant friction between her husband, her son and her father-in-law. Salim blames Khusro for it – his son's stubborn refusal to be 'loyal and loving' to him. Khusro has no voice in history, but if it is true that Akbar nurtured a not-so-secret desire to place his grandchild on his throne, it would be no wonder if Khusro became contemptuous of his seemingly worthless father; even less surprising if he held his mother's suicide against Salim.

In brief: Khusro and his father were bitter rivals, and, as inevitably as tobacco found addicts in Hindustan, their fighting elephants were soon eclipsed by the spectacle of Salim's and Khusro's supporters attacking each other. Akbar was 'exceedingly angry, vexed, and enraged', writes Asad Beg, at the scene – his conversation with God interrupted by unruly mobs.

Figure 16.1   Akbar, Salim and Khusro. Salim has brought his father a trained falcon, but Akbar is no longer the young boy who derived such joy from his hunts. Instead, he looks a bit hunted himself, trapped between the ambitions of his lone remaining son, Salim, and his favourite grandson, Khusro (standing behind). Artist unknown, c. 1602–04. *Source*: The Cleveland Museum of Art, Public domain.

It isn't clear when this fight happened, but it was either soon before it or soon after, in 'the beginning of winter, when the air was cold, and the constitution became torpid', that Akbar caught a stomach bug.[23]

As he grew increasingly weak, two of Akbar's closest friends and most powerful amirs, Man Singh and Aziz, called a meeting of the senior nobility. The two men – Khusro's maternal uncle and father-in-law respectively – reminded the council that Akbar's feelings towards Salim were 'notorious', and that the emperor 'by no means wishes [his son] to be his successor'. Instead, they proposed Khusro for the throne.[24]

Salim has been much decried through history for his dissolute ways, but the prince with an eye for art and a taste for wine was of a more flinty disposition than he is given credit for. Salim had managed to win himself strong support during his past few years in Allahabad. Partly this may have been the result of his natural affability, but also, he had been courting conservative Muslim allegiance, even issuing a farman countermanding Akbar's orders to shut down some mosques and prevent prayers in them. 'It was improper on his part to have acted in this manner', the prince had declared.[25]

As a result, if Khusro had powerful backers at the council, so did Salim. The Sayyids of Barha, a clan of Indian Muslims recruited to Akbar's court and hugely valuable to his empire, spoke in Salim's favour and left the meeting. Others followed suit.

Salim was camped across the river. He had been warned not to enter the palace, according to Asad Beg, or he would be imprisoned – or worse – by Man Singh and Aziz. The prince was waiting to hear the council's decision, wondering whether to stay or flee, when the amirs began to arrive, one by one. By the end of the day, the tide had turned so completely in Salim's favour that even Aziz 'came in great shame and paid his respects'.[26]

Man Singh, meanwhile, took Khusro out of the Agra fort and prepared his boats: if need be, they would escape to Bengal.

It is hardly possible that Aziz and Man Singh decided to make Khusro emperor all on their own. As Munis Faruqui writes, 'Almost to the end of his reign . . . Akbar seems to have held out hope that Salim's imperial claims might somehow be thwarted.'[27]

Was he disappointed, now, to see his son walk in? Or did he reconcile himself to the fact that it was, after all, the son he had prayed for who was at his deathbed, seeking his blessings? Abul Fazl might have been able to explain it in a way that soothed the dying emperor: even Akbar, he might have said, could not undo the destiny that Akbar's prayers had invoked.

There was little time for regrets, in any case. The emperor 'was still breathing', writes Asad Beg, but only just.

At his father's signal, Salim put on Akbar's turban and robes, strapped Akbar's sword around his waist. The sword had belonged to Babur, and Babur, too, had given it to Humayun as he lay dying and uncertain of what his son would make of Hindustan.

Asad Beg says that Akbar watched Salim put on these symbols of his rule, watched the attendants prostrate themselves before their new ruler, and '. . . closed his life'. Another near-contemporary historian called Ni'matullah

Figure 16.2 A posthumous portrait of an aged Akbar, possibly commissioned by his grandson Shahjahan. Note the winged angels above him and the lion and cow resting at peace by his feet. Attributed to Govardhan, c. 1640-50. *Source*: The Cleveland Museum of Art, Public domain.

Khan Harvi, however, describes the emperor as much more alive to the happenings around him; maybe even, in the end, approving of them.[28]

It wasn't only the symbols of rule, turban, robe and sword, that Akbar gave Salim; it wasn't only an official transfer of power that occurred by his bed. Akbar gave Salim more personal tokens of farewell, too: his own rosary and amulets. And then, pulling his long-estranged, lone remaining son into his arms, Akbar gave Salim a final, forgiving kiss.

In October 1605, sixty-three years to the month since the light of the world first filled his eyes, the Niru'un died. He might have been pleased by the chronogram for the date of his demise, playing as it does on his name, as Akbar loved to do.

Wafaat-i-Akbar shud.

'Akbar died', it might read; or 'There was a mighty death'. His worst enemies would have agreed, while sighing in relief: both meanings were true.

Epilogue

'Of God, people have said that He had a son; of the Prophet they have said that he was a sorcerer
Neither God nor the Prophet has escaped the slander of men. Much less I!'

> – Akbar in a letter to Abdullah of Turan, *Akbarnama*

'In our free Hall, where each philosophy
And mood of faith may hold its own, they blurt
Their furious formalisms, I but hear
The clash of tides that meet in narrow seas, –
Not the Great Voice not the true Deep.'

> – Alfred, Lord Tennyson, 'Akbar's Dream'

Akbar did not want to die. He practised ascetic austerities – eating little, and of a predominantly 'Sufiyana' diet that excluded meat, sleeping little, and hailing celibacy as a virtue: 'Had I been wise earlier, I would have taken no woman from my own kingdom into my seraglio, for my subjects are to me in the place of children.' In the eventuality that he must die, even if he lived 100, 200 or 1000 years, Akbar had shaved a spot on his head, believing that this provided for his soul to escape through his skull, and return to live another great emperor's life.

Far from living several times the span of a normal life, as he had been promised, Akbar died at the unexceptional age of sixty-three, and, as far as we know, he has yet to return to rule the world. But the emperor who sought immortality had one last trick up his sleeve. He was a bibliophile, after all, and he knew that books last longer than any human life, any dynasty, any age.

In the late 1580s, Akbar commissioned histories. He asked his aunt, Gulbadan, to write her memoirs, he asked his father's water-bearer, Jouher, and one of his old soldiers, Bayazid Biyat. And, of course, he asked Abul Fazl, who collected many of these other writings (Bayazid, in fact, dictated his history to one of Abul Fazl's clerks), interviewed older relatives, attendants and the emperor himself, trawled through the annals of Central Asia, Persia and Hindustan, and produced one of the most monumental works of literature that exists in the world – not only an account of Akbar's life but a political, theological, even mythological basis for the emperor's existence and rule.

The research involved was tremendous. It was only in November of 1595, many years after Akbar had commissioned the work, that Abul Fazl sat down to write. 'A great joy seized me', he says of those days. 'My heart renewed its vigour, and my useless pen drew a wondrous sketch.' Writers will know how rare this feeling is, and how wonderful, and may not be surprised that by April of the following year, in barely six months, Abul Fazl, thus absorbed, had written the first thirty years of Akbar's life.[1]

Abul Fazl was invited to present his work in court. 'Assemblies were convened for praise and censure of my labour, and cries of "bravo" and "boo" rang out.' His enemies and competitors 'sat gnashing their teeth in envy'.[2]

One of them may well have been Badauni who, not content with merely scowling at Abul Fazl's nonsense, decided to write his own version of events. In the opening pages of his secret history, Badauni states he will write an account of 'these 40 years from the accession of Akbar',[3] implying that he began to write in 1596, the very year that Abul Fazl presented his manuscript.

No sooner, that is, had one man written a story of Akbar than another began to compose a counter to it.

Badauni was quite clear about his reasons for writing his rejoinder: 'my inducement to write this has been nothing but sorrow for the faith, and heart-burning for the deceased Religion of Islam'. Akbar's alleged abandonment of Islam and his Muslim subjects is, indeed, a recurring and bitter theme in some reports of Akbar's rule. A prominent Islamic theologian of the time, Shaikh Ahmad Sirhindi, wrote of how 'The infidels are demolishing mosques and building their own places of worship in their stead'. Among these were a mosque and a dargah by the lake of Kurukshetra, where Akbar had once watched ascetics at war. 'Both have been destroyed by the infidels and in their place they now have a big temple.'

That was not the end of it; if Shaikh Ahmad is to be believed, it wasn't only Muslim shrines but Muslim ways of life that were being taken over by Hindu custom and practice:

Again, the infidels perform their rituals . . . freely while the Muslims find themselves helpless and unable to execute ordinances of the sharia. On the day of Ekadashi when Hindus abstain from eating and drinking, they see to it that the Muslims also do not cook, sell or buy anything in the towns. On the contrary, in the month of Ramzan, they cook and sell breads in the bazaars openly.[4]

Such was the animosity against the emperor that not all his critics confined their complaints to paper; some dreamt of more direct action. In 1582, the year that brought about the pitiful end of Abdun Nabi and Makhdum-ul-Mulk, the Jesuit Fathers of the first mission left Akbar's court. Monserrate writes of this journey that he narrowly escaped being murdered by a soldier who, on learning that 'the priest was a Christian and had been summoned by the King to teach him Christianity . . . plainly declared that, if he got a chance, he would kill not only the Priest but the King as well'.[5]

Some five years later, Abul Fazl records a murderous attack on a Shia priest called Mulla Ahmad in Lahore. In December 1587, a 'hot-headed young [Sunni] man' called Mirza Fulad Beg Barlas, sick and tired of Mulla Ahmad's discourses on Shias and Sunnis, waylaid the priest and 'cut off his arm'. It must have been a dark night: Fulad Beg thought he'd cut off Mulla Ahmad's head, and left. The priest picked up his arm, went to a doctor, and managed to stay alive long enough to have his assailant arrested. Abul Fazl was part of the investigation and writes that even though 'leading persons' (that is, Akbar's women relatives) petitioned for mercy, Fulad Beg was executed – tied to an elephant's foot and paraded through the city. Mulla Ahmad died of his wounds a little later.

Badauni tells a more revealing tale. Evidently, Fulad Beg had support against the Shia priest – chronograms for his murder included 'Bravo! the dagger of Steel' and 'Hell-fire Pig'. Badauni witnessed Mulla Ahmad's death and swears that 'I saw his face look actually like that of a pig' as he breathed his last. More to the point, Badauni writes that Akbar sent an official to ask Fulad Beg what had possessed him to attack the priest – was it religious zeal? Fulad Beg replied, 'If zeal for religion had been my motive, I should have turned my hand against a greater one than he.' No wonder, with the man voicing such a clear threat to Akbar's own life, that the emperor ignored his harem's plea for mercy.

But the anger of such men did not die with them. Centuries later, Jawaharlal Nehru wrote of how the Muslim League 'kept aloof' from the fourth-centenary celebrations of Akbar's birth.

It wasn't only orthodox Muslim opinion that sided against Akbar, however. The Jesuit Fathers of the third mission, led by Father Xavier, believed that God himself was raining punishments upon the heretical emperor: the death of his son, Murad; then a great fire in Lahore that ravaged the palace – so much so, it was said, that 'gold, silver, and other metals melted . . . [and] ran down the streets like streams of water'.[6]

Colonial and nationalist historians might have written with modern detachment of Akbar's heterodoxy, but picked other quarrels with the emperor, condemning his appetite for power, or accusing him of duplicity. Thus, by 1922, J. S. Hoyland and S. N. Banerjee, writing their introduction to Monserrate's memoirs and comparing Akbar unfavourably with the Mauryan emperor Ashoka, declared that 'modern researches' had undone the idea of Akbar as an ideal 'philosopher-king': 'His character with its mixture of ambition and cunning has now been laid bare.'

Among nationalist historians, Akbar and Ashoka may have been two 'greats' who united the diversity of newly independent India, but not all historians of this school were able to fully disguise an instinctive suspicion of the Muslim ruler. R. C. Majumdar damns him by exception – the only good man in a dynasty of kings 'notorious for their religious bigotry'.[7] A. L. Srivastava's censure is more a slip of the pen. In a biography that credits Akbar with establishing 'national Indian' schools of every kind, from music to architecture, Srivastava also describes the emperor, in his youth, as a 'good, though tolerant, Muslim' – as if the two qualities contradict each other quite naturally.[8]

And now, a century later, another troop of adversaries rallies against Akbar, politicians, columnists and makers of memes, leaders and foot soldiers of Hindutva straining to strip Akbar of his usual suffix, 'the great', and hand it to a more deserving – or, let us say, more Hindu – king, like Hemu or Rana Pratap.

Akbar was not a perfect man, the insan-i-kamil of Abul Fazl's resplendent prose. His appetite for conquest was, indeed, insatiable, though it is strange to expect anything less from a sixteenth-century monarch.[9] He was not above a covert assassination or two; nor above proclaiming his Islamic credentials to Abdullah of Turan while encouraging Muslim clerics in his own court to drink wine.[10] For all his reforms of revenue, administration and welfare that so distressed his warlords, for all his controversial experiments with faith, Akbar was not as radical on questions of caste. The emperor is said to have coined the term '*halalkhor*' (literally, one who eats what is lawful, more broadly, 'one who earns an honest living'[11]) for sweepers – that is, Dalits, 'untouchables'. The name anticipates another, '*harijan*' (born of God), which the third 'great' of Indian history, Mahatma Gandhi, popularized for a while. Both terms carry an air of ineffectual benevolence: neither change in terminology effected a change in the lives of those whom it renamed.[12]

Akbar was not a perfect man, but he was as great as any man can be, in that he strove for perfection not through power, but through its just exercise.

This was what lay at the crux of Akbar's enquiries into faith. 'The King was always pondering in his mind which nation has retained the true religion of God; and to this question he constantly gave the most earnest thought', writes Father Monserrate. The question – How I wish for the coming of some pious man, who will resolve the distractions of my heart! – possessed the emperor, in his solitary meditations, in the gladiatorial combats of the Ibadat Khana, in the perplexing fits that sometimes overtook him.

A less imaginative man might well have remained caught in this imperative, that only one faith can make one empire, but Akbar, striding into storms of ideas and opinions as audaciously as he rode into the monsoon-heavy waters of the Ganga, was not that man. 'By God', he once exclaimed when Father Monserrate himself thought he might have gone too far in his criticism of Islam, 'I am not the man to have my feelings outraged by these things.' He was, instead, the man to have his intelligence aroused. As men of many faiths argued around him, Akbar stopped looking for the one true belief that would bring peace to all men. Instead, he turned the whole proposition on its head and decided to make that very peace for all, the sulh-i kul, the principle tenet of his rule.

Akbar may not have found one true God, but he had found his way.[13]

When Akbar took the throne in 1556, writes Stephen Dale, he 'reigned over, but did not rule, a modest, insecure north Indian state'. It was hardly a few cities – Lahore, Sirhind, Delhi and Agra, and a narrow corridor of land between them. A half-century later, when Akbar died, 'his conquests and institutional innovations [had] bequeathed to his successors a stable, populous empire, whose wealth dwarfed that of his Safavid and Ottoman contemporaries'.[14]

The Mughal realm stretched far in space, from Kabul and Kashmir to Burhanpur, from Surat and Sindh to Orissa – and it was the rare foreign court where the wealth and power of the 'Great Mogor' was unknown – but it stretched even farther in time. Two and a half centuries after Akbar's death, in 1857, it was the truncated Mughal court in Delhi that remained the greatest symbolic threat to the British Raj, and today, it is the Mughals, still, who arouse most envy and spleen among votaries of the Hindu Rashtra.

What gave the empire such longevity, such seemingly eternal relevance? Akbar, despite his best efforts, is long gone, along with his dynasty; their appearance in textbooks is being curtailed, the naming of roads after them is contested. But the *Akbarnama* remains.

As those cries of 'bravo' and 'boo' rang out, a sympathetic critic came to Abul Fazl and asked him what the point was of writing such a book. 'Why do you take such pains, and why do you write in such a style? Will one out of thousands come into existence who will read this glorious volume aright, and be instructed by the new magic of its method? From whom do you expect the effectual recognition of the Truth?' His friend advised the historian to write for a wider market.

As is often the case with writers, Abul Fazl was pleased by the praise but unimpressed by the advice. He was writing for a special audience, for the 'Unique One of Time'. 'What have I to do with a crowd?'[15]

A great deal, as it happens.

It is Abul Fazl whom Harbans Mukhia credits with 'the construction of "harmony" as the encompassing ideological frame that would remain the keystone of the Mughal state's legitimacy and its posthumous legacy'. Long after the last Mughal died forlorn in Rangoon, the Akbar and the Mughal empire of Abul Fazl's book have lived on in the Indian imagination, surviving assaults from every front – not because Abul Fazl valorizes the perfection of one man, but rather because he locates that perfection in the fragile hope of peace for all, a phrase that echoes in the guiding tenet of the Indian dream, once familiar to every Indian schoolchild: unity in diversity.

In Jaunpur, young Banarasidas, budding poet, fell unconscious when he heard that Akbar had died. He was sitting on a staircase when 'The news struck him like a blow upon the heart'. Banarasi fainted and fell; 'He cracked his head and began bleeding profusely. / The word "God" slipped from his mouth.'[16] His parents were frantic, Banarasi's mother ran to put burnt cloth to his wound. Outside, meanwhile, the whole city was experiencing Banarasi's shock and his parents' panic. 'The people, bereft of their emperor, felt orphaned and helpless', the jeweller's son wrote later. 'The townsfolk were afraid, / Their hearts troubled, their faces pale with fear.'

Riots broke out and the town shut down. Worried about robberies and insurrections, people locked up their houses and shops, buried their fine clothes and jewels, accounting books and cash. Men put on rough blankets, 'The women too began to dress plainly.'

As it happens, there was no need to fear. 'No thieves or robbers were to be seen anywhere, / People were needlessly afraid.' Peace returned; 'A letter came from Agra saying that all was well' – announcing Salim's accession.

So often while Akbar lived – when he had his epileptic epiphany in Punjab, when he got off his horse during a polo match – rumours of his death or ill health had led to immediate revolts in the more restless pockets of his empire. And yet, so strong was the scaffolding on which Akbar had built his realm that when the emperor did die, his own mighty death did not shake it.

One man, however, was shaken to the core. Banarasi recovered from his wound. Like the rest of Jaunpur, he breathed in relief as the letter announcing Salim's peaceful succession 'was read from house to house'. But later on, sitting alone on his terrace, Banarasi had other thoughts.

The seventeen-year-old Jain of eclectic faith had only recently been disappointed by his purchase of a mantra meant to bring gold to his door. Soon after, he had taken to worshipping Shiva. But now he asked himself why: 'When I swooned and fell, / Shiva did not help me then.' Banarasi stopped his daily puja to the Lord.

Abul Fazl might have liked the story, and Akbar too: that his death bred doubt in his young subject. Perhaps, they might have said, Akbar's soul did escape into the world through that patch on his skull. Perhaps his famously, notoriously, adventurous spirit found its way to Jaunpur, flew up to the pensive poet on his roof and whispered in his ear: Question. Doubt. Scandalize.

The Mughal Empire at Akbar's Demise, 1605

Notes

CAST OF CHARACTERS

1. 'Mirza' came to mean 'prince' or 'young nobleman'. At this time, however, it was used to identify descendants of Timur. Everyone from Babur to Humayun and his brothers, from Akbar to all his cousins spread far and wide across Central Asia and spilling into Afghanistan, Persia, China and Hindustan would be 'mirzas'.
2. Anaka means 'foster mother'.
3. Ataka means 'foster father'.
4. Koka means 'milk brother'.

CHAPTER 1

1. Unless otherwise specified, all quotations from the *Akbarnama* are from the translation by Henry Beveridge: Abu'l Fazl, *The Akbarnama of Abu'l Fazl* (completed by Inayatullah), trans. Henry Beveridge, vols 1, 2 and 3 (first published 1902–1939; Low Price Publications, 2017).
2. Occasionally, as here, I have quoted from a more recent translation of the *Akbarnama* by W. M. Thackston: Abu'l Fazl, *The History of Akbar*, trans. W. M. Thackston, vols 1–6 (Murty Classical Library of India, Harvard University Press, 2015, 2016, 2017, 2018, 2019, 2020). This phrase appears in volume 5.
3. In the dismissive words of Akbar's court historian, Abul Fazl.
4. 'Mirza' would come to mean 'prince' or young nobleman. Thus, for example, a Rajput heir to Amber is referred to as Mirza Raja Jai Singh in Jahangir's time. At this time, however – and thus in this book – 'mirza' denotes a descendant of Timur.
5. Haider Mirza Doghlat, 'Tarikh-i Rashidi', in *The History of India, As Told by Its Own Historians*, trans. H. M. Elliot, vol. 5 (Trübner and Co., 1873). This translation is of extracts from Haider's history. I have also consulted a translation of the full work by E. Denison Ross.

6. Sometime between October 1507, when Babur made an unsuccessful attempt to conquer Hindustan, and March 1508, when Babur's first son, Humayun, was born, Babur declared himself 'padishah', or emperor, thus distinguishing himself from the profusion of mirzas – Timurid relatives and rivals – in Central Asia and its outskirts. The title was rather more optimistic than true, both in Babur's case and even more so in that of his luckless son, Humayun, but it stuck through the generations and fulfilled its promise in Akbar.

7. Among the deserters were Muhammad Sultan Mirza, to whom Babur had given Kannauj in fief, along with his sons Ulugh Mirza and Shah Mirza. This was not the first time that these Mirzas and their descendants betrayed Babur's family, and it would not be the last.

8. *The Akbarnama of Abu'l Fazl*, vol. 1.

9. Jouher, *The Tezkereh al Vakiat, or Private Memoirs of Moghul Emperor Humayun by Jouher*, trans. Major Charles Stewart (Oriental Translation Fund, 1832).

10. Ibid.

11. The horse was borrowed from Tardi Beg, of whom – and of whose horses – more follows.

12. Gulbadan, Humayun's sister, relates this exchange in her memoir of her brother's tumultuous reign, the *Humayun-nama*. In it, and not surprisingly, Hindal emerges as the author's clear favourite. Gulbadan Begum, *The History of Humayun (Humayun-nama)*, trans. Annette S. Beveridge (The Asiatic Society, 1902).

13. *The Akbarnama of Abu'l Fazl*, vol. 1. Jouher writes that it was Askari who struck Yadgar Nasir with his whip first.

14. Haider Mirza Doghlat, 'Tarikh-i Rashidi', trans. H.M. Elliot.

15. It may be that Kamran's disinclination to fight on his brother's behalf was at least partly the result of a famous episode from Humayun's life: that of the water carrier whom he made king. Kannauj was the site of Humayun's second defeat at Sher Shah's hands; the first was at Chausa, once again upon the banks of the Ganga. Much of Humayun's camp – including some of his harem – had been swept into the river by Sher Shah's advance; one of his daughters drowned, one of his wives was taken prisoner, and Humayun himself only escaped with the help of a water carrier and his buoyant canteens. As a reward, Humayun declared he would seat the man upon his own throne for a day – a flamboyant and eccentric gesture that deserves its pride of place in popular tellings of Humayun's life and character. At the time, however, and particularly since Sher Shah's advance upon the capital wasn't slowing down, it must have appeared like criminal negligence. 'Gifts and favours of some other kind ought to be the servant's reward', wrote Kamran to his brother, plainly irritated. 'What propriety is there in setting him on the throne? At a time when Shir Khan is near, what kind of affair is this to engage your Majesty?' (Gulbadan Begum, *The History of Humayun*). Soon after, Humayun left to battle Sher Shah in Kannauj, and a disgusted Kamran packed up and left for Lahore.

16. Haider minced no words in his rebuke, by his own account:

Formerly, when matters could have been arranged with ease, you put obstacles in the way, by your want of constancy and of purpose. At present it is impossible to achieve anything, without encountering untold difficulties.

I will now lay before you what seems to me your wisest course. It involves great hardships, but it is you who has made hard what was once so easy.

He then proceeded to propose his own conquest of Kashmir. See Mirza Muhammad Haider Dughlat, *The Tarikh-i-Rashidi: A History of the Moghuls of Central Asia*, trans. E. Denison Ross, ed. N. Elias (Sampson. Low, Marston & Co., 1895).
17. Ibid.
18. Abu'l Fazl, *The History of Akbar*, vol. 1, trans. W. M. Thackston.
19. Gulbadan notes here a bit of historical revisionism from within the harem. Humayun's future wife, Hamida Banu Begum, held that the emperor wrote these lines for his brother, Kamran. It is Gulbadan, however, who was at the scene, not Hamida; in the words of her translator, Annette Beveridge, 'Gulbadan puts the difference of opinion gently but does not surrender, and leaves her readers to draw their own inferences.'
20. Gulbadan tells this story; I have changed its words somewhat, but kept its meaning. Shaikh Ahmad of Jam (1048–1141) was a celebrated Sufi buried in Torbat-e Jam, Iran. Humayun's mother, Maham, was descended from him, and Humayun's vision was somewhat tautological, therefore. Any child of Humayun's would be of the Persian philosopher's blood.
21. She was named Bakshi Banu.
22. And most of Lahore with them, it seems. Annette Beveridge writes that 200,000 men and women are said to have fled the city at news of Sher Shah's approach. See Gulbadan Begum, *The History of Humayun*.
23. The courtier is quoted in Ali Anooshahr, 'The King Who Would Be Man: The Gender Roles of the Warrior King in Early Mughal History', *Journal of the Royal Asiatic Society*, vol. 18, no. 3, 2008.
24. Nizamuddin Ahmad, 'Tabakat-i Akbari', in *The History of India, As Told by Its Own Historians*, trans. H. M. Elliot, vol. 5 (Trübner and Co., 1873).
25. *The Akbarnama of Abu'l Fazl*, vol. 1.
26. Ibid.
27. See Annette Beveridge's introduction to Gulbadan Begum, *The History of Humayun*.
28. Ibid. The lines are from Sa'di's *Gulistan* quoted by Babur in his *Baburnama*.
29. Abu'l Fazl, *The History of Akbar*, vol. 1, trans. W. M. Thackston.
30. Mirza Muhammad Haider Dughlat, *The Tarikh-i-Rashidi*, trans. E. D. Ross.
31. Gulbadan Begum, *The History of Humayun*.
32. Ibid.
33. Ibid.
34. Ibid.
35. Even Gulbadan seems to want to gloss over her brother's disgusted departure, writing that Humayun 'gave Mirza Hindal leave to go'.
36. Abul Fazl, for example, writes that Humayun sent two emissaries, Mir Samandar followed by Rai Mal Sauni, to Jodhpur, the raja's capital, and both returned with reports of Maldeo's doubtful loyalty.

37. Abul Fazl offers a more favourable perspective on the raja, possibly because, at the time the historian was writing, Marwar was a friendly ally of the Mughal empire. Thus, he writes that Raja Maldeo was 'in the first instance well-intentioned, and desirous of doing service' but that news of Humayun's reduced circumstances coupled with threats from an increasingly powerful Sher Shah, 'diverted [him] from the right path'. Nizamuddin Ahmad is even more sympathetic to the raja's plight, and allows that Humayun's weak army was a serious impediment to Maldeo's loyalty, for the raja did not have 'sufficient forces of his own to withstand Sher Khan'.

38. Nizamuddin Ahmad, 'Tabakat-i Akbari'.

39. Gulbadan Begum, *The History of Humayun*.

40. Ibid.

41. *The Akbarnama of Abu'l Fazl*, vol. 1.

42. Gulbadan Begum, *The History of Humayun*.

43. Ibid.

44. Jouher, *The Tezkereh al Vakiat*. Food was almost as precious as water on this journey. Jouher tells of how, as they were camped by a small lake on the border of Sindh and Rajasthan, a deer ran into the camp. The thought of a good meal spread a great delight through the company: 'What a delicious prize this deer would be!' cried Humayun as he got on his horse to hunt it. The deer ran into the water, and Jouher, showing both courage and a shrewd presence of mind, leaped in after it, calling out his condition, 'One quarter is mine.' Of course, Humayun agreed, and Jouher grabbed the deer and held on until it was killed.

45. Ibid.

46. Ibid.

47. *The Akbarnama of Abu'l Fazl*, vol. 1. Abul Fazl, delicately though scarcely credibly, ascribes the plunder to Rana Prasad and applauds the 'perfect kindness, liberality and justice' by which Humayun kept only a small portion of this loot for his staff and returned 'the bulk of it to [its] low-minded, narrow-souled owners'. Gulbadan, meanwhile, writes that Humayun had to borrow 80,000 *ashrafis* (gold coins) from Tardi Beg who, unsurprisingly, stipulated a callous 20 per cent rate of interest on the loan.

48. Gulbadan Begum, *The History of Humayun*.

49. *The Akbarnama of Abu'l Fazl*, vol. 1.

50. Shah Husain's own father, meanwhile, had lost Qandahar to Babur – one reason why Shah Husain was so disinclined to help Babur's son.

51. *The Akbarnama of Abu'l Fazl*, vol. 1.

52. As explained by Henry Beveridge in *The Akbarnama of Abu'l Fazl*, vol. 1.

53. The lines from 'Once Humayun became emperor' to 'a successor in turn' are extracted, with some modification, from an article I wrote for *The Hindu Businessline*, 'Gulbadan Begum's story', published 21 June 2019.

54. Chagatais were descendants of Chinghis Khan's second son, Chagatai. Babur was a Chagatai, too, on his mother's side, and a Timurid – a descendant of Timur – on his father's. Many writers and historians consider this something of a genealogical jackpot for Babur and his progeny, combining as it did both Mongol (Chinghizid) and Turkish (Timurid) nobility in their veins. The view is not unchallenged. More on this later.

55. Gulbadan Begum, *The History of Humayun*.

56. Jiji was the first anaka to hold Akbar, but not the first to nurse him. She had not delivered her own son yet, so had no milk to give. A substitute nurse and servant of Humayun's, Daya Bhawal, was ordered to take her place and became, therefore, Akbar's first wet nurse.

CHAPTER 2

1. Gulbadan Begum, *The History of Humayun (Humayun-nama)*, trans. Annette S. Beveridge (The Asiatic Society, 1902).

2. Abu'l Fazl, *The Akbarnama of Abu'l Fazl* (completed by Inayatullah), trans. Henry Beveridge, vol. 1 (First published 1902–1939; Low Price Publications, 2017).

3. Jouher, *The Tezkereh al Vakiat, or Private Memoirs of Moghul Emperor Humayun by Jouher*, trans. Major Charles Stewart (Oriental Translation Fund, 1832).

4. Gulbadan Begum, *The History of Humayun*.

5. Afzal Husain, *The Nobility under Akbar and Jahangir: A Study of Family Groups* (Manohar Publishers, 1999). Abul Fazl brings Bairam Khan into the narrative during Humayun's conquest of Champaner fort in Gujarat in 1535 – sometimes considered Humayun's greatest show of military skill and audacity. He climbed up the fort's high walls with a few hundred men and took it by surprise as much as by force.

6. The story goes that Bairam Khan was on the road with Abul Qasim, a man 'remarkable for the beauty of his person', when they were stopped by one of Sher Shah's noblemen, who thought, reasonably enough, that the strapping Abul Qasim must be the man his king had wanted to recruit. Though Bairam yelled out who he was, the gallant Abul Qasim would have none of it; he was killed and Bairam escaped. *The Akbarnama of Abu'l Fazl*, vol. 1.

7. Jouher, *The Tezkereh al Vakiat*. It is an example of the treacherous currents that flowed between the Mughal princes, their courtiers and their thrones that this agitated Uzbek was a retainer of Askari's, sent to spy on Humayun. Instead, and luckily for the latter, he gave the game away.

8. Ibid.

9. *The Akbarnama of Abu'l Fazl*, vol. 1.

10. Ibid.

11. Sultan Begum would form a far closer bond with Akbar than his uncle, so much so that chroniclers of Akbar's life, including even Abul Fazl, speak of her with approval.

12. *The Akbarnama of Abu'l Fazl*, vol. 1.

13. Ibid.

14. Ibid.

15. According to Abul Fazl, Babur 'was much pleased' with the invention.

16. Jouher, *The Tezkereh al Vakiat*.

17. The founder of Shah Tahmasp's Safavid dynasty, Shah Ismail, also founded a cadre of devoted followers called the Qizilbash, 'redheads' – 'a name given to them because they wore a distinctive turban with a red baton and twelve folds that

symbolized the Imams of Twelver Shi'ism' (Stephen F. Dale, *The Muslim Empires of the Ottomans, Safavids, and Mughals* [Cambridge University Press, 2010]). Thus, the modern historian Azfar Moin has argued that the crown Shah Tahmasp forced on Humayun's head was not so much an emblem of Shiism but rather of the shah's own Safavid dynasty, and that this ceremony in the shah's court was not so much an induction into a rival sect but rather a literal 'uncrowning' of Humayun, by which Shah Tahmasp made the exiled emperor his 'disciple and slave' (Azfar Moin, *The Millennial Sovereign: Sacred Kingship & Sainthood in Islam* [Columbia University Press, 2012]). More on this later.

18. Jouher, *The Tezkereh al Vakiat*.

19. Gulbadan Begum, *The History of Humayun*. Nizamuddin Ahmad writes that the shah's murderous thoughts were inspired by his younger brother, Bahram Khan, who was 'offended' when Humayun offered his own brothers' lack of loyalty as the reason for his exile (Nizamuddin Ahmad, 'Tabakat-i Akbari', in *The History of India, As Told by Its Own Historians*, trans. H. M. Elliot, vol. 5 [Trübner and Co., 1873]). William Erskine relates an anecdote that clarifies the nature of Humayun's offence. Shah Tahmasp was hectoring his guest over dinner, declaring that Humayun would have been better off had he not let his brothers get out of hand. Afterwards, the shah summoned Bahram, whose duty it was to bring a basin and water for Tahmasp to wash his hands, and, as the younger brother bent to his task, the shah declared, 'This is the way in which you ought to have treated your brothers.' Humayun's enthusiastic concurrence with his tactless host is what angered Bahram Khan, and not without reason. See William Erskine's *A History of India Under the Two First Sovereigns of the House of Taimur: Báber and Humáyun* (Longman, Brown, Green and Longmans, 1854).

Humayun's fate was both uncertain in his own eyes and a mystery to the family he'd left behind. His uncle Haider, who had, indeed, marched on Kashmir and taken it as he'd wanted to, wrote in his account of Central Asian kings: 'The Emperor, after endless hardships and incalculable misfortunes, passed on to Irak, but up to the present time it is not known what has become of him.' See Mirza Muhammad Haider Dughlat, *The Tarikh-i-Rashidi: A History of the Moghuls of Central Asia*, trans. E. Denison Ross, ed. N. Elias (Sampson. Marston & Co., 1895).

20. Jouher, *The Tezkereh al Vakiat*. Jouher stayed with Akbar when Humayun fled at Askari's approach, and accompanied the boy to Qandahar, then rejoined his padishah in Herat.

21. Humayun was lucky to have these gifts to give, and wise to be submissive in the face of the shah's many provocations. Some years later, another refugee king in Tahmasp's court would be far less fortunate: Sultan Bayazid of Turkey, along with his four sons and 12,000 followers, was first given shelter then killed at the shah's orders (*The Akbarnama of Abu'l Fazl*).

22. Ibid., vol. 1.

23. Ibid.

24. Abu'l Fazl, *The History of Akbar*, vol. 2, trans. W. M. Thackston (Murty Classical Library of India, Harvard University Press, 2016). They met in Kabul's Shahrara Garden.

25. *The Akbarnama of Abu'l Fazl*, vol. 1.
26. Ibid.
27. Abu'l Fazl, *The History of Akbar*, vol. 2, trans. W. M. Thackston.
28. *The Akbarnama of Abu'l Fazl*, vol. 1.
29. 'Goats' might be a mistranslation; as my editor, Nandini Mehta, informs me, it is sheep, not goat, that was and remains the most popular meat in the Central Asian diet.
30. Jouher, *The Tezkereh al Vakiat*. Cow flesh was considered as unappetizing as horsemeat, it seems, not only by the Central Asian Timurids but also by the Indian Muslims they conquered. One of the latter, Abdul Qadir Badauni, describes the predicament of a besieged Deccani amir called Muqarrab Khan, whose forces were 'reduced to eating the flesh of horses, camels, and cows, and the matter touched the life, and the knife reached the bone' See Abdul Qadir Badauni. *Muntakhab-ut-Tawarikh* (Selections from Histories), vol. 2, trans. W. H. Lowe (First published 1884–98; Atlantic Publishers and Distributors, 1990).
31. *The Akbarnama of Abu'l Fazl*, vol. 1.
32. Freer Gallery of Art: https://asia.si.edu/object/F1939.57/
33. Abu'l Fazl, *The History of Akbar*, vol. 2, trans. W. M. Thackston.
34. *The Akbarnama of Abu'l Fazl*, vol. 1.
35. Ibid.
36. Iqtidar Alam Khan, *The Political Biography of a Mughal Noble: Mun'im Khan Khan-i Khanan, 1497–1575* (Orient Longman, 1973).
37. Babur, *The Baburnama: Memoirs of Babur, Prince and Emperor*, trans. W. M. Thackston (Modern Library, 2002).
38. *The Akbarnama of Abu'l Fazl*, vol. 1.
39. Ali Anooshahr's wonderful essay, 'The King Who Would Be Man: The Gender Roles of the Warrior King in Early Mughal History', *Journal of the Royal Asiatic Society*, vol. 18, no. 3, 2008, examines how their contemporaries perceived the relative 'manliness' of Humayun and Kamran. Anooshahr argues that the 'crucial distinction in gender roles' at this time among this class was 'not between effeminate and manly, but between not-yet-man and adult male'. The latter would not, for example, marry for desire but for duty. Thus, the political failure of Humayun's marriage to Hamida, which cost him Hindal's loyalty, stands in sharp contrast with Kamran's manoeuvres to 'consolidate his own power through marriage-alliances' – as now with Sindh.
40. *The Akbarnama of Abu'l Fazl*, vol. 1.
41. Ibid.
42. Ibid.
43. This time, with his son.
44. *The Akbarnama of Abu'l Fazl*, vol. 1.
45. Ibid.
46. Gulbadan Begum, *The History of Humayun*.
47. Only a few months after this meeting, Humayun received a letter from his young uncle Haider. Years ago, at their last meeting in panic-stricken Lahore, Haider had suggested conquering Kashmir. He had followed through on his plan, marching into the mountains with 4000 men; and would rule Kashmir for over a decade. Now,

he wrote to remind Humayun that he had a whole empire to recuperate in Hindustan; Humayun agreed in principle and did nothing about it. Moreover, only months after sending a polite, non-committal reply to Haider, Humayun wrote off letters of his own – to Kamran, Askari, Hindal and Sulaiman – reminding them of their plans for Balkh and inviting them to join his army. Hindustan, it seems, was off the agenda.

48. *The Akbarnama of Abu'l Fazl*, vol. 1.

49. Ibid.

50. Humayun's love and concern for his son pervades the chronicles. During his siege of Qandahar, for example, the padishah had asked for Akbar's auspicious horoscope as a way of comforting his fears for his son's future. Hamida was equally protective. When Akbar was six years old, he had a toothache that Humayun's eldest wife, Haji Begum, proposed to treat with a new paste. Hamida tried to smuggle Akbar away. She was 'in an agony lest [Haji Begum] should give me the medicine' Akbar remembered, but was unable to refuse the senior queen. Akbar, meanwhile, 'would not leave' Haji Begum's side. Luckily for the frantic Hamida, Haji Begum understood her fears; she ate some of the paste herself before rubbing it on Akbar's tooth. See *The Akbarnama of Abu'l Fazl*, vol. 3.

51. He was sent to Mecca, a euphemism for exile at the time, and died en route, sometime between October 1557 and October 1558.

52. *The Akbarnama of Abu'l Fazl*, vol. 1.

53. Young Akbar was given to borrowing headgear, it seems. He credits himself with inventing the *kornish* – a bow in which one hand touches the lowered head, as if offering it in tribute – telling the story of how he was wearing a hat of Humayun's while bowing to his father. Akbar had to hold on to the oversized hat as he bent down, and so the salute came about. See Abul Fazl, *The Ain-i-Akbari*, vol. 1, trans. H. Blochmann (first published 1927; Low Price Publications, 2014).

54. *The Akbarnama of Abu'l Fazl*, vol. 1.

55. Though Abul Fazl insists that Humayun's letter was 'not at all of a censuring or cautioning character', the historian in him grapples with the devotee, and he manages to quote one line from the rebuke – a quotation by a thirteenth-century poet, Shaikh Nizami: 'Sit not idle, 'tis not the time for play/ 'Tis the time for arts and for work.'

56. Khan, *The Political Biography of a Mughal Noble*. The story was told by Bayazid.

57. *The Akbarnama of Abu'l Fazl*, vol. 1.

58. Vincent Smith writes that Akbar was originally named Badruddin ('the full moon of religion') because he was born on a full-moon night, 23 November, not 15 October as officially stated. The change of date would '[frustrate] the calculations of hostile astrologers'. See Vincent A. Smith, *Akbar the Great Mogul, 1542–1605* (Clarendon Press, 1917).

59. *The Akbarnama of Abu'l Fazl*, vol. 1.

60. The Gakkhars ruled over parts of what is now the province of Punjab in Pakistan.

61. Abul Fazl's aspersions may well have something to do with the fact that Sultan Adam lost both favour and his kingdom under Akbar's rule. Jouher remembers

it differently. According to him, the sultan came to pay homage, if rather late, but excused himself with the fact that he had a guest whom he could hardly leave unsupervised. 'You have done right,' Humayun replied, 'that was of more consequence'.

62. Jouher, *The Tezkereh al Vakiat.*

63. Gulbadan Begum, *The History of Humayun.*

64. When Ghulam Ali, a paymaster, tried to pull rank on Ali Dost, the latter replied that Ghulam Ali wouldn't give out a single coin without Humayun's explicit leave, so why should Ali Dost carry out such an irreversible act 'without a personal order from his Majesty? Perhaps tomorrow the King may say, "Why did you put out the eyes of my brother?" What answer could I give? Depend upon it', he concluded, 'I will not do it by *your* order.' See Jouher, *The Tezkereh al Vakiat.*

65. Humayun noticed his water bearer's unhappy mood and sent a man to ask why Jouher had returned to his tent (from Kamran's) without orders. Had he left his task unfinished? Jouher replied (waspishly?), '[T]he business I had been sent on was *quite completed.*' Humayun seems to have understood what his servant was feeling, perhaps he was a little abashed. He sent word back: there was no need for Jouher to return to Kamran's tent; let him, instead, 'get the water ready for me to bathe'. Ibid.

66. S. Roy, 'Humayun', in *The Mughul Empire,* ed. R. C. Majumdar (Bharatiya Vidya Bhavan, 1974).

67. *The Akbarnama of Abu'l Fazl,* vol. 1.

68. Sometimes Islam Shah.

69. Abul Fazl is quite clear on these two counts: that Humayun left on his conquest after he heard of Salim Shah's death, and that he marched out of Kabul in mid-November 1554. It is generally accepted that Salim Shah died on 22 November 1554.

70. Jouher, *The Tezkereh al Vakiat.*

71. *The Akbarnama of Abu'l Fazl,* vol. 1. Muazzam's treachery was discovered after the battle and he was arrested.

72. Roy, 'Humayun'.

73. The lines are by a fifteenth-century poet called Shaikh Azari.

74. This much-quoted witticism appears in Stanley Lane-Poole's *Mediaeval India under Mohammedan Rule, 712–1764* (T. Fisher Unwin, 1903).

CHAPTER 3

1. The Cleveland Museum of Art: https://www.clevelandart.org/art/2013.292.a

2. Abu'l Fazl, *The Akbarnama of Abu'l Fazl* (completed by Inayatullah), trans. Henry Beveridge, vol. 2 (first published 1902–1939; Low Price Publications, 2017).

3. Six years later, Akbar would kill a lioness, again with a sword, again single-handed.

4. As must any nobleman or noblewoman of the age. Babur's grandmother, for example, had an unwelcome male visitor stabbed to death and thrown out of the door, not batting an eyelid (Ira Mukhoty tells the story in *Daughters of the Sun: Empresses, Queens and Begums of the Mughal Empire* [Aleph, 2018]). It is a moot point whether

the world has grown more or less violent over the last 400 years. Would sixteenth-century soldiers, inured to blood, be horrified, nevertheless, by the sheer scale of the carnage that nuclear bombs inflict?

5. News of Humayun's fall had arrived a few days ago; Bairam had turned his army around immediately, abandoning the march to Mankot for Delhi. Only days later, another messenger arrived. It was too late; Humayun was dead.

6. Abdul Qadir Badauni, *Muntakhab-ut-Tawarikh* (Selections from Histories) vol. 2, trans. W. H. Lowe (first published 1884–98; Atlantic Publishers and Distributors, 1990).

7. The Mughal troops had taken over a local *eidgah*, a compound meant for prayer gatherings. Ibid.

8. *The Akbarnama of Abu'l Fazl*, vol. 2.

9. That is, from the Prophet Muhammad himself.

10. *The Akbarnama of Abu'l Fazl*, vol. 1. 'Shah Abu'l-Ma'ali traced his descent from the sayyids of Termiz. His personal beauty made the good and right-thinking look for goodness of nature, and his forwardness was tolerated on account of his courage. Consequently he became a favourite with [Humayun].'

11. *The Akbarnama of Abu'l Fazl*, vol. 1. It is also possible that Abul Ma'ali instigated Humayun's trip to Qandahar by suggesting that Bairam was plotting against him. Nizamuddin writes that Humayun's chiefs tried to sow discord between Humayun and Bairam, so much so that Humayun ordered Munim Khan to take over Qandahar as governor. 'But Munim Khan remonstrated, and said that an expedition to Hindustan was resolved upon, and if the chief men were offended and alienated, disaffection would arise in the army. After the conquest of Hindustan that course might be pursued which the necessities of the time might require.' See Nizamuddin Ahmad, 'Tabakat-i Akbari', in *The History of India, As Told by Its Own Historians*, trans. H. M. Elliot, vol. 5 (Trübner and Co., 1873).

12. *The Akbarnama of Abu'l Fazl*, vol. 1.

13. Badauni, *Muntakhab-ut-Tawarikh*, trans. W. H. Lowe.

14. Ibid.

15. Harbans Mukhia, *The Mughals of India* (Blackwell Publishing, 2004; Indian reprint by Wiley India, 2018).

16. Abu'l Fazl, *The History of Akbar*, vol. 3, trans. W. M. Thackston (Murty Classical Library of India, Harvard University Press, 2017).

17. *The Akbarnama of Abu'l Fazl*, vol. 2.

18. Ibid.

19. Badauni, *Muntakhab-ut-Tawarikh*, trans. W. H. Lowe.

20. Muhammad Adil's real name was Mubariz Khan. His assumed title, which means 'just', did not sit well with his subjects, apparently, who preferred to call him 'Andhali, which means "blind"'. Ibid.

21. Vincent A. Smith, *Akbar the Great Mogul, 1542–1605* (Clarendon Press, 1917).

22. *The Akbarnama of Abu'l Fazl*, vol. 1. Abul Fazl would have resented the comparison between Adil and Akbar.

23. While Hemu was leading his army ever closer to Delhi, Sulaiman had arrived to besiege Munim Khan in Kabul. Short of both troops and provisions, Munim Khan

'and his few starving soldiers' made a great show of plenty when Sulaiman's envoy came to the city, to trick him into believing that Kabul was well prepared to wait out a long siege. See Iqtidar Alam Khan, *The Political Biography of a Mughal Noble: Mun'im Khan Khan-i Khanan, 1497–1575* (Orient Longman, 1973). Decades later, Jahangir describes one of his generals throwing elaborate banquets on the turrets of his fort to befuddle the besieging force below.

24. Badauni, *Muntakhab-ut-Tawarikh*, trans. W. H. Lowe.
25. Mahomed Kasim Ferishta, *History of the Rise of the Mahomedan Power in India till the Year A.D. 1612*, vol. 2, trans. John Briggs (R. Cambray & Co., 1909).
26. Badauni, *Muntakhab-ut-Tawarikh*, trans. W. H. Lowe.
27. *The Akbarnama of Abu'l Fazl*, vol. 2.
28. Ibid.
29. Ibid.
30. Abu'l Fazl, *The History of Akbar*, vol. 3, trans. W. M. Thackston.
31. *The Akbarnama of Abu'l Fazl*, vol. 2.
32. Ibid.
33. Nizamuddin Ahmad, 'Tabakat-i Akbari'.
34. Badauni, *Muntakhab-ut-Tawarikh*, trans. W. H. Lowe.
35. *The Akbarnama of Abu'l Fazl*, vol. 2.
36. Abu'l Fazl, *The History of Akbar*, vol. 3, trans. W. M. Thackston.
37. *The Akbarnama of Abu'l Fazl*, vol. 2.
38. Ibid.
39. For Abul Fazl, this second innings at Panipat occurred 'so that the conquest of Hindustan would take place all over again', this time under its rightful ruler, Akbar. But then, there are few setbacks in Mughal history that Abul Fazl won't describe as ordained for Akbar's greater glory; even the debilitating defeat at Kannauj was a merely 'unpleasant event' meant to 'ward off the evil eye' in anticipation of Akbar's birth. See Abu'l Fazl, *The History of Akbar*, vols 1 and 3, trans. W. M. Thackston.
40. Gunpowder is the popular explanation for Babur's victory, but it is disputed. Stephen Dale, for example, writes that Ibrahim Lodi's defeat was mostly the work of Babur's Mongol cavalry, mounted archers sent to 'outflank and envelop the enemy'. Thus, writes Dale, 'This was not primarily a gunpowder victory, for Babur himself reports that his new artillery pieces fired only a "few shots". Firearms may have contributed to his triumph by helping to defend his centre, but Mongol flanking attacks won the battle, as they had so many times before in Central Asia.' Stephen F. Dale, *The Muslim Empires of the Ottomans, Safavids, and Mughals* (Cambridge University Press, 2010).
41. *The Akbarnama of Abu'l Fazl*, vol. 2.
42. Harbans Mukhia, *The Mughals of India*.
43. As Hemu was wounded by accident, so he was arrested by chance. Nizamuddin writes that one Shah Kuli Khan saw Hawai wandering driverless, thought of taking the elephant, whom he did not recognize, and sent his mahout to mount it. 'The driver then perceived that there was a man lying wounded in the howda and upon examination this person proved to be Himun himself. Shah Kuli Khan, fully alive to the importance of his discovery, drove the elephant, along with several others which had been captured in the field, to the presence of the Emperor.'

44. *The Akbarnama of Abu'l Fazl*, vol. 2.

45. Akbar's eldest son, Salim, later Jahangir, relates this story in *The Jahangirnama: Memoirs of Jahangir, Emperor of India*, ed. and trans. W. M. Thackston (Oxford University Press with the Smithsonian Institution, 1999).

46. The fief was Tardi Beg's, in fact, and its loss may well have accounted for his desire to leave Hindustan after the fall of Delhi.

47. Badauni, *Muntakhab-ut-Tawarikh*, trans. W. H. Lowe.

48. *The Akbarnama of Abu'l Fazl*, vol. 2.

49. 'Bharmal [Bihari Mal] acted shrewdly at this juncture', as Afzal Husain writes in *The Nobility under Akbar and Jahangir: A Study of Family Groups* (Manohar Publishers, 1999).

50. *The Akbarnama of Abu'l Fazl*, vol. 2.

51. Azfar Moin, *The Millennial Sovereign: Sacred Kingship & Sainthood in Islam* (Columbia University Press, 2012).

52. Abu'l Fazl, *The History of Akbar*, vol. 3, trans. W. M. Thackston.

53. *The Akbarnama of Abu'l Fazl*, vol. 2.

54. Ibid.

55. Ibid.

56. Abu'l Fazl, *The History of Akbar*, vol. 3, trans. W. M. Thackston.

57. As Afzal Husain notes, Bayazid lists eleven members of Shamsuddin's family in Humayun's entourage when he came to India, but Abul Fazl doesn't mention even one. This might be because 'the Atakas as yet held minor positions among nobles and were more or less members of the personal staff of Prince Akbar' – Abul Fazl listed only high-ranking officers, while Bayazid noted 'even menial servants' (Husain, *The Nobility under Akbar and Jahangir*).

58. *The Akbarnama of Abu'l Fazl*, vol. 2.

59. Ali Quli and his brother Bahadur, along with their father Haider Sultan Shaibani, had joined Humayun during his Persian exile (Husain, *The Nobility under Akbar and Jahangir*). Their lineage was as exalted as the Chagatais': they were Shaibanid Uzbeks, claiming descent from Chenghiz Khan via Chagatai's elder brother Juchi.

60. Notes on 'The Grandees of the Empire' in Abu'l Fazl, *The Ain-i-Akbari*, vol. 1, trans. H. Blochmann (first published 1927; Low Price Publications, 2014).

61. 'Grief's my friend, blood's my drink, pain's my sweetmeat, my food's my heart', it goes on. Badauni, *Muntakhab-ut-Tawarikh*, trans. W. H. Lowe.

62. Ibid.

63. Babur, *The Baburnama: Memoirs of Babur, Prince and Emperor*, trans. W. M. Thackston (Modern Library, 2002).

64. *The Akbarnama of Abu'l Fazl*, vol. 2.

65. Badauni, *Muntakhab-ut-Tawarikh*, trans. W. H. Lowe.

66. *The Akbarnama of Abu'l Fazl*, vol. 2.

67. Badauni, *Muntakhab-ut-Tawarikh*, trans. W. H. Lowe.

68. The Walters Art Museum: https://art.thewalters.org/detail/32482

69. *The Akbarnama of Abu'l Fazl*, vol. 2.

70. Ibid.

71. Ali Anooshahr, 'The King Who Would Be Man: The Gender Roles of the Warrior King in Early Mughal History', *Journal of the Royal Asiatic Society*, vol. 18, no. 3, 2008.
72. *The Akbarnama of Abu'l Fazl*, vol. 2.
73. Badauni, *Muntakhab-ut-Tawarikh*, trans. W. H. Lowe.
74. Nizamuddin Ahmad, 'Tabakat-i Akbari'.
75. As Abul Fazl writes, 'The frown which for some time had been behind his brow came out, and he mediated something against [Pir-Muhammad].' See *The Akbarnama of Abu'l Fazl*, vol. 2.
76. Ibid.
77. Ibid.
78. Which would still tally, as Beveridge notes, with Abul Fazl's statement that Maham served Akbar 'from the cradle'. Note on 'Maham Anaga', *The Akbarnama of Abu'l Fazl*, vol. 1.
79. Notes on 'The Grandees of the Empire', in Abu'l Fazl, *The Ain-i-Akbari*, vol. 1.
80. Ibid.
81. Badauni, *Muntakhab-ut-Tawarikh*, trans. W. H. Lowe.
82. *The Akbarnama of Abu'l Fazl*, vol. 2.
83. Badauni, *Muntakhab-ut-Tawarikh*, trans. W. H. Lowe.
84. Badauni writes that Akbar moved against Bairam 'because he had not absolute power in his own kingdom, and sometimes had no voice in some of the transactions relating to expenses of the Exchequer, and because there was no privy purse at all, and the servants of the Emperor had but poor fiefs, and were kept in the depths of poverty, while the Khan Khanan's were in ease and luxury'.
85. Abu'l Fazl, *The History of Akbar*, vol. 3, trans. W. M. Thackston.
86. *The Akbarnama of Abu'l Fazl*, vol. 2.
87. Abu'l Fazl, *The History of Akbar*, vol. 3, trans. W. M. Thackston.
88. In fact, Abul Fazl never mentions Abul Qasim again, although Kamran's son would live on for many years, and with him would live his claim to the throne. If, after all, Humayun could claim Kabul, Abul Qasim could certainly claim Delhi. One day, Akbar would put a swift and secret end to this possibility; for the moment, however, it's unclear whether Akbar had thought about his cousin any more than Bairam had.
89. Badauni, *Muntakhab-ut-Tawarikh*, trans. W. H. Lowe.
90. *The Akbarnama of Abu'l Fazl*, vol. 2.
91. Badauni, *Muntakhab-ut-Tawarikh*, trans. W. H. Lowe.
92. Abu'l Fazl, *The History of Akbar*, vol. 3, trans. W. M. Thackston.
93. Annette Beveridge's introduction to Gulbadan Begum, *The History of Humayun (Humayun-nama)*, trans. Annette S. Beveridge (The Asiatic Society, 1902).
94. The promise of rewards is reported by Nizamuddin Ahmad.
95. *The Akbarnama of Abu'l Fazl*, vol. 2.
96. Ibid.
97. Reported variously by Abul Fazl, Badauni and Nizamuddin.
98. Badauni calls him a 'paragon of greatness', while Abul Fazl applauds the fact that 'From his lack of bigotry and his broadmindedness he was called in India a Shia

and in Persia a Sunni . . . the zealots of each sect used to censure him.' It is generally held, besides, that Abdul Latif's unorthodox theological positions were among the early influences that inspired Akbar's own future unorthodoxies.

99. *The Akbarnama of Abu'l Fazl*, vol. 2.

100. Ibid.

101. The quotations from Akbar's letter are from Abu'l Fazl, *The History of Akbar*, vol. 3, trans. W. M. Thackston.

102. *The Akbarnama of Abu'l Fazl*, vol. 2.

103. He is said to have found refuge in the small kingdom of Talwara, ruled by one Raja Ganesh.

104. *The Akbarnama of Abu'l Fazl*, vol. 2.

105. Badauni describes Ram Das as 'a second Miyan Tan Sen' and writes of how 'the beauty of his voice continually brought tears to [Bairam Khan's] eyes'. It may be that Akbar inherited some of his own love of music from his regent.

106. Badauni, *Muntakhab-ut-Tawarikh*, trans. W. H. Lowe.

107. *The Akbarnama of Abu'l Fazl*, vol. 2.

108. Ibid.

109. Ibid.

110. Ibid.

111. Ibid. These lands in Punjab were divided among Shamsuddin and his relatives.

112. Ibid.

113. Ibid.

CHAPTER 4

1. Victoria and Albert Museum: https://collections.vam.ac.uk/item/O9289/akbar -and-abdur-rahim- painting-anant

2. Abu'l Fazl, *The History of Akbar*, vol. 5, trans. W. M. Thackston (Murty Classical Library of India, Harvard University Press, 2019). The fact may have distressed the loyal historian, who makes at least one passing remark about 'the lack of wisdom that often afflicts unbalanced tall people' (*The History of Akbar*, vol. 2).

3. Fr. Antonio Monserrate, *The Commentary of Father Monserrate, S.J. on his Journey to the Court of Akbar*, trans. J. S. Hoyland, annotations S. N. Banerjee (Oxford University Press, 1922).

4. Baz Bahadur, 'the most accomplished man of his day in the science of music and in Hindi song', according to Nizamuddin, is said to have learnt music from Muhammad Adil, the Suri king who spotted Hemu's military talent, and also tutored the legendary Tansen. If that is true, the Afghan king left behind a remarkable cultural legacy, if no trace of his short-lived dynasty. See Nizamuddin Ahmad, 'Tabakat-i Akbari', in *The History of India, As Told by Its Own Historians*, trans. H.M. Elliot, vol. 5 (Trübner and Co., 1873), and Vincent A. Smith, *Akbar the Great Mogul, 1542–1605* (Clarendon Press, 1917).

5. Abu'l Fazl, *The Akbarnama of Abu'l Fazl* (completed by Inayatullah), vol. 2, trans. Henry Beveridge (first published 1902–1939; Low Price Publications, 2017).

6. Nizamuddin Ahmad, 'Tabakat-i Akbari'.

7. Michael H. Fisher, *A Short History of the Mughal Empire* (I.B. Tauris, 2016).

8. Abdul Qadir Badauni, *Muntakhab-ut-Tawarikh* (Selections from Histories), vol. 2, trans. W. H. Lowe (first published 1884–98; Atlantic Publishers and Distributors, 1990).

9. '[I]n accordance with the Indian custom' (*The Akbarnama of Abu'l Fazl*, vol. 2).

10. Ibid.

11. Iqtidar Alam Khan, *The Political Biography of a Mughal Noble: Mun'im Khan Khan-i Khanan, 1497–1575* (Orient Longman, 1973).

12. Ibid.

13. *The Akbarnama of Abu'l Fazl*, vol. 2.

14. Adham Khan had been meaning to besiege a fortress nearby, in Gagraun, for a while, and this seemed a good day for it. Little did he know that Akbar had managed a quick and bloodless conquest of Gagraun on his gallop down to Sarangpur.

15. *The Akbarnama of Abu'l Fazl*, vol. 2.

16. Ibid.

17. Ibid.

18. Abu'l Fazl, *The History of Akbar*, vol. 3, trans. W. M. Thackston.

19. Ibid.

20. *The Akbarnama of Abu'l Fazl*, vol. 2.

21. Ibid.

22. Abu'l Fazl, *The History of Akbar*, vol. 3, trans. W. M. Thackston.

23. *The Akbarnama of Abu'l Fazl*, vol. 2.

24. Ibid.

25. Victoria and Albert Museum: https://collections.vam.ac.uk/item/O9408/akbar-painting-basawan and https://collections.vam.ac.uk/item/O9403/akbar-painting-basawan.

26. *The Akbarnama of Abu'l Fazl*, vol. 2.

27. Ibid.

28. Ibid.

29. Afzal Husain, *The Nobility under Akbar and Jahangir: A Study of Family Groups* (Manohar Publishers, 1999).

30. Now Jaipur.

31. Nizamuddin Ahmad, 'Tabakat-i Akbari'.

32. *The Akbarnama of Abu'l Fazl*, vol. 2.

33. Norman P. Ziegler, 'Some Notes on Rajput Loyalties during the Mughal Period', in *The Mughal State: 1526–1750*, eds. Muzaffar Alam and Sanjay Subrahmanyam (Oxford University Press, 1998).

34. 'The Happy Sayings of His Majesty', in Abu'l Fazl, *The Ain-i-Akbari*, vol. 3, trans. Col. H. S. Jarrett (First published 1927; Low Price Publications, 2014).

35. Badauni, *Muntakhab-ut-Tawarikh*, trans. W. H. Lowe.

36. Husain, *The Nobility under Akbar and Jahangir*.

37. *The Akbarnama of Abu'l Fazl*, vol. 2. The description of the battle that follows is based on Abul Fazl's account.

38. There are too many Dalsingars in the *Akbarnama* to say for certain, but it is tempting to believe that this particular Dalsingar was the very animal that Akbar first drove as a boy, now taking him into his maiden battle.

39. The raja gave the padishah a drink of water, memorable enough to be chronicled in the *Akbarnama*.

40. The ambassador's father was the shah's uncle and vakil.

41. Victoria and Albert Museum: https://collections.vam.ac.uk/item/O9419/akbar -receives-the- iranian-ambassador-painting-lal

42. Rafi al-din's description is quoted in Harbans Mukhia, *The Mughals of India* (Blackwell Publishing, 2004; Indian reprint by Wiley India, 2018).

43. *The Akbarnama of Abu'l Fazl*, vol. 2.

44. Mukhia, *The Mughals of India*.

45. Bayazid cited by Henry Beveridge in *The Akbarnama of Abu'l Fazl*, vol. 2.

46. *The Akbarnama of Abu'l Fazl*, vol. 2.

47. Abu'l Fazl, *The History of Akbar*, vol. 3, trans. W. M. Thackston.

48. *The Akbarnama of Abu'l Fazl*, vol. 2.

49. Harbans Mukhia, commenting on Akbar's abuse of Adham Khan with a word 'picked up straight from the gutter' notes how, in his fury, Akbar spoke Hindustani. 'Clearly, Akbar's command of Persian did not quite match the intensity of the moment.'

50. A painting of the scene, Victoria and Albert Museum: https://collections.vam .ac.uk/item/O9740/ adham-khan-painting-miskin

51. Bayazid, quoted by Annette Beveridge in her introduction to Gulbadan Begum, *The History of Humayun (Humayun-nama)*, trans. Annette S. Beveridge (The Asiatic Society, 1902).

CHAPTER 5

1. Abdul Qadir Badauni, *Muntakhab-ut-Tawarikh (Selections from Histories)*, vol. 2, trans. W. H. Lowe (first published 1884–98; Atlantic Publishers and Distributors, 1990). Pir Muhammad was escaping Burhanpur, which he had recently sacked with his usual brutality. 'That city also he took by storm', writes Nizamuddin, 'and gave orders for a general massacre. Many of the learned men and saiyids of the place he caused to be decapitated in his presence.' This time, however, an alliance of local rulers – joined, as luck would have it, by Baz Bahadur – retaliated, forcing Pir Muhammad to flee. As he was wading across the Narmada with his commanders, they passed by a caravan of camels, one of whom 'came up and bit the horse upon which he was riding. He was thrown off into the water and drowned, thus receiving the recompense of his deeds.' See Nizamuddin Ahmad, 'Tabakat-i Akbari', in *The History of India, As Told by Its Own Historians*, trans. H. M. Elliot, vol. 5 (Trübner and Co., 1873).

2. Abu'l Fazl, *The Akbarnama of Abu'l Fazl* (completed by Inayatullah), vol. 1, trans. Henry Beveridge (First published 1902–1939; Low Price Publications, 2017).

3. Michael H. Fisher, *A Short History of the Mughal Empire* (I.B. Tauris, 2016).

4. Akbar wasn't just asking for a one-time tribute and deference from these men, he was trying to ensure a steady supply of funds to his treasury. Thus, Shamsuddin Ataka's appointment as vakil was accompanied by a cabinet reshuffle of sorts, in

which Itimad Khan, an accountant previously employed by Sher Shah Suri, began to work with Akbar's ataka on 'realising the state's share [of revenue from the fiefs] that had long been in default'. The nobility was not pleased, particularly not Maham's faction. This may well be one of the reasons why Adham murdered Shamsuddin. See Iqtidar Alam Khan, *The Political Biography of a Mughal Noble: Mun'im Khan Khan-i Khanan, 1497–1575* (Orient Longman, 1973).

5. Stephen F. Dale, *The Muslim Empires of the Ottomans, Safavids, and Mughals* (Cambridge University Press, 2010).

6. Ali Anooshahr, 'Mughals, Mongols, and Mongrels: The Challenge of Aristocracy and the Rise of the Mughal State in the *Tarikh-i Rashidi*', *Journal of Early Modern History*, vol. 18, 2014.

7. Babur, writes Michael H. Fisher, 'regarded most of his contemporary Mongols as uncultured and fierce but unreliable warriors, with a strong penchant for predatory looting of foe and friend'.

Humayun, meanwhile, seems to have held the aristocratic 'Moghul' in some contempt. Having returned to Hindustan, he rewarded the faithful Jouher with a fief and sent him off with this cautionary tale, saying, 'Young man, listen to this story as a piece of advice.' A Moghul having received an appointment' began his supposed duty by snatching a blanket from the shoulders of a citizen. Upon the man's remonstrating, he said, 'You scoundrel, don't you know that I have been sent by Government to collect?' Jouher's translator notes that 'The Moghuls are made the butts of numerous anecdotes.' See Jouher, *The Tezkereh al Vakiat, or Private Memoirs of Moghul Emperor Humayun by Jouher*, trans. Major Charles Stewart (Oriental Translation Fund, 1832).

8. Khan, *The Political Biography of a Mughal Noble.*

9. *The Akbarnama of Abu'l Fazl*, vol. 2.

10. Nizamuddin Ahmad, 'Tabakat-i Akbari'.

11. *The Akbarnama of Abu'l Fazl*, vol. 2.

12. In a painting of the scene, Akbar seems to have caught the arrow mid-flight, there is no hint of a wound on his clean, white clothes, while the sniper lies dead in the foreground, drenched in blood.

13. *The Akbarnama of Abu'l Fazl*, vol. 2.

14. Abu'l Fazl, *The History of Akbar*, vol. 3, trans. W. M. Thackston (Murty Classical Library of India, Harvard University Press, 2017).

15. *The Akbarnama of Abu'l Fazl*, vol. 2.

16. Afzal Husain, *The Nobility under Akbar and Jahangir: A Study of Family Groups* (Manohar Publishers, 1999).

17. *The Akbarnama of Abu'l Fazl*, vol. 2.

18. Ghazi Khan Tannuri was the second prisoner (along with Abul Ma'ali) that Bairam Khan released before his angry bid for Punjab. Years after the canny regent's defeat and death, his plans were still playing out.

19. *The Akbarnama of Abu'l Fazl*, vol. 2.

20. Ibid.

21. Abu'l Fazl, *The History of Akbar*, vol. 4, trans. W. M. Thackston.

22. The conquering king as lord, master and husband of the conquered land was a common metaphor of the times. Norman P. Ziegler notes how, in Rajput texts, 'The

kingdom itself was conceived of as the product of marriage between a ruler, who was both God and master (*thakur*) and husband (*dhani*), and the land (*dharti* – from Sanskrit *dharitri* – "a female bearer"), which was his wife.' The metaphor is complicated, naturally, if the ruler is a queen. See Norman P. Ziegler, 'Some Notes on Rajput Loyalties during the Mughal Period', in *The Mughal State: 1526–1750*, eds. Muzaffar Alam and Sanjay Subrahmanyam (Oxford University Press, 1998).

23. *The Akbarnama of Abu'l Fazl*, vol. 2. The account of the battle that follows is Abul Fazl's, unless I have indicated otherwise.

24. Shaikh Illahdad Faizi Sirhindi, 'Akbarnama', in *The History of India, As Told by Its Own Historians*, trans. H. M. Elliot, vol. 6 (Trübner and Co., 1875).

25. *The Akbarnama of Abu'l Fazl*, vol. 2.

26. The pots were filled with gold coins, possibly from the time of Alauddin Khilji. See *The Akbarnama of Abu'l Fazl*, vol. 2, and Mahomed Kasim Ferishta, *History of the Rise of the Mahomedan Power in India till the Year A.D. 1612*, vol. 2, trans. John Briggs (R. Cambray & Co., 1909).

27. *The Akbarnama of Abu'l Fazl*, vol. 2. The following descriptions of Akbar's time in the forest and his hunt for Abdullah the Uzbek are based on Abul Fazl's account.

28. Abu'l Fazl, *The History of Akbar*, vol. 4, trans. W. M. Thackston.

29. *The Akbarnama of Abu'l Fazl*, vol. 2.

30. Badauni, *Muntakhab-ut-Tawarikh*, trans. W. H. Lowe. Badauni also notes that, by the time of his writing some three decades later, 'of that city and edifice not a trace now is left'.

31. Rohtas, less than 300 kilometres south-east of Jaunpur, in Bihar, is among the many impregnable fortresses that fill the Indian landscape, towering tributes to the power and wealth once guarded by their thick walls and jutting turrets. Rohtas had the advantage, too, of encompassing fertile land and plenty of water – 'such an abundance', Badauni wrote, that 'if one drives a nail into the ground . . . water comes up'. Naturally, Akbar would have been happy to have it for his own.

32. *The Akbarnama of Abu'l Fazl*, vol. 2.

33. Husain, *The Nobility under Akbar and Jahangir*.

34. Khan, *The Political Biography of a Mughal Noble*.

35. According to Abul Fazl, Akbar preferred to offer the job to Ali Quli's brother, Bahadur, who was, in fact, appointed vakil for a brief and unspecified time.

36. To this end, having chased Abdullah the Uzbek out of Malwa, Akbar did not merely appoint a new governor to the region but also left behind a group of imperial overseers to watch over him. As Nizamuddin writes, 'an order was made directing a party of the Imperial followers who remained behind in Mandu to stay in that province along with Karra Bahadur [the new governor], and zealously serve His Majesty'.

37. *The Akbarnama of Abu'l Fazl*, vol. 2.

38. Worse, Abul Fazl writes that when Kamran was eventually exiled, he spoke to Humayun about his children, and that Humayun 'gladly promised to care for them'. Little did Kamran realize that it was his nephew who would decide his cousins' fate.

39. Ferishta, for example, writes that '[Kamran] left three daughters and one son, Abool Kasim Mirza, who, some time after his father's decease, was put to death by order of Akbur, in the fort of Gualiar'.

40. *The Akbarnama of Abu'l Fazl*, vol. 2.

41. Notes on 'The Grandees of the Empire' in Abu'l Fazl, *The Ain-i-Akbari*, vol. 1, trans. H. Blochmann (First published 1927; Low Price Publications, 2014).

42. Nizamuddin Ahmad, 'Tabakat-i Akbari'.

43. Akbar shrugged off their complaints. 'Every one of you has a Hindu to manage his private affairs', he said, according to Badauni. 'Suppose we too have a Hindu, why should harm come of it?'

44. With some tact, it must be said, Akbar renamed the office when he gave it to Muzaffar Khan. Of late, however, writes Iqtidar Alam Khan in his revealing biography of Munim Khan, the Khan-Khanan had been finding himself pushed out of the spotlight by 'exceptionally able men' who were also, for the most part, 'non-Turani upstarts' – that is, men who shared neither Munim's Central Asian ethnicity, nor his Chagatai lineage. Most galling of these promotions would have been that of the Khorasani Muzaffar Khan (Khan, *The Political Biography of a Mughal Noble*).

45. Bayazid, quoted in Khan, *The Political Biography of a Mughal Noble*.

46. *The Akbarnama of Abu'l Fazl*, vol. 2.

47. In fact, Ali Quli sent a woman called Agha Sarv-qad to open negotiations. Agha Sarv-qad was 'a one-time intimate friend' of Munim's, writes Iqtidar Alam Khan, and Ali Quli had tasked her with getting the Khan-Khanan to agree to talks and to spy on his troops. For all Munim Khan's recent demotions in court, he was an able and experienced soldier and strategist. In turn, therefore, Munim, 'cleverly using his friendship with the lady', discovered Ali Quli's own increasing desire to end hostilities thanks to growing 'demoralisation' among his supporters. See Khan, *The Political Biography of a Mughal Noble*.

48. *The Akbarnama of Abu'l Fazl*, vol. 2.

49. Ibid. Badauni declares this inevitable as the commander hailed from Mashhad, a city known for the arrogance of its people, and quotes a little verse in support of his claim: 'O men of Mashhad, with the exception of your Imam / May the curse of God rest on each one of you!' (The eighth Imam, Imam Reza, is buried here, and Mashhad is a venerated pilgrimage for Shias.)

50. Badauni, *Muntakhab-ut-Tawarikh*, trans. W. H. Lowe. Again, this owed a great deal to the fact that neither Muizzulmulk nor Todar Mal was Turani, unlike Munim Khan.

51. Ibid.

52. 'Khan-khanan [Munim Khan], with the assistance of Mir Abdul Latif, Mulla Abdulla Makhdum-ul Mulk, who was Shaikh-ul Islam of Hind, and Shaikh Abdu-n Nabi the Sadr, again made intercession for Khan-zaman [Ali Quli] and the Emperor, in his great kindness, once more pardoned his offences' (Nizamuddin Ahmad, 'Tabakat-i Akbari'). Two of these men, Makhdum-ul-Mulk and Abdun Nabi, would suffer the fate of the Uzbeks themselves, one day.

53. *The Akbarnama of Abu'l Fazl*, vol. 2.

54. Khan, *The Political Biography of a Mughal Noble*.

55. *The Akbarnama of Abu'l Fazl*, vol. 2.

56. Ibid.

57. Ibid.

58. Ibid.

59. Ibid.

60. Annette Beveridge proposes the marriage in her introduction to Gulbadan Begum, *The History of Humayun (Humayun-nama)*, trans. Annette S. Beveridge (The

Asiatic Society, 1902). Abul Fazl will not have it, however; he reports that the vakil, Haidar Qasim Kohbur, was no more than that.

61. The exchange of verses quoted by Badauni, *Muntakhab-ut-Tawarikh*, trans. W. H. Lowe.

62. Abu'l Fazl, *The History of Akbar*, vol. 4, trans. W. M. Thackston.

63. *The Akbarnama of Abu'l Fazl*, vol. 2.

64. Even after such proof of his villainy – and testament, perhaps, to the undeserved esteem a sayyid could command – Abul Ma'ali was given a prime burial spot near the tomb of Babur's sister and Akbar's loving aunt, Khanzada (and her would-be-king husband Mahdi Khwaja) no less. See *The Akbarnama of Abu'l Fazl*, vol. 2.

65. Ibid.

66. Ibid.

67. Ibid.

68. Badauni, *Muntakhab-ut-Tawarikh*, trans. W. H. Lowe: 'And they contrived a fiery ball with which one could play on a dark night.'

69. According to Nizamuddin, Sulaiman chased after Hakim, leaving the siege of Kabul to his daughters – no less formidable, it seems, than his queen.

70. Badauni, *Muntakhab-ut-Tawarikh*, trans. W. H. Lowe.

71. *The Akbarnama of Abu'l Fazl*, vol. 2.

72. Ibid.

73. The hunt was not the only sign of Akbar's concern at Hakim's attempt at Lahore, no matter how ineffective. Akbar spent time in the city and touring the region. He also ordered his nobility to travel across the province, undoing any damage that Kabuli soldiers may have done, and ensuring thereby that Hakim gained no popular support. See *The Akbarnama of Abu'l Fazl*, vol. 2.

74. Badauni, *Muntakhab-ut-Tawarikh*, trans. W. H. Lowe. 'Khushkhabar Khan is bad news, for never was there / In the world such an ugly fellow as he / He died in the water, although they say / And from the water all things live.'

75. *The Akbarnama of Abu'l Fazl*, vol. 1.

76. Ibid., vol. 2.

77. Nizamuddin Ahmad, 'Tabakat-i Akbari'.

78. *The Akbarnama of Abu'l Fazl*, vol. 2.

79. Abul Fazl will not say what these objections were, preferring to diagnose a broad spectrum of malaise, 'cowardice, laziness and opportunism', among Akbar's advisers.

80. *The Akbarnama of Abu'l Fazl*, vol. 2.

81. Ibid.

82. Munim Khan was not at the battle. He was left behind in charge of Agra, possibly because he was considered too close to the Uzbeks; also, possibly, because Akbar trusted his old ataliq to keep the capital calm during his absence.

83. Badauni, *Muntakhab-ut-Tawarikh*, trans. W. H. Lowe.

84. *The Akbarnama of Abu'l Fazl*, vol. 2.

85. Badauni, *Muntakhab-ut-Tawarikh*, trans. W. H. Lowe.

86. *The Akbarnama of Abu'l Fazl*, vol. 2.

87. Badauni, *Muntakhab-ut-Tawarikh*, trans. W. H. Lowe.

88. *The Akbarnama of Abu'l Fazl*, vol. 2.

CHAPTER 6

1. Abdul Qadir Badauni, *Muntakhab-ut-Tawarikh* (Selections from Histories), vol. 2, trans. W. H. Lowe (first published 1884–98; Atlantic Publishers and Distributors, 1990).

2. Nizamuddin Ahmad, 'Tabakat-i Akbari', in *The History of India, As Told by Its Own Historians*, trans. H. M. Elliot, vol. 5 (Trübner and Co., 1873).

3. Abu'l Fazl, *The Akbarnama of Abu'l Fazl* (completed by Inayatullah), vol. 2, trans. Henry Beveridge (First published 1902–1939; Low Price Publications, 2017). Badauni's version of events supports Nizamuddin's.

4. Col. G. B. Malleson, *Akbar and the Rise of the Mughal Empire* (Clarendon Press, 1908).

5. Badauni, *Muntakhab-ut-Tawarikh*, trans. W. H. Lowe.

6. *The Akbarnama of Abu'l Fazl*, vol. 2.

7. Ibid.

8. From July 1564, when Akbar set out against Abdullah the Uzbek in Malwa, to June 1567, when he defeated Ali Quli and Bahadur.

9. Akbar 'killed a thousand animals in sport', Nizamuddin reports.

10. Lt-Col. James Tod, *Annals and Antiquities of Rajasthan, or the Central and Western Rajput States of India*, vol. 1, ed. William Crooke (Oxford University Press, 1920). Other later historians have agreed, broadly, with this claim, though in less florid terms. Thus, for example, Michael H. Fisher writes: 'Historically . . . many martial immigrants (from elsewhere in South Asia or from Central Asia) claimed Rajput status after they had settled or conquered and became local landholders or rulers.' See Michael H. Fisher, *A Short History of the Mughal Empire* (I.B. Tauris, 2016).

11. William Crooke in his introduction to Tod, *Annals and Antiquities of Rajasthan*, vol. 1.

12. Richard M. Eaton, *India in the Persianate Age: 1000–1765* (Allen Lane, 2019). Eaton uses a fascinating episode from an early fifteenth-century Sanskrit poem, the *Hammira Mahakavya*, both to explain the 'crystallization' of Rajput identity as 'territorially based, closed clans . . . nurturing a warrior ethos' in the sixteenth century onwards, and to demonstrate how fluid this identity was previously. Thus, the *Hammira Mahakavya* describes a fourteenth-century soldier called Muhammad Shah ('Mahimasahi') 'transitioning from an ethnic Mongol, to an Indian Muslim, and finally to a kshatriya warrior'. Muhammad Shah comes to the Delhi Sultanate from Central Asia in the late thirteenth century; participates in a conquest of Gujarat in 1299; then rebels with fellow Mongols and finds refuge in Ranthambore, ruled by Hammira, last of the Chauhans. When the then sultan, Alauddin Khilji, besieges Ranthambore, Muhammad Shah kills his own family before going out into his final battle. He is found wounded by Khilji, who offers him his life, but Muhammad Shah refuses to submit. So he dies: the Mongol vowing allegiance to the Chauhan with his last breath.

13. *The Akbarnama of Abu'l Fazl*, vol. 3.

14. Possibly from Paramara rulers.

15. As Tod writes, 'The close of Bappa's career is the strangest part of the legend.' This is how it goes: 'Advanced in years, [Bappa Rawal] abandoned his children and his country, carried his arms west to Khorasan, and there established himself, and married new wives from among the "barbarians", by whom he had numerous offspring.' Thus, he battled and defeated 'all the kings of the west, as in Ispahan, Kandahar, Kashmir, Irak, Iran, Turan, and Kafiristan', married all their daughters 'by whom he had one hundred and thirty sons, called the Nausshahra Pathans'. When Bappa Rawal died, having lived a full hundred years, the legendary king was buried at the foot of the legendary Mount Meru.

16. Tod, *Annals and Antiquities of Rajasthan*, vol. 1.
17. *The Akbarnama of Abu'l Fazl*, vol. 2.
18. Maulana Ahmad and others, 'Tarikh-i Alfi', in *The History of India, As Told by Its Own Historians*, trans. H. M. Elliot, vol. 5 (Trübner and Co., 1873).
19. *The Akbarnama of Abu'l Fazl*, vol. 2.
20. Maulana Ahmad and others, 'Tarikh-i Alfi'.
21. *The Akbarnama of Abu'l Fazl*, vol. 2.
22. Cynthia Talbot, 'Justifying Defeat: A Rajput Perspective on the Age of Akbar', *Journal of the Economic and Social History of the Orient*, vol. 55, 2012.
23. Maulana Ahmad and others, 'Tarikh-i Alfi'.
24. Ibid.
25. *The Akbarnama of Abu'l Fazl*, vol. 2.
26. Ibid.
27. Badauni, *Muntakhab-ut-Tawarikh*, trans. W. H. Lowe.
28. Scenes from Chittorgarh, Chester Beatty: https://viewer.cbl.ie/viewer/image/In _03_134/1/ LOG_0000
29. Maulana Ahmad and others, 'Tarikh-i Alfi'.
30. Abu'l Fazl, *The History of Akbar*, vol. 4, trans. W. M. Thackston (Murty Classical Library of India, Harvard University Press, 2018).
31. *The Akbarnama of Abu'l Fazl*, vol. 2.
32. 'The devoted men . . . were admiring the skill and rare failure of one of the musketeers of the fort who had injured many of the ghazis.' See *The Akbarnama of Abu'l Fazl*, vol. 2.
33. Ibid.
34. Ibid.
35. Nizamuddin Ahmad, 'Tabakat-i Akbari'.
36. Badauni, *Muntakhab-ut-Tawarikh*, trans. W. H. Lowe.
37. Many years later, Abul Fazl would describe Sangram as 'the first of his Majesty's private guns'; Akbar killed 1019 animals with it. See Abu'l Fazl, *The Ain-i-Akbari*, vol. 1, trans. H. Blochmann (First published 1927; Low Price Publications, 2014).
38. *The Akbarnama of Abu'l Fazl*, vol. 2.
39. Ibid.
40. Ibid.
41. Maulana Ahmad and others, 'Tarikh-i Alfi'.
42. *The Akbarnama of Abu'l Fazl*, vol. 2.

43. Iqtidar Alam Khan, 'The Nobility under Akbar and the Development of His Religious Policy, 1560–80', *Journal of the Royal Asiatic Society of Great Britain and Ireland*, no. 1/2, April 1968.

44. Iqtidar Alam Khan, *The Political Biography of a Mughal Noble: Mun'im Khan Khan-i Khanan, 1497–1575* (Orient Longman, 1973). For more on these 'upstarts', see footnote 44 in Chapter 5.

45. 'When Babur arrived' in Hindustan, writes Michael H. Fisher, 'a substantial minority of people living in South Asia were Muslims: some were immigrants and their descendants, but most were converts . . . Some prominent converts later claimed biological descent from the Prophet Muhammad or another revered Arab, boasting honorifics like Sayyid or Shaikh, despite their Indic biological ancestry.' These would be the 'Shaikhzadas' – literally 'sons of Shaikhs'. 'Indian Muslims' also comprised 'settled Indo-Afghans'. See Fisher, *A Short History of the Mughal Empire*.

46. Khan, 'The Nobility under Akbar and the Development of His Religious Policy, 1560–80'.

47. Ibid.

48. The briefly rebellious and increasingly reliable Asaf Khan was left to govern Chittorgarh.

49. 'When we reflect what he did, the age in which he did it, the method he introduced to accomplish it', writes Col. G. B. Malleson, 'we are bound to recognise in Akbar one of those illustrious men whom Providence sends, in the hour of a nation's trouble, to reconduct it into those paths of peace and toleration which alone can assure the happiness of millions'. See Malleson, *Akbar and the Rise of the Mughal Empire*. Meanwhile, Vincent A. Smith has this to say: 'Akbar regarded the assertion of independence by any ruling prince within the reach of his arm as a personal affront to be expiated by ruthless conquest.' See Vincent A. Smith, *Akbar the Great Mogul, 1542–1605* (Clarendon Press, 1917).

50. 'The Happy Sayings of His Majesty', in Abu'l Fazl, *The Ain-i-Akbari*, vol. 3, trans. Col. H. S. Jarrett (First published 1927; Low Price Publications, 2014).

51. *The Akbarnama of Abu'l Fazl*, vol. 2.

52. See Talbot, 'Justifying Defeat: A Rajput Perspective on the Age of Akbar'.

53. Ibid.

54. Lt-Col. James Tod, *Annals and Antiquities of Rajasthan, or the Central and Western Rajput States of India*, vol. 2 (Higginbotham & Co., 1880).

55. Norman P. Ziegler, 'Some Notes on Rajput Loyalties during the Mughal Period', in *The Mughal State: 1526–1750*, eds. Muzaffar Alam and Sanjay Subrahmanyam (Oxford University Press, 1998). It is from this 'chakar', presumably, that we get the commonly used Hindustani term, *naukar-chakar*.

56. *The Akbarnama of Abu'l Fazl*, vol. 2.

57. It was around this time, too, that Baz Bahadur – a decade after he lost his kingdom and his beloved Rupmati to Adham Khan and Pir Muhammad's unsparing attack, having spent long years seeking shelter and alliances, once even with the Rana of Mewar – decided there was nothing for it but to join Akbar's court.

58. Rajasthan, as Norman P. Ziegler describes it, was not a rich land of itself, being 'a relatively isolated frontier region of marginal agricultural importance'. It

was, however, 'a strategic transitional zone situated between larger cultural centres in Gujarat and on the north Indian plain, criss-crossed by trade routes running between these larger centres'.

59. *The Akbarnama of Abu'l Fazl*, vol. 1.

CHAPTER 7

1. Abu'l Fazl, *The Akbarnama of Abu'l Fazl* (completed by Inayatullah), vol. 2, trans. Henry Beveridge (First published 1902–1939; Low Price Publications, 2017).

2. Nizamuddin Ahmad, 'Tabakat-i Akbari', in *The History of India, As Told by Its Own Historians*, trans. H. M. Elliot, vol. 5 (Trübner and Co., 1873).

3. Fr. Antonio Monserrate, *The Commentary of Father Monserrate, S.J. on His Journey to the Court of Akbar*, trans. J. S. Hoyland, annotations S. N. Banerjee (Oxford University Press, 1922).

4. 'The pious King, who used not to make any other requests to God, became a wisher for this great boon.' See *The Akbarnama of Abu'l Fazl*, vol. 2.

5. Monserrate, *The Commentary of Father Monserrate*.

6. Chester Beatty / Wikimedia Commons: https://commons.wikimedia.org/wiki /File:Balchand._ Akbar_inspecting_construction_for_his_new_capital_Fatehpur_S ikri,_Akbarnama,_1603-5,_ Chester_Beatty_Library.jpg

7. *The Akbarnama of Abu'l Fazl*, vol. 2.

8. Abdul Qadir Badauni, *Muntakhab-ut-Tawarikh* (Selections from Histories), vol. 2, trans. W. H. Lowe (first published 1884–98; Atlantic Publishers and Distributors, 1990).

9. Nor was it Muzaffar Khan's love for 'a young man', thwarted by Akbar two years earlier. At the time, the accountant had declared himself a dervish, renouncing the world to tend to his broken heart, but he returned, evidently, and there seem to have been no hard feelings on either side. The beloved's fate is unrecorded. See *The Akbarnama of Abu'l Fazl*, vol. 2.

10. *The Akbarnama of Abu'l Fazl*, vol. 2.

11. Abu'l Fazl, *The Ain-i-Akbari*, vol. 1, trans. H. Blochmann (First published 1927; Low Price Publications, 2014). The historian adds that if any player 'lost his patience and got restless, he had to drink a cup of wine'.

12. *The Akbarnama of Abu'l Fazl*, vol. 2.

13. Ibid.

14. Itimad Khan had been making overtures to Akbar for a while, it seems. When the padishah was besieging Chittorgarh, he received a gift from the Gujarati khan: a 'sea-elephant' – presumably from Africa – 'which had exceedingly long ears' (*The Akbarnama of Abu'l Fazl*, vol. 2).

15. *The Akbarnama of Abu'l Fazl*, vol. 3.

16. Editor's note in Shaikh Illahdad Faizi Sirhindi, 'Akbarnama', in *The History of India, As Told by Its Own Historians*, trans. H. M. Elliot, vol. 6 (Trübner and Co., 1875).

17. Stephen F. Dale, *The Muslim Empires of the Ottomans, Safavids, and Mughals* (Cambridge University Press, 2010).

18. Shaikh Illahdad Faizi Sirhindi, 'Akbarnama'.

19. See Afzal Husain, *The Nobility under Akbar and Jahangir: A Study of Family Groups* (Manohar Publishers, 1999).

20. Victoria and Albert Museum: https://collections.vam.ac.uk/item/O9594/akbar -painting-mahesh

21. Badauni, *Muntakhab-ut-Tawarikh*, trans. W. H. Lowe.

22. Ibid.

23. *The Akbarnama of Abu'l Fazl*, vol. 3.

24. Ibid.

25. Ibid. In an earlier edition, I had assumed that these thorny plants were cacti. I am grateful to Pradip Krishen for pointing out to me that all cacti are, in fact, native to the Americas, and that it was virtually impossible for these to have been transplanted and growing wild in sixteenth-century Gujarat. The thorny plants that obstructed Akbar's way were Euphorbias (*Euphorbia caducifolia*), indigenous to this region. Henry Beveridge and W.H. Lowe, translators of the *Akbarnama* and Badauni's history respectively, are careful to note the distinction. The Persian word for the plant was *zaqqum* and Beveridge translates it as 'thorn bushes', with a note to identify it as 'euphoria antiquorum'. Lowe (who translates it incorrectly as 'prickly pear' but also identifies it as 'euphorbia of the ancients') notes that 'al-zaqqum' is 'a tree said in the Quran to grow in the midst of Hell.'

26. Badauni, *Muntakhab-ut-Tawarikh*, trans. W. H. Lowe.

27. Nizamuddin Ahmad, 'Tabakat-i Akbari'.

28. *The Akbarnama of Abu'l Fazl*, vol. 3. Evidently, Ibrahim's fellow Mirzas annoyed him with their harsh appraisal of his performance against Akbar: 'a discussion arose among the brothers about Ibrahim's defeat at Sarnal. From criticism they came to violent language, and from that to a quarrel. Ibrahim Husain [Mirza], who was skilful as a swordsman and distinguished for his want of sense, was displeased with his brothers and separated from them, and foolishly resolved to make an attack on the capital. His haughty brothers, from their evil destiny, were glad of the departure of such a brother and did not try to appease him.'

29. Monserrate, *The Commentary of Father Monserrate*. Such was the wealth and renown of the ports of Gujarat that Ralph Fitch, an early English traveller to Akbar's court, came bearing a letter from Queen Elizabeth addressed to the 'King of Cambay'. See William Foster, ed., *Early Travels in India: 1583–1619* (Low Price Publications, 1921).

30. *The Akbarnama of Abu'l Fazl*, vol. 3.

31. Ibid.

32. Could it be that Gulrukh gave her daughter to Baglana in a bargain of her own? She would have trusted Akbar not to harm the girl; and the boy, her son, might yet grow up to stake a claim in his grandfather Kamran's name.

33. *The Akbarnama of Abu'l Fazl*, vol. 3; the commander was Saif Khan, elder brother of one of Akbar's milk brothers, Zain Koka.

34. Jahangir, *The Jahangirnama: Memoirs of Jahangir, Emperor of India*, ed. and trans. W. M. Thackston (Oxford University Press with the Smithsonian Institution, 1999).

35. Abu'l Fazl, *The History of Akbar*, vol. 5, trans. W. M. Thackston (Murty Classical Library of India, Harvard University Press, 2019).
36. Ibid.
37. *The Akbarnama of Abu'l Fazl*, vol. 3.
38. Chester Beatty / Wikimedia Commons: https://commons.wikimedia.org/wiki/File:Akbar_Fights_with_Raja_Man_Singh.jpg
39. *The Akbarnama of Abu'l Fazl*, vol. 3.
40. Badauni, *Muntakhab-ut-Tawarikh*, trans. W. H. Lowe.
41. Abu'l Fazl, *The History of Akbar*, vol. 5, trans. W. M. Thackston.
42. Victoria and Albert Museum: https://collections.vam.ac.uk/item/O9429/husain-quli-and-akbar- painting-basawan
43. The other, a nonentity called Shah Mirza, was part of this alliance but plays no real role in the events that follow.
44. *The Akbarnama of Abu'l Fazl*, vol. 3.
45. Nizamuddin describes him riding in a cart, one night, being massaged to soothe the pain; for most of the journey, day and night, Akbar was in his saddle.
46. *The Akbarnama of Abu'l Fazl*, vol. 3. Akbar was not angry because they were lost but because his men had tried to dodge his orders. Akbar had wanted the imperial escort to take them via Sirohi. Only recently, however, a Mughal general – Mir Muhammad Khan, Aziz's uncle – was grievously injured by the Rajputs of Sirohi, one of whom stabbed him near his collarbone as Mir Muhammad offered them *paan*, betel leaves, in friendly farewell. Akbar had reacted to Sirohi's resistance with punitive missions, and the area was quiet now. Still, his companions did not think it wise to risk a journey through it in such small numbers. They persuaded the escort to pretend he was going via Sirohi, while taking another route. The escort obliged, promptly lost his way and gave the whole game away.
47. *The Akbarnama of Abu'l Fazl*, vol. 3.
48. Ibid.
49. Badauni, *Muntakhab-ut-Tawarikh*, trans. W. H. Lowe.
50. The Abyssinians had long been a force in the region. These particular troops were led by the son of a chief called Wali Khan, accused of murdering Chenghis Khan, the Gujarati king whose demise had spurred Akbar's conquest of this land. Chenghis Khan's mother had come to Akbar demanding justice for her son, and Akbar had had Wali Khan executed. His son, then, had both a personal and a political grudge against the padishah.
51. *The Akbarnama of Abu'l Fazl*, vol. 3.
52. Abu'l Fazl, *The History of Akbar*, vol. 5, trans. W. M. Thackston.
53. Ibid.
54. Ibid.
55. *The Akbarnama of Abu'l Fazl*, vol. 3.
56. Ibid.
57. Nizamuddin Ahmad, 'Tabakat-i Akbari'.
58. Ibid.
59. *The Akbarnama of Abu'l Fazl*, vol. 3.
60. Badauni, *Muntakhab-ut-Tawarikh*, trans. W. H. Lowe.
61. *The Akbarnama of Abu'l Fazl*, vol. 3.

CHAPTER 8

1. Abdul Qadir Badauni, *Muntakhab-ut-Tawarikh* (Selections from Histories), vol. 2, trans. W. H. Lowe (first published 1884–98; Atlantic Publishers and Distributors, 1990). This particular phrase, however, is translated by H. M. Elliot in the extracts of Badauni's work published in *The History of India, As Told by Its Own Historians*, vol. 5 (Trübner and Co., 1873).

Badauni's secret history was published after the emperor's demise, naturally, and promptly banned by his successor, thus becoming an instant hit. See Azfar Moin, *The Millennial Sovereign: Sacred Kingship & Sainthood in Islam* (Columbia University Press, 2012).

2. Abu'l Fazl, *The Akbarnama of Abu'l Fazl* (completed by Inayatullah), vol. 1, trans. Henry Beveridge (First published 1902–1939; Low Price Publications, 2017).

3. Nizamuddin Ahmad, 'Tabakat-i Akbari', in *The History of India, As Told by Its Own Historians*, trans. H. M. Elliot, vol. 5 (Trübner and Co., 1873).

4. His battle cry was 'Either martyrdom or victory', because, as he explained to anyone who asked why he wouldn't put victory first, Husain Khan would rather 'see the glorious departed, than the lords who remain alive'. See Badauni, *Muntakhab-ut-Tawarikh*, trans. W. H. Lowe.

5. Husain Quli tried to mollify the disappointed warrior by showing him around the battlefield, telling him all the stories, and letting him chase after Mirza Ibrahim. It may be that Husain Quli was feeling a bit guilty. Husain Khan had written to him before he arrived, asking him to delay the battle by a day: '. . . if you would let me be a participator in this victory, and postpone the battle one day, it would be only friendly'. Husain Quli had replied with a friendly enough yes but ignored the request.

6. Badauni, *Muntakhab-ut-Tawarikh*, trans. W. H. Lowe.

7. P. P. Sinha, *Raja Birbal: Life and Times* (Janaki Prakashan, 1980).

8. Akbar described Birbar thus in a letter to another of his favourites, Abdur Rahim. See Sinha, *Raja Birbal*.

9. Now better known as Kangra.

10. Harbans Mukhia, citing S. R. Sharma's record of a local tradition, writes that Akbar sent a golden umbrella for the temple's deity as a way to 'make amends' for the bloody siege. See Harbans Mukhia, *The Mughals of India* (Blackwell Publishing, 2004; Indian reprint by Wiley India, 2018). The *Akbarnama*, too, records that Akbar wanted to visit the Nagarkot temple in the twenty-sixth year of his reign, 1581–82, a decade or so after the battle at the shrine. The road was difficult but no one dared dissuade the emperor until Akbar himself had a dream telling him to return. At this, writes Abul Fazl, 'A great delight took possession of everyone'. See *The Akbarnama of Abu'l Fazl*, vol. 3.

11. Such ideas of a second (and final) coming were common across religions and the globe. Christopher Columbus's search for a new route to India, by which he stumbled upon the Americas, derived some of its urgency from the belief in an imminent return of the messiah. As Reginald Stackhouse explains it, Columbus's sponsors, the Spanish royalty, hoped that the 'fabled wealth of the East would give them up front financing against the infidel – and prepare for Christ's coming at Jerusalem'.

Columbus himself hoped that a shortcut to the east would allow Christian missionaries to get there faster and thus 'meet the provision for world evangelization before the Lord could return' (Reginald Stackhouse, 'Columbus's Millennial Voyage', *Christian History*, no. 61, 1999).

12. Specifically in the court of Sher Shah Suri's son and successor, Salim Shah.

13. Heinrich Blochmann in his introduction to Abu' l Fazl, *The Ain-i-Akbari*, vol. 1, trans. H. Blochmann (First published 1927; Low Price Publications, 2014). Outspoken and intelligent, Shaikh Ala'i 'charmed' Salim (or Islam) Shah, Sher Shah's son and successor, along with many of his courtiers, including Shaikh Mubarak. 'It is not clear', writes Blochmann, whether Abul Fazl's father 'joined the sect from religious or from political motives' – the latter would have been to 'break up the party of the learned at the Court, at whose head Makhdum-ul-Mulk stood'. The court clerics would not take such a challenge lying down, of course. Makhdum-ul-Mulk persuaded Salim Shah to banish Shaikh Ala'i.

Soon, however, the shah reversed his decision and recalled the shaikh, asking him only to whisper that he had recanted his Mahdawi beliefs. The shaikh refused and Salim Shah had no choice but to order him to be whipped. The punishment was not intended to be lethal, but it killed the shaikh. Immediately, a great cyclone hit Salim Shah's camp; afterwards, Shaikh Ala'i's body was found buried in flowers. Such a clear sign of divine blessing did little, presumably, to discourage the Mahdawis, nor to bolster the court clergy's popularity. As Blochmann writes, 'Makhdum-ul-Mulk was never popular after that'.

14. Blochmann's introduction to Abu'l Fazl, *The Ain-i-Akbari*, vol. 1.

15. Ibid.

16. H. M. Elliot's translation in *The History of India, As Told by Its Own Historians*, vol. 5. W. H. Lowe's translation (which is what I quote unless otherwise indicated) is more sympathetic; in it, Badauni seems to be saying that the cleric's books were precious to him like 'ingots' – not bricks – of gold. There is nothing ambiguous, however, about Badauni's disgruntlement with the court clergy.

17. Blochmann's introduction to Abu'l Fazl, *The Ain-i-Akbari*, vol. 1. A 'number of Turks came and surrounded our abode', Abul Fazl would write, years later, in the *Akbarnama*, remembering the moment with vestigial anxiety, perhaps.

18. And defence, then as now, had one of the biggest claims on government resources. Gunpowder was expensive. So were horses, which had to be imported and were 'constantly needing replacement due to uncongenial equine conditions' in South Asia. See Michael H. Fisher, *A Short History of the Mughal Empire* (I.B. Tauris, 2016).

19. Jouher, *The Tezkereh al Vakiat, or Private Memoirs of Moghul Emperor Humayun by Jouher*, trans. Major Charles Stewart (Oriental Translation Fund, 1832). The annals suggest that one of the essential features of armies at this time, big or small, was a body of accountants. Thus, the handful of men who accompanied Humayun on his Persian exile included no less than three accountants (plus an assorted muster of men including a librarian, bartender, keepers of bedding and the strongbox, and Jouher the ewer-bearer, of course).

20. As Michael H. Fisher explains it, when Babur arrived in Hindustan, only about four decades earlier, 'the land itself had limited economic value' because there was

so much of it that was 'potentially arable' but uncultivated. 'Control over people', therefore, 'was more valuable than control over land' – exploitative governments or zamindars would only force farmers to leave and settle elsewhere. See Fisher, *A Short History of the Mughal Empire*.
21. Ibid.
22. Ali Anooshahr, 'Mughals, Mongols, and Mongrels: The Challenge of Aristocracy and the Rise of the Mughal State in the *Tarikh-i Rashidi*', *Journal of Early Modern History*, vol. 18, 2014.
23. *The Akbarnama of Abu'l Fazl*, vol. 3.
24. Ibid.
25. Nizamuddin Ahmad, 'Tabakat-i Akbari'.
26. Or listening to a 'beautiful voice' read out tales of 'spiritual love' that often made Akbar cry, writes Abul Fazl, as the stars rose above and water lapped against the boat's sides.
27. Nizamuddin Ahmad, 'Tabakat-i Akbari'.
28. 'On that dreadful night', writes Nizamuddin, 'a foretaste of the day of judgment, the inhabitants [of Patna] were in a state of bewilderment and despair. Some endeavoured to escape by the river, but through the crowding and struggling many of them were drowned. Others endeavoured to fly by land, but were crushed under the feet of elephants and horses in the narrow lanes and streets.'
29. Munim Khan was 'already about eighty' at this time. See Iqtidar Alam Khan, *The Political Biography of a Mughal Noble: Mun'im Khan Khan-i Khanan, 1497–1575* (Orient Longman, 1973).

CHAPTER 9

1. Michael H. Fisher describes the 'lengthy and contested process' of turning *iqta* land, that is, fiefs, into *jagirs*: 'In order to gain more direct data about actual yields, around 1575, the central administration resumed most such [iqta] grants, with the former grantee receiving in lieu a cash salary from the imperial treasury. Many former grant holders objected, particularly those whose incomes actually exceeded their official grant. About five years later, after the central administration had secured more accurate agricultural productivity figures . . . it reissued most of the reassessed revenue assignments as jagirs – the term henceforth widely used for the temporary assignment of land revenue and other taxes from a designated territory. Jagirdars ("jagirholders") then collected these revenues or parceled them out among their followers.' See Michael H. Fisher, *A Short History of the Mughal Empire* (I.B. Tauris, 2016).
2. Ali Anooshahr, 'The King Who Would Be Man: The Gender Roles of the Warrior King in Early Mughal History', *Journal of the Royal Asiatic Society*, vol. 18, no. 3, 2008.
3. Abu'l Fazl, *The Akbarnama of Abu'l Fazl* (completed by Inayatullah), vol. 2, trans. Henry Beveridge (First published 1902–1939; Low Price Publications, 2017).
4. Abdul Qadir Badauni, *Muntakhab-ut-Tawarikh* (Selections from Histories), vol. 2, trans. W. H. Lowe (first published 1884–98; Atlantic Publishers and Distributors, 1990).

5. It was his brother, Faizi, who took him home eventually. Abu'l Fazl, *The History of Akbar*, vol. 5, trans. W. M. Thackston (Murty Classical Library of India, Harvard University Press, 2019).

6. Nawab Samsam-ud-Daula Shah Nawaz Khan and his son Abdul Hayy, *The Maathir-ul-Umara: Biographies of the Muhammadan and Hindu Officers of the Timurid Sovereigns of India from 1500 to about 1780 AD*, trans. Henry Beveridge, revision, annotation and completion Baini Prashad, vols 1 and 2 (The Asiatic Society, 1941, 1952).

7. Except his trousers, which were burnt, being too intimate, perhaps, to be handed down.

8. The phrases quoted in this sentence are from H. M. Elliot's translation of extracts from Badauni's work published in *The History of India, As Told by Its Own Historians*, vol. 5 (Trübner and Co., 1873).

9. R. C. Majumdar, 'Preface', in *The Mughul Empire*, ed. R. C. Majumdar (Bharatiya Vidya Bhavan, 1974).

10. 'The Happy Sayings of His Majesty', in Abu'l Fazl, *The Ain-i-Akbari*, vol. 3, trans. Col. H. S. Jarrett (First published 1927; Low Price Publications, 2014).

11. Guru Arjan Dev completed the Adi Granth in 1604. This was the first edition of what would become the Guru Granth Sahib, the holy book of the Sikh religion.

12. B. B. Majumdar, 'Hindu Religion', in *The Mughul Empire*, ed. R. C. Majumdar (Bharatiya Vidya Bhavan, 1974).

13. Editors' introduction to Fr. Antonio Monserrate, *The Commentary of Father Monserrate, S.J. on His Journey to the Court of Akbar*, trans. J. S. Hoyland, annotations S. N. Banerjee (Oxford University Press, 1922).

14. Banarasidas, *Ardhakathanak (A Half Story)*, trans. Rohini Chowdhury (Penguin Books, 2009).

15. The free movement of people across Hindustan is another aspect of life at this time that Banarasi's autobiography reveals. The poet's father, for example, was born in Narwar, raised in Jaunpur, got his first job in Bengal, his second in Agra, and was married in Meerut – all by the age of eighteen or so. Banarasi travelled fairly extensively, too. As a young man, he went from Jaunpur to Agra, hoping to start his own jewellery business. The poet had little talent for trade, however. He lost most of the jewels he'd taken with him, 'Tied into his underpants': the pearls tucked along with the drawstring of his pyjama rolled away, mice ran off with his rubies. Banarasi was soon bankrupt, sitting at home reading his poems to a small group of men, one of whom was a *kachauriwalla* who gave Banarasi a seer of *kachauris*, fried bread with a filling, on credit. 'He told no one of his situation / But lived on the kachauris he bought on credit.' See Banarasidas, *Ardhakathanak*.

16. The story of the brahmin and the qazi is told in H. M. Elliot's translation of Badauni in *The History of India, As Told by Its Own Historians*, vol. 5.

17. The description of Abdun Nabi's arrogance and power is from Badauni, *Muntakhab-ut-Tawarikh*, trans. W. H. Lowe.

18. Badauni tells of another grudge that Akbar held against his sadr. Once, there was a discussion on how many wives Akbar might have by law and the emperor quoted Abdun Nabi as having said nine. When asked to confirm, however, the shaikh equivocated,

saying he only meant that the question was debated. 'This annoyed His Majesty very much. "The Shaikh," said he, "told me at that time a very different thing to what he tells me now." He never forgot this.' Badauni, *Muntakhab-ut- Tawarikh*, trans. W. H. Lowe.

19. Equally wittily, Badauni once wrote of how 'jealousy, hypocrisy, and envy' were 'to the saints of Hindustan, in their feelings towards one another . . . the very necessaries of life'. Ibid.

20. Shaikh Tajuddin would invent the flattering custom of '*zamin-bos*', kissing the floor when greeting the emperor, an obeisance very similar to the *sijda*, prostration in prayer, that became de rigueur in Akbar's court.

21. Badauni, *Muntakhab-ut-Tawarikh*, trans. W. H. Lowe.

22. Ibid., Translator's note.

23. Badauni, *Muntakhab-ut-Tawarikh*, trans. W. H. Lowe.

24. Abul Fazl's thoughts on the distressed debaters in the Ibadat Khana are from Abu'l Fazl, *The History of Akbar*, vol. 6, trans. W. M. Thackston.

25. Ibid.

26. *The Akbarnama of Abu'l Fazl*, vol. 3. The description of the battle that follows is based on Abul Fazl's account.

27. Harbans Mukhia, *The Mughals of India* (Blackwell Publishing, 2004; Indian reprint by Wiley India, 2018). Or, as Abul Fazl puts it, 'A separate volume would be required to describe the intuition into mysteries of the "gift of God".'

28. *The Akbarnama of Abu'l Fazl*, vol. 3. This and the descriptions of Akbar's miracles that follow are based on Abul Fazl's accounts.

29. As Abul Fazl puts it, the deer's trust was a natural consequence of Akbar's 'graciousness and kindness', which not only attracted people of 'various sects and ethnic groups [to] gird their loins in [his] service' but made even wild animals 'calm and tame' in his presence. I'm quoting from Thackston's translation (Abu'l Fazl, *The History of Akbar*, vol. 5); Beveridge is so disgusted with Abul Fazl's 'rhapsody', as he calls it, that he only offers a summary of it.

30. 'From early youth, in compliment to his wives, the daughters of Rajahs of Hind, he had within the female apartments continued to offer the hom, which is a ceremony derived from sun-worship' (Badauni, *Muntakhab-ut-Tawarikh*, trans. W. H. Lowe).

31. Lt-Col. James Tod, *Annals and Antiquities of Rajasthan, or the Central and Western Rajput States of India*, vol. 1, ed. William Crooke (Oxford University Press, 1920).

32. Rana Pratap's descendants, writes James Tod, 'cherish a recollection of the deeds of their forefathers, and melt, as they recite them, into manly tears' – and few of the colonel's readers will doubt that he, too, left such recitations with wet eyes. See Tod, *Annals and Antiquities of Rajasthan, or the Central and Western Rajput States of India*, vol. 1.

33. Harkha Bai was Man Singh's aunt, not his sister. The error may be a slip of Tod's agitated pen. Man Singh's sister would marry a 'Turk' who was also her cousin, Akbar's eldest son, Salim.

34. Allison Busch, 'Portrait of a Raja in a Badshah's World: Amrit Rai's Biography of Man Singh (1585)', *Journal of the Economic and Social History of the Orient*, vol. 55, 2012.

35. The poet's name was Mulla Sheri.
36. Busch, 'Portrait of a Raja in a Badshah's World'.
37. Badauni, *Muntakhab-ut-Tawasrikh*, trans. W. H. Lowe.

CHAPTER 10

1. Azfar Moin, *The Millennial Sovereign: Sacred Kingship & Sainthood in Islam* (Columbia University Press, 2012).
2. Abdul Qadir Badauni, *Muntakhab-ut-Tawarikh* (Selections from Histories), vol. 2, trans. W. H. Lowe (first published 1884–98; Atlantic Publishers and Distributors, 1990).
3. J. F. Richards, 'The Formulation of Imperial Authority under Akbar and Jahangir', in *The Mughal State: 1526–1750*, eds. Muzaffar Alam and Sanjay Subrahmanyam (Oxford University Press, 1998).
4. Harbans Mukhia, *The Mughals of India* (Blackwell Publishing, 2004; Indian reprint by Wiley India, 2018).
5. 'The Happy Sayings of His Majesty', in Abu'l Fazl, *The Ain-i-Akbari*, vol. 3, trans. Col. H. S. Jarrett (First published 1927; Low Price Publications, 2014).
6. Abu'l Fazl, *The Akbarnama of Abu'l Fazl* (completed by Inayatullah), vol. 3, trans. Henry Beveridge (First published 1902–1939; Low Price Publications, 2017).
7. Ibid.
8. Ibid.
9. Badauni, *Muntakhab-ut-Tawarikh*, trans. W. H. Lowe.
10. There were twenty-six types of coins during Akbar's rule, all of which Abul Fazl describes in the *Ain-i-Akbari*. Most commonly used among them were the gold *mohur*, silver rupee and copper *dam*. See Abu'l Fazl, *The Ain-i-Akbari*, vol. 1, trans. H. Blochmann (First published 1927; Low Price Publications, 2014).
11. *The Akbarnama of Abu'l Fazl*, vol. 3. The symbolic present of coins to the nobility was followed by a great distribution, 'handful by handful, and skirt by skirt' to the gathered crowd.
12. Abu'l Fazl, *The History of Akbar*, vol. 5, trans. W. M. Thackston (Murty Classical Library of India, Harvard University Press, 2019).
13. On earrings as a sign of enslavement, Annemarie Schimmel writes, 'the Persian expression *halqa be-gush*, "ring in the ear", means "slave"'. See Annemarie Schimmel, *The Empire of the Great Mughals: History, Art and Culture* (Reaktion Books, 2004, reprinted in 2010).
14. Nizamuddin Ahmad, 'Tabakat-i Akbari', in *The History of India, As Told by Its Own Historians*, trans. H. M. Elliot, vol. 5 (Trübner and Co., 1873).
15. Badauni, *Muntakhab-ut-Tawarikh*, trans. W. H. Lowe.
16. Ibid.
17. Ibid.
18. Ibid. Badauni quotes the whole mahzar in his book.
19. Translator's note in Abu'l Fazl, *The History of Akbar*, vol. 6, trans. W. M. Thackston.

20. Iqtidar Alam Khan, 'The Nobility under Akbar and the Development of His Religious Policy, 1560–80', *Journal of the Royal Asiatic Society of Great Britain and Ireland*, no. 1/2, April 1968.
21. Much as, one might say, Henry VIII declared himself Supreme Head of the Church of England a half-century earlier.
22. Mukhia, *The Mughals of India*.
23. As for the Adam under consideration, he was 'tall, wheaten in colour', died in India, and was buried in Sri Lanka. See Abu'l Fazl, *The History of Akbar*, vol. 1, trans. W. M. Thackston.
24. Richard M. Eaton, *India in the Persianate Age: 1000–1765* (Allen Lane, 2019). This paragraph is extracted, with some modification, from an article I wrote for *The Hindu Businessline*, 'Between bread and empire', published 8 May 2020.
25. This last phrase from Abu'l Fazl, *The History of Akbar*, vol. 6, trans. W. M. Thackston.
26. Ibid.
27. Ibid.
28. Corrine Lefèvre, 'In the Name of the Fathers: Mughal Genealogical Strategies from Babur to Shah Jahan', *Religions of South Asia*, vol. 5, no. 1/2, 2011.
29. Stephen F. Dale, *The Muslim Empires of the Ottomans, Safavids, and Mughals* (Cambridge University Press, 2010).
30. Abu'l Fazl, *The History of Akbar*, vol. 1, trans. W. M. Thackston.
31. The trip was no reassurance whatsoever to Badauni and his friends. '[S]ensible people smiled', writes the unhappy historian, 'and said, "It was strange that His Majesty should have such a faith in the Khwajah of Ajmir, while he rejected the foundation of everything."' Badauni, *Muntakhab-ut- Tawarikh*, trans. W. H. Lowe.
32. *The Akbarnama of Abu'l Fazl*, vol. 3.
33. Ibid.
34. Ibid.
35. See T. C. A. Raghavan, *Attendant Lords: Bairam Khan and Abdur Rahim, Courtiers and Poets in Mughal India* (HarperCollins, 2017).

CHAPTER 11

1. As Stephen Dale writes: Akbar 'evolved from a twelve-year-old Timurid prince supervised by his own atabeg . . . Bairam Khan, to the triumphant status of a dominant South Asian emperor, himself a padishah in reality rather than in aspiration, as Babur had been when he assumed this title while ruling uneasily in Kabul in 1506'. See Dale, *The Muslim Empires of the Ottomans, Safavids, and Mughals* (Cambridge University Press, 2010).
2. Introduction to Gulbadan Begum, *The History of Humayun (Humayun-nama)*, trans. Annette S. Beveridge (The Asiatic Society, 1902).
3. Abu'l Fazl, *The Akbarnama of Abu'l Fazl* (completed by Inayatullah), vol. 3, trans. Henry Beveridge (First published 1902–1939; Low Price Publications, 2017). Haram Begum, too, had a forbidden love. According to Abul Fazl, 'the skirt of Haram

Begam's chastity [was stained] by insinuations about her and Haidar Ali Beg who was her beloved brother'. Ibrahim, no less ruthless than his mother, had her lover killed.

4. Nizamuddin Ahmad, 'Tabakat-i Akbari', in *The History of India, As Told by Its Own Historians*, trans. H. M. Elliot, vol. 5 (Trübner and Co., 1873).

5. Shahrukh's father, Ibrahim, died circa 1560, and he may have married Khanim soon after Kamran's death in October 1557. Shahrukh, then, would have been born in 1558 or later, and could not have been more than seventeen years old in 1575, when Sulaiman arrived in Fatehpur.

6. *The Akbarnama of Abu'l Fazl*, vol. 3.

7. Ibid.

8. The nineteenth-century administrator J. A. Bourdillon echoed the feelings of these disgruntled chiefs when he described Bengal as a 'hell full of good things'. See Vincent A. Smith, *Akbar the Great Mogul, 1542–1605* (Clarendon Press, 1917).

9. *The Akbarnama of Abu'l Fazl*, vol. 3.

10. Akbar did, in fact, try to tempt Sulaiman with Bengal in place of Badakhshan, but the old warlord showed little joy at news 'of this great boon', writes Abul Fazl. Instead, later that year, swept along by the 'high wind of [his] passion' for 'revenging himself on Mirza Shahrukh', Sulaiman left Fatehpur – apparently on the Haj, but really to seek Persian help for his quest to return home. His many Timurid relatives may have fought for the wealth and opportunities of Hindustan, but Mirza Sulaiman, consumed by 'love for the stony land of his birth', wasn't interested.

11. *The Akbarnama of Abu'l Fazl*, vol. 3.

12. Ibid.

13. Badauni may have counted his blessings along with the gold coins. He had almost lost the precious Ram Prasad on his way, when the elephant became stuck in a morass near Amber. '[T]he more it went forward, the deeper it sank in the clay. And since this was my first service of such a nature, I was in a terrible fix.' Finally, some locals came to Badauni's aid, telling him to pour water into the clay to help the elephant out. Fortunately, the trick worked. See Abdul Qadir Badauni, *Muntakhab-ut-Tawarikh* (Selections from Histories), vol. 2, trans. W. H. Lowe (first published 1884–98; Atlantic Publishers and Distributors, 1990).

14. Abu'l Fazl, *The Ain-i-Akbari*, vol. 1, trans. H. Blochmann (First published 1927; Low Price Publications, 2014).

15. *The Akbarnama of Abu'l Fazl*, vol. 3.

16. Abu'l Fazl, *The History of Akbar*, vol. 6, trans. W. M. Thackston (Murty Classical Library of India, Harvard University Press, 2020).

17. *The Akbarnama of Abu'l Fazl*, vol. 3.

18. This was Abul Fazl's rank at the time of Badauni's writing; by the end of his career, Abul Fazl would be a '*panch-hazari*', having attained a mansab of 5000, the highest possible rank for an amir under Akbar.

19. J. F. Richards, 'The Formulation of Imperial Authority under Akbar and Jahangir', in *The Mughal State: 1526–1750*, eds. Muzaffar Alam and Sanjay Subrahmanyam (Oxford University Press, 1998).

20. Rosalind O'Hanlon, 'Kingdom, Household and Body. History, Gender and Imperial Service under Akbar', *Modern Asian Studies*, vol. 41, no. 5, September 2007.

21. Iqtidar Alam Khan, 'The Nobility under Akbar and the Development of His Religious Policy, 1560–80', *Journal of the Royal Asiatic Society of Great Britain and Ireland*, no. 1/2, April 1968.

22. 'As gardeners adorn gardens with trees', writes Abul Fazl, 'and move them from one place to another, and reject many, and irrigate others, and labour to rear them to a proper size, and extirpate bad trees, and lop off evil branches, and remove trees that are too large, and graft some upon others . . . so do just and far-seeing kings light the lamp of wisdom by regulating and instructing their servants . . .' Or, as Iqtidar Alam Khan explains it in less flowery terms, 'Shortly after the suppression of the Uzbek revolt, the concentration of the officers belonging to the Atka Khail in the Punjab was also broken. From the account of Bayazid, it appears that Akbar was keenly conscious of the significance of this policy. To his mind the transfer of the Atka Khail from the Punjab was a greater achievement than the punishments meted out to Adham Khan.' Iqtidar Alam Khan, *The Political Biography of a Mughal Noble: Mun'im Khan Khan-i Khanan, 1497–1575* (Orient Longman, 1973).

23. *The Akbarnama of Abu'l Fazl*, vol. 3.

24. 'They shaved their heads, put on their high caps, and broke out into revolt', Nizamuddin continues. See 'Tabakat-i Akbari'.

25. *The Akbarnama of Abu'l Fazl*, vol. 3.

26. Badauni, *Muntakhab-ut-Tawarikh*, trans. W. H. Lowe.

27. Notes on 'The Grandees of the Empire', in Abu'l Fazl, *The Ain-i-Akbari*, vol. 1.

28. According to Iqtidar Alam Khan's calculation, in 1580–81, when the Bengal rebellion began, thirty-two of his Persian noblemen supported Akbar, twelve joined the rebels and three were neutral. See 'The Nobility under Akbar and the Development of His Religious Policy, 1560–80'.

29. Ibid.

30. Abu'l Fazl, *The History of Akbar*, vol. 6, trans. W. M. Thackston.

31. *The Akbarnama of Abu'l Fazl*, vol. 3.

32. Abu'l Fazl, *The History of Akbar*, vol. 6, trans. W. M. Thackston.

33. *The Akbarnama of Abu'l Fazl*, vol. 3.

CHAPTER 12

1. Munis D. Faruqui, 'The Forgotten Prince: Mirza Hakim and the Formation of the Mughal Empire in India', *Journal of the Economic and Social History of the Orient*, vol. 48, no. 4, 2005.

2. Lahore, after all, was held by Kamran in Kabul during Humayun's first stint on the Hindustani throne. Thus, as Faruqui argues, Punjab 'was a part of [Hakim's] patrimony that had been stolen following the untimely death of Humayun and the unequal partition of the Mughal Empire by Akbar's partisans'. Faruqui, 'The Forgotten Prince'.

3. Edward Maclagan, *The Jesuits and the Great Mogul* (Burns Oates & Washbourne, 1932).

4. Fr. Antonio Monserrate, *The Commentary of Father Monserrate, S.J. on His Journey to the Court of Akbar*, trans. J. S. Hoyland, annotations S. N. Banerjee (Oxford University Press, 1922).

5. It isn't clear if Pereira saw these paintings himself. It is improbable that Akbar invited the priest to dinner. More likely, the emperor told him about the art; thus Pereira could say to Monserrate that 'when naming them [Akbar] showed his true sentiments by putting Muhammad last' (Monserrate, *The Commentary of Father Monserrate*). This too may be a bit of wishful thinking by the priests – Akbar may have named him last because Muhammad was, in fact, the last prophet. More interesting is that Akbar had a painting of him hung on his walls, a heresy in Islam, without exciting any comment, it seems, from his critics – not even Badauni.

6. Abdul Qadir Badauni, *Muntakhab-ut-Tawarikh* (Selections from Histories), vol. 2, trans. W. H. Lowe (first published 1884–98; Atlantic Publishers and Distributors, 1990).

7. Abu'l Fazl, *The Akbarnama of Abu'l Fazl* (completed by Inayatullah), vol. 3, trans. Henry Beveridge (First published 1902–1939; Low Price Publications, 2017).

8. Rudolf, a young Italian of noble birth who joined the Jesuits against his parents' wishes, was something of an absent-minded masochist, given to dressing in hair shirts, flogging himself, and misplacing his books and glasses. 'He burned with a great desire for a martyr's death', writes Monserrate. 'For he often said, "Will these Musalmans never martyr us?" To which the other priest used to reply, "The King is too fond of us; no one dare touch us." At this Rudolf used to frown as if in deep chagrin.' The priest got his wish not long after his return to Goa from Akbar's court, when he was lynched by a mob in Cuncolim. About two centuries later, in 1893, the single-mindedly pious Rudolf also got his due: he was beatified.

9. Azfar Moin, *The Millennial Sovereign: Sacred Kingship & Sainthood in Islam* (Columbia University Press, 2012).

10. Fr. Pierre Du Jarric, *Akbar and the Jesuits: An Account of the Jesuit Missions to the Court of Akbar*, trans. C. H. Payne (First published 1926; Low Price Publications, 2008).

11. *The Ain-i-Akbari*, vol. 1.

12. Arif Qandahari quoted in Irfan Habib, 'Akbar and Technology', in *Akbar and His India*, ed. Irfan Habib (Oxford University Press, 1997).

13. *The Ain-i-Akbari*, vol. 1. Abul Fazl is not the only one to vouch for the purity of Akbar's coinage. A later and far more critical historian, Vincent Smith, too, writes that 'Akbar deserves high credit for the excellence of his extremely varied coinage, as regards purity of metal, fullness of weight, and artistic execution. The Mogul coinage, when compared with that of Queen Elizabeth or other contemporary sovereigns in Europe, must be pronounced far superior on the whole. Akbar and his successors seem never to have yielded to the temptation of debasing the coinage in either weight or purity. The gold in many of Akbar's coins is believed to be practically pure.' Vincent A. Smith, *Akbar the Great Mogul, 1542–1605* (Clarendon Press, 1917).

14. *The Ain-i-Akbari*, vol. 1.

15. Ibid.

16. Monserrate, *The Commentary of Father Monserrate*.

17. *The Ain-i-Akbari*, vol. 1. For all the curiosity, rationality and debate that filled this pre-modern world, its mysteries were not yet undone by science. Abul Fazl's description of the origins of amber is a lovely example of how rational explanation could coexist with magic in the sixteenth century. Thus, he writes: 'It is said that on some mountains a great deal of honey is to be found, so much in fact that it runs into the sea; the wax rises to the surface, when the heat of the sun reduces it to a solid state.' Honey comes from bees, which make it from scented flowers, Abul Fazl goes on. Therefore, amber is naturally scented – and sometimes bees are trapped in it.

18. Habib, 'Akbar and Technology', in *Akbar and His India*.

19. Badauni, *Muntakhab-ut-Tawarikh*, trans. W. H. Lowe.

20. Ibid. The export of horses, on the other hand, was forbidden, as Heinrich Blochmann notes in the *Ain-i-Akbari* (vol. 1). Horses were not native to Hindustan but were of great value to its armies. 'Droves after droves' of them were imported from Iran and Turan, writes Abul Fazl in the *Ain-i-Akbari* – at the time of his writing, there were 12,000 horses in Akbar's own stables. Among the men employed to take care of them was the '*sipandzoz*', whose job was to light *sipand*, rue, to keep the evil eye away from the prized animals. See Abu'l Fazl, *The Ain-i-Akbari*, vol. 1, trans. H. Blochmann (First published 1927; Low Price Publications, 2014).

21. Badauni, *Muntakhab-ut-Tawarikh*, trans. W. H. Lowe.

22. *The Ain-i-Akbari*, vol. 1.

23. 'It became the current custom', writes Badauni, despairingly, '. . . to wear the rakhi on the wrist, which means an amulet formed out of twisted linen rags'. See Badauni, *Muntakhab-ut-Tawarikh*, trans. W. H. Lowe.

24. Monserrate, *The Commentary of Father Monserrate*.

25. 'Urdu' was the Turki word for 'camp' and etymological origin of the English word 'horde' (Translator's note in *The Commentary of Father Monserrate*). Now, it is the name of an Indian language that grew from the mingling of many tongues in such camps.

26. 'Camels are as nimble and skilful in a battle, if I may say so, as horses', writes Monserrate. 'Nor are they less fierce. They fight with teeth and feet. If they catch hold of any one, they kneel upon him so hard and long, pounding and crushing him, that their wretched victim is destroyed.' Monserrate, *The Commentary of Father Monserrate*.

27. Besides dancing, elephants could also be trained to shoot arrows from a bow and discharge a matchlock, according to Abul Fazl (*The Ain-i-Akbari*, vol. 1).

28. Abu'l Fazl, *The History of Akbar*, vol. 6, trans. W. M. Thackston (Murty Classical Library of India, Harvard University Press, 2020).

29. *The Akbarnama of Abu'l Fazl*, vol. 3.

30. The very first accountant that Akbar hired to sort out his finances was the *khwajasara*, eunuch, Itimad Khan. Itimad Khan was murdered, too, in 1578, having aggravated the ill effects of his 'conceit' by demanding the return of some loans (*The Akbarnama of Abu'l Fazl*, vol. 3).

31. *The Akbarnama of Abu'l Fazl*, vol. 3.

32. Abu'l Fazl, *The History of Akbar*, vol. 6, trans. W. M. Thackston.

33. *The Akbarnama of Abu'l Fazl*, vol. 3.

34. Abu'l Fazl, *The History of Akbar*, vol. 6, trans. W. M. Thackston.
35. Ibid.
36. *The Akbarnama of Abu'l Fazl*, vol. 3.
37. Abu'l Fazl, *The History of Akbar*, vol. 6, trans. W. M. Thackston.

CHAPTER 13

1. Abu'l Fazl, *The Akbarnama of Abu'l Fazl* (completed by Inayatullah), vol. 3, trans. Henry Beveridge (First published 1902–1939; Low Price Publications, 2017).
2. Some Qaqshals never gave in. Among them was Dastam Qaqshal, who was killed in 1585, and is worth a mention for his endearingly named elephant Son Kaduh, Golden Pumpkin, now taken into the imperial stables.
3. Abul Fazl calls him 'Nannu', but this undignified diminutive cannot reduce the tragic heroism of the uncrowned prince. Muzaffar Shah, last of the Muzaffarid dynasty, used as a pawn by various Gujarati nobles, was arrested during Akbar's first conquest of Gujarat in 1572. He managed to escape in 1578 and had raised enough support to pose a serious challenge to the government in Gujarat five years later. Abdur Rahim's suppression of Muzaffar Shah's uprising in 1583–84 is what gained him his father Bairam's title, Khan-Khanan. Muzaffar Shah, meanwhile, continued to battle for his father's throne for the next decade – a Jesuit mission travelling through Gujarat would note the ravages of war, 'towns and large cities which were mostly in a state of ruin, particularly the mosques, which had not been rebuilt' (Fr. Pierre Du Jarric, *Akbar and the Jesuits: An Account of the Jesuit Missions to the Court of Akbar*, trans. C. H. Payne [First published 1926; Low Price Publications, 2008]). Eventually, in the winter of 1592, Muzaffar Shah was betrayed by one of his allies and arrested by the Mughals. As he was being escorted to court, the prince asked to relieve himself. Muzaffar covered himself with a canopy and took out a razor. He carried the blade with him at all times, knowing he would die before he gave up his fight. The fight was over now, the empire had prevailed. Muzaffar Shah 'Gujarati' put the blade to his own throat and ended his life (Abul Fazl, Badauni and Ferishta all tell versions of this story).
4. Michael H. Fisher, *A Short History of the Mughal Empire* (I.B. Tauris, 2016).
5. Abu'l Fazl, *The History of Akbar*, vol. 6, trans. W. M. Thackston (Murty Classical Library of India, Harvard University Press, 2020).
6. Abdul Qadir Badauni, *Muntakhab-ut-Tawarikh* (Selections from Histories), vol. 2, trans. W. H. Lowe (first published 1884–98; Atlantic Publishers and Distributors, 1990).
7. 'The Happy Sayings of His Majesty', in Abu'l Fazl, *The Ain-i-Akbari*, vol. 3, trans. Col. H. S. Jarrett (First published 1927; Low Price Publications, 2014). Abul Fazl writes that the duty of kings is to emulate how the sun sheds its light upon the world and makes life possible. He follows this with a pitying aside on the 'weak-minded zealots who, with much concern, talk of His Majesty's religion as of a deification of the Sun, and the introduction of fire-worship[.] But I shall dismiss them with a smile.' See Abu'l Fazl, *The Ain-i-Akbari*, vol. 1, trans. H. Blochmann (First published 1927; Low Price Publications, 2014).

8. Abu'l Fazl, *The History of Akbar*, vol. 6, trans. W. M. Thackston.

9. Annemarie Schimmel, *The Empire of the Great Mughals: History, Art and Culture* (Reaktion Books, 2004, reprinted in 2010).

10. It was the conquest of Gujarat and access to its ports that allowed the women to make the pilgrimage. Characteristically, Akbar expanded the scope of their journey to include the less privileged of his subjects – according to Nizamuddin, all 'pious poor' who wanted to join Gulbadan were given the means to. In fact, Nizamuddin writes that Akbar created the post of a Mir Haji to conduct annual state-sponsored pilgrimages to Mecca. 'Never before had any monarch provided for the annual departure of a caravan from India', he writes, 'nor had any one furnished means to the needy, to enable them to perform the pilgrimage'. See Nizamuddin Ahmad, 'Tabakat-i Akbari', in *The History of India, As Told by Its Own Historians*, trans. H. M. Elliot, vol. 5 (Trübner and Co., 1873). Ironically, and perhaps because these expeditions were so well endowed, Mughal pilgrims were not very popular with Mecca's government. Its 'Ottoman governors', writes Michael Fisher, 'reported that Mughal visitors distributed so much charity as to disrupt the local economy, remained too long, did not respect Ottoman sovereignty, and were spying for a joint Mughal–Portuguese invasion of Yemen'. See Fisher, *A Short History of the Mughal Empire*.

11. Badauni, *Muntakhab-ut-Tawarikh*, trans. W. H. Lowe.

12. There is one Mughal history, the *Iqbalnama*, that tells a slightly different story. In this version, Abdun Nabi was put in Abul Fazl's charge, who had the judge strangled, thus slaking an old thirst for revenge against his enemy. The *Iqbalnama* also says that Abdun Nabi had spent his time in Mecca spreading tales of Akbar and his heresies and that this was the real cause of Akbar's anger against him (Translator's note in *The Akbarnama of Abu'l Fazl*, vol. 3).

13. Later, the Father goes further, writing that Akbar's treatment of his nobility was such that each one 'believes himself to be regarded not only as a contemptible creature but as the very lowest and meanest of mankind'. See Fr. Antonio Monserrate, *The Commentary of Father Monserrate, S.J. on His Journey to the Court of Akbar*, trans. J. S. Hoyland, annotations S. N. Banerjee (Oxford University Press, 1922).

14. The 'vassal' was Muzaffar Mirza of Qandahar. Decades ago, when Akbar gained his precarious throne, the Mughals had had to let Qandahar revert to Shah Tahmasp (who would have argued, of course, that they had no claim to the city in the first place, since it was taken for Humayun by the shah's troops led by his infant son). It speaks volumes for the rising Mughal star that, in 1595, Qandahar submitted to Akbar without a shot being fired – Muzaffar Mirza came to court and meekly accepted a mansab of 5000 in Sambhal ('which is larger than Qandahar', as Abul Fazl doesn't fail to note).

15. Du Jarric, *Akbar and the Jesuits*. To this day, it is not uncommon for visitors to Akbar's grave in Sikandra to leave a small offering of money, just as worshippers do at shrines of many faiths across the subcontinent.

16. Ibid.

17. *The Ain-i-Akbari*, vol. 1.

18. *The Ain-i-Akbari*, vol. 3. Akbar's antipathy towards meat would reach such an extent, in fact, that he also declared that 'Butchers, fishermen and the like who have

no other occupation but taking life should have a separate quarter and their association with others would be prohibited by fine'. For weeks on end, Akbar would eat no meat, or only a little for 'the spirit of the age' (*The Ain-i-Akbari*, vol. 1).

19. Famously, Akbar only drank water from the Ganga, although Abul Fazl may have had a slight preference for the Yamuna's water, of which he wrote that it 'has few like it for . . . lightness and digestibility'. *The Akbarnama of Abu'l Fazl*, vol. 2.

20. *The Ain-i-Akbari*, vol. 1.

21. Nizamuddin Ahmad, 'Tabakat-i Akbari'.

22. Monserrate, *The Commentary of Father Monserrate*.

23. Ibid.

24. The weighing ceremony, *majlis-i-wazn* (Nizamuddin, 'Tabakat-i Akbari'), may have been borrowed from the Indian custom of *tula-daan*. The *Akbarnama* mentions such weighing ceremonies on Akbar's lunar birthdays in previous years, but it was now, in 1582, that he added a solar birthday ceremony to his calendar – and, perhaps, began to observe the custom more publicly.

25. Iqtidar Alam Khan, *The Political Biography of a Mughal Noble: Mun'im Khan Khan-i Khanan, 1497–1575* (Orient Longman, 1973).

26. The emperor wasn't just dispossessing the high-ranking and powerful officials in his realm, however; he was, once again, reinforcing them in their place with regard to the throne. As J. F. Richards argues, escheat was '[c]ontrary to the precepts of canonical law for the inheritance of free Muslims, but permissible of course for slaves' – that is, when Akbar took over an amir's property, he was confirming his nobility's 'enslavement' to the throne. See J. F. Richards, 'The Formulation of Imperial Authority under Akbar and Jahangir', in *The Mughal State: 1526–1750*, eds. Muzaffar Alam and Sanjay Subrahmanyam (Oxford University Press, 1998).

27. *The Akbarnama of Abu'l Fazl*, vol. 3.

28. Birbar and Abul Fazl may have been playing to another facet of Akbar's personality with their suggestions: Birbar proposed men spread across the realm sending secret reports to court; Abul Fazl thought that the daroghas of every town should take a census of the inhabitants and throw out 'the do-nothings, the mischievous, and the bad'. Ibid.

29. Abul Fazl writes in the *Ain-i-Akbari* (vol. 1) that improvement in 'the condition of man' depends 'on the advancement of agriculture, on the order kept in the king's household, on the readiness of the champions of empire, and the discipline of the army'.

30. *The Akbarnama of Abu'l Fazl*, vol. 3.

31. As the historian A. L. Srivastava puts it, Harkha 'exerted great influence on Akbar and his policy'. See A. L. Srivastava, *A Short History of Akbar the Great (1542–1605)* (Shiva Lal Agarwala & Co., 1957).

32. Editors' introduction to Monserrate, *The Commentary of Father Monserrate*.

33. Banarasidas, *Ardhakathanak (A Half Story)*, trans. Rohini Chowdhury (Penguin Books, 2009).

34. The Jain monk, writes Pushpa Prasad, was able to win over the brahmins: 'Vijayasen Suri proved from the Jain scriptures the falseness of the accusation and convinced the Brahmans, Shaikhs (Muslim scholars), the emperor and others, that

the Jain conception was similar to that expounded in the Samkhya philosophy of the Brahmans.' See Pushpa Prasad, 'Akbar and the Jains', in *Akbar and His India*, ed. Irfan Habib (Oxford University Press, 1997).

35. The historians add that Akbar asked Guru Amar Das to pray for him during the siege of Chittorgarh. See editors' introduction to Monserrate, *The Commentary of Father Monserrate*.

36. Iqtidar Alam Khan, 'The Nobility under Akbar and the Development of His Religious Policy, 1560–80', *Journal of the Royal Asiatic Society of Great Britain and Ireland*, no. 1/2, April 1968.

37. Ibid.

38. Munis Faruqui argues that this final change in Akbar's policies (not only with regard to the jizya but the rule of his diverse realm) was influenced far more than is usually admitted by his half-brother's defeat (in 1581) and subsequent death (in 1585): 'Once rid of the menacing shadow cast by Mirza Hakim, Akbar no longer felt compelled to tailor his imperial initiatives to woo disparate political and religious constituencies. Indeed, the death of Mirza Hakim, I argue, is a hitherto overlooked element in the exploration of how and why Akbar conclusively moved from a pro-Islamic stance to the liberal and eclectic stance for which he is widely remembered.' Munis D. Faruqui, 'The Forgotten Prince: Mirza Hakim and the Formation of the Mughal Empire in India', *Journal of the Economic and Social History of the Orient*, vol. 48, no. 4, 2005.

39. 'He was singular for theoretical and practical knowledge', writes Abul Fazl (*The Akbarnama of Abu'l Fazl*, vol. 3).

40. Translator's note in *The Ain-i-Akbari*, vol. 1.

41. Ibid.

42. Translator's introduction to *The Ain-i-Akbari*, vol. 1.

43. Translator's note in Badauni, *Muntakhab-ut-Tawarikh*, trans. W. H. Lowe. Richard Eaton notes that Humayun, too, had adopted the ritual of a darshan at dawn – 'showing his face to the public just as the sun showed itself to the king'. Humayun also gave pride of place to the sun on his 'courtly carpet', where it was coloured gold and placed at the very centre of all planets. Richard M. Eaton, *India in the Persianate Age: 1000–1765* (Allen Lane, 2019).

44. The figure of the eternally 'oppressed brahman' makes more than one cameo appearance in the chronicles of Akbar's reign. In 1586, one of Akbar's generals, Qasim Khan, marched into Srinagar and discovered yet another prophecy of this kind. Some 900 years previously, the story goes, Kashmir was ruled by 'wine-sellers' – a community of low or no caste, presumably, for a brahmin called Shiv Dat was terribly 'distressed by the vogue of the polluted'. Shiv Dat decided to summon a '*baital*', a spirit, for help. This was no small matter: the ritual involved sitting on a human corpse by the light of a lamp lit in a human skull, burning human fat while strewing human teeth upon the dead body. At this, writes Abul Fazl, 'if the heart of the necromancer does not fail him, the corpse begins to move'. Shiv Dat had made all the arrangements and left the corpse at a tanner's house. As it happens, the baital arrived before the brahmin's return, and told the tanner that the current 'oppressors' would be succeeded by Kayasths, then Muslims, and finally, at the eighth generation of Chak rulers, there

would come one whose 'thoughts, actions and speech are devoted to the accomplishment of the Divine Will'. *The Akbarnama of Abu'l Fazl*, vol. 3.

45. Srivastava, *A Short History of Akbar the Great (1542–1605)*.

46. P. P. Sinha, *Raja Birbal: Life and Times* (Janaki Prakashan, 1980).

47. See Prasad, 'Akbar and the Jains'. The monk went on: 'Thieves and robbers were conspicuous by their absence in his empire. His glory was as white as the moon because he had defeated all his enemies. His religious zeal never made him intolerant.'
Akbar seems to have held the Jains in equally high esteem. A Sanskrit inscription on the Adiswara temple in Kathiawar, Gujarat, is quoted by Monserrate's editors to demonstrate the Jains' achievements in Akbar's court. The inscription records how, in 1582, a Jain teacher called Hiravijaya persuaded Sahi Akbbara 'to issue an edict forbidding the slaughter of animals for six months, to abolish the confiscation of the property of deceased persons, the Sujijia tax (the Jizia) and a Sulka, to set free many captives, snared birds and animals, to present Satrunjaya to the Jainas, to establish a Jaina library, and to become a saint like King Srenika (Bimbasara c. 582–554 BC)'. See editors' introduction to Monserrate, *The Commentary of Father Monserrate*.

48. Allison Busch, 'Portrait of a Raja in a Badshah's World: Amrit Rai's Biography of Man Singh (1585)', *Journal of the Economic and Social History of the Orient*, vol. 55, 2012.

49. Azfar Moin, *The Millennial Sovereign: Sacred Kingship & Sainthood in Islam* (Columbia University Press, 2012).

50. Ibid.

51. Faruqui, 'The Forgotten Prince'.

52. Translator's note in *The Ain-i-Akbari*, vol. 1.

53. In this reply, Man Singh may also have explained, succinctly if unwittingly, the difficulty that the Jesuit Fathers, far from court, would face in finding converts. Akbar had long promised the various Jesuit missions that came to him that the Fathers would be free to live and proselytize in his realm, but it was clearly not an easy promise to keep – Akbar only issued a farman to this effect in 1602, two decades after the first Jesuit mission arrived in Fatehpur. It was also in 1602, shortly before the edict was issued, that the third Jesuit mission tells a story of conversion in Lahore, which sheds some light on the troubles the Fathers faced in recruiting a new flock in Hindustan.
It all began when a young brahmin pandit in Lahore was convinced by Father Pigneiro to adopt the Christian faith. The pandit's family was terribly upset (as the Fathers write, 'the Brachmanes, who are, more than all others given to idolatry, exhibited the greater resentment when any of their children became Christians'). The whole clan arrived to take their son back home, the pandit's mother throwing herself at his feet, while the young man waved a sword above his head ('he was . . . new to the teaching of our Saviour', write the Fathers, and hadn't quite grasped Christ's message of non-violence). Eventually, the family left, with the pandit's mother flinging her grandchild upon the steps of the church in despair. A few days later, when his clan came back, the pandit flung his janeu, sacred thread, at his mother in return, and cut off his topknot. At their wits' end, the family complained to the sadr of Lahore, accusing Father Pigneiro of eating human flesh, stealing children and practising black magic. The sadr was unable to bring about any peace between the two parties, so

the pandit was taken to a Hindu 'Coxi', possibly 'qazi', judge. Thousands lined the streets of Lahore and peered from balconies, 'many having shut up their shops that they might come and see what was taking place'. The Hindu qazi had collected funds for the pandit to bathe in the Ganga and wash away his sins, but the young convert showed little appreciation for his efforts. Indeed, he spat in disgust and – here echoing the essence, if not the spirit, of Man Singh's argument against Akbar's 'religion' declared: 'It is a very strange thing that when any Gentile wishes to become a logue [yogi], or a Mahometan, there is none to stand in his way; but when he wishes to become a Christian, it seems that the Devil and hell are leagued against him, to turn him from his purpose.'

The pandit stuck to his guns, though he had to give up all claims to his inheritance to do so. And so ended 'the most noteworthy episode in the lives of the Christians during the year 1602'. See Du Jarric, *Akbar and the Jesuits*.

54. Badauni, *Muntakhab-ut-Tawarikh*, trans. W. H. Lowe.

55. See Richards, 'The Formulation of Imperial Authority under Akbar and Jahangir', and Faruqui, 'The Forgotten Prince'.

56. Abu'l Fazl, *The History of Akbar*, vol. 6, trans. W. M. Thackston.

CHAPTER 14

1. Abdul Qadir Badauni, *Muntakhab-ut-Tawarikh* (Selections from Histories), vol. 2, trans. W. H. Lowe (first published 1884–98; Atlantic Publishers and Distributors, 1990).

2. 'For this reason His Majesty, in imitation of the usages of these Lamahs, limited the time he spent in the Haram, curtailed his food and drink, but especially abstained from meat.' Ibid.

3. Ibid.

4. Abu'l Fazl, *The Akbarnama of Abu'l Fazl* (completed by Inayatullah), vol. 3, trans. Henry Beveridge (First published 1902–1939; Low Price Publications, 2017).

5. Abu'l Fazl, *The History of Akbar*, vol. 6, trans. W. M. Thackston (Murty Classical Library of India, Harvard University Press, 2020).

6. *The Akbarnama of Abu'l Fazl*, vol. 3.

7. Fr. Antonio Monserrate, *The Commentary of Father Monserrate, S.J. on His Journey to the Court of Akbar*, trans. J. S. Hoyland, annotations S. N. Banerjee (Oxford University Press, 1922).

8. For several months after he came to Punjab in the second half of 1585, Akbar camped by the Indus – a lot of it at 'the blacksmiths' shop in looking after gunmaking', writes Abul Fazl – either awaiting an opportunity to cross over to Turan or discouraging any movement eastwards from Abdullah Khan. When Akbar resumed his march in mid-1586, his nobility thought they were heading home to Fatehpur. It must have come as a rude shock when Akbar led them to Lahore instead.

9. William Foster, ed., *Early Travels in India: 1583–1619* (Low Price Publications, 1921).

10. Munis D. Faruqui, 'The Forgotten Prince: Mirza Hakim and the Formation of the Mughal Empire in India', *Journal of the Economic and Social History of the Orient*, vol. 48, no. 4, 2005.

11. Richards writes that 'For the Indo-Muslim rulers of Hindustan prior to Akbar . . . possession and political domination of Delhi was of supreme importance . . . Akbar reversed this fixed concern, fusing, instead, all authority within himself and ultimately within the dynasty which succeeded him.' See J. F. Richards, 'The Formulation of Imperial Authority under Akbar and Jahangir', in *The Mughal State: 1526–1750*, eds. Muzaffar Alam and Sanjay Subrahmanyam (Oxford University Press, 1998).

12. 'The Happy Sayings of His Majesty', in Abu'l Fazl, *The Ain-i-Akbari*, vol. 3, trans. Col. H. S. Jarrett (First published 1927; Low Price Publications, 2014).

13. Peter Hardy, 'Abul Fazl's Portrait of the Perfect Padshah: A Political Philosophy for Mughal India – or a Personal Puff for a Pal?' *Islam in India: Studies and Commentaries*, vols 1 and 2, ed. Christian W. Troll (Vikas, 1985).

14. *The Akbarnama of Abu'l Fazl*, vol. 3.

15. Afzal Husain, *The Nobility under Akbar and Jahangir: A Study of Family Groups* (Manohar Publishers, 1999).

16. Hardy, 'Abul Fazl's Portrait of the Perfect Padshah'.

17. *The Akbarnama of Abu'l Fazl*, vol. 3.

18. P. P. Sinha, *Raja Birbal: Life and Times* (Janaki Prakashan, 1980).

19. Abu'l Fazl, *The History of Akbar*, vol. 6, trans. W. M. Thackston. Jafar Beg was a Persian refugee whose brother, Ghiyas Beg, followed him to Hindustan, bringing with him a newborn daughter called Mihrunissa – the future empress Nurjahan.

20. Sinha, *Raja Birbal*.

21. *The Akbarnama of Abu'l Fazl*, vol. 3.

22. Ibid. The story of Birbar's fatal campaign that follows is based on Abul Fazl's account.

23. Badauni, *Muntakhab-ut-Tawarikh*, trans. W. H. Lowe.

24. Ibid.

25. Abul Fazl estimates the Mughal losses at 500, Nizamuddin at 8000. Khafi Khan, a Mughal historian of the seventeenth and eighteenth centuries, puts the figure at 40,000 to 50,000 (Translator's note in *The Akbarnama of Abu'l Fazl*, vol. 3).

26. Sinha, *Raja Birbal*.

27. Ibid.

28. Badauni, *Muntakhab-ut-Tawarikh*, trans. W. H. Lowe.

29. *The Akbarnama of Abu'l Fazl*, vol. 3.

30. Ibid.

31. Ibid.

32. Abu'l Fazl, *The History of Akbar*, vol. 6, trans. W. M. Thackston.

33. 'I asked the date of his decease from the Old Man of Intellect: / Cheerfully replied the wise Old Man: "He is gone to Hell."'

34. Sinha, *Raja Birbal*.

35. *The Akbarnama of Abu'l Fazl*, vol. 3.

36. Abu'l Fazl, *The Ain-i-Akbari*, vol. 1, trans. H. Blochmann (First published 1927; Low Price Publications, 2014).

37. *The Akbarnama of Abu'l Fazl*, vol. 3.

38. On one of his journeys back from Kashmir, Akbar said, 'It is forty years since I saw snow, and there are many men with me, born and bred in Hind, who have never seen it. If a snow-storm should come upon us in the neighbourhood of Pakhali, it would be a kind dispensation of Providence.' Nizamuddin tells the story and writes that the snowstorm Akbar had wished for did occur. See Nizamuddin Ahmad, 'Tabakat-i Akbari', in *The History of India, As Told by Its Own Historians*, trans. H. M. Elliot, vol. 5 (Trübner and Co., 1873). It wasn't only his men but also his elephants who struggled with his travels into unfamiliar terrain. Father Xavier of the third Jesuit mission to Akbar's court provides this memorable description of an elephant negotiating its way uphill: 'Sometimes, feeling insecure on its feet, owing to the load which it carried, it supported itself with its trunk, making it serve the purpose of a staff.' See Fr. Pierre Du Jarric, *Akbar and the Jesuits: An Account of the Jesuit Missions to the Court of Akbar*, trans. C. H. Payne (First published 1926; Low Price Publications, 2008).

39. Vincent A. Smith, *Akbar the Great Mogul, 1542–1605* (Clarendon Press, 1917).

40. Jahangir, *The Jahangirnama: Memoirs of Jahangir, Emperor of India*, ed. and trans. W. M. Thackston (Oxford University Press with the Smithsonian Institution, 1999).

41. Banarasidas, *Ardhakathanak* (A Half Story), trans. Rohini Chowdhury (Penguin Books, 2009).

42. 'The Happy Sayings of His Majesty', in Abu'l Fazl, *The Ain-i-Akbari*, vol. 3.

43. *The Akbarnama of Abu'l Fazl*, vol. 3.

44. Every city and district of the empire had 'vigilant and truthful men' appointed to prevent 'forcible burning', writes Abul Fazl (*The Akbarnama of Abu'l Fazl*, vol. 3).

45. Ibid.

46. Jahangir, *The Jahangirnama*.

47. Stephen Dale, *Babur: Timurid Prince and Mughal Emperor, 1483–1530* (Cambridge University Press, 2018). There is a wonderful example of the family's respect for elder women from Jahangir's life. Gulrukh Begum, daughter of Kamran and widow of the equally ill-fated Mirza Ibrahim, had eventually reconciled herself to Akbar's ascendancy and joined his court. She had even asked for her daughter to marry the eldest prince, Salim. Years later, when Salim ruled as Jahangir, he went to visit his mother-in-law. At the emperor's arrival, Gulrukh gave him a robe of honour. It was a complete inversion of the usual protocol but Jahangir, 'preferring the observance of the code (Tora) to the maintenance of royal dignity, did obeisance and took the robe'. See Nawab Samsam-ud-Daula Shah Nawaz Khan and Abdul Hayy, *The Maathir-ul-Umara: Biographies of the Muhammadan and Hindu Officers of the Timurid Sovereigns of India from 1500 to about 1780 AD*, trans. Henry Beveridge, revision, annotation and completion Baini Prashad, vols 1 and 2 (The Asiatic Society, 1941, 1952).

48. Abu'l Fazl, *The History of Akbar*, vol. 6, trans. W. M. Thackston.

49. Badauni, *Muntakhab-ut-Tawarikh*, trans. W. H. Lowe.

50. Harbans Mukhia, *The Mughals of India* (Blackwell Publishing, 2004; Indian reprint by Wiley India, 2018).

51. If Akbar was influenced by his Rajput kin and allies' investment of honour in their women, it is unclear if there was any reciprocal Central Asian influence on the Rajputs. Man Singh, for example, served in the Mughal court from the age of eleven; he was one of Akbar's greatest generals and his nephew by marriage, and also Jahangir's brother-in-law. Man Singh may have expanded the Mughal empire but he didn't absorb any of the Mughals' antipathy towards sati: when the Rajput amir died in 1614, sixty women burned with him. See Annemarie Schimmel, *The Empire of the Great Mughals: History, Art and Culture* (Reaktion Books, 2004, reprinted in 2010).

52. Ruby Lal, *Domesticity and Power in the Early Mughal World* (Cambridge University Press, 2005).

53. Ruby Lal, 'Settled, Sacred and All-Powerful: Making of New Genealogies and Traditions of Empire under Akbar', *Economic and Political Weekly*, vol. 36, no. 11, 17–23 March 2001.

54. *The Ain-i-Akbari*, vol. 1.

55. Mukhia, *The Mughals of India*.

56. *The Akbarnama of Abu'l Fazl*, vol. 3.

57. Du Jarric, *Akbar and the Jesuits*. The painting was a copy of the Madonna from the Church of St Maria del Popolo, which is said to have miraculous powers. The Fathers had hung it up in their chapel in Agra for Christmas when news of its display reached Akbar and he asked to see it.

58. Nizamuddin Ahmad, 'Tabakat-i Akbari'.

59. *The Akbarnama of Abu'l Fazl*, vol. 3.

60. The Fathers had begun to suspect that all Akbar's debates on religious matters were actually brainstorming sessions for a 'new religion with matter taken from all the existing systems' and they no longer wished to 'give him the pearls of the Gospel to tread and crush under his feet'. See Monserrate, *The Commentary of Father Monserrate*.

61. Nephew of the better-known St Francis Xavier.

62. Du Jarric, *Akbar and the Jesuits*.

63. S. Roy, 'Akbar', in *The Mughul Empire*, ed. R. C. Majumdar (Bharatiya Vidya Bhavan, 1974).

64. Jahangir, *The Jahangirnama*.

65. *The Ain-i-Akbari*, vol. 1.

66. *The Akbarnama of Abu'l Fazl*, vol. 3.

67. Ibid.

68. Translator's note in *The Akbarnama of Abul Fazl*, vol. 3. Henry Beveridge writes that Murad also asked for books and was promised the forthcoming translation of the Mahabharata.

69. Badauni, *Muntakhab-ut-Tawarikh*, trans. W. H. Lowe.

70. Ibid.

71. See Husain, *The Nobility under Akbar and Jahangir*.

72. Translator's note in *The Akbarnama of Abu'l Fazl*, vol. 3.

Notes   351

73. *The Akbarnama of Abu'l Fazl*, vol. 3.
74. Ibid.
75. Ibid.
76. Mahomed Kasim Ferishta, *History of the Rise of the Mahomedan Power in India till the Year A.D. 1612*, vol. 2, trans. John Briggs (R. Cambray & Co., 1909).
77. *The Akbarnama of Abu'l Fazl*, vol. 3.
78. *The Ain-i-Akbari*, vol. 1.
79. *The Akbarnama of Abu'l Fazl*, vol. 3.
80. Ibid.
81. Muzaffar Alam and Sanjay Subrahmanyam, 'The Deccan Frontier and Mughal Expansion, ca. 1600: Contemporary Perspectives'. Journal of the Economic and Social History of the Orient, vol. 47, no. 3, 2004.

CHAPTER 15

1. Banarasidas, *Ardhakathanak* (A Half Story), trans. Rohini Chowdhury (Penguin Books, 2009).
2. Freer Gallery of Art: https://asia.si.edu/object/F1960.27
3. Jahangir, *The Jahangirnama: Memoirs of Jahangir, Emperor of India*, ed. and trans. W. M. Thackston (Oxford University Press with the Smithsonian Institution, 1999).
4. Abu'l Fazl, *The Akbarnama of Abu'l Fazl* (completed by Inayatullah), vol. 3, trans. Henry Beveridge (First published 1902–1939; Low Price Publications, 2017).
5. Abdul Qadir Badauni, *Muntakhab-ut-Tawarikh* (Selections from Histories), vol. 2, trans. W. H. Lowe (first published 1884–98; Atlantic Publishers and Distributors, 1990).
6. Translator's note in Abu'l Fazl, *The Akbarnama of Abu'l Fazl*, vol. 3.
7. In 1586, Abul Fazl had drawn lots with Birbar to go to Swat, wanting to 'shut the mouths of . . . envious persons'. In 1591, when he fell ill, he wrote that 'as I was inclined to perform military service, my disposition . . . became sad'. The next year, when Abul Fazl was promoted to a mansab of 2000, he wrote, 'I hope that I may return some thanks by the tongue of action.' Now was his chance to prove himself.
8. Technically, Chand Bibi was regent to the king but 'secretly that chaste lady was ruler', as Abul Fazl writes.
9. *The Akbarnama of Abu'l Fazl*, vol. 3. It may be, as some historians speculate, that it was not Daniyal but his ataliq, Abdur Rahim, who wanted to prevent Abul Fazl from enjoying too much success in the Deccan. The two men became bitter rivals over the following months.
10. Ibid.
11. Shaikh Illahdad Faizi Sirhindi, 'Akbarnama', in *The History of India, As Told by Its Own Historians*, trans. H. M. Elliot, vol. 6 (Trübner and Co., 1875).
12. Translator's note in *The Akbarnama of Abu'l Fazl*, vol. 3.

13. Fr. Pierre Du Jarric, *Akbar and the Jesuits: An Account of the Jesuit Missions to the Court of Akbar*, trans. C. H. Payne (First published 1926; Low Price Publications, 2008).

14. *The Akbarnama of Abu'l Fazl*, vol. 3.

15. Shaikh Illahdad Faizi Sirhindi, 'Akbarnama'.

16. *The Akbarnama of Abu'l Fazl*, vol. 3.

17. Ibid.

18. Du Jarric, *Akbar and the Jesuits*.

19. *The Akbarnama of Abu'l Fazl*, vol. 3.

20. Ibid. The Jesuit chronicle of events – accepted by some historians, rejected by others – alleges that it wasn't valour but deceit that won Asirgarh. 'His inability to approach the fort greatly vexed the Mogor', they write, so that Akbar, 'finding the lion's skin ineffective, changed it for that of the fox'. Bahadur was lured out of the fort with false promises, his generals were bribed; the whole affair, indeed, was a damning example of Akbar 'making use of the arts of cunning and deceit, of which he was a master'. The Jesuits may have had a slight prejudice in the matter, however, since Akbar had asked them to try and get him Portuguese ammunition from Goa – having left behind his own siege-guns, not anticipating a battle against Khandesh. The Fathers had refused, and Akbar, furious, ordered them out of his sight. The priests were planning to leave when one of Akbar's amirs told them not to go – it would only enrage the emperor further. Instead, he said to lie low until the storm blew over. 'They followed his advice, and in a short time the King's wrath subsided, and they were completely restored to his favour.' See Du Jarric, *Akbar and the Jesuits*.

21. Translator's note in *The Akbarnama of Abu'l Fazl*, vol. 3.

22. With Daniyal went 3000 Badakhshanis 'who had recently come from Turan' and seem to have been serving a year's duty in the Deccan as price of admission to Hindustan. Ibid.

23. Abul Fazl ascribes a very similar augury to Akbar, writing of how the emperor declared that Abdur Rahim, his protégé and Khan-Khanan, would have three sons. In fact, Abdur Rahim would have four, but Abul Fazl doesn't linger on the fact.

24. Fr. Antonio Monserrate, *The Commentary of Father Monserrate, S.J. on his Journey to the Court of Akbar*, trans. J. S. Hoyland, annotations S. N. Banerjee (Oxford University Press, 1922).

25. Du Jarric, *Akbar and the Jesuits*.

26. Harbans Mukhia, *The Mughals of India* (Blackwell Publishing, 2004; Indian reprint by Wiley India, 2018).

27. *The Akbarnama of Abu'l Fazl* (completed by Inayatullah), vol. 3.

28. Henry Beveridge argues that Inayatullah's addendum was most likely written during the reign of Salim's son, Khurram (titled Shahjahan), considering the 'animus shown' towards Salim. If so, Inayatullah and Shahjahan were treading a delicate path. Such was the force of the destiny that Abul Fazl had conjured for Akbar and his dynasty that Inayatullah would find himself papering over Salim's insubordination with the very 'veil' that once obscured Akbar's own light. Salim would, after all, inherit Akbar's throne, and so, Inayatullah would write: 'Though the action of the

Prince outwardly appeared to be entirely alien from governing, yet God had special designs with regard to him so that by such conduct he should be selected for reigning.' See *The Akbarnama of Abu'l Fazl*, vol. 3.

29. S. Roy, 'Akbar', in *The Mughul Empire*, ed. R. C. Majumdar (Bharatiya Vidya Bhavan, 1974).

30. Jahangir, *The Jahangirnama*.

31. *The Akbarnama of Abu'l Fazl* (completed by Inayatullah), vol. 3.

32. Asad Beg, 'Wikaya-i Asad Beg', in *The History of India, As Told by Its Own Historians*, trans. H. M. Elliot, vol. 6 (Trübner and Co., 1875).

33. Abu'l Fazl, *The Ain-i-Akbari*, vol. 1, trans. H. Blochmann (First published 1927; Low Price Publications, 2014).

34. The only other person allowed near Akbar at this time was a Jain scholar called Bhanu Chandra. See Pushpa Prasad, 'Akbar and the Jains', in *Akbar and His India*, ed. Irfan Habib (Oxford University Press, 1997).

CHAPTER 16

1. The painting is beautifully analysed by the art historian Kavita Singh in Scroll.in (https://scroll.in/article/1000463/as-jahangir-contemplates-a-portrait-of-his-father-a-reversal-of-our-ideas-about-dreams-and-reality).

2. Munis D. Faruqui, *The Princes of the Mughal Empire, 1504–1719* (Cambridge University Press, 2012).

3. Munis D. Faruqui, 'The Forgotten Prince: Mirza Hakim and the Formation of the Mughal Empire in India', *Journal of the Economic and Social History of the Orient*, vol. 48, no. 4, 2005.

4. Faruqui, *The Princes of the Mughal Empire*.

5. Ibid.

6. Abu'l Fazl, *The Akbarnama of Abu'l Fazl* (completed by Inayatullah), vol. 3, trans. Henry Beveridge (First published 1902–1939; Low Price Publications, 2017).

7. Faruqui, *The Princes of the Mughal Empire*.

8. Fr. Pierre Du Jarric, *Akbar and the Jesuits: An Account of the Jesuit Missions to the Court of Akbar*, trans. C. H. Payne (First published 1926; Low Price Publications, 2008).

9. Jahangir, *The Jahangirnama: Memoirs of Jahangir, Emperor of India*, ed. and trans. W. M. Thackston (Oxford University Press with the Smithsonian Institution, 1999).

10. *The Akbarnama of Abu'l Fazl* (completed by Inayatullah), vol. 3.

11. Du Jarric, *Akbar and the Jesuits*. At the time of Badauni's writing, it was Akbar's former tutor Abdul Latif's son, Mir Ghiyasuddin Naqib Khan, who was employed in 'reading history, and all books of verse and prose, both day and night' to the emperor.

12. Abu'l Fazl, *The Ain-i-Akbari*, vol. 1, trans. H. Blochmann (First published 1927; Low Price Publications, 2014).

13. Annemarie Schimmel, *The Empire of the Great Mughals: History, Art and Culture* (Reaktion Books, 2004, reprinted in 2010).

14. So much so, in fact, that Shah Abbas's court poet Kausari 'regrets that the centre of Persian literature had shifted from Persia to Hindusthan'. See S. Roy, 'Akbar', in *The Mughul Empire*, ed. R. C. Majumdar (Bharatiya Vidya Bhavan, 1974).
15. Abdul Qadir Badauni, *Muntakhab-ut-Tawarikh* (Selections from Histories), vol. 2, trans. W. H. Lowe (first published 1884–98; Atlantic Publishers and Distributors, 1990).
16. Asad Beg, 'Wikaya-i Asad Beg', in *The History of India, As Told by Its Own Historians*, trans. H. M. Elliot, vol. 6 (Trübner and Co., 1875). The following story of Asad Beg's appearance in court is based on his own account.
17. *The Akbarnama of Abu'l Fazl* (completed by Inayatullah), vol. 3.
18. Jahangir, *The Jahangirnama*.
19. *The Akbarnama of Abu'l Fazl* (completed by Inayatullah), vol. 3.
20. Ibid.
21. Ibid.
22. *The Akbarnama of Abu'l Fazl*, vol. 2.
23. *The Akbarnama of Abu'l Fazl* (completed by Inayatullah), vol. 3.
24. Asad Beg, 'Wikaya-i Asad Beg'.
25. Iqtidar Alam Khan, 'Akbar's Personality Traits and World Outlook: A Critical Appraisal', in *Akbar and His India*, ed. Irfan Habib (Oxford University Press, 1997).
26. Asad Beg, 'Wikaya-i Asad Beg'.
27. Faruqui, *The Princes of the Mughal Empire*.
28. Described by Faruqui, *The Princes of the Mughal Empire*: 'Even if Ni'matullah Khan Harvi's *Tarikh-i Khan Jahan wa Makhzan-i Afghani* (written in the mid-1610s) cannot top the drama of *Waqa'i' Asad Beg*, it more than makes up for it by offering fresh details of the "event". Thus we now learn that the sword gifted by Akbar to Salim belonged to Babur, who passed it down to Akbar's father Humayun just prior to his own death. As well as his sword, Akbar also gave Salim his personal rosary and good luck amulets as well as a warm hug and kiss.'

EPILOGUE

1. Abu'l Fazl, *The Akbarnama of Abu'l Fazl* (completed by Inayatullah), vol. 2, trans. Henry Beveridge (First published 1902–1939; Low Price Publications, 2017).
2. Abu'l Fazl, *The History of Akbar*, vol. 4, trans. W. M. Thackston (Murty Classical Library of India, Harvard University Press, 2018).
3. Abdul Qadir Badauni, *Muntakhab-ut-Tawarikh* (Selections from Histories), vol. 2, trans. W. H. Lowe (first published 1884–98; Atlantic Publishers and Distributors, 1990).
4. Harbans Mukhia, *The Mughals of India* (Blackwell Publishing, 2004; Indian reprint by Wiley India, 2018).
5. Fr. Antonio Monserrate, *The Commentary of Father Monserrate, S.J. on His Journey to the Court of Akbar*, trans. J. S. Hoyland, annotations S. N. Banerjee (Oxford University Press, 1922).

6. Fr. Pierre Du Jarric, *Akbar and the Jesuits: An Account of the Jesuit Missions to the Court of Akbar*, trans. C. H. Payne (First published 1926; Low Price Publications, 2008).

7. R. C. Majumdar, 'Preface', in *The Mughul Empire*, ed. R. C. Majumdar (Bharatiya Vidya Bhavan, 1974).

8. A. L. Srivastava, *A Short History of Akbar the Great (1542–1605)* (Shiva Lal Agarwala & Co., 1957).

9. As Abul Fazl put it, 'According to the religion of sovereignty and the canons of world-conquest, contentment (or moderation) in regard to the subjugation of countries is blameworthy and disapproved of, just as covetousness is in ascetics.' *The Akbarnama of Abu'l Fazl*, vol. 3.

10. In a carefully worded letter to Abdullah of Turan, written in 1586, Akbar declared that 'Places which from the time of [the] rise of the sun of Islam . . . had not been trod by the horse-hoofs of world-conquering princes and where their swords had never flashed have become the . . . homes of the faithful'. He went on to write that temples of the 'infidels and heretics have become mosques and holy shrines for the masters of orthodoxy' – a claim at which Shaikh Ahmad Sirhindi, at least, would have scoffed. By contrast, at a feast in Akbar's court in 1590, two clerics drank wine and Akbar recited a little verse for the occasion: 'In the era of the fault-forgiving king / The Qazi drained flagons, the Mufti quaffed cups.' See *The Akbarnama of Abu'l Fazl*, vol. 3.

11. See Joel Lee's essay on the evolution of the term 'halalkhor' from Akbar's age to the present day (Joel Lee, 'Who Is the True Halalkhor? Genealogy and Ethics in Dalit Muslim Oral Traditions', *Contributions to Indian Sociology*, vol. 52, no. 1, 2018). Abul Fazl, describing the various ranks of employees in the imperial stables, writes of the sweepers that they are called 'halalkhur' and that 'His Majesty brought this name en vogue'. See Abu'l Fazl, *The Ain-i-Akbari*, vol. 1, trans. H. Blochmann (First published 1927; Low Price Publications, 2014).

12. It is debatable whether either Akbar or Gandhi wanted to bring about such radical systemic change. Gandhi's essay on 'The Ideal Bhangi' is notorious, and Akbar, again, may have anticipated some of its sentiments when he said: 'In the struggle to maintain universal order it may be appropriate for one person to be a sweeper and another a dog keeper in order for them to be safe from the temptations of the flesh and to keep their minds pure.' See Abu'l Fazl, *The History of Akbar*, vol. 5, trans. W. M. Thackston. Henry Beveridge did not translate the reams of advice of which these lines are a part, arguing that the discourse held 'nothing . . . characteristic of Akbar'.

13. Iqtidar Alam Khan writes that the fact that Akbar's 'fits' stopped after 1578 or so, 'when Akbar had developed a new world view identified with sulh-i kul, goes to suggest that these had something to do with the mental tensions of the earlier phase of his life'. See Iqtidar Alam Khan, 'Akbar's Personality Traits and World Outlook: A Critical Appraisal', in *Akbar and His India*, ed. Irfan Habib (Oxford University Press, 1997).

14. Stephen F. Dale, *The Muslim Empires of the Ottomans, Safavids, and Mughals* (Cambridge University Press, 2010). Joseph E. Schwartzberg's *A Historical Atlas of*

South Asia includes a detailed map of the expansion of Akbar's empire. It is available to view on the Digital South Asia Library: http://www.columbia.edu/itc/mealac/pritchett/00maplinks/mughal/dsal/dsal.html

15. *The Akbarnama of Abu'l Fazl*, vol. 2

16. Banarasidas, *Ardhakathanak* (A Half Story), trans. Rohini Chowdhury (Penguin Books, 2009).

Select Bibliography

THE MUGHALS IN THEIR OWN WORDS

Babur. *The Baburnama: Memoirs of Babur, Prince and Emperor*, trans. W.M. Thackston. Modern Library, 2002.

Gulbadan Begum. *The History of Humayun (Humayun-nama)*, trans. Annette S. Beveridge. The Asiatic Society, 1902.

Jahangir. *The Jahangirnama: Memoirs of Jahangir, Emperor of India*, ed. and trans. W.M. Thackston. Oxford University Press with the Smithsonian Institution, 1999.

Mirza Muhammad Haider Dughlat. *The Tarikh-i-Rashidi: A History of the Moghuls of Central Asia*, trans. E. Denison Ross, ed. N. Elias. Sampson Low, Marston & Co., 1895.

AKBAR IN (AND AROUND) HIS TIME

Abdul Qadir Badauni. *Muntakhab-ut-Tawarikh (Selections from Histories)*, vol. 2, trans. W.H. Lowe. First published 1884–98; Atlantic Publishers and Distributors, 1990.

Abu'l Fazl. *The Ain-i-Akbari*, vols 2 and 3, trans. Col. H.S. Jarrett, corrected and further annotated by Sir Jadunath Sarkar. First published 1927 and 1949; Low Price Publications, 2011 and 2014.

Abu'l Fazl. *The Ain-i-Akbari*, vol. 1, trans. H. Blochmann, ed. Lt-Col. D.C. Phillott. First published 1927; Low Price Publications, 2014.

Abu'l Fazl. *The Akbarnama of Abu'l Fazl* (completed by Inayatullah), vols 1, 2 and 3, trans. Henry Beveridge. First published 1902–39; Low Price Publications, 2017.

Abu'l Fazl. *The History of Akbar*, vols 1–6, trans. W.M. Thackston. Murty Classical Library of India, Harvard University Press, 2015, 2016, 2017, 2018, 2019, 2020.

Banarasidas. *Ardhakathanak (A Half Story)*, trans. Rohini Chowdhury. Penguin Books, 2009.

Du Jarric, Fr. Pierre. *Akbar and the Jesuits: An Account of the Jesuit Missions to the Court of Akbar*, trans. C.H. Payne. First published 1926; Low Price Publications, 2008.

Elliot, H.M. trans., ed. and completed by John Dowson. *The History of India, As Told by Its Own Historians*, vol. 5. Trübner and Co., 1873. Including: 'Humayun-nama' by Khondamir; 'Tarikh-i Rashidi' by Haider Mirza Doghlat; 'Tarikh-i Alfi' by Maulana Ahmad and others; 'Tabakat-i Akbari' by Nizamuddin Ahmad; 'Muntakhab-ut-Tawarikh or Tarikh-i Badauni' by Abdul Qadir Badauni.

Elliot, H.M. trans., ed. and completed by John Dowson. *The History of India, As Told by Its Own Historians*, vol. 6. Trübner and Co., 1875. Including: 'Akbarnama' by Shaikh Illahdad Faizi Sirhindi; 'Waki'at' by Shaikh Faizi; 'Wikaya-i Asad Beg' by Asad Beg; 'Tarikh-i Hakki' by Shaikh Abdu'l Hakk; 'Zubdatu't Tawarikh' by Shaikh Nuru'l Hakk; 'Rauzatu't Tahirin' by Tahir Muhammad; 'Muntakhabu't Tawarikh' by Hasan bin Muhammad; 'Ma'asir-i Rahimi' by Muhammad Abdu'l Baki; 'Anfa'ul Akhbar' by Muhammad Amin.

Foster, William, ed. *Early Travels in India: 1583–1619*. First published 1921; Low Price Publications, 2012.

Jouher. *The Tezkereh al Vakiat, or Private Memoirs of the Moghul Emperor Humayun*, trans. Major Charles Stewart. Oriental Translation Fund, 1832.

Mahomed Kasim Ferishta. *History of the Rise of the Mahomedan Power in India till the Year A.D. 1612*, vol. 2, trans. John Briggs. R. Cambray & Co., 1909.

Monserrate, Fr. Antonio. *The Commentary of Father Monserrate, S.J. on his Journey to the Court of Akbar*, trans. J.S. Hoyland, annotations S.N. Banerjee. Oxford University Press, 1922.

EIGHTEENTH-CENTURY AND COLONIAL HISTORIANS

Beale, Thomas William. *The Oriental Biographical Dictionary*. The Asiatic Society, 1881.

Khan, Nawab Samsam-ud-Daula Shah Nawaz, and Abdul Hayy. *The Maathir-ul-Umara: Biographies of the Muhammadan and Hindu Officers of the Timurid Sovereigns of India from 1500 to about 1780 AD*, vols 1 and 2, trans. Henry Beveridge, revision, annotation and completion Baini Prashad. The Asiatic Society, 1941, 1952.

Maclagan, Edward. *The Jesuits and the Great Mogul*. Burns, Oates & Washbourne, 1932.

Malleson, Col. G.B. *Akbar and the Rise of the Mughal Empire*. Clarendon Press, 1908.

Smith, Vincent A. *Akbar the Great Mogul, 1542–1605*. Clarendon Press, 1917.

Tod, Lt-Col. James. *Annals and Antiquities of Rajasthan, or the Central and Western Rajput States of India*, vol. 1. Edited and introduced by William Crooke. Oxford University Press, 1920.

Tod, Lt-Col. James. *Annals and Antiquities of Rajasthan, or the Central and Western Rajput States of India*, vol. 2. Higginbotham & Co., 1880.
Von Garbe, Richard. *Akbar, Emperor of India: A Picture of Life and Customs from the Sixteenth Century*, trans. Lydia G. Robinson. The Open Court Publishing Company, 1909.

MODERN HISTORIANS

Alam, Muzaffar, and Sanjay Subrahmanyam, eds. *The Mughal State: 1526–1750*. Oxford University Press, 1998.
Alam, Muzaffar, and Sanjay Subrahmanyam. 'The Deccan Frontier and Mughal Expansion, ca. 1600: Contemporary Perspectives'. *Journal of the Economic and Social History of the Orient*, vol. 47, no. 3, 357–389, 2004.
Anooshahr, Ali. 'Mughals, Mongols, and Mongrels: The Challenge of Aristocracy and the Rise of the Mughal State in the *Tarikh-i Rashidi*'. *Journal of Early Modern History*, vol. 18, 559–577, 2014.
Anooshahr, Ali. 'The King Who Would Be Man: The Gender Roles of the Warrior King in Early Mughal History'. *Journal of the Royal Asiatic Society*, vol. 18, no. 3, 327–340, 2008.
Busch, Allison. 'Portrait of a Raja in a Badshah's World: Amrit Rai's Biography of Man Singh (1585)'. *Journal of the Economic and Social History of the Orient*, vol. 55, 287–328, 2012.
Collier, Dirk. *The Great Mughals and Their India*. Hay House Publishers, 2016 (reprinted 2017).
Dale, Stephen F. *Babur: Timurid Prince and Mughal Emperor, 1483–1530*. Cambridge University Press, 2018.
Dale, Stephen F. *The Muslim Empires of the Ottomans, Safavids, and Mughals*. Cambridge University Press, 2010.
Davar, Satish K. 'The Making of Fatehpur Sikri'. *Journal of the Royal Society of Arts*, vol. 123, no. 5232, 781–805, November 1975.
Eaton, Richard M. *India in the Persianate Age: 1000–1765*. Allen Lane, 2019.
Faruqui, Munis D. 'The Forgotten Prince: Mirza Hakim and the Formation of the Mughal Empire in India'. *Journal of the Economic and Social History of the Orient*, vol. 48, no. 4, 487–523, 2005.
Faruqui, Munis D. *The Princes of the Mughal Empire, 1504–1719*. Cambridge University Press, 2012.
Fisher, Michael H. *A Short History of the Mughal Empire*. I.B. Tauris, 2016.
Gascoigne, Bamber. *A Brief History of the Great Moghuls: India's Most Flamboyant Rulers*. Constable & Robinson Limited, 1971 (reprinted 2002).
Grewal, J.S. 'The Sikh Movement during the Reign of Akbar'. *Akbar and His India*, ed. Irfan Habib. 243–255, Oxford University Press, 1997.
Habib, Irfan. 'Akbar and Technology'. *Akbar and His India*, ed. Irfan Habib. 129–148, Oxford University Press, 1997.

Hardy, Peter. 'Abul Fazl's Portrait of the Perfect Padshah: A Political Philosophy for Mughal India – or a Personal Puff for a Pal?' *Islam in India: Studies and Commentaries*, 2 vols, ed. Christian W. Troll. 114–137, Vikas, 1985.

Husain, Afzal. *The Nobility under Akbar and Jahangir: A Study of Family Groups.* Manohar Publishers, 1999.

Khan, Iqtidar Alam. 'Akbar's Personality Traits and World Outlook: A Critical Appraisal'. *Akbar and His India*, ed. Irfan Habib. 79–96, Oxford University Press, 1997.

Khan, Iqtidar Alam. 'The Nobility under Akbar and the Development of His Religious Policy, 1560–80'. *Journal of the Royal Asiatic Society of Great Britain and Ireland*, no. 1/2, 29–36, April 1968.

Khan, Iqtidar Alam. *The Political Biography of a Mughal Noble: Mun'im Khan Khan-i Khanan, 1497–1575.* Orient Longman, 1973.

Kohli, P. *A Short History of Akbar and Mughal Administration in India.* S. Chand & Co., 1949.

Lal, Ruby. 'Historicizing the Harem: The Challenge of a Princess's Memoir'. *Feminist Studies*, vol. 30, no. 3, 590–616, Fall 2004.

Lal, Ruby. 'Settled, Sacred and All-Powerful: Making of New Genealogies and Traditions of Empire under Akbar'. *Economic and Political Weekly*, vol. 36, no. 11, 941–958, March 17–23, 2001.

Lal, Ruby. *Domesticity and Power in the Early Mughal World.* Cambridge University Press, 2005.

Lee, Joel. 'Who is the True Halalkhor? Genealogy and Ethics in Dalit Muslim Oral Traditions'. *Contributions to Indian Sociology*, vol. 52, no. 1, 1–27, 2018.

Lefèvre, Corinne. 'In the Name of the Fathers: Mughal Genealogical Strategies from Babur to Shah Jahan'. *Religions of South Asia*, vol. 5, no. 1/2, 409–442, 2011.

Majumdar, R.C. ed., J.N. Chaudhuri and S. Chaudhuri assistant eds. *The Mughul Empire.* Bharatiya Vidya Bhavan, 1974. Including: 'Preface' by R.C. Majumdar; 'Humayun' by S. Roy; 'Hemu: A Forgotten Hindu Hero' by R.C. Majumdar; 'Akbar' by S. Roy; 'Mewar' by A.K. Majumdar; 'Muslim Resistance to Mughul Imperialism (I)' by A.K. Majumdar; 'Hindu Religion' by B.B. Majumdar; 'The Sikh Religion' by Hari Ram Gupta; 'Islam' by M.W. Mirza.

Moin, A. Azfar. *The Millennial Sovereign: Sacred Kingship & Sainthood in Islam.* Columbia University Press, 2012.

Mukhia, Harbans. *The Mughals of India.* Blackwell Publishing, 2004; Indian reprint by Wiley India, 2018.

Mukhoty, Ira. *Daughters of the Sun: Empresses, Queens & Begums of the Mughal Empire.* Aleph Book Company, 2018.

Naim, C.M. 'Popular Jokes and Political History: The Case of Akbar, Birbal and Mulla Do-Piyaza'. *Economic and Political Weekly*, vol. 30, no. 24, 1456–1464, 17 June 1995.

Narayan, Saarang. 'From Jalaluddin to Akbar: Analyzing the Akbarid Notion of Kingship'. *Inquiries Journal/Student Pulse*, vol. 8, no. 1, 2016.

O'Hanlon, Rosalind. 'Kingdom, Household and Body. History, Gender and Imperial Service under Akbar'. *Modern Asian Studies*, vol. 41, no. 5, 889–923, September 2007.

Prasad, Pushpa. 'Akbar and the Jains'. *Akbar and His India*, ed. Irfan Habib. 97–108, Oxford University Press, 1997.

Raghavan, T.C.A. *Attendant Lords: Bairam Khan and Abdur Rahim, Courtiers and Poets in Mughal India*. HarperCollins, 2017.

Richards, J.F. 'The Formulation of Imperial Authority under Akbar and Jahangir'. *The Mughal State: 1526–1750*, eds. Muzaffar Alam and Sanjay Subrahmanyam. 126–167, Oxford University Press, 1998.

Schimmel, Annemarie. *The Empire of the Great Mughals: History, Art and Culture*. Reaktion Books, 2004 (reprinted 2010).

Sinha, P.P. *Raja Birbal: Life and Times*. Janaki Prakashan, 1980.

Srivastava, A.L. *A Short History of Akbar the Great (1542–1605)*. Shiva Lal Agarwala & Co., 1957.

Talbot, Cynthia. 'Justifying Defeat: A Rajput Perspective on the Age of Akbar'. *Journal of the Economic and Social History of the Orient*, vol. 55, 329–368, 2012.

Tripathi, R.P. 'The Turko-Mongol Theory of Kingship'. *The Mughal State: 1526–1750*, eds. Muzaffar Alam and Sanjay Subrahmanyam. 115–125, Oxford University Press, 1998.

Ziegler, Norman P. 'Some Notes on Rajput Loyalties during the Mughal Period'. *The Mughal State: 1526–1750*, eds. Muzaffar Alam and Sanjay Subrahmanyam. 168–210, Oxford University Press, 1998.

Index

Page references for figures are italicized

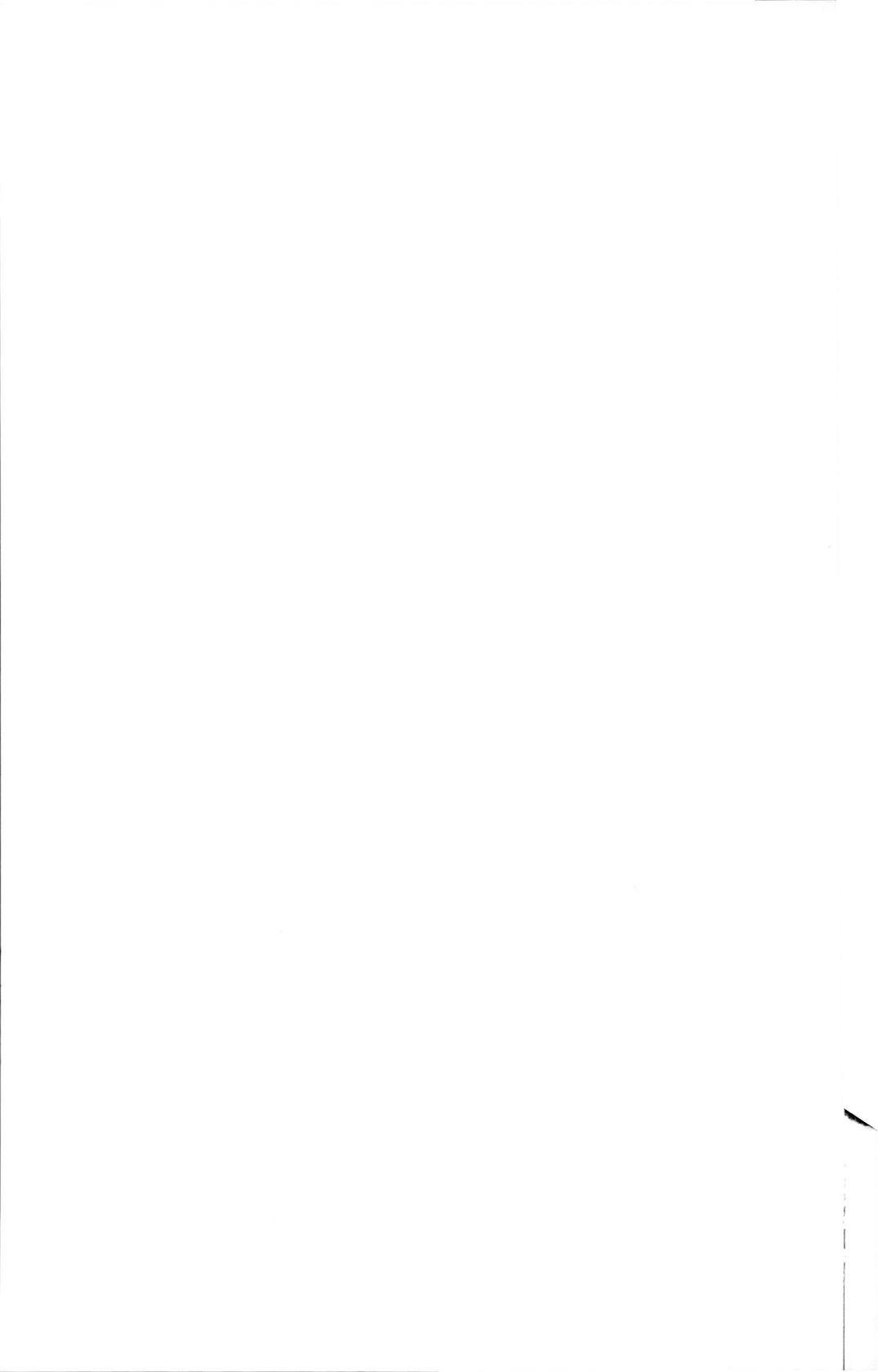